Janez Juhant,
Bojan Žalec (Eds.)

Art of Life

Theologie Ost – West

Europäische Perspektiven

herausgegeben von

Prof. Dr. Janez Juhant
(Universität Ljubljana)
und Prof. Dr. Albert Franz
(Universität Dresden)

Band 14

LIT

ART OF LIFE

Origins, Foundations and Perspectives

With contributions of
Ulrich Beck, Wilhelm Schmid,
Santiago Sia, Karl M. Woschitz
and others

edited by

Janez Juhant and Bojan Žalec

LIT

Cover Picture: Anka Doblekar, Photomontage

Gedruckt auf alterungsbeständigem Werkdruckpapier entsprechend
ANSI Z3948 DIN ISO 9706

Bibliographic information published by the Deutsche Nationalbibliothek
The Deutsche Nationalbibliothek lists this publication in the Deutsche Nationalbibliografie; detailed bibliographic data are available in the Internet at http://dnb.d-nb.de.

ISBN 978-3-643-90043-2

A catalogue record for this book is available from the British Library

Zweigniederlassung Zürich 2010
Klosbachstr. 107
CH-8032 Zürich
Tel. +41 (0) 44-251 75 05
Fax +41 (0) 44-251 75 06
e-Mail: zuerich@lit-verlag.ch
http://www.lit-verlag.ch

LIT VERLAG Dr. W. Hopf
Berlin 2010
Fresnostr. 2
D-48159 Münster
Tel. +49 (0) 2 51-620 320
Fax +49 (0) 2 51-922 60 99
e-Mail: lit@lit-verlag.de
http://www.lit-verlag.de

Distribution:

In Germany: LIT Verlag Fresnostr. 2, D-48159 Münster
Tel. +49 (0) 2 51-620 32 22, Fax +49 (0) 2 51-922 60 99, e-mail: vertrieb@lit-verlag.de

In Austria: Medienlogistik Pichler-ÖBZ, e-mail: mlo@medien-logistik.at

In Switzerland: B + M Buch- und Medienvertrieb, e-mail: order@buch-medien.ch

In the UK: Global Book Marketing, e-mail: mo@centralbooks.com

In North America by:

Transaction Publishers
New Brunswick (U.S.A.) and London (U.K.)

Transaction Publishers
Rutgers University
35 Berrue Circle
Piscataway, NJ 08854

Phone: +1 (732) 445 - 2280
Fax: + 1 (732) 445 - 3138
for orders (U. S. only):
toll free (888) 999 - 6778
e-mail: orders@transactionpub.com

Acknowledgments

We thank to all persons who contributed to the appearing of the book. Our special thanks go to: the reviewers, Professor Dietmar Mieth from University of Tübingen, Professor Christian Gostečnik and Professor Matjaž Potrč from University of Ljubljana; to Samo Grčman for the layout; to Valerija Japelj, who helped by the final corrections of the book; last, but not least, to all the authors of the book.

Our special thanks go to Slovenian Book Agency, which financially supported the appearing of the book.

Janez Juhant and Bojan Žalec, the editors
Ljubljana, July 2010

CONTENTS

INTRODUCTION: *ARS VIVENDI* FOR THE PRESENT TIMES

Nowadays problems are many, urgent and burning and the reflection on them and ideas how to overcome them are - in this age of acting rather than thinking - needed more than ever. It should be clear by now that the strategy "Rather do something then just think and talk" is false, inadequate, populist, demagogical and ideological. But how can we explain that to somebody who doesn't reflect upon his actions? For that reason the first and probably main aspiration of the book is to stimulate creative reflection on some difficult questions which are often put in the background. Yet, the questions that the book considers have never been totally neglected because as long as we live as humans that is not possible. All civilizations have cultivated some kind of *ars vivendi,* and also our own (present) is no exception. Just think about Socrates, Plato, Aristotle, Hellenistic philosophy, Christian tradition, Nietzsche, William James, existentialism, works of a contemporary philosopher John Kekes or the title of the latest book of the famous sociologist Zygmunt Bauman.

We believe that it is plane that some virtues must necessarily be cultivated if we want to survive and live as humans. But what do nowadays *humanity, prudence, justice, temperance, courage, faith, hope, love* ... and last, but not least, *life* and *meaning of life* amount to? However, all these questions converge in the following: "What is good life?" – or, as many would put it today, the life of quality - and "How to reach it?" Certainly, no easy and non-complex understanding of these questions is possible and correspondingly there are no such answers. In this book we offer a scientific contribution (provided by scholars cultivating several scientific approaches and disciplines, mostly belonging to social science and humanities) to multilayered background from which alone the genuine sense of proper attitude toward them can grow. We thank all the contributors for taking a part in this demanding endeavor.

At one hand the present society more deeply than ever interferes with secrets of life. Yet at the other hand, there are signs of non-mastering the life, escaping in the opposite direction, to non-life. There are even sings of turning to death. The former Pope John Paul II has often spoken about our culture as a culture of death. How can we consider the art of life as a challenge for solving difficult problems of man's life in the time being? Such questions are considered by the authors of the present book.

The book starts with essays of two well-known thinkers. The first is a sociologist, Professor Ulrich Beck, whose book *The Risk Society: Towards a New*

Modernity already now belongs to classical works of social science. The second, philosopher Wilhelm Schmid in 1998 published a very well accepted book titled *Lebenskunst* (a German word for *art of life*).

Ulrich Beck considers religion from the aspect of its potentials for peace and violence. His starting point is the fact that religions have two faces. The first is marked with cosmopolitan fraternity, which transcendences nations and classes, the other with the demonization of the religiously other. In the course of his essay he develops seven thesis dealing with religion in the context of the second (religious) modernity, trying to illuminate the specifics of religion in modernity, the process of its individualization (religion of one's own God), the questions of violence, tolerance, and of relation between peace and truth. **Wilhelm Schmid** presents holistic grounds of the art of life and he stresses and investigates the importance of contexts. The conditions of those contexts depend on understanding of one's life, but also on societal, educational, political and cultural conditions of one's own life and especially on one's own interpretations of them. **K. Mathäus Woschitz** deals with the Greek pair 'Dionysian/ Apollonian' as the fundamental basis of the understanding of man. 'Dionysic' refers to the living, eruptive and 'dark' side of human life. Apollo is a god of culture, order, rationality and planned life. These fundamental moments of human life also nowadays can't be neglected in order to cultivate really integral and hence fruitful anthropological reflection and understanding. **Janez Juhant** deals with the dialogical supposition of good life. It is a fact that our life is a dialogical one, but because man's capacity for a dialogue is not given but acquired, the dialogue form depends on particular cultural background. Because the societal life today is more competitive and combatable than dialogue-friendly there are more and more of "thirds", of excluded. To make possible the overcoming of clashes and the protection of the growing number of victims it is necessary to take side with the victims of globalisation. The starting point and the motivation for **Bojan Žalec**'s essay consists in the fact of the growing influence of the media and informational technology on the modern life. He is interested in it from the ethical point of view. The background of his reflection represents existentialistic and phenomenological philosophy (of man's being in the world), supplemented by Girard's mimetic theory and modern cognitive science. **Zvezdan Pirtošek** deals with human feelings from the point of view of the modern brain science. Happiness is functionally related to the corresponding brain structures, areas and chemical substances (dopamine in the central role). The essay of **Santiago** and **Mirian F. Sia** exemplifies the philosophical grammatical approach to the meaning of life and to the human seeking of it. The authors use as their model some grammatical entities like sentence and punctuation marks in their quest to understand the main subject of their essay. **Vojko Strahovnik** deals in a comparative way with Kekes' and Bauman's views about the art of life. While Kekes develops his ideas by considering several types or examples of good life, Bauman analyses the (post)modern society in order to grasp the possibilities of a good life.

Branko Klun follows Heidegger's phenomenological analysis in his consideration of the problem of the meaning of life and its criterion. It seems that this criterion couldn't be an objective one but only the one given by life itself as a whole, estimated by the bearer of life. **Tomas Kačerauskas** deals with some aspects of the phenomenological-existential analysis of man in Husserl, Heidegger and Arendt. **Gábor Kovács** shows the Arendt's concept of man in his catchiness in the political realm. Hannah Arendt has dealt with the question how man can preserve his humanity in complex social and political circumstances. **Robert Petkovšek** deals with Michel Henry's phenomenological analysis of the post-modern access to truth. Henry stresses that the fundamental truth is not only discovered on visible things, but that truth is to be defined as Life: Life is self-revelation. **Zdenka Zalokar Divjak** investigates the spiritual grounds of man as playing an important role in man's leading a meaningful life.

Tadej Strehovec uses the mimetic theory of René Girard to show how the societal (especially scientific) development is caught in violence, which has its victims. This is apparent in medicine, biotechnology and environment. The pseudo messianism of the sacrifice of the innocent can't bring a fortunate future. **Tonči Matulić** continues the idea of the previous author arguing that the so called post-historian ideology as a part of the post-modern ideology reduces man's existence to "mere *conditio humana*", which must be rejected as "a just human project". **Gunter Prüller-Jagenteufel** shows (in his taking side with the poor) the negative consequences of one-sided globalisation for ordinary people in Latin America. He pleads for a society in which everybody could live as a subject. **Anton Jamnik** criticises the so called "wild liberalism", which gives more opportunities to the strongest in the society and suspends the ethics. **Mateja Pevec Rozman** lists the constituents and characteristics of the modern society and of good life, stressing the importance of virtues, engagement and of others. **Tomaž Erzar** and **Katarina K. Erzar** deal with the possibilities of healing of trauma in the context of its trans-generational transferring. They are stressing the central role of the attachments of a child to his parents, of dysfunctional (wounded) parents and of the necessity of veridical reconstruction of the story constituted by the mentioned elements for a successful therapy. Presenting Schweitzer's concept of life as a whole, embracing all living creatures **Roman Globokar** presents the ethics of respect to life developed by Albert Schweitzer. As pace Hans Jonas also according to Schweitzer the proper understanding of the meaning of life is very important to deal more successfully with the present problems of surviving of mankind and solving ecological problems. **Stanislav Slatinek** deals with the problem of one`s good name in the media. He concludes that preservation of the right to a good name should be much more cultivated.

Drago Ocvirk deals with the difference between Christian and Islamic way of faith. The Christian is invited to participate on God's love in Jesus Christ, the Moslem has to subordinate himself to God's will in the Islamic community. **Mari Jože Osredkar** presents the ways of salvation of man. He argues for the thesis that the salvation in different traditions means the salvation of a soul and he differentiates the eastern and the Christian way of salvation, which means the salvation through the (O)other. **Avguštin Lah** analyses how to live with God in a world without God. **Béla Mester** pursues the stoic concept *adiaphora* (indifferent things) in the Christian thought on liberty in the 16th-17th Century and considers its possible role in the political life today. The topics of **Maja Milčinski's** article are Asian notions of life, death, impermanence and universal life, the Mohist tradition of haven, transcendence (as a state of undifferentiated state of consciousness, language and the void space). She considers the mystical and meditative Asian methods in their connection to the possibility of mature acceptance of death and impermanence and of a full life grounded on it. **Romualdas Dulskis** compares the Christian and the Daoistic way of life. He concludes that the Christians stresses that life's purpose is getting of the blessedness by God. According to Daoists the last aim of life is emptiness and full freedom. Christians believe that this happens through Jesus (Mark 9:43-47).

Gabriella Pusztai enumerates the contributions of the churches to the higher education in former communistic countries. In the post-communist era churches brought new visions, new contents, new teachers and opened possibilities of higher education for formerly neglected regions. **Andrej Šegula** analyses the postmodern anti-authoritarian tendencies and concludes that religious education should adapt its concepts to those changes. **Erika Prijatelj** describes the phases of man's reflexive thinking and maturing. She claims that every step toward becoming adult is a possibility towards independence of a person, given that a young person is at each stage of education actively and critically engaged in relation with others. **Alina Pătru** considers the crossing of the western and eastern religious culture in

Transylvania and presents the region as an example of cooperation and peaceful cohabitation. **Inna Naletova** uses the analysis of three successful Russian films from the post-Soviet period in arguing for her thesis about the pilgrimage as a way of life that can help people to overcome the difficult periods of their lives.

The articles deal with concrete everyday problems of people at one hand, but also with the most fundamental ones. The book might help to deepen the understanding of the questions covered by the key word life, and might also contribute to the cultivation of personal art of life.

The editors

GENERAL

THE TWO FACES OF RELIGION*

Ulrich Beck, Munich/London

"God needs no passport", argues Peggy Levitt. Many religious institutions where founded on universal claims and have always been "global players". Today, however religious universalism and globalism often takes predominance over its national forms. Religions, like capitalism, politics and climate change, are no longer firmly rooted in a particular country. This happens because religion in contrast to nation is the ultimate boundary cross. "God needs no passport" because faith traditions give their followers symbols, rituals and narratives they use to create alternative sacred landscapes, marked by holy sites, shrines and places of worships. Some groups and persons of different religion think of themselves as religious global citizens. Faith is their membership card. Religious global citizenship has a lot in common with its political equivalent. In exchange for obeying the law and following the religious rules members gain participation, protection, representation and access to resources and power.

But we should not forget: there are two faces of religion. For all the humanity of religion there, too, is a totalitarian temptation inherent in it. Out of the universalism of religion there arises a cosmopolitan fraternity which transcends class and nation, but also demonization of religious others throughout history – fault lines that go back about two thousand years to the origins of the monotheistic religions, Christianity, Judaism, Islam. God can equally civilise and barbarise human beings. I would like to ask: If religion often sharply divides us, why can't it also be the bricks with which we bridge these divides? I will present seven theses to discuss this question.

First thesis: Within the scientific disciplines of the social sciences and the humanities, especially in the field of the theories of modern society the explicit

* This essay tries to summarize my complex argument in *A God of One's Own: Religion's Capacity for Peace and Potential for Violence.*

study of religions is underdeveloped. This is, of course, not the case for the sociology of religion, which is a very lively field of research and discussions. The relative neglect of religion in the context of globalization may be due to the fact that religions usually ground themselves in tradition as opposed to modernization. But the main reason is the close relation between secularization and theories of modernity, which has let many social scientists to expect religion to be irrelevant in the modern world. If we want to understand religion in the modern world we have to understand the *globalization-paradox of religion*: religion is *not* just incidentally global in extent, a by-product of the globalization of more powerful structures like mass media, capitalism and the modern state. Rather the formation and global spread of religion in general, and the monotheistic religions in particular, is *an essential defining characteristic of those religions from their beginnings*. Indeed, some religions have been "global players" for more than two thousand years. The history of today's religions claim is an indicator of just how long the process of globalization itself has been going on.

And there is a clue to it: you cannot understand, at least the monotheistic religions Judaism, Christianity and Islam, in a national gaze. The social sciences need a cosmopolitan outlook in order to understand the coexistence or conflicts of religions even in the national and local contexts. This paradigm shift from a "methodological nationalism" to a "methodological cosmopolitanism" is necessary to conceptualize the mobilizing forces, conflicts and visions of religions and their specific contribution in constructing norms and structures of the emerging world society. Thus, in order to understand the meta-power game that redefines power in the global age, we have to take into account, besides global capital, civil society movements, state actors and international organizations, the role of religions as modernizing or anti-modernizing forces in the coming post-secular world society.

Second thesis: For religion one feature is absolute: Faith – measured against it all other social differences and oppositions are unimportant. The New Testament says: "All men are equal before God." This equality, this annulment of the boundaries separating people, groups, societies, cultures is the social foundation of (Christian) religions. A further consequence, however, is this: A new fundamental distinction and hierarchy is established in the world with the same absoluteness that social and political distinctions were annulled: the distinction between *believers* and *non-believers*. The non-believers (likewise in accordance with the logic of this duality) are denied the equality and dignity of human beings. Religions can build bridges between people where hierarchies and borders exist;

at the same time they create new religion-determined chasms where there were none before.

It was Paul, a Hellenistic Jew who, more than any other figure in the Jesus movement, turned Christianity from a Jewish sect into a global religious force with a universalistic vision. He pulled down the walls: "There is neither Jew nor Greek, there is neither bond nor free, there is neither male nor female."

The humanitarian universalism of believers is based on the identification with God – and on a demonization of the opponents of God who, as Paul and Luther put it, are "servants of Satan". This ambivalence of tolerance and violence can be broken down into three elements: World religions a) overcome given hierarchies and boundaries between nations and ethnic groups; they are in a position to do so, to the extent that b) they create a religious universalism, in the face of which all national and social barriers become less important; there simultaneously arises, however, the danger c) that instead of ethnic, national and class barriers, barricades are now raised between believers in the right faith on the one hand and believers in the wrong faith and non-believers on the other.

a) The way that the monotheistic religions deal with the otherness of the others is fundamentally different from all forms of vertical differentiation in which an attempt is made to organise social otherness in terms of a hierarchical relation of superiority and subordination. That is to say, the society of religion is an anti-racist society. But it is more than that. It even dissolves the boundaries and distinctions, which everyday realism and sociological realism share: Class, estate, ethnicity, generation, nation. How is that possible?

b) Through *religious universalism*. This represents the opposite principle to the hierarchical subordination of others. Both universal Christianity and universal Islam – as image of man and as missionary duty – raise boundary-crossing into a programme. All worldly distinctions pale in the face of the one, the only point of view that counts, the eternal salvation of man and his soul. In this respect belief comes significantly close to human rights, because the bond with God is available to every human being and so is divested of any ethno-centric limitation.

c) But the seed of religiously motivated violence derives from this very same universalism of the equality of believers, which denies to the believer in a different faith or to the non-believer what it promises the believer: human dignity, equality in a world of strangers. The One Gods and their eternal truths create the violence-laden categories of the damned, of the brutes or the sub-human – "heretics", "heathens", "apostates", "the superstitious", "worshippers of idols" etc. (Jan Assmann; Arnold Angenendt). The "evil" for which these "children of darkness" stand, indicates actions and thoughts beyond all powers of the imagination, beyond all justification, beyond all possibility of defence.

That is the fear that's spreading: That the reverse of the failure of secularisation is the threat of a new dark age. Religion kills.

The history of European colonisation is of course the primary historical example of how the category of unbelievers, who were to be converted for the sake of the salvation of their own souls, permitted unimaginable atrocities and acts of violence and cruelty to be carried out and "legitimated". Columbus expressed it with quite undisguised brutality. To him the spreading of the faith "and the enslavement of the non-believers were indissolubly linked".

But the demonization of the religious other can also be effectively illustrated by the "mixed marriages war" between Catholic and Protestant Christians which raged in the long 19th century and into the 20th century. With the establishment of national equality the boundary of hate and contempt between Catholic and Protestant Christians of the same nationality – who, contrary to all declarations of love within marriage, family, parenthood, attacked and excluded one another as "false faith communities of heretics" – had again and again to be proclaimed with fiery words and actions.

In particular, it appeared to both Catholic and Protestant churchmen a betrayal of their own religion to abandon the education of children to the other religion: "Whoever does not merely have the name of a Protestant Christian, but also that Protestant faith, for whose sake thousands once suffered a martyr's death, he also knows, what this faith is worth (...). Whoever, whether out of indifference or to gain some kind of worldly good, abandons his children to the Catholic Church, not only sins most gravely against their souls, but himself also ceases to be a Protestant Christian, he may no longer allow God's Word to dwell in his house, he may no longer with his family worship his God and Saviour in spirit and in truth." The historian Tilmann Bendikowski (2002) has reconstructed many such stories, at whose core is the message: "So heed this, dear Christian – beware of mixed marriage!" What unites both churches is that by condemning and combating mixed marriage they have erected and maintained a "confessional apartheid".

This confessional fundamentalism which refuses to see and acknowledge the other Christian in the "other believer" is increasingly being rejected, not least by active believers. Here, as Hans Joas (2007) has written, a "reversal of the burden of proof" (Daniel Deckers) has taken place with respect to ecumenical co-operation: "What increasingly has to be justified is its absence, not its occurrence."

Third thesis: Even the question: What is religion? displays a European bias. Because religion is understood as a substantive, by which a clearly defined social set of symbols and practices is assumed, constituting a monotheistic either/or – one can only either believe in it or not believe it, and one cannot, if one is a member of one church, simultaneously belong to another. It is, therefore, useful and necessary to introduce a distinction between "religion" and "religious" as substantive and as adjective.

The substantive "religion" organises the religious field in accordance with an either/or logic. The adjective "religious", on the other hand, organises it in accordance with a both/and logic. To be religious is not based on adherence or non-adherence to a particular group or organisation; it defines, rather, a particular attitude to the existential questions concerning the position and the understanding of self of human beings in the world. That raises the question: Is it primarily "religion" which displays the Janus face of brotherly love and deadly enmity, but perhaps not "religious"? Can the violence-laden, monotheistic either/or be relativised, undermined, defused by the syncretic tolerance of both/and?

The authority in principle of revived faith is the sovereign self, which assembles a "god of its own". What is emerging as a result is certainly not the end of religion, but the advent of a new kind of subjective faith anarchy transcending all religious boundaries, which less and less fits inside the dogmatic frameworks which the institutionalised religions provide. The unity of religion and religious is breaking up. Indeed, religion and religious are coming into conflict.

In Western societies, which have internalised the autonomy of the individual, human beings are creating ever more independently those little narratives of belief – "the god of one's own" – which fit one's "own" life and "own" horizon of experience. This "god of one's own", however, is no longer the One God, dictating salvation by appropriating (hi)story and authorising intolerance and force. The principle of the religious melange is accompanied by the principle of a subjective polytheism. The blurred forms of faith of a "god of one's own" could (to borrow and adapt a formulation of Odo Marquard (1995)) give rise to a subjectively willed and realised division of powers even "within the absolute", directed against the sole claim of the monotheistic religions. Are we seeing a regression of the monotheism of religion to a polytheism of the religious governed by the principle of "a god of one's own"?

This syncretic tolerance is not only spreading in the sphere of detached religiosity, but can also be practised quite naturally in institutional forms, as can be observed, for example, in Japan. People there don't regard it as a problem to visit a Shinto shrine at certain times of the year, to arrange a marriage in accordance with Christian ceremonies and to be buried by a Buddhist monk. The disbelieving astonishment at that comes from within a monotheistic horizon of God monogamy ("Thou shalt have no other gods before me!"), which is quite foreign to Japanese eclecticism with respect to religions, but also generally in East Asia, including China. Peter L. Berger (2006), the sociologist of religion, quotes the summing-up of the Japanese philosopher Nakamura: "The West is responsible for two fundamental errors. One is monotheism – there is only one god, and the other is the Aristotelian principle of opposition – something is either A or not-A. Every intelligent person in Asia knows that there are many gods and that things can be both A and not-A at the same time."

Fourth thesis: Hence in the European context there appears the paradox of a second, religious, modernity: The emptying of the churches and the religious re-enchantment of human beings' thoughts and actions, the weakening of religious organisations and the strengthening of a 'liquid' (Zygmunt Bauman) religiosity represent two sides of the same development. This is also evident in that the claim of the institutions to testify to the true doctrine is being placed in doubt by the faithful themselves. Thus, in a country-wide survey of the religious convictions of Catholics and Protestants in Switzerland, only two per cent of those asked agreed with the following statement: "All religions should be respected, but only mine is true." The younger generations are profoundly affected by this weakening of religious orthodoxy. According to a survey conducted in 1998 in France six per cent of all those interviewed and only four per cent of 18-29 year-olds believe their religion to be the only true one (see Hervieu-Léger 2006).

In other words: The individualised believers are literally walking out on the old fathers of the church and their dogmas – just as politically and morally committed young people are abandoning the trade unions, the political parties and traditional associations. Accordingly there is the danger of a *false conclusion* being drawn from declining and ageing membership, that the younger generation are dulled and indifferent, even though behind and between the established organisational categories new forms of morality, politics and religiosity are developing. In order to describe them, however, sociology requires a new perspective and conceptual terminology.

Certain questions, however, have to be asked: Is the personal religiosity of a god of one's own – without an authoritative point of reference outside the individual – still capable of challenging the status quo? Is the starting-point of any revolt not shifted within the individual, with the consequence that attitudes to circumstances are changed, but not the circumstances themselves? Is it even the case, perhaps, that religious navel-gazing as a collective attitude is linked to an incapacity to co-operate?

The individualisation of belief does not exclude the *standardisation* of belief, quite the contrary. That is evident from the commodity character of the "religion products" on offer and their standardised rather than individual consumption. The individualisation of belief, therefore, accords with a religious symbolic economy, which is increasingly penetrated by the laws of the market. "More than half of Swiss Catholics still faithful to the Church, who attend mass every Sunday, have no difficulty combining traditional eschatological ideas of Christianity with elements of the Buddhist belief in reincarnation. [...] A Catholic shamanism allows the living a notably friendly relationship with the dead. It may be concluded, that the magicians, faith-healers and palm-readers, as the well as the people they help, are good Catholics." (Graf 2004) So we arrive at the paradox, that in highly individualised faith cultures, every person attributes to themselves, (according to their own image of themselves), the authenticity of their spiritual narrative of belief, while seen from the outside, on the one hand this takes its course in altogether standardised forms, on the other the boundaries between the religions become blurred. It is in this sense that it is possible to say: The individualised pattern of faith is the collective standard consciousness, which, nevertheless, is hardly able any longer to examine the ego as such, precisely because it sees itself as individualised self-consciousness.

What does standardisation mean? One indicator of it – at least in the European world of Christendom – is the empirically demonstrable growth in significance of a "minimum creed". It can be summarised as follows: "God loves you, Jesus saves you, you can be healed!" This requires no theological interpretation, must rather prove itself in terms of personal faith experiences and practices. In the search for faith, "this 'evaporation of doctrine' combines with the spread of emotional forms of religiosity. They explicitly demand that the intellect be 'consigned to the back seat' and a much higher value attached to emotional experiences of the presence of the Holy Ghost. This theological minimalism, which reduces the transcendence relationship to a purely emotional and personalised experience of closeness to the divine being, permits the efficient adaptation of religious doctrinal contents to modern individualism's demand for personal self-realisation." (Hervieu-Léger 2006)

So what does a god "of one's own" mean? It is not at all, as might be too quickly assumed, of a product of "post-modernity". Instead "a god of one's own" represents a climax of a long process of individualisation, which is built into Christianity itself and in the course of which the autonomy of the individual is asserted *against* the collective definition of religiosity.

Fifth thesis: If religions have always surmounted seemingly unshakeable territorial and national boundaries and opened up new gulfs between believers and non-believers, what then is new? In today's world the density of communications technologies, resulting in everyone being everyone's neighbour, leads to contact between and interpenetration of the world religions and this in turn to a *clash of universalisms*, to omnipresent conflicts of revelatory truths, as well as to tendencies to the mutual demonization of other believers, whose human dignity is questioned. Each believing and non-believing person, whatever his or her faith or non-faith, sees himself simultaneously in the home of the believers (or atheists) and potentially an outlaw (like the non-believer in the eyes of the religious others). This compulsory shift arouses and feeds diffuse fears, thanks to which political differences and conflicts can become religiously charged and explode in violence.

Clash of universalisms means: In one's own life just as in worldwide debates unavoidable legitimation and reflexivity pressures arise, whereas previously circular self-certainty prevailed. To refuse these explanatory pressures, that is, to pursue with all possible means the restoration of certainties of faith which have become questionable, becomes the basic concern of fundamentalist movements in all religions everywhere in the world.

Here a new divisive social differentiation and line of conflict opens up, affecting all religions, one which will perhaps be extremely important in future: that is, between such currents of belief and such groups which allow room for the reflexivity of doubt, indeed see in it an element of the saving of religion and those who, in order to repel doubt, barricade themselves in the constructed "purity" of their faith. "Hard religions have a lot to offer the consumer. By requiring a great deal of religious commitment, adherence to moral norms which must be strictly observed and considerable financial contributions they make available, to those unsettled by a confusing plurality and frightened by uncertainties, a strong, stable identity, robust interpretations of the world and the times, orderly family structures and dense networks of solidarity." (Graf 2004)

Combating the "dictatorship of relativism", Pope Benedict XVI defends the Catholic hierarchy of truth. It approximates to the logic of a card game: faith trumps reason; Christian faith trumps all other forms of faith (Islam in particular); Roman Catholic faith is the jack of spades which trumps all other (fellow) Christian players; and the Pope is the ace (of spades) of Catholic orthodoxy.

Sixth thesis: The nationalisation of God results in the naturalisation of intolerance and violence.

The widespread discussion of nationalism as a "substitute religion" ultimately trivialises what happened in the 19th and 20th centuries, that is, the "Germanisation of Christianity", and the consequences this has had, down to the present day, for internal and intra-religious relations with others and for religious tolerance. Because the deliberate fusion of nation and religion annuls both principles of toleration: the principle of ethnic-national tolerance and the principle of inter-religious tolerance.

There are some who say: A Christianity which becomes tolerant surrenders itself. "Because what is true of nations, is also true by analogy of religions and confessions: No strong identity without a clearly defined enemy." (Graf 2004)

However: Anyone who imports the national either/or principle into Christianity is getting rid off the Christian universalism which recognises no distinction between nations and races, whose core indeed is the individual's sovereignty of faith, which is detached from all blood bonds by religion. The antidote to the demonization of the national other and to national intolerance is the idea of Jesus Christ, which is synonymous with pulling down ethnic and national walls. (Angenendt 2007)

The point of the Protestant sacralisation of the nation, is that, along with the "naturalisation" of the national friend/foe logic it constructs (and continues to construct) the "naturalness" of intolerance towards the national and religious other as real and insurmountable. The end result was the perversion of Christianity: Whoever refused to participate in the war of one Christian nation against another, was held not only to be a national "sinner", but a Christian one as well, proving himself incapable of Christian brotherly love, that is, of Christian mortal enmity.

Wherever images of a national enemy dominate, tolerance between religions is the first thing to die. Thus the persecution of the Jews in Nazi Germany right up to the point of their deportation was, for the "Confessing Church" [i.e. those sections of the Protestant churches in Germany which *resisted* incorporation in the Nazi state apparatus], "confirmation anew of a Jewish fate already laid down in the Bible", as Arnold Angenendt (2007) puts it. The aggressive anti-semitism of Protestant congregations conformed to an anti-semitism ordained by the state. Accordingly from 1941 "some congregations banned Christian bearers of the yellow star from attending services."

There is by now an extensive historical and theological literature which has reconstructed and criticised these processes of a theologisation of the nation and of a nationalisation of theology. What remains underexposed so far, is the "methodological nationalism" of historical writing and, linked to that, the continuing consequences for the assessment of the potential for tolerance in Christian attitudes to national and religious others.

"Methodological nationalism" means: The unreflected adoption in the observing language and perspectives of historiography and theology of the principles of political nationalism of actors. In other words: The Carl Schmitt error rules people's heads. The unified friend/foe logic of demarcation is accepted for both nation and religion and so "realistically" excludes the world and religious alternatives of transnational and inter-religious tolerance from the horizon of the possible. It is in this respect that Protestant theological nationalism has theoretically impregnated the understanding of religion and distorted it in a national political way. The result has been that right up to the present the crucial question as to religion's potential for tolerance has been answered in the negative, without it really having being addressed and thought through at all.

Seventh thesis: Assuming that the expectation of secularism – more modernity means less religion – is mistaken, then the question arises: How will a type of inter-religious tolerance become possible, in which brotherly love does not mean mortal enmity? I mean a type of tolerance, whose goal is not truth but peace? (Gray 2007)

Anyone who asserts truth as the supreme goal of tolerance may be striving for consensus and harmony, but is simultaneously damning all those who do not wish to bow to this "truth". If, on the other hand, the goal of consensus and harmony is regarded as being neither realistic, nor even worth striving for at all, then that inevitably throws up the question: How does – beyond the revealed truths of the religions – a "cosmopolitan tolerance" become possible? And what possible, active contributions can the world religious actors and movements themselves make? Are there models, starting points, in the history of religion which can be drawn on today?

This is indeed the case, as Jan Assmann (2007) explains with reference to the model of "double religion" that arose from the European reception of Egyptian religion in the 18th century. " From the news of an Egyptian written culture the 18th century put together the idea of a 'double religion', having the generally accessible exterior aspect of a polytheistic popular religion and, accessible only to initiates, the interior aspect of a philosophical monotheism. While the populace paid homage to the many gods who, it was believed, kept watch over the observance of the laws, rewarding and punishing, and protected the state both internally and externally, the initiates dedicated themselves to the hidden, sole deity, on whose seated statue in the temple at Sais was written, according to Plutarch: 'I am all that was, is and shall be and my veil no mortal could ever uncover.' [...]

This acute awareness of a double membership, as citizen of the state and citizen of the world, Catholic and philosopher, corresponded to the intellectual situation of an age of a first breakthrough of globalisation, [an age] which was learning to think along cosmopolitan lines and to see the peoples of the earth as one community. [...] At the very moment of the birth of the first 'world religions', Judaism and Christianity, based on the profession of the one name alone, there formed as a counter-movement a world religion in the true sense, which admittedly could never exist as religion, but only as cosmopolitan wisdom as to the secret convergence of all religions."

The idea of a double religion was later taken up by Mahatma Gandhi and turned into world-changing politics. To him double religion means practising a kind of "passing over" into the religion and culture of the others, in order to be capable of seeing the world, including the world of one's own religion, through the eyes of others. Gandhi's biography provides an example of this adventure of "methodological conversion". As a young man Gandhi went to England to study law. The "detour" by way of a heartland of the Christian West didn't alienate him from Hinduism but deepened his understanding and avowal of it. Because it was in England, on visiting a friend, that Gandhi began to read the *Bhagavad Gita*, in an English translation by Edwin Arnold with the title *The Song Celestial*. It was to prove an illuminating experience for him. Only subsequently did he begin an intensive study of the Hindu text in Sanskrit. He was also deeply impressed by Arnold's book *The Light of Asia* which recounted the life of Buddha. So it was through the eyes of his Western friends that he was moved to discover the spiritual wealth of his own Hindu tradition.

This is also reflected in the increase in transnational ways of life, in which the comparison of religious philosophies, doctrines and practices becomes an existential stimulus. In her book *The Inheritance of Loss* (2006) Kiran Desai describes one such scene of the existential comparison of religion.

"Sai eavesdropped instead on Noni talking to the librarian about *Crime and Punishment*: 'Half awed I was by the writing, but half I was bewildered,' said Noni, 'by these Christian ideas of confession and forgiveness – they place the burden of the crime on the victim! If nothing can undo the misdeed, then why should sin be undone?'

The whole system seemed to favour, in fact, the criminal over the righteous. You could behave badly, say you were sorry, you would get extra fun and be reinstated in the same position as the one who had done nothing, who now had both to suffer the crime and the difficulty of forgiving, with no goodies in addition at all. And, of course, you would feel freer than ever to sin if you were aware of such a safety net: sorry, sorry, oh so sorry.

Like soft birds flying you could let the words free.

The librarian, who was the sister-in-law of the doctor they all went to in Kalimpong, said: 'We Hindus have a better system. You get what you deserve and you cannot escape your deeds. And at least our gods look like gods, no? Like Raja Rani. Not like this Buddha, Jesus – beggar types.'

Noni: 'But we, too, have wriggled out! Not in this lifetime, we say, in others, perhaps...'

Added Sai: 'Worst are those who think the poor should starve because it's their own misdeeds in past lives that are causing problems for them..."

The German writer Lessing wrote the play *Nathan the Wise* (1779) in which the question of tolerance between Christianity, Judaism and Islam is of central importance. In the play's famous "Ring Parable" he, in a way, further develops the model of double religion. Lessing profoundly distrusted the dream of One Truth, which the philosophers have dreamed throughout history. Because when it comes to truth it's never just truth alone which is at issue, but much more, that is, *humanity*, or as we would have to say today: *peace*.

Lessing already recognised the conflict between the One Truth and a cosmopolitan acknowledgment of the truths of many religions. But the "wisdom" of Nathan is based on the ruse of pursuing both priorities at the same time – the absolutist truth of religion *and* that of peace.

So no one should be in possession of the *one* ring! That would be the Devil's victory. So two things must exist: the One Ring *and* the many rings, which every son, who inherits this ring from his father, must take to be the One Ring. Every ring, therefore, is the "Only" Ring, which doesn't exist. Consequently no one can ever know which is the True One Ring. But all know that there are many One Rings, and that they possess one of the many One Rings.

If Lessing had been forced to choose between the One Ring and no ring, he would certainly have chosen to have no ring. His Ring Parable was constructed in such a way, that the One Ring, if it ever existed, has been lost forever amidst the indistinguishability of the many One Rings, which the religions of humanity evidently need.

The "problem" of Islam in a "secular" Europe is being nervously debated and argued about on all sides. Fears of foreigners and outsiders and the impossibility of "multicultural co-existence" are being articulated. Yet the "ruse" of co-operation is being ignored: It is possible – in accordance with the idea of double religion, Gandhi's "methodological conversion" and Lessing's Ring Parable – to distinguish between *orthodoxy* and *interaction*. This can be observed in action in certain localities, let's say in London and Berlin, but above all in the United States, in particular in the big cities. Although there's a great deal of talk of the deadly hostility between religious fundamentalisms, and this talk is repeatedly given mass media currency by spectacular actions, it is evident, that an everyday pragmatism of *inter-religious cosmopolitan common sense* is at work here as the basis of a religious-secular co-operation which transcends boundaries. And that is because its usefulness convinces all those involved. It is not disputes between dogmas, but the pragmatism of co-operation across the barricades of dogmatic dispute, that allows problems which weigh on everyone to be addressed. This is true of educational projects as it is of issues of the care of the poor, the protection of minorities or those relating to (illegal) migrants.

Below the level of demarcation battles of the religious warriors on the world media stage this *ruse of co-operative surplus value* is stealthily gaining in reality and significance. Groups may be intolerant with respect to the theology of the others, but at the same time work creatively together in order to promote shared public concerns – the Ring Parable applied. The endlessly disputing theological guardians of doctrine could learn from this "*Vernunft* of double religion". Is this irony of the separation of dogma and practice possible not only locally, but also on the world stage? In the search for pragmatic answers to the challenges of world risk society – the danger of nuclear war, climate change, global poverty?

Today the question, to what extent truth can be replaced by peace, is a crucial one for the continued existence of humanity. But is the hope for a brotherly (and sisterly) love without deadly enmity not the most improbable, naive, foolish, absurd thing one can hope for?

References and bibliography

Angenendt, A. 2007: Toleranz und Gewalt. Das Christentum zwischen Bibel und Schwert, Münster: Aschendorff.

Arnold, E. (trans.) 1885: The Song Celestial or Bhagavad-Gita, Boston: Roberts Brothers.

Arnold, E. 1890: The Light of Asia, or the Great Renunciation, London: Kegan Paul, Trench, Trübner.

Assmann, J. 2003: Die mosaische Unterscheidung oder der Preis des Monotheismus, München: Hanser.

Assmann, J. 2007: '»Religio duplex«. Zur europäischen Rezeption der ägyptischen Religion', in: Simm, H.-J. (ed.): Die Religionen der Welt. Ein Almanach zur Eröffnung des Verlags der Weltreligionen, Frankfurt am Main: Verlag der Weltreligionen.

Beck, U. 2010: A God of One's Own: Religion's Capacity for Peace and Potential for Violence, Cambridge, UK/Malden, MA: Polity Press.

Bendikowski, T. 2002: '»Eine Fackel der Zwietracht«. Katholisch-protestantische Mischehen im 19./20. Jahrhundert', in: Blaschke, O. (ed.): Konfessionen im Konflikt. Deutschland zwischen 1800 und 1970: ein zweites konfessionelles Zeitalter. Göttingen: Vandenhoeck & Ruprecht.

Berger, P. L. / Mathewes, C. T. 2006: 'An Interview with Peter Berger', The Hedgehog Review. Critical Reflections on Contemporary Culture 8: After Secularization, 152-161.

Desai, K. 2006: The Inheritance of Loss, New York: Atlantic Monthly Press.

Graf, F. W. 2004: Die Wiederkehr der Götter. Religion in der modernen Kultur, München: C.H. Beck.

Gray, J. (2007): Black Mass. Apocalyptic Religion and the Death of Utopia. London: Penguin Books.

Hervieu-Léger, D. 2006: 'In Search of Certainties: The Paradoxes of Religiosity in Societies of High Modernity', The Hedgehog Review. Critical Reflections on Contemporary Culture 8: After Secularization, 59-68.

Joas, H. 2007: 'Die Zukunft des Christentums', Blätter für Internationale Politik 8'07, 976-984.

Lessing, G. E. 1955 [1779]: Nathan the Wise: A Dramatic Poem in 5 Acts, New York: Ungar.

Levitt, P. 2007: God Needs No Passport: Immigrants and the Changing American Religious Landscape, New York: The New Press.

Marquard, O. 1995: 'Lob des Polytheismus', in: id.: Abschied vom Prinzipiellen, Stuttgart: Reclam.

SOME FUNDAMENTAL QUESTIONS OF THE ART OF LIVING

Wilhelm Schmid, Berlin

Is the life we live our "own"? It is influenced by factors over which we have hardly any control, by forces that seem to treat us as they please. Nonetheless, this life becomes our own – on its last day at the latest. Only we ourselves will bring it to a conclusion, whoever or whatever may have influenced it. We alone are responsible – to ourselves – for this life; no one else will assume this responsibility, certainly not when our life has reached its final moment. The art of living is the seriousness of the attempt to make our life our own in good time, perhaps even to fashion it into a "well-lived life," because we know only we can do so.

Far from being "easy," the art of living is the hard work of enhancing our own autonomy, as well as helping others with theirs, for example by mentorship. The fact that some people casually consider the art of living to be "superficial" can be traced to the lack of serious reflection on it in modern times. In fact, the art of living is "philosophical"; the very term itself (*techne tou biou* in Greek, *ars vitae* in Latin) originates from philosophy and was in use even in ancient times. The attempt to invent again a "philosophy of the art of living" ties in to this ancient concept. That such an attempt has met with interest in the most diverse segments of society (an unexpectedly integrative effect of the art of living) is no doubt owing to our current situation: The end of ideologies, the end of some dreams, socialist as well as capitalist, the end of the overly optimistic utopias associated with science and technology in the 19th and 20th centuries – these have, to an unsuspected extent, abandoned human beings to their own devices. Nothing and no one will ever create the perfect world, a world in which life is unproblematic; ideologies and utopias have instead ushered in new problems that many don't know how to deal with. And even if an "ideal" society were someday achieved – why the naive belief it would be more or less obvious how to live one's life?

The endeavor to reestablish the art of living is the attempt at a response to this naive belief. Important for this, however, is the modality used: not proceeding *normatively*, creating norms and general obligations, but *optatively*, opening up options and possibilities. The suggestions made here should be read in light of this modality: Thus the aim is not to prescribe the contents of the art of living, as in the early history of philosophy, but to highlight conditions and possibilities for filling in such content. Not only the choice in favour of the art of living itself, but also the choice and acquisition of particular life skills, is up to the subject of the art of living.

Philosophical reflection can enhance our skill in the art of living, and our ability to lead our lives with some mastery and awareness. The search for reasons and justifications, the clarification of concepts, the discovery of structures and fundamental connections, the evaluation of conditions, and the distinguishing of possibilities – all of these are philosophical undertakings. In this sense, philosophy can help to clarify a life situation; it helps us to understand better what happens, what options an individual does or does not have. The most crucial assistance to living is provided at the level of thought, for all too often we are the victims not of outer, anonymous powers or inner, psychic structures, but of a mode of thought that allows us to think one way and one way only about a particular matter. Thought can influence our attitudes and behavior, and free us from predicaments.

1. So, the first question is a structural one, it aims at the contexts in which the art of living can find full expression: *In what contexts do I live? How can contexts be created in which I can live as I choose?* A fundamental aspect of the art of living is seeing your own existence against the horizon of overarching structures; social contexts in particular come into view here, and they are permeated throughout by power structures. Attention must be directed at the power that is exercised over you, yet also at the power that you yourself are able to exercise so as not to become a mere minion of a prevailing power, but rather to work to reverse power relationships, and finally to handle your own power with care and not to collaborate thoughtlessly in relations of dominance. When there is dissatisfaction with existing structures, altering them can require the coordinated action of many individuals over a prolonged period, commensurate with the scope and the longevity of structures that cannot be transformed all at once. Social engagement can aim at improving the structural conditions and possibilities for forming life, your own as well as that of others: It is the concern of a "politics of the art of living".

2. The second question is the question of options: *What choice do I have?* The art of living, however it may be arranged in terms of its contents, is based entirely on the choice made by the subject of the art of living. True, there may initially be worry in the face of the question of whether there is a choice at all. The problem of the modern age seems to be that situations in which a choice has to be made are multiplying beyond what individuals are prepared for. So it becomes important to explain just what a choice is and in what way it is to be distinguished from a decision. The most important precondition for making a choice, it seems, is to

take account of its limitation by structural conditions and not to situate it in empty space. A choice, then, opens or closes off a horizon of possibilities, giving an individual life, as well as a common life in a "society of choice", a direction. We need to distinguish the elements of a sensible choice: sensitivity, feeling, judgement, and prudence.

3. In the background all the while is the third question, the subject-question: *Who am I?* Here I mean the question about the self-understanding of the subject of the art of living who chooses and forms him- or herself. The idea of self-formation can be shown to be a constitutive element of philosophical subject-concepts; it goes together with the idea of self-consciousness, which can be found at the center of all such concepts. Yet the subject need not, contrary to a modern conviction, be constituted according to standards of identity, and he or she need not, contrary to a postmodern conviction, pass completely into dissolution, but instead can organize him- or herself in another way, the way of integrity and coherance. His or her self-organization and self-formation are a matter of his or her self-concern. At the same time, it becomes apparent that the subject cannot obtain self-understanding on its own, but only in relation to others and in discussion with them; that the subject is formed in part by others and does not make something out of itself merely through its self-concern; that its self-formation therefore also includes the forming of its relationships to others, and its self-concern likewise concern for others. By extension, concern for others becomes concern for society and its inner constitution.

4. The course you take in life is opened up by the fourth question, the hermeneutical question: *What understanding of life do I have?* Interpretations of your own life and the world in which it takes place make it possible for you to conduct your life. The work of interpretation clarifies what is of importance for the self, what isn't, what seems important and what unimportant, and in what way life is to be carried out in light of each of these considerations. The work of interpretation also aims at becoming acquainted with the phenomena and contexts of the world in which your life takes place, and at deciphering, at knowing, how something is to be understood. In the one case as well as in the other it isn't the simple deduction of an objective meaning that is at issue; rather, the work of interpretation consists in producing meaning yourself and giving sense to your life. By means of interpretation, you work out the knowledge you need for your life, so that you know how to live; in contrast to the form of knowledge of the sciences, the distinctiveness of "life knowledge" lies not at least in its conscious perspectivity. The main focus of pedagogical work in the passing on of life knowledge is imparting

the hermeneutical abilities the student needs in order to derive life knowledge for himself.

5. The crucial fifth and basic question has nothing to do with the possibilities for forming one's life, or with the details of the execution; rather, it calls their *sense* into doubt from the outset: *Why form one's life at all?* This question resonates unspoken for one who regards the undertaking of the art of living as senseless from the start, and in principle such senselessness cannot be disputed. With regard to sense or senselessness, the individual itself must decide. However, a weighty argument for forming one's life can be drawn from ancient philosophy: Why form your life? *On account of its shortness.* That is the *final argument* – "final", because it still remains at the end, when all others have been played through; "final", because it relates to "the end". It gains particular force in cultures in which the individual is no longer preserved in the bosom of a community and in the traditional, endless succession of generations, but instead feels the full power of death. Death does not inevitably mean that life as such is at an end, just that it is at an end in this form. Death is a limit, but it doesn't exist "in itself" – it depends on the idea you form of it; this in turn depends on the culture in which you live. Only modern man dies in horrible loneliness; only for him is death the absolute limit of life; only for him does his own death mark "actuality." In regard to death, the philosophy of the art of living follows the ancient Stoic philosophy rather than its modern adaptation in Heidegger: it is concerned with a consciousness of the limitedness of life, not with a "being unto death".

What we owe to death is thus the limitation of life. If this limit were not present, forming your life would be unimportant. The explosive power this realization holds, not only in terms of the individual but also in terms of politics, is displayed in revolts and revolutions. It was displayed in 1989 in then-East Germany, when people asserted their own lives as the only ones they had; rather than let their lives go to waste, they sought to realize their dreams in their own lifetimes. Death as the limit of life called upon them to live, and to live in a fulfilled way. This didn't require any fixation on death, just a consciousness of the limit it sets. The limit to life is at the same time the condition of its possibility: You ruin life when you want to have it forever, just as you ruin a pleasure when you want to enjoy it perpetually. Every pleasure would last an eternity if it could, but eternity would be its death. This is true of life as well. Even if immortality becomes possible, it will hardly be desirable – it can mean only the quiescence of life. For why live life now if you can do so in the distant future as well? Why do anything at all? If there were no death, you would have to invent it in order not to lead an immortally boring life that consisted in endlessly postponing living. Hence the affirmation of the limitation: so as to not let life simply go on, but really to live it as long as it lasts. Put pointedly: It is the limit provided by death to which we owe the joy of living. To philosophize is to learn how to live in the consciousness of this limit.

6. The sixth and concluding question is the practical one: *What, specifically, can I do? How can I conduct my life?* That is the form the fundamental question of ethics ("What should I do?") assumes in the art of living. With this question, the first step is taken toward assuming possession of your life in order to fashion a life of your own out of a life in the abstract. Since the freedom to conduct your life individually is an idea of the modern age, we have to discuss the conditions and possibilities of life in its modern meaning; in need of special attention are the inner contradictions of the modern age itself, which raise for the conduct of life the question of a life with contradictions. Yet the central problem is the modern understanding of freedom. Not only has this understanding, because of its extremely broad concern for liberation, neglected work on forms of freedom; it has also sought to negate the contradictory structure constitutive of freedom. Because the problem has only intensified in the "postmodern age", the search for an *other modern age* (term of Ulrich Beck, used in his book "Risikogesellschaft. Auf dem Weg in eine andere Moderne", Frankfurt am Main 1986) – an other modern age whose concern it is to work out a *practice* of freedom and within whose milieu the subject of the art of living strives to conduct its life itself, implement a lifestyle, and acquire a form of life – begins not least in the examination of the challenge that modern and postmodern media and information technologies represent for the question of how to conduct one's life.

This question concerns both the basic attitude you can assume and life as you live it everyday; in each case, it's a matter of utilizing exercises and techniques with the help of which your life can be given form. They should be regarded only as examples, such as exercises for forming habits, or techniques for dealing with desires; further techniques are aimed at dealing with pain, and a separate exercise depicts living with death, the object of our utmost concern. On account of the shortness of life, practice in dealing with the peculiar phenomenon of time has a fundamental character. The techniques of trial have an experimental character; their deliberate employment leads directly to an essayistic way of life. Techniques for dealing with emotions, such as anger, can be refashioned by reaching back to the ancient philosophy of the art of living. For the acquisition of an artful mode of dealing with contradictions, techniques of irony should be brought in. The technique of reversal bears a clear connection to the problems of the modern and postmodern ages, and helps us to put negative thinking in the place of rampant positive thinking. And finally, perhaps as a Cassandra of a coming epoch, melancholy enters the art of living and raises the question of techniques for dealing with it; in response to this question, the classic technique of the art of living is recalled: composure. We need "ultimate composure" for ecological relationships, which are fundamental for life and provide the only framework within which an art of living can find expression. A composed way of living is also a mode of the "art of living in cyberspace". Qualities that often count in the popular imagination as elements of the art of living – health, serenity, and happiness – require an examination of their own, lest we uncritically adopt the modern understanding of these concepts. For instance, the concept of happiness seems, as a goal, to be above all criticism. Yet it is often equated with the pleasant and successful life, and usually stands for a feeling of well-being, for a festive mood of "feeling good", as well as for happiness in the here and now, although what would seem to matter is living largely not in the here and now. And, finally, we need to speak about the popular goal of the art of living: "living well"; this must be reinterpreted, however, from a philosophical point of view.

And what can "living well", "living beautifully" mean in this context? As with the concept of the art of living itself, "living well" is a forgotten concept of ancient ethics and aesthetics that needs to be reintroduced into the debate, in order to get beyond the all-too-uncritically conceived "good life" or even "successful life." In the history of philosophy, for Plato just as for Diogenes or Epicurus and the Stoics, this was a common formula: "to live well", "to live beautifully" (*kalos zen*). A man who said he wasn't fit for philosophy promptly received the reply from Diogenes: "Why do you live then, if you aren't concerned about living well?" To be concerned about living well is to not simply drift through life, following the law of inertia, but instead to intervene in one's existence and consciously work it out. In the tradition of humanism, the idea of living well has played a leading role. Against this background, the philosophically reflective art of living is not meant as a fair-weather art of living that could serve as a luxury for those who already have everything else. Instead, it is meant as an existential art of living, according to which every ethic begins with the attitude and behavior of the individual himself, so as to work on the individual's own life and, together with others, on a common life in society.

The practitioner of the art of living distinguishes himself by leading a fulfilled life. He is more thorough than others, for he seeks to reflect on himself and his life and to understand the "reasons" for his life. He is perhaps more far-sighted than others, for he lives, at once passionately and serenely, in the broad horizon of the wide variety of experiences he has had and potentially could have. He is one of whom prudence can be expected, but one who remains curious enough to risk new, uncertain experiences again and again. He is one who in every respect is on the move. In this way, he's in the middle of life and at the same time far outside it, so that he can see things and himself from outside, an experience just as painful as pleasurable. But we shouldn't speak of the art of living with too much pathos, for as a rule it is experienced as something absent. The art of living isn't something we have, but rather something we lack, and will dreadfully lack time and time again.

References and Bibliography

Schmid, W. *Ökologische Lebenskunst. Was jeder Einzelne für das Leben auf dem Planeten tun kann*, Suhrkamp Taschenbuch, Frankfurt a. M. 2008.

-------------- *Glück – Alles, was Sie darüber wissen müssen und warum es nicht das Wichtigste im Leben ist*, Insel Verlag, Frankfurt a. M. 2007, 8th edition 2009. Translations: Dutch (2008), Latvian (2008), Danish (2008), Finnish (2009), Italian (2009).

Die Fülle des Lebens. 100 Fragmente des Glücks, Insel Taschenbuch, Frankfurt a. M. 2006, 2th edition 2007. Translations: Dutch (2007).

-------------- *Die Kunst der Balance. 100 Facetten der Lebenskunst*, Insel Taschenbuch, Frankfurt a. M. 2005, 4th edition 2007. Translations: Dutch (2005), Latvian (2006).

-------------- *Mit sich selbst befreundet sein. Von der Lebenskunst im Umgang mit sich selbst*, Suhrkamp Verlag, Reihe Bibliothek der Lebenskunst, Frankfurt a. M. 2004, Taschenbuch 2007. Translations: Dutch (2004).

-------------- *Schönes Leben? Einführung in die Lebenskunst*, Suhrkamp Verlag, Reihe Bibliothek der Lebenskunst, Frankfurt a. M. 2000, 6th edition 2004, Taschenbuch 2005. Translations: Latvian (2001), Dutch (2001), Serbian (2001), Italian (2007).

-------------- *Philosophie der Lebenskunst – Eine Grundlegung*, Suhrkamp Taschenbuch Wissenschaft, Frankfurt a. M. 1998 (10th edition 2007).

THE LIFE IN THE WORLD OF DIONYSUS AND APOLLO: THE GREEK UNDERSTANDING OF THE TRAGIC AND THE DELPHIC THEOLOGY OF THE HUMANITY

Karl Matthäus Woschitz, Graz

1. Introductory remark

On the small shoreline of Asia Minor - for some more valuable than the whole continent - more than two and a half millenniums ago the mythology was let aside and the philosophical way to knowledge was paved.

A great comic poet Aristophanes brings the inquiring of the so-called pre-Socratic philosophers with pointing out the sentence: "You dethroned Zeus, and Vortex, the turbulence, is the king". With the wh-questions *what, how and why* the restless inquiring comes into the world with all irritations. As Hans Blumenberg puts it into the sentence: "It is one's own fault to ask *why* and being annoyed by the answer. "Why-questions accompany and seam to be the path of philosophy and theology:

Cur Deus homo, Why did God become a man?, the question asked by Augustinus and Anselm of Cantenbury;

"Why there is being at all and not rather nothing", asks Martin Heidegger. But there is also the mystical marveling of Meister Eckhart "without why": "God knows no why (lat. quare), but rather he is Why of everyone and everything" (Expos. in Joh.).

And the German baroque poet Angelus Silesius (1624-1677) speaks in the saying of epigrammatic Alexandrine: "The rose (Christ) is without why, it blooms because it blooms".

While being accompanied with the questions all his life, man's desire to comprehend the meaning(s) is inevitable.

But each culture whether it is understood religiously or irreligiously is associated with the three questions, comprehension of which could be (through its social reflection) only partially understood:

Is it the phenomenon of coincidence with good fortune and bad fortune and the inherent question of how could an indeterminable be determined and unreachable obtained.

The Greek tragedy circles around the question of unquestionable fate that stands also over the actions of Gods and human activity.

- The second phenomenon is that of guilt with the question about *unde malum,* the question about the source of evil with its attempts to overcome it.

- The third question asks about the phenomenon of death, after morality of a life balance - with a longing that murderer should not triumph over his victim. The question of afterwards and transcendent meta-world is being connected with this.

The conceptual confrontation: 'Apollo – Dionysus' is personified by the two leading antique Greece concepts in the sense of existence and world's interpretation. Apollo symbolizes the harmoniously organized common life of Polis, the fullness of wisdom's limitation in ethics, the distance, which holds moderation, but also the vivid formation in art, the reflection of philosophy and the investigation in science. Through the mouth of his in Delphi, Apollo sets his moral demands, supervises the observance of moral commandments and so becomes the holder of mental purity and human justice. The atonement for the crime lies in his hand as well.

Dionysus, the God of wine, fertility, the orgy, which grabs people "in neck-breaking stupor". He is the God of man's advancement in his existence. In the Dionysian experience of ecstasy (*ek stasis* = going out, and enthusiasm /*en-theos* = being imbued by God) the life principle becomes experienced substance: the intimacy of man is spreading out of itself and turns itself outward while in the enthusiasm God is grasped by a man and takes the place of human consciousness in mystical unification.

The question why Apollo and Dionysos will be discussed in details further on.

If we re asking about freedom, responsibility, identity, creativity, as well as culture and religion, and knowledge of a human, Karl Raimund Popper's "three worlds theory" („Drei-Welten-Theorie") can offer us some guidance.

Born in 1902 in Vienna and in 1937 from Austria emigrated philosopher Popper is amongst the most influential thinkers of our time.

Popper's critical rationalism turns itself towards supposed self security of the philosophical enterprise of his time, and tries to show the hypothetical character of human theories formation with the central concept of "fallibilism" ("Falsifizierbarkeit").

In collection of his essays "Objective Knowledge" from 1972, in which his central positions are represented, Popper in chapter three sketches his so-called three worlds theory („Drei-Welten-Theorie")". In this model, world 1 is the world of the physical objects and states in space and time. It is the empirical outer world of objects and processes (Popper 1974: 106 ff.).

World 2 is the mental world, the world of our mental states, of our subjective perceptions, thoughts, feelings, thought processes and human consciousness, of thinking, speaking, consent and of objection, but also of self-identity.

World 3 or the "Third World" is the cultural world, the world of objective thought contents, the cultural and religious traditions, poetic, philosophical, theological and religious thoughts and works, architecture, works of art and the symbolic structures, music, but also the world of meaningfulness of life and its references. As being a reflection of a man, the world 3 is for Karl Popper extensively autonomous.

All the three worlds are in mutual interaction. Whereas the world 2, the world of consciousness of a man, bearing the role of a bounding link, occurs as a tradition, symbolizing, interpreting and communicating. In his personal-being and his language, man sets himself in relation to the world, to a man and to the more-than-humanity (God). World 3, the venerable world of great and enduring thoughts, the home of a man told in his stories and myths, theories and his religion; it is like a reflection of the Chinese sign for a house: "heart and spirit under the roof". Karl Popper in the following lines presents a plea for the preservation of world 3:

"What I regard as the most important point is not the sheer autonomy and anonymity of the third world, or the admittedly very important point that we always owe almost everything to our predecessors and to the tradition which they created: that we thus owe to the third world especially our rationality – that is our subjective mind, the practice of critical and self-critical ways of thinking, and the corresponding dispositions. More important than all this, I suggest, is the relation between ourselves and our work, and what can be gained for us from this relation…As it happens with our children, so it does with our theories… On human level, this trying out is done almost entirely in the third world, by attempts to represent, in the theories of this third world, our first world, and perhaps our second world, more and more successfully; by trying to get nearer to the truth –to fuller, a more complete, a more interesting, logically stronger and more relevant truth –relevant to our problems" (Popper 1974: 147-8).

"What may be called the second world – the world of the mind – becomes, on human level, more and more the link between the first and third world: our actions in the first world are influenced by our second-world grasp of the third world. This is why it is impossible to understand the human mind and the human self without understanding the third world (the 'objective mind' or 'spirit'); and why it is impossible to interpret either the third world as a mere expression of the second, or the second as the mere reflection of the third" (Popper 1974: 148-9).

We owe our reason, our critical and self-critical thinking and action to the interaction with the world 3. We owe our spiritual growth to it.

2. The Greek Mystery of the Apollo and Dionysus religion: Order and ecstasy (To the world 3)

Culture-theoretically considered Apollo and Dionysus, the two half-sib gods, both children of Zeus with symbolic forms of Leto and Semele, the two elementary powers and poles in man, the strivings of the will (Dionysus) and the world seizing power of imagination (Apollo), the dynamic life in its irrational being-out-of-himself and the Minion attempts of integration and sublimation. Generally spoken, the faith of Greeks has been seen its gods as in-worldly acting powers and figures, furthermore as primordial and mirror images of the human and its interpretations of encountered reality.

In this aesthetically (*aisthesis* – visually seen, obvious) sketched religion with its configurations of the polytheistic divine world overflowing us deeply, in-dogmatic religion told in a "poetic" shape, in which the longings, questions, anxieties of a human are projected to a meta-horizon. In this sense Friedrich Schiller's sentence of Hellenic religion is summarized: "In its gods a man paints himself". The concept of god is a predicate concept, i.e. where the almighty, the powerful meets a man or seizes him; it is the divine. Not God is love, as in the 1st letter of John in the New Testament or the Papal Letter from Benedict XVI. *Caritas in Veritate*, but rather the Love is God, as well as *Dike*, Right, *Eirene*, Peace, Strife and Envy.

R. M. Rilke puts it in a double verse:

> "There are only gods. Through their mirrors
> we draw out from background of animals and plants".

In the Greek polis-religion of rule and order with its cults of gods, symbolized in Apollo, the Dionysus religion and its mystery cults, an element of genuine mystics, a religion of ecstasy and mystical unification as deification, breaks into it. In his treatise "*De natura deorum*" (3.58) Cicero writes: *Dionysos multos habemus*, we have many figures of Dionysus, and thus points to the vast diversity of this deity that stands for ecstatic-inebriated life experience, but also for fertility and vegetative growth, for life enhancement as well as for transgression of civilization standards and boundaries, for the poetic inspiration and the irrational, but also for solving, purifying and scarifying actions of mysteries. Central art forms of

Greek tragedy and comedy as well as the dithyramb, the Dionysian dance song are originated in the cult of Dionysus. A special festival culture was devoted to him, so that this god of life enhancement stands at the beginning of the entire European theater culture.

The conjecture of Friedrich Nietzsche still has a validity today, when he says, "that also we - contemporary people being able to recognize, and we godless and anti-metaphysicians,... still take our fire from conflagration, which was lighted by the millennium old faith, by Christian faith, which was also Plato's faith, stating that God is the truth, that the truth is divine" (Nietzsche, 1972: 208).

In his first work *The Birth of Tragedy from the Spirit of the Music* (1872) Friedrich Nietzsche (1844-1899) – philosopher of upheaval and demon of crisis endeavors to expose the hidden topic of 'birth' in all metamorphoses of the zeitgeist, in order to show that the Western culture in its vital primordial grounds in two basic drives is anchored: the Apollonian spiritual power and order and the Dionysian inebriation and ecstasy.

Apollo stands for measure and limitation in space and time, for the wisdom of standards and the vivid form in the artistic formation.

However, Dionysus stands for the emotional, passionately moved, dreamlike, ecstatically drunken (cf. King Midas). Therewith Nietzsche makes him for the leading concept of a philosophy of life and modern irrationalism.

The last legible letters that Nietzsche wrote before he tragically submerged into the night of his insanity fantasies, are subscribed with "Dionysus" or with "The crucified". In a short, bright moment of the awakening; he sent his friend Overbeck a letter containing only a single sentence, which sounds like a Dionysian cry of rapture (Verzückung): "Sing me a new song: the world is transfigured and all the heavens rejoice!"

In this identification with the Bacchic ecstasy the tragic philosopher finds himself as to become a particle of the self-changing cosmos, the unification of self and non-self, of human, God and nature. In such being-out-of-self, the first cause (Urgrund) arises, the One (das Eine) as a truth before all differentiation, the One that is at once all and nothing of all apparently existing things.

A) Apollo the son of Zeus and of mortal Leto, was born on the island Delos (which reveals). He, the Greek god of light was presented in the timeless form of youthfulness and blossom, in form of expression of the timeless life-fullness and meaningfulness.

Apollo, the god of light, is a bearer of attributes of reason, temperance, and also a symbol of intellectual maturity and the protector of the flying spirit. He is the god who pulls himself away, so to say a deus absconditus, and who returns back with the first swallows to his epiphany. As a divine Archeget, he leads the muses at dance and singing and accompanies them on his guitar, lyre – relentless to Marsyas, the flute player, who challenged him to the contest. His string-music as a component of harmony, but also of philosophical abstraction, had a purifying and clarifying effect on soul and body, an aspect that was basic for the Pythagorean circles, therefore we can talk with a theology of number about a Pythagorean Apollo-religion (cf. Paestum in south Italy).

In Doric temple, Vitruv sees an abstract image of god Apollo himself. This is the architecture of pure reason, order, proportions of the masculine body.

The Apollo's cult sanctuary and oracle sanctuary in Delphi, on the southern slope of Parnass, was his central consecration sites and the place where the secret of the Greek is presented on the most tangible way.

a) In the ban circle of Apollo's temple, votive pictures (Weihebilder) were set up in order to give him the human resemblance and beauty and in order to be in his vicinity. At the time of his government, Emperor Nero, had ordered to bring 500 of the most famous statues to Rome and Plinius the Elder estimated that there were still 3000 statues.

b) In the most interior site of Apollo's temple stood the stone monument of Omphalos, the navel of the world, which was in every day ceremony covered with a woolen fabric. A navel, being the scar of a cut that separates a child from the blood stream of mother. It reminds one on the old mistress from Delphi »Gaia«, the mother of the earth, the bearer and donor of life.

Omphalos is a symbol of birth, a bleeding wound, the step and the exile into the time, in the corruptible (Hinfällige) and transitory - as it was the Greek's »original sin.« The step in space and time is moved in Delphi into the present of Apollo and into the **Konnex** of Delphic theology and idea of humanity connected with him. Its core sentence sounds: *Gnothi seauton, theneton onta,* recognize yourself in your own mortality, your boundaries; recognize that you are a mortal. This epitome of the Delphic theology and wisdom – the consideration of the mortal (fragment 590 of Sophocles) should be a regulative for man; his thinking, feelings, endeavors and activities.

c) To the *delphika parangelmata*, to the Delphic sayings furthermore belongs: "Not too much of everything" (*meden agan*) as a measure of the middle, which is true: "Temperance is the best" (*metron ariston*), as counterweight to the fundamental sin of hybris, the arrogance, which disregards and breaks the defined boundary (cf. Myth of Daedalus and Icarus). Hence, it holds the truth: "Be prudent " (*sophronei*), the virtue of prudence, which is praised by Sophocles in his "Antigone" (683ff.) as the biggest of the divine gifts to the human heart; in this virtue it completes itself the humane in all its shapes and measures.

Another imperative of Delphic theology sounds: "Mind the given" (*kairon hora*).

d) In the Delphic oracle, the mouth of Apollo's prophetess Pythia mediated between the questions of mortals and the answers of the god's prophets, first of all with the divine *yes or no*, but later with enigmatic sayings that need interpretation, and which should decoded as the answers to give direction.

e) Apollo, the god of order and definition (*definire* = to set limits) is not only the god of clear prudence and ethos, but rather the god who sends evil and banishes evil, who creates suffering and heals suffering. Above all, he is also the god of purification where healing was considered as a special form of purification, cathartics. As "impure" was considered everything that endangered or offended order and was in opposition with a common value. The ethical purity of the Delphic Apollo religion finds its reverberation and its development in the platonic philosophy. Apollo is the divine light coming from the sky that gives to things clear and sharp outlines, the god of the pure reason and the dawning thought.

B) Dionysus, the ease of feeling, experience and perception, the experience of sense enthusiasm, (*en-theos*), the acceptance of the god by the drunkenness in itself, being overwhelmed by him, ecstatically dragged out of oneself, over entire apollonian reasonableness. It was Homer who already called Dionysus "a raving god" (***mainomenos,*** Il 6,132), one who can draw his cultic worshipers in ritual raving under the spell of "divine madness" (*theia mania*). Dionysus is also the god of transformations and disguise, but also of the painful consciousness of emerging and passing away, of die and become (Stirb und Werde), which is at the same time a trans-rational ground of being of all things affirmed.

Dionysus works with juices of fruits, its crown being the juicy grapevine, with which one drinks the god himself and therefore changes oneself. In the Dionysian frenzy, the irrationality of death and life is celebrated at the same time, due to its double essence it belongs to, on one hand, a boiling life abundance along with the life-giving power of procreation, and on the other hand, to a raving wildness and tremendousness of annihilation. He himself is the embodiment (Inbild) of this fate, for he was torn up and consumed by Titans after instigation of Hera.

a) The god of inebriating wine is also the god of poetic tragedy, the god of tragic triumph. A specific festival culture was staged to his honor. If the empire of Apollo was the lyrical song, a voice that sings alone, then the empire of Dionysus is the game of a tragic action in which several voices and the choir speak together and are placed on the stage, (*Theo-ater Koilon*), a dark "*ecce homo*", see, the (tragic) man.

The Greek tragedy, the timeless and splendid creation of Greeks, was dedicated to Dionysus. It had – in order to show his honor – a cultic, god-official character and served to his function of a savior, as Dionysus Lysios.

b) In the action of "transfer" in fear and trembling" the spectators should have experienced in a kind of healing psycho-hygiene as a relief, hence, a catharsis, purification. The myth presented in the performance is "performative" art of mimetic literature in order to present existential affectedness.

c) In tragedies staged to the honor of Dionysus there are unfolded great topics of *conditio humana et deorum*: in Aeschylus, the power and glory of divine acting, Zeus and his Dike, the justice; in Sophocles the questions of human aristocracy and its humaneness, but also a man standing under the blessing and curse of fate, represented in Oedipus, *oi-dipous*, woeful biped, woeful man;

Oedipus = woe, biped, woe man, the wisest of the men, who knew to solve the riddle, is at the same time the most tragic: After he had blinded himself – the patricide husband of his own mother - he represents a part of the frights of this world.

d) Anecdote: How overwhelmed were the listeners in the theater, notes a chronicler, when an actor a short omicron stretched to a broad omega, thousands jumped out the seats because of excitement.

e) Dionysus is also the god of a "mask", the symbol of his appearance form, which was hung on a tree or pillar. In the mask, distance and vicinity is represented at the same time: a distance in rigidity of the sightless and voiceless with the emptiness of eyes and mouth on the one hand, but also a vicinity, on the other, a through-sounding voice of a person (*personare*) of the concealed countenance. The mask transforms and unites. It transforms a dead-like rigidity into the talking life.

f) Dionysus' myth is a genetic and a cosmic myth; as a genetic myth it explains the double nature of man, the Dionysian-divine part and the titanic negative one. Zeus had burned the Titans, who had torn up and consumed Dionysus's child, with a lightening to ashes and a man had been formed from it. As the cosmic myth, it explains a dismemberment and composing of Dionysus's child in the cyclical returning and renewal of life, the annual die and be in nature.

The Dionysian "apocalypse" of the ecstasy, however, leaves in unity all the three time modes: past, present and the future, but also the self and non-self, the divine and the nature of man in the experienced and inebriated moment of the "now" in one.

g) Also in the mysteries of Dionysus, the idea of transformation reigns. In the ecstatic crossing over, the mystery of Dionysus (cf. pictures of Villa dei misteri in Pompeii) touches the secret of one as the truth behind the many. In this mystical religious form of Antique and its main-discipline both lines of Antique piety intertwine, the myth and the ritual. It is a ritualistic religiosity with sacred actions (orgia) and contemplative intuition and self-immersing into the contemplated (epopteia).

In this, (the actor/myste in a performance) goes in the specific relation to the deities of mysteries- and to their fate "die and become" (cf. Osiris, Attis, Dionysus, Demeter/Persephone,) to participate on their part. In such mysteries-religiosity changes the doer's (mist) self-identification. In the Bacchantes of Euripides it meets the blessing:

"Blessed, those fortunate, knowing of god's consecration and leading a pure life" (Bakh 73-75).

In those fortunate connectedness of Mysteries' deity and actor/myste with life and death, two mark-stones are notified, which have been the limits and the line of separation in the meeting of "die and be". The relation of 'God-man' comes to existential level .

Cicero says that - regarding to centuries of old practice of mysteries of Eleusis - those people were directed to humanity, to the right lifestyle and "for better hope in dying" (cum spe meliore moriendi, De leg. 2.36).

3. Epilog

The third great preserver of the classic archetype Friedrich Hölderlin (1770-1843), besides Goethe and Schiller, in his philosophical aphorisms in his essay "Over religion" places Dionysus, "god of myth", simply into the middle of action, with the Dionysian appeal that "everyone celebrates mythically a higher life of community". And in his elegy "Bread and Wine", the most important post-antique Dionysus poem, makes Dionysus the cipher of mythologically embodied life context, the universal synthesis with the image of Christ.

The hymn: In day-night metaphorics, "night" means the unfulfilled time of the present, and "day" means the time of fulfilling perfection. The Poet brings "Demetera's gift of bread and Dionysus's gift of wine into comprehensive synthesis to the Eucharistic gifts of Jesus Christ and his commemorative meal, in which there still lives "the quiet and unifying thankfulness". A community-forming "joy within the spirit" (V. 134) is celebrated.

With the two mythological figurations, the god of light - Apollo, the image of measure and limit, prudence and order as well as rationality and perfect arcadic existence on one hand, and Dionysus, the figuration for desire of crossing the limits, wild motion and ecstatic de-individualization on the other, "And always in the unbound goes the longing" – in the last hymn "Mnemosyne" of Friedrich Hölderlin – the antique Greece structured the polar tension in a man and brought it into a conceptual opposition. Both antipodes were somehow related to each other and were divided at the same time, as Plutarch reports (de E 389c), the delphic festival year, Dionysus - the winter and spring months, and Apollo - the summer months. This polar unifying contrast in man has retained its relevance till today – due to experiences of the modern times civilization.

References and Bibliography

Nietzsche, Friedrich, (1972) *Werke* (ed. by K. Schlechta), Vol. 2.

Popper, Karl R. (1974) *Objective Knowledge. An Evolutionary Approach*, Oxford: Oxford University Press.

Translated from German by Janez Juhant and Mateja Repanšek Tkalec

ON LIVING WITH: DIALOGUE AS THE WAY TO THE ART OF PERSONAL AND COMMON LIFE

Janez Juhant, Ljubljana

The clash of civilizations as a menace

The development of modern society is about to encounter serious problems, apart from the fact that "the clashes of civilizations" are intensifying. Some serious questions have emerged: will be there enough resources for the survival of the coming generations? Will people who have enough to eat be ready to share the existing food supply? And how will future generations live? We have already problems with the emissions of CO_2 and there is a growing problem of pollution. How to provide the sources of energy, water and other necessary resources for the survival of all men?

There are still clashes between peoples about the manner of distributing the present supply of essential raw materials, sources of energy and water. The wars or oppression in Tibet and Rwanda, the conflicts between Russia and other states of the former Soviet Union, especially with the NATO allies, between South and North Korea, Japan and China, and other South-East Asian countries, between Iran and other Islamic states and Israel stem from the difficult task of finding a language of cooperation which would enable sharing of goods among all people. The dispute between Slovenia and Croatia, two relatively small countries, is about the redistribution of economical power gained by traffic ways in the Adriatic Sea.

The main problem is the lack of dialogue on these questions. All partners lack the willingness to train in the ways of dialogue. There are many reasons behind this. The liberal thinking as a basis of the modern production system does not take care for underprivileged groups. Particularly children, women, and powerless people in general are excluded from the process of dialogue. They are not able to participate in these modern processes on equal grounds. As John Rawls pointed out, there should be equal positions for all people and everybody should have general access to the main societal positions and sources. But differences in the so-called global world make it difficult to provide everybody with an equal starting point (Rawls 1971). The liberal manner of the Darwinian paradigm encourages the exclusion and rivalry, and it seems to be the predominant mode of the political, economic and other societal life as such. This, however, promotes exclusion of the weak. So the prevailing formula of modern life is not cooperation but exclusion.

The modern liberalistic way of life, the ways of negotiation in the politics and in other individual and societal areas of human endeavour do not address real problems of being, nor promote dialogue, because the tendencies of protectionism, exclusion and discriminations prevail. Yet the global development demands dialogue and cooperation. It seems there is no other way than a living dialogue about the civic and cultural foundations of our development.

The "lack of feelings"

Cooperation and dialogue must be learnt. Young people should be introduced to dialogue in order to experience their human being and to learn to deal with it. If these prerequisites of free dialogue in lives of families and other basic structures of society are not granted, man cannot develop his human capacities to live as a human being.

How can man develop the ability for dialogic communication? This happens mostly in the first years of one's life. If children grew up among animals they could not develop any of these foundations of human life. Similarly, children growing up in dysfunctional or asocial families experience difficulties in contacts with others. The modern way of life provides children with few or no possibilities to socialise with their parents or other relational persons. They are predominantly using non-living means of communications – electronic media and internet – their abilities for genuine human communication is thus stunned. Consequently, young people are unable to deal with their feelings, though this is a sine qua non for normal human communication. They cannot be consistently familiarised with the main elements of human being and they are weak or incapable to perform any inter-human exchange. If they are not enabled to develop their first emotional life, they will not be able to mend it later.

The popularity of talk-shows, therapeutic workshops and other communication services comes as no surprise, as they are trying to compensate for this serious human deficiency in modern society (Gerjolj, Erzar/Kompan). Because of this marriages are not stable, young people are not capable of a steady living dialogue nor can they share their problems (Slatinek 2008:). The same holds true in other areas of life.

Who will enable man in his human condition and teach him the way of dialogue? In modern non-personal relations parents and relational persons lack time and opportunities to enable their children to learn the forms of dialogue. Most of our daily life is enacted only through business and other impersonal activities. The "lack of feeling" is compensated by searching for special events, "full adventures", "enriched" by alcohol, drugs and sexual exploits, all of which are a way to compensate for the lack of feelings exchange. These all are consequences of the modern competitive and excluding society.

Criticising this "one-sided way" society, Joachim Bauer in his book *Prinzip Menschlichkeit* ("A Principle of Humanity", 2006) denounces Darwin's "war of nature" as a principle of inhumanity. Darwin's notion that man and the entire nature are inherently determined to struggle for life, and that this struggle means war of all against all, is not in accordance with human nature, it is indoctrinated. Yet this is exactly how Richard Dawkins (2006) revives Darwinism by stressing that the "selfish gene" directs our actions. Bauer stresses that life is enabled by cooperation, while Darwin and Dawkins ignore this fact of life. They maintain that in Western culture struggle and fight prevailed over cooperation and connectedness. According to Bauer, we can find ample examples of this cooperation in nature, as well as in our own lives. Bauer points out: "The model of Darwin neglects the fundamental characteristic of phenomena which stays at the beginning of all biology, the phenomenon of the cooperation " (Bauer 2006: 128).

The process of dialogue as a condition for a good life

Joachim Bauer considers man a being of dialogue. He is of the opinion that human genes are predisposed to cooperation and not struggle. The man is by his nature predisposed to cooperate and not to exclude others. There are no proofs that human genes are by nature made to exclude others. On the contrary: Bauer as a physician confirms that genes are willing to cooperate. Aggression is caused by lack of cooperation and love. Cooperation is so important for us that, as Bauer stresses, our brains do not agree with uncooperative unfairness; they consider such behaviour punishable (Bauer 2006: 185).

Life of nature and man is according Bauer to a large extent cooperation and not exclusion, it means that man is willing to cooperate and not to fight. This view of dialogic life seems to oppose the way Rene Girard regards the genesis of life. He emphasises that from the beginning of human civilization the struggle of all against all seems to be the prevailing mode of existence, and modern society also confirms this.

The scapegoat

Rene Girard is dealing with desiring and phenomenon of malice as a crucial problem of all societies. As we know, for Buddhists desires are the cause of malice.

Man desires objects because others possess them. To get objects means to compete with others who own them. The primary objects of desire are food, territory and women (Palaver 2003: 69). This desire for possession stimulates the one who desires to imitate (*mimesis*) his rival with the objects of his desire. This is, according to Girard, the main characteristic of individuals and groups. This can be easily seen in children. When one child is playing with a toy or a tool, the other will want to play with the same toy or tool. The same struggle occurs between families, groups, nations. All this should follow strict and exact societal rules. When a crisis erupts due to scarcity of goods, members of a society have to search for solutions to avoid clashes or wars.

Girard, like Thomas Hobbes, is convinced there is some "natural violent condition". It is the state of war, all against all. This is the mimetic crisis (Girard: *mimetic furor*, *emballement mimétique*, *effervescence collective*). The cultural history knows different examples of this crisis and the culture is in fact a way of dealing with these crises or, which is the same, a way such crises could be solved. Different societies worked out precise mechanisms to deal with these societal situations, which are in some cases very dangerous. People are bound to find the so-called "scapegoat" to overcome a crisis.

According to Girard, there are two principal ways to solve the "mimetic crisis":

The first is more usual and present throughout the history of mankind and is described both in ancient myths and modern literature. In times of crisis people find a scapegoat to avoid clashes or war of all against all. Girard speaks about *the mimesis of reunification* or about *the mimesis of reconciliation*. But this could be achieved only with a scapegoat. To avoid the mimetic or sacrificial crisis, it is necessary to channel the mimetic desire (Girard: 1987: 26).

The other is a Christian solution. Christianity differs from other teachings in that it takes the position of victims. Through Jesus Christ offerings Christians are invited to intercede on behalf of the poor. The so-called "mimetic situation" has to be overcome by willingly accepting the position of the weak.

Nothing without sacrifice

These observations by Joachim Bauer and René Girard, as well as the experiences of our daily lives, help us see the gravity of the mimetic crisis. Modern man was by Darwin's theory and galloping technology pushed into the current competition and rivalry. According to Girard, man as such is always a rival because he desires the objects of his fellowmen. Societies have always encountered the problem of how to overcome this rivalry. The other has been always the standard against which one measures himself. In the same sense the other is one's rival, because he wants to posses the same "things", the same goods, his rival is trying to obtain. Rivalry emerges because goods are limited in quantity. Rivals have to reach a peaceful solution to sustain their societal order and to prevent shortages of goods. Yet this cannot be done without sacrifice.

In modern liberal society the situation changes, especially in the post-communist societies. They display increasing tendencies toward rivalry, ousting the other and taking goods for oneself, societal equidistance is thus weakened. These tendencies are augmented by economist and financial decision-makers. Multinational companies and their owners are gathering ever more economic and financial power, thus ousting the other. The society is consequently divided into the player and the excluded – "the third". The modern society is a quite well adapted society, yet it does not take care of all its members. Involved in the system are the so-called "*double-binds*". Apart from them, there are those who do not participate in societal connections, "the third". The old societies knew only the rivalry between *double-binds*. All conflicts and use of force usually occur between *double-binds*, it means the society consisted only of rivals who have "to solve the problem". They had to act according to the sacrificial or mimetic crisis to preserve the well-adapted society.

According to Girard, the essence of *mimesis* is insincerity, as the society functions with some insincere suppositions. It accepts the covert suppositions of desires and the pertaining rivalry. Insincerity is the basis of new myths referring to these desires. To overcome this insincerity, people should be always aware of their obligations to this mythic past. Against this background, people were in the past always reminded to uphold stable societal relations, it means one should not question this mythical supposition but preserve and to cultivate it. All people in these primordial societies took part in the mimetic sacrificial mystery and were thus all equal. They were obliged to sustain the equivalence of society. Lack of goods was inconceivable as it would have disastrous consequences.

Paul Demouchel shows how Girard's mimetic theory works in modern global conditions. This society tolerates scarcity of goods but it has also invented the third, the excluded. The societies of old also included rivals, "the principle of solidarity was the anti-mimetic brake" (Demouchel/Depuy 1999: 234). The mimetic crisis channelled desires to prevent shortages of goods. Desires are nowadays subordinated to "perpetual growth". The members of the global world society are trained to accept economic growth as the solution for all societal problems. But this philosophy (and psychology) could be sustainable only under the condition the world community is prepared to sacrifice its weak members. The excluded are not able to participate in this process. Even more – they are sacrificed for this development. In this "process of perpetual growth" the modern society has been sacrificing ever more victims. Modern systems were built on the supposition that scapegoats were never in short supply, there would be always enough of them. Nazism invented Jews and Slavs, communism could not do without class-enemies. The today's "world-liberalistic" multinational system produces large numbers of homeless powerless children, people living on the street and in overcrowded suburbs. They are not hungry for the lack of food in the world but for the lack of will to expose the insincere suppositions of modern society and to include all people in the world's development.

Here the question arises of how to find in the modern global world positive options, so people would be willing to cooperate and include "*the third*". Either there is an alternative solution to this problem or we will simply wait for the homeless masses to come to our Shengen border or to other doors, knocking and appealing to our conscience. This means: if we are not willing to cooperate with them and through dialogue solve the main problems of mankind, like the distribution of food, resources and territory, we invite global clashes.

However, solving of sacrifice crises demands willingness to sacrifice. **This is human or Christian aspect of the question.** Man should not give in to the dead systems but should as a being of dialogue and cooperation find ways to solve these tensions. Yet man is an ambivalent being. He is a rival on one hand and a partner in dialogue on the other – from the anthropological point of view. Whether he is prepared to overcome his natural tendency to rivalry depends on his socialisation and cultural background. Christianity teaches the way of love and empathy and tries to enable man to live this way. Girard is convinced that Christianity is a teaching of the non-violent mimesis ("imitation non violent" - Palaver 2003: 278).

What does it mean? Is the Christian way really a way of man which enables man to become a being of dialogue? If man learns or carries out dialogue, he will empower himself for an authentic human life. This could be reached through feeling and the exchange of human feelings. But how could man overcome the natural egoistic tendency to compete? With other words: how can man solve mimetic crises, especially in case of the modern liberal way of life? Things make us live according to the art of rivalry and grabbing. If modern civilisation is a civilisation of competition, how could one be limited, made ready to give way to the other and be humane? Is it possible to act or live in a society without having to obey and uphold only competitive rules, is it possible to accept the other even though he is not able to take part in this competitive societal game? With the words of Pope Benedict XVI.: Are only the logics of competitive exchange possible or are there the political logics of dialogue and "the logic of unconditional gift", too? (Benedict XVI. 2009: Nr. 37)

The real being

Erich Fromm worked out the importance of being versus having. Fromm enumerates the elements of the genuine being: relatedness, creativity, rootedness, a sense of identity and a frame of orientation (Fromm 2007: 71ff). This confirms that man's being is deepened in the wholeness of being. We have to attain genuine being. In his expositions about the art of life in Eckhartian way, Dietmar Mieth (2007) says that the way to live for Master Eckhart was not to live for (worumwillen) but to live ex. The man is fully engaged in living for, in Frommian mode he lives to have. He is working for his purposes but he cannot live from (ex) his grounds. For Master Eckhart life is flowing from the unity of being, and this unity is God. A man who would act in different manner should transform himself: he should act from the inner, not from the outer. To act from the inner, man needs to be open to his inner ground. For Eckhart this inner ground is God. This is the birth of the Son of God in the soul of man.

The real being is a being distanced from appearances. Appearances entangle or blind man. The real life is the life in the real being, which is God. It means that nothing (including people) is final and we have to open to the real being, which is God. Understanding and love open us to this reality. According to Johannes Tauler, to live in love means the real conversion. Love is the only living power; 1 Cor 13, 3: "If I give away all I have, and I deliver my body to be burned, but I have not love, I gain nothing." Love is empathy for the other, it means to be ready for the art of dying (to himself = *ars moriendi*). In the end he has to live without desiring anything, he has to die to everybody and everything.

The Christian way opens us to the real being. This is a prayer, it is a dialogue. We cannot make progress without dialogue with the other (man and God). As childhood experiences show, dialogue opens us to our real being. The experience of a child is the experience of a living dialogue and a living being. This is a dimension of God's kingdom, of full humanity and the source of a real and full life. The way to come to it is always sincere dialogue which does not end at man's borders but remains open for unlimited openness. To come to this stage of development, man needs to pass "the dark night", as mystics said. This "dark night" could be endured by dying to oneself.

Ars moriendi vs. ars of grabbing

Christian thinkers of Middle Ages spoke a lot about the art of dying (*ars moriendi*). They perceived man as a dialectics of rest and motion (Flasch 2000: 185). Man is a mobile being and because of it more of a not-being as a being, as master Eckhart pointed out (Flasch 2000: 266). But "man should renounce the world, the self and God". He should be just moved from life itself. In this sense man is without plans, without systems, without way; his life should be abandoning movement within, becoming still. Such life is a life without works, without honours for your deeds. This life is a life of renouncement.

Why should man live this life? Why should he die to himself? And why should modern man in the times of worldly prospects, progress and welfare think of dying to himself or renouncing himself?

First of all: according to Martin Heidegger (1967: 55) man is a being for death. This is the basic dimension of man. Man has to give up in order to get anything in his life. A child will be conceived and born through the parent's giving of each other. All important and worthy things have their price. From this point of view, man is a being for death. Man should be ready to accept life as an open but limited (by death) process, as a motion and readiness to give up his own power to govern life and to accept the possibilities of otherness.

This involves accepting oneself and the other as limited and in the same sense readiness to empathize with the other, which means to die to oneself. This brings possibilities for dialogue between partners. Edith Stein stressed the importance of empathy for the survival of mankind. She accepted her fate as a sacrifice for her nation and a sacrifice for the salvation of the German nation. But is this empathy possible without such faith as Edith Stein had? Only free existence prepared to be given to the other (Levinas) can be emphatic.

The outer world cannot give man such primary experience. A child will learn the empathy only through inner meetings with other person (Erzar/Kompan). A child will be open to experiences of empathy by the parents. If (s)he is learning to express his/her feelings, (s)he will give himself up to the other, learn to live in love, as well as meet God. Such childhood is the purpose – to change the habits of modern consumptive life and to come to the sources of life. This will be reached by dialogue.

Dialogue as acknowledgement of the other and a way to the sources

The Christian culture is a culture of dialogue. The Old Testament speaks about the dialogue between Jahwe and his people. Partners tried to establish just relations. In the New Testament Jesus was practising dialogue even though he did not use the word "dialogue". The first Christian councils spoke about the dialogue in God as the Trinity. The relations in God are dialogical. This was the model for man, who is made according to God's image. In Western culture dialogue is the result of its long practice in Christianity, despite the fact that Christian communities did not always accept dialogical manners and also quarrelled and waged wars. Yet dialogue remained a means of overcoming conflicts between them. The Second Vatican Council also officially proclaimed dialogue as a form of meeting between different religions.

Dialogue is today regarded as a basic means for solving the world's conflicts, since we can choose between dialogising and destroying our civilisation. To follow the way of dialogue means to have sufficient ground for dialogue. Could it be only the fear of clashes between civilisations? Could it be the fear of wars or other violent conflicts? Dialogue opens a deeper insight into the mystery of man. Through dialogue among men and dialogue with God we find our mystical sources, which enable and persuade us to change our short-sighted and one-sided view of the world.

Dialogue and mystics

Many thinkers stressed that the 21st century will be either mystical or it will not exist at all. "Mystical" means the same as religious. Karl Rahner spoke about mystical in the sense that man should be open to the inexpressible. The real dialogue is expressed by poetic, mystic words, words that transcend usual daily experience.

Karl Jaspers speaks about "the ciphers of the transcendence." They are expressed through religion, philosophy and art. They are called ciphers because they express the last experience of man. This experience touches the limits of man's worldly experience and opens him to the inexpressible. Alois Haas distinguishes between the Buddhist and the Christian mystical experience. The Buddhist experience is nirvana, which means passing into the eternal "time and space", it is "void". The Christian experience of the self is a dialogue about Christians striving for the Otherness. It is the transcendence for the other world to come and openness to the Unknown. It is *via negationis* (Rahner, 1961: 56). We have not heard the last word but we research reality in openness to the other (Other). Dialogue needs a new language and strives for the union with God. "The meaning of man's mystic union with God is all-extensive and total and have to do with totality of man's capacity" (Hass 2007: 25). There are different mystics and thus different paths to this unity, but it is important that these paths will be reached through finding new words (Theresa from Avilla). According to Master Eckhart, the word has tremendous power, "with the word could be wonders done" (Haas 2007: 107). Man plays a very important role in all processes of the world, he is a mediator of the world. This mediator's role can be performed in dialogue "among all opposites of the world" (Haas 2007: 268).

What can be the meaning of all this mystic inclusion in relation to dialogue? My aim is to stress that life has shadowy sides which should be opened in dialogue – this means integration, openness to all aspects of life. If we are ready to dialogize, we are taking into account the limited situation of our life in order to open ourselves earnestly in all our public and personal relations to new and deeper interconnectedness of our lives. It is a child who is open and accepts all things in life, willing to be influenced from different directions. We cannot take the world as the innocent, but in order to cope within and to deal with the world as such, we have to acquire childrenhood of God. Life as a technical project remains limited. The full life of man could be attained only by dialogue with all opposites of man's life and by preserving equidistance. Dialogue between two people and between man and God is the foundation of our lives which ensures our happiness.

Happiness

"And is happiness simply a matter of now anyway? Perhaps, as Aristotle sometimes suggests, happiness is better understood as an attribute, not of a present moment of one's life, but of whole life – the wisdom in the ancient Greek saying that we should call no man happy until he is dead" (Murphy 2009: 66). The Eckhardian, or be it the Christian attitude, is that the happiness is a paradox. Man will be happy if he is opening his life in dialogue to the otherness, yet it implies giving up his life. What it really means could be dialogised and could not be exhausted during our earthly existence, though we have no other access to it. So:

I am going to travel inwards
I am travelling into me
Into the inner core of my being
Where you are dwelling

At this deepest point of my being
You are still there before me
You are creating and reviving
Strengthening without ceasing
My Whole person.

Dag Hammarskjöld (1905-1961), Secretary-General of the United Nations

References and Bibliography

Bauer, J, 2006 *Prinzip Menschlichkeit*, Hamburg: Hoffmann und Campe.

Benedict XVI. (2009*) Caritas in Veritate*. Ljubljana: Družina (Cerkveni dokumenti 127)

Fromm, E., (2007) *To Have or to Be*, New York: Continuum Books (1976)

Demouchel,P./Depuy J.-P. *Die Hölle der Dinge. René Girard und die Logik der Ökonomie*. Thaur/Münster: Verlagshaus/LIT.

Flasch, K. (2000) *Das philosophische Denken im Mittelalter*. Stuttgart:Reclam.

Girard, R. (1987) *Thinks Hidden since the Foundation of the World.* Stanford: University Press.

Haas, Alois M. (2007) *Mystik als Aussage. Erfahrungs-, Denk- und Redeformen christlichen Mystik*. Frankfurt/Leipzig: Verlag der Weltreligionen.

Heidegger, M, (1967) *Existence and Being* (with an introduction and analysis by W. Brock), Chicago: Gatway.

Mieth, D. (2007) *Meister Eckhart Jahrbuch,* Vol.1. Stuttgar-Kohlhammer Verlag, 71-96.

Murphy, Jeffrie G. (2009) "The Unhappy Immoralist", in: Cahn, Steven M. (ed.) *Exploring Ethics,* New York: Oxford Univ. Press, 64-67

Palaver, W. (2003) *René Girards mimetische Theorie*, Münster/Thaur: LIT/Thaur.

Girard, R. (1997) *Wenn all das beginnt ... Dialog mit Michael Treguer* (translated from French by P. Veldboer). Thaur/Münster, 29.

Rahner, K. (1961) *Schriften zur Theologie* IV, Einsiedeln: Benzinger.

MEDIA, REALITY SHOWS, VIRTUES, AND THE PITFALLS OF THE INTERNET

Bojan Žalec, Ljubljana

> *"A week ago we could read about touching news. Abraham Biggs, nineteen years old boy from Florida, committed a suicide before the eyes of the users of the World Wide Web. Some of them didn't believe that the situation was serious, the others stimulated him; the third were even giving him advices about the quantity of consumed tablets sufficient for certain death. His misfortune was that his call was directed exactly to the World Wide Web. Nobody responded."*[1]

Why is the question I deal with in the paper important? Maybe its importance looks obvious to many. However I want to stress one special reason based on the fact that human being is a mimetic creature. We are both, creatures and mimetic beings as well. By the term 'creature' I refer to the fact that we are created beings, dependent beings, that we are brought and raised up in some environment, community, nation, culture etc. By the 'mimetic being' I mean that we imitate some other being during the whole our life, from the beginning. And we should imitate if we want to follow the Jesus' message that we should be like children.[2] So the examples play the crucial role in the shaping of human creatures. They play the crucial role at several areas, at several levels. As the efforts to bring up children in a family essentially depend on examples, so the success in the cultural competition or struggle substantially depends on the examples that people follow. That is way charismatic persons are so valuable and literally indispensible for being successful on the market of ideas.

Examples or paradigms are crucial. However, in the age of the electronic media it is impossible to control the exposure to examples we don't approve, neither of ourselves nor of persons that we care about; we can only limit it. The electronic media and the internet radically increased such an exposure. Let's take

1 Strahovnik 2009. Trans. by B. Žalec.

2 »Nothing is more mimetic than the desire of a child, and yet it is good. Jesus himself says it is good. Mimetic desire is also desire for God« (Girard, 2004, 64).

the example of TV series, reality shows and computer games compared to theater plays or movies. Certain empirical research has indicated that a population of children from 7-10 prefers the TV series over the movies. The reason has been the more intense identification with characters and the happenings in the series than in the movies. What is the reason for it? One plausible answer given is that movies have the beginning and the end, but series don't have it, at least not in the way like movies. So they more resemble the real life and that increases the identification.[3] Also computer games do not have such an end (you can play them only till your own end). That is in a way true also for life stories of protagonists involved in reality shows, competitions for the best new talent, for the best new model etc. If you nowadays switch on the TV and overview channels, what you see most frequently is just that kind of program. This just confirms the fact, which is verified also by empirical measuring, that such shows and series are the most popular program contents (beside some sports, football at first place). They are of course also the cheapest way to enormous profit, but relatively low costs of their realization obviously do not suffice to explain their success, or with the other words, why they function. What they have in common is that people can identify with the main characters. Then they imitate them or try to imitate them and they take them seriously. The media are frameworks or places that allot veracity to models, examples, events. The fact that characters appear in the media, in reality shows, in computer games etc. allot them the status of examples or it causes the fact that people imitate them. The same is true for newspapers. Somebody tells you that one person has committed a crime, that somebody is involved in affair etc. You ask: "How do you know that it is true?"

"It's in Delo!" (Slovene main daily newspaper), "It was on POP TV!" (Slovene main commercial TV) and similar are the lightning-like convinced answers. The context creates the behavior of people and people are of course capable of split life or "schizophrenia". In the moment of reflection or if they want to show their prudence, people will say, of course, that nowadays we cannot just believe to everything that is stated or presented in the media. Yet these are their "theoretical"

3 Klun, 2002, 51, xii. I thank for the information about the research and the explanation to my college, psychologist and education scientist Stanko Gerjolj from the Faculty of Theology in Ljubljana.

or "intellectual" moments. In every day practice and that means most of the time most of people behave as persons who take the information in the media as true. The context, not their theories, determines the behavior of people.[4]

I said earlier that we, humans are mimetic creatures. But that is not the whole story. We must say even more: The human dynamism, "the dynamics of the entire personality" is what René Girard called a mimetic desire (2004, 268). I would like to stress an important but sometimes neglected fact about the Girard's theory of mimetic desire: the mimetic desire as such is not something bad, quite to the contrary: it is something intrinsically good, even when bad, because "it's the opening out of oneself (op. cit., 64)", the extreme openness to other. "It is everything" (ibid.)[5]. Some philosophers have stressed the importance of drives for life: destroy the drives and you will destroy the life. Something similar we can say about the mimetic desire. The mimetic desire is a huge basic power, like drives. But similarly like drives it is just a quantity or scalar, not a vector in the sense that it can be directed as to the bad as to the good things. The object of our desire can be something bad or good.

Another danger of the media and the internet can be understood in the terms of malicious glee or delight in misfortune, bad luck or misery of the other. Why do reality shows attract people? Many people draw analogies between such shows and gladiator fights. Today gladiator fights are illegal but the need in people for

4 Another example: an acquaintance of mine has told me about his experience from the USA, where he spent some time living in his friend's house. Every week the same story was repeating: They are both religious Christians and every Sunday they went shopping. My acquaintance's American friend bought an enormous quantity of food every Sunday and every next Sunday he threw most of it in the garbage for most of the time they ate in restaurants. But every new Sunday and every week the American friend repeated the procedure. On the question "Why?" he offered no answer except "Let it just be so, it is right so." The cultural context of consumer's society has produced its effect. Already Karl Marx observed: It is not true that being determines the consciousness, it is rather the opposite. I would agree with him in the sense that it is the context, the praxis, the background and not the person's theory that determines her behavior. There are many examples provided by religious people that amount to the evidence for that thesis: they are for instance believers in transcendence or creationists during the Sunday mass, but six days in the week they behave like pure imanentists or non-creationist evolutionists. This last point is often stressed by Stanko Gerjolj.

5 »It can be murderous, it is rivalrous; but it is also the basis of heroism, and devotion to others, and everything« (Girard, 2004, 64).

similar experiences is still present, combined with the need for consciousness that there are people that are even greter losers, fools, victims in any case even worse off than I am.[6] The same holds true for the success of spectacular news, yellow press etc. The internet has added in this respect another possibility. People can visit home pages, forums etc. and write for instance many bad things, offensive words to some mighty, successful or famous person and they can feel better. Maybe somebody would observe that we can see such ventilation from the positive side, because people in such a way let loose a lot of bad feelings that might be otherwise unleashed otherwise, in a more dangerous way, in real life. The adequacy of such an opinion which lays a bet on a kind of "catharsis" is very dubious from the point of view of formation of a personality and of acquiring skills, competencies and virtues for resolving problems in the real life. The observer of reality shows is passive observer out of context. He is not really involved in solving the problems. Such a satisfaction is an instant satisfaction. The same is true for the above mentioned "catharsis" on the internet. What kind of persons will become young people who will take a shelter from the problems in their real life in such instant "catharsis" and satisfaction in the virtual world? You cannot learn the art of life from the media and in the virtual reality.[7] There are also political and other interests for redirecting people's energy and attention from their real problems to problems in the virtual world where they can achieve quick and easy but only instant satisfaction and oblivion of their real problems yet in no way their solution. Further, many participants in reality shows report that mostly bad things, conflicts, fights, quarrels are presented in the shows and most of what has happened among the participants and can be characterized as good, nice, kind etc. is omitted. So the shows one-sidedly intensify the conflicting, competitive, malicious side of human nature over its cooperative and benevolent side. So they nicely fit with philosophies, ideologies and doctrines that stress only the "dark", competitive, violent features and potentials of human nature. Several Nazi, market, (quasi)Darwinian ideologies etc. are among them. The stressing of such one

6 Such delight is stronger if the person stroke by bad luck or misery is (till the moment of misfortune) better off: successful, beautiful, educated, rich ... This is one of the reasons why the reality shows with (in a sense) successful persons are particularly popular.

7 Some of the things said above were observed also by the Slovene pop singer star Jan Plestenjak in the talk show »Nočni klub« (Night club) at the Slovene national TV.

sided picture of human nature can cause the process of self-fulfilling prophecy (see Kohn, 1992, 29). From the philosophical point of view, the success of reality shows can be reflected in the light of Christian tradition and the Girard's theory of mimetic desire. The malicious gill is a counterpart of envy, which is after pride the most fundamental of cardinal sins. The Girard's theory of mimetic desire can be observed as a variant and supplementation of this traditional Christian wisdom.

The crucial importance of the media was established long time before our informational age. Already in the middle of the 19th century Søren Kierkegaard found out that his age was nihilistic and that the cause for such a state of affairs was the public sphere given rise by the press (Kierkegaard, 2009, 93). The public alienates individuals (op. cit., 91), it "creates no situation and no community" (ibid.). Kierkegaard's time was quite primitive compared to our age regarding the influence of the media and development of the technology yet his visionary mind predicted the state of affairs we live in today, and his reflection has been fruitfully used by the American philosopher Hubert Dreyfus (2003) in his analysis of the benefits and drawbacks of the internet.

Kierkegaard described his age as nihilistic. He didn't use that term but the phenomenon of nihilism is detected: Our age, claimed Kierkegaard, is the age that levels all the things (Kierkegaard, 2009, 84). The context or the background of the age is such that things cannot appear as better or worse. We find the following chracterization: "The present age is essentially a *sensible, reflecting age, devoid of passion, flaring up in superficial, short-lived enthusiasm and prudentially relaxing in indolence*" (op. cit., 68). We may mention also legalism, anonymity, lack of commitment, boredom, lacking of exposure, lack or avoiding the risk among the features of it pointed out by Kierkegaard. Maybe the terms listed already ring the bell regarding the nature of our age.

Let us turn to the analysis of the internet from the ethical philosophical perspective. When the internet has became a practical reality, many enthusiasts or optimists believed that it would bring several benefits into the area of retrieval of information, education, that it would increase the inclusion of excluded people in a society, that it would connect people, democratize community, create agoras, decrease the feelings of loneliness and depression etc. As Dreyfus (2003) has successfully shown not much of the mentioned really became a reality, rather the opposite came true.

Retrieving of information is problematic without the help of human beings, because computers do not operate on the semantic but rather only on the syntactic (or formal) level. They are burdened with the relevance problem because they cannot distinguish which datum is relevant and which is not in the case of formally or syntactically similar data. The spam on the internet confirms every day how perennial and till now insolvable is the relevance problem for the computers. Regarding the psychical well being of people we should point out that the researches carried out in the USA surprised the optimists. Populations have been researched before and after the use of the internet. The feeling of loneliness and depression has increased after the start of the use of the internet (Dreyfus, 2003, 3). In another research people have estimated that the internet has improved the quality of their lives but at the same time they have confessed that it caused that they spent less time with their family or their friends (ibid.).

Ad education: We may start by reminding you about the difference between the feeling when you enjoy a play in the theater at the one hand and when you watch it on the TV at the other. TV watching lacks a thousand important elements which we cover with the terms such as context, atmosphere etc. The same is true for teaching and a good teacher is like a good actor. He is sensitive regarding the atmosphere, regarding the public and he takes some measures when the atmosphere is bad, when public/pupils are bored etc. Such a sensation of the public/pupils/students is not possible through the internet or by the way of TV broadcast. As has been stressed for instance by the sociologist Thomas Luckmann, a dialogue is something that far surpasses a verbal communication between human beings. It is something very primitive and bodily (Luckmann, 1990). The same scientist, not surprisingly one of the best connoisseurs of phenomenology among sociologists, stressed the importance of the face to face encounters and communication (ibid.). The Italian philosopher Umberto Galimberti, scholar who knows very well the philosophy of Nietzsche, who has been the famous partisan of the body and of Heidegger too, has written an influential book (2007). When he considers what is wrong in our modern schools, he asks the reader: "Teachers come into the classroom. But do they look pupils in the face at all?" How can you look a single pupil (not even to think of pupils) into face or into eyes by the way of the internet or by the way of the Skype? For a full communication, for a dialogue, for empathy a bodily presence and a bodily contact are necessary. Our body in the environment enables us to see at the same time the whole and the detail, it automatically moves in the space to get the best position, as Merleau-Ponty (2008) has pointed out, it can tell us things which cannot be known otherwise.[8] We can speak about the wisdom of the body. Nevertheless we should not forget that empathy is bodily grounded phenomenon. The finding of the mirror neurons responsible for it is a strong piece of evidence for it.[9]

Let's consider now the political sphere. I remember the evening when the independence of Slovenia was declared. Till that day I had known only from books what joy and civil feast really means. That evening I went to the Ljubljana down town. Despite justified fear people were smiling, singing, embracing, joy and happiness were among us. Such an atmosphere is not possible without bodily contact among people and it represents a huge human and political capital. Bodily presence and bodily contact are crucial for people`s connectedness. I also remember the difference I noticed when I went to Italy from the socialist Slovenia. In Italy people were gathering at squares, also at the evenings, sitting there, talking, kids were playing around etc. I didn't notice any such gathering at squares in our socialist country (but I noticed "squared" life in the sense of *uomo quadrato* (a relatively old Italian satiric term for a TV spectator)). Physically connected people are powerful and dangerous. They should be scattered and isolated in apartments or gathered under control. One of the best protections of our freedom is that we gather physically. The lesson about the importance of the body should be especially taken into account by churches in the times of the spreading of phenomenon to which Ulrich Beck (2008) refers by the term "one's own God", which can be experienced in the bodily isolation of our own room or in the darkness of the cyberspace. Nevertheless, particularly we in the Roman Catholic Church, burdened by dramatic projections about the number of priests in the future should, seriously and with greatest care consider our future religious life in the light of the importance of the body.

8 Santiago Sia has commented that internet is for him a very good mean for easy and good communication with his family. I don't doubt that's true but we should not forget that his communication with his family members can be such even through the internet thanks just to the direct, physical, bodily (grounded) relations that he already had or has with them.

9 For the mirror neurons and empathy see works of Gallese, Fadiga, Fogassi, Rizolatti, Craighero. See also Pfeifer & Dapretto, 2009. A good and accessible work on the topic is Bauer, 2005. See also Ratcliffe, 2009, especially the chapter »Mirror Neurons and Intersubjectivity«, pp. 332-335.

Ad creating cyber agoras: What is the essence of agora democracies? Publicity, transparency, personal exposure, commitment and responsibility arising from them. What we find in the cyberspace is just the opposite of the mentioned: anonymity[10], no exposure, no necessary commitment, no responsibility. You can take arbitrary name and safely hidden under such a name saying whatever you like. Every man has the right to a good name. Probably never before in the history this right has been so endangered as it is now by the phenomenon of the media and the internet. Kierkegaard has suggested an unconditional commitment to the cause as an antidote to the nihilism. The internet can destroy any serious commitment and hence contribute to the flourishing of nihilism. True democracy cannot be realized by nihilists lacking any (capacity) for unconditional commitment and sacrifice.

Courage is the most important virtue for Gandhi. He has once written that in case that one must choose between the absence of violent acts and lack of courage, he must pick the courage.[11] Courage is virtue that can be learned only in the context when you are exposed. The internet seriously hinders the development of this fundamental (Gandhi) or - in the Christian tradition - cardinal virtue (fortitude).[12] The same should be true for passion (Kierkegaard's age was pace him, as also quoted above, famously passionless.) The adequate passion and the adequate courage are both essential components of fortitude. At the same time the internet with its limitless offer negatively effects the development of modesty and temperance (which is as fortitude one of the four Christian cardinal virtues).

10 Vojko Strahovnik has mentioned to me - as a counter example to the thesis about anonymity - the example of a Slovene citizen who has sent a rather frightening mail to the president George Bush Jr. and he has been than traced out and officially persecuted. But such examples are at the practical level rather exceptions as the president of the USA himself is a very special case. Usually nobody is traced out no matter what she or he has said.

11 »I do believe that where there is only a choice between cowardice and violence, I would advise violence. Hence also do I advocate training in arms for those who believe in the method of violence. I would rather have India resort to arms in order to defend her honor than that she should in a cowardly manner become or remain a helpless witness to her own dishonor« (Gandhi, 1995, 62).

12 For the importance of the fortitude in the context of the condition and perspectives of the modern Church see Juhant, 2005, Ch. 10.2.

Can we really imagine human love (lat. *caritas*) without bodily contact, exposure, courage and risk, without adequate passion?

Ulrich Beck - in his already mentioned book *Der eigene Gott* (2008) - noticed that tolerance implies suffering. I think he is right. Why? There are, according to the conception I accept, two necessary conditions in order to speak about tolerance: 1. The phenomenon we tolerate must be such that we do not like it, it might be almost unbearable to us. Thus its presence might be more or less painful for us. 2. We tolerate it despite the fact that we have power to eliminate it. One cannot learn what a pain is on the internet. The attractiveness of it is just the avoidance of a pain, the experiencing of exciting events without any pain and without any risk. But the real tolerance (like true love) involves just these two, pain and risk. So you cannot acquire the virtue of tolerance by the way of the internet. Yet, for the things being even worst, the internet (and other media) might create the illusion by its users that they are tolerant when in fact they lack the capacity for it. The self-image about us as being really capable of tolerance might be just an unjustified pride, lacking every real basis.

The virtue of proper tolerance might be easily confused with indifference, but they are not the same: 1. the former implies responsibility towards the other(s), the latter doesn't; 2. we can't be indifferent to something what is unpleasant or even painful for us, yet we can tolerate it. Following Levinas Branko Klun[13] wrote: »The responsibility for the other is better than tolerance; it is the true good and the original call <*die ursprüngliche Berufung*> of man (Klun, 2006, 92 (my translation))". Here Klun refers to tolerance in the sense of indifference. However, the proper tolerance is a kind of responsible attitude. Not every responsible relationship contains tolerance, but every proper tolerance involves some kind of responsibility. There are kinds of responsibility without tolerance, but no proper tolerance without responsibility. Properly tolerant attitude is a special kind of responsible attitude. So there is no exclusion between tolerance and responsibility (quite to the contrary). Only indifference is irresponsible. It seems very important to me to take into account those differences otherwise we might - in the name of refusal of indifference - discard also the proper tolerance. The later is however a

13 For the consideration of responsibility and tolerance in the context of the paradigm of the post-modern philosophy see Klun, 2006, 91-93.

special and indispensable kind of responsibility, which can't be efficaciously substituted by any other kind of responsibility. Internet adventurism, "voyeurism", malice, or even sadism are all indifferent and irresponsible (as we can see in the case of Abraham Biggs). The feeling of responsibility destroys the enjoyment that the persons who practice them search for.

References and Bibliography

Bauer, J. (2005) *Warum ich fühle, was du fühlst. Intuitive Komunikation und das Geheimnis der Spiegelneurone.* Hamburg: Hoffmann und Campe Verlag.

Beck, U. (2008) *Der eigene Gott: Von der Friedensfähigkeit und dem Gewaltpotential der Religionen.* Frankfurt am Main: Verlag der Weltreligionen im Insel Verlag.

Dreyfus, H. L. (2003) *On the Internet.* London and New York: Routledge.

Galimberti, U. (2007) *L'ospite inquietante: Il nichilismo e i giovani.* Milano: Fetrinelli.

Gandhi, M. K. (1995) *The Wisdom of Gandhi* (compiled by T. S. Settel), New York: Citadel Press.

Girard, R. (1996) *The Girard Reader* (ed. by J. G. Williams), New York: A Herder & Herder Book.

Juhant, J. (2005) *Globalisierung, Kirche und postmoderner Mensch.* Münster: Lit Verlag.

Kierkegaard, S. (2009) *Two Ages: The Age of Revolution and the Present Age, A Literary Review, Kierkegaard's Writings, XIV*, ed. and trans. with introduction and notes by H. V. Hong and E. H. Hong, Princeton, New Jersey: Princeton University Press.

Klun, B. (2006) "Der Anspruch des Anderen. Überlegungen zum 'postmodernen' Guten", in: J. Juhant & B. Žalec (eds.), *Person and Good: Man and His Ethics in the Postmodern World*, Münster: Lit, pp. 83-94.

Klun, N. (2002) *Televizija in oglaševanje v odnosu do otroka*, Diplomska naloga, Ljubljana: Teološka fakulteta Univerze v Ljubljani.

Kohn, A. (1992) *No Contest. The Case Against Competition.* Boston and New York: Houghton Mifflin Company.

Luckmann, T. (1990) "Social Communication, Dialogue and Conversation", in: I. Marková and K. Fopp (eds.), *The Dynamics of Dialogue.* New York (etc.): Harvester Wheatsheaf., pp. 45-61.

Merleau-Ponty (2008) *Phenomenology of Perception* (trans. by. C. Smith). London and New York: Routledge.

HAPPINESS AND THE BRAIN

Zvezdan Pirtošek, Ljubljana

Introduction

There are many definitions of happiness. Happiness could be defined as a state of well being and contentment which is perceived as pleasurable and satisfying experience. Many psychologists would describe it as one of the basic human emotions – innate, pan-cultural, evolutionary old, shared with other species, with a distinct feeling, physiology and behaviour. Philosophers, poets, common people – many have their own particular definition of happiness. In the last few decades, neuroscientists have joined the ranks with their view of happiness being the result of brain activity. The experience of being happy has been linked to the pleasure and reward systems (Kringelbach and Berridge 2009).

Anatomical basics of the nervous system

From a perspective of a neuroscientist hapiness is a brain process. Basic knowledge of the anatomy and physiology of the central nervous system is crucial for comprehension of the neurological substrates of happiness.

The nervous system is divided anatomically into the central nervous system and the peripheral nervous system. The central nervous system is made up of the spinal cord, brainstem, diencephalon and telencephalon. The brainstem is comprised of three areas: the medulla oblongata, the pons and the midbrain (mesencephalon).

The telencephalon consists of two cerebral hemispheres. Each of the hemispheres is divided into four separate lobes: frontal, parietal, temporal and occipital. In the centro–medial regions of the brain is the limbic system, which comprises parts of the frontal, temporal and parietal lobe and is crucial for the emotional processes and memory. Important structures in the limbic system are the cingulate gyrus, hippocampus, septum and amygdala.

The diencephalon consists of the thalamus, the hypothalamus (the structure below the thalamus) and the epithalamus (the structure above the thalamus), which includes the pineal (glandula pinealis) and habenula. Seated deep in the brain are grey matter nuclei collectively known as the basal ganglia, consisting of the striatum (caudate nucleus and putamen), globus pallidus and the accumbens.

The brainstem is the connection between the spinal cord and the cerebrum. It is comprised of three areas: the medulla oblongata, the pons and the midbrain (mesencephalon). On the base of the midbrain is a functional part of the basal ganglia - the substantia nigra with cells that produce dopamine and give rise to fibers that project to the caudate nucleus and to the putamen. These fibers make up the nigrostriatal pathway (connection of the substantia nigra and the basal ganglia). Mesocortical and mesolimbic pathway connect the surrounding structures in the midbrain with the frontal and limbic lobe respectively.

Programming and execution of motor, oculomotor, cognitive and emotional actions which contribute to the feelings of happiness are strongly dependent on circular connections between subcortical structures (especially the basal ganglia and the thalamus) and the frontal cortex. The frontal cortex, particularly its prefrontal component is the apex of the brain-behaviour relationship where the programmes, intentions, and decisions finally transform into acts. These connections - called cortico-subcortico-frontal loops - are anatomical substrates underlying the relationship between higher aspects of behaviour and the brain. There are five pathways (loops), transferring either limbic, motor, oculomotor or cognitive information, following the same principle: the information from various parts of the cortex converge to the basal ganglia, from there to the nuclei of the thalamus and finally to different parts of frontal cortex (Alexander et al 1986).

Happiness as a brain process depends on deep subcortical as well as superficial cortical structures. Among these are very important structures involved in the process of reward related behaviour and hedonism in the mesencephalon, basal ganglia, limbic system and the prefrontal cortex:

Midbrain (mesencephalon): structures with predominance of dopamine as a neurotransmiter:

- substantia nigra
- ventral tegmental area
- mesolimbic pathway
- mesocortical pathway

the basal ganglia

- ventral striatum (nucleus accumbens)
- dorsal striatum

limbic system (cingulate gyrus, hippocampus, septum, amygdala)

prefrontal cortex

- ventromedial and orbitofrontal prefrontal cortex
- dorsolateral prefrontal cortex

From pleasure and desire to reward and happiness

The concept of 'happiness' is difficult to operationalize from the neurophysiological perspective. Therefore some neurophysiologists operationalize the concept of happiness by introducing the difference between pleasure and desire. Common to both of them is reward. Reward is the active process of the brain that reacts to a pleasant stimulus. However, some would describe happiness as pleasure without desire.

The concept of pleasure and the pleasure centres have historically emerged in the 1950s when psychologists James Olds and Peter Milner working at McGill University in Canada, found that rats would repeatedly - even up to 2000 times per hour - press levers to receive tiny jolts of current injected through electrodes implanted in the dopaminergic mesolimbic pathways. While pressing the lever, they would stop almost all other normal behaviours, including feeding, drinking and sex. Dopamine was quickly dubbed the brain's »pleasure chemical«. However, recent work by Kent Berridge, at the University of Michigan in the US suggests a distinction between desire and pleasure - wanting and liking - in terms of both the brain regions and the neurochemical substances that mediate these subjective states: the dopamine system appears to encode desire while the endogenous opioid system is closer to pleasure (Berridge 2009).

Common to both, pleasure and desire, is reward. Reward is the active process of the brain that reacts to a pleasant stimulus and is closely related to happiness. However, some would describe happiness as pleasure without desire. The motivational rewarding aspect of happiness is extremely important in the evolution since it allows the development of the behaviour pattern for successful survival. Appart from being the basis for the feeling of happiness motivational rewarding system importantly shapes several cognitive processes (i.e. learning) and has developed in the brain of human and primates as a distinct system.

Key happiness - related areas of the brain

Central components of the rewarding system are in the limbic cortico-subcortico-frontal loop: dopaminergic neurons in the mesencephalon, ventral striatum and ventral pallidum, anterior cingulate gyrus, prefrontal cortex (especially orbitofrontal and dorsolateral part) and amygdala. Limbic and all other loops follow the somatotopic organisation through the whole pathway in a distinct and occasionally convergent course therefore operating in parallel and integrative manner (Bevan et al., 1996).

Distinct parts of the limbic cortico-subcortico-frontal loop represent different aspects of the rewarding behaviour: anterior cingulate gyrus and orbitofrontal cortex are active in the prediction of the mistake in the rewarding process, evaluation and choosing among current and long term benefit; cells in the ventral parts of the basal ganglia respond to expectation and detection of the reward. Disturbance in dopaminergic and opioid transmission in the ventral stiatum (accumbens) in rats causes compulsive behaviour exclusively for the reward - food and pharmacological substances (Le Moal, 2007), which defines accumbens as a very "hedonistic" structure. Mogenson (Mogenson et al., 1980) suggests that the nucleus accumbens determines the goal of action which we want to perform (food, drink, sex, material assets, reputation...) or which we want to avoid (pain, suffering...) and chooses among alternative goals and behaviours. This structure represents the intersection of motivation and action. Ventral striatum and dopaminergic pathways in the midbrain are interconnected and have similar function.

The anterior cingulate cortex (ACC) also seems to be involved in processing of happiness, monitoring conflicts and triggering other brain circuits to carry out more detailed processing when they occur.

Evolutionary more recently developed brain region, with connections to deep limbic and basal ganglia regions and with connections to both the opioid and dopamine systems is the prefrontal cortex, particularly orbitofrontal and dorsolateral prefrontal areas. Although the prefrontal cortex by itself does not generate pleasure (as learned from the lobectomy patients who can still feel pleasure).

However, as found by neuroimaging, the orbitofrontal cortex contains regions that correlate with subjective reports of pleasure. The human orbitofrontal cortex (OFC) plays an important role in representing taste, flavor, and food reward. The primary role of the OFC in taste is thought to be the encoding of affective value and the computation of perceived pleasantness. OFC integrates multiple sensory inputs and computes reward value to guide feeding behavior. This cortex may have originally represented nutrients and toxins, but gradually became involved in more general aspects of response and goal selection encoding higher order rewards, such as the beauty of a face (O'Doherty et al 2003) and the joy of a Brahms symphony (Blood et al 2001 and 1999). It receives input information on reward from hierarchically lower regions (limbic system, ventral striatum, orbital and medial parts of prefrontal lobe) and integrates them with cognitively relevant data. Cognitive functions of the prefrontal cortex include behaviour pattern inhibition, changing a set, cognitive and motor behaviour and planning (Goldman-Rakic and Leung 2002). Final goal is to perform sensible, useful and adaptive behaviour which is necessary for higher aspects of happiness.

The role of neurotransmitters, hormones and genetics in pleasure & reward

Dopamine plays the central role in the reward system. It is located in the ventral tegmental area with terminals in the nucleus accumbens. Dopaminergic neurons encode two sets of information (i) current disproportion between expected and actual reward and (ii) long-term maintained signal, which correlates with uncertainty or reliability of the reward.

Dopaminergic system can be studied with the electrophysiological methods. Electrophysiological studies demonstrated that the dopaminergic neurones are active primarily in events connected with reward and new stimuli. If the stimuli are aversive the dopaminergic activity stops. In the reward related situations the activity is pulsatile, phasic and it correlates with disproportion between the expected and actual reward (reward prediction error) and represents a type of learning. Different aspects of reward (the size, the likelihood, delay) are processed and integrated separately.

Rewarding systems are strongly influenced through dopaminergic system by hormones and genetic characteristics (especially those in-/directly related to dopamine and enzymes involved in metabolism of dopamine). However, other neurotransmitters are involved in pleasure processing and its transfer to higher aspects of happiness characteristic for humans - endogenous opioids, serotonine, stress related hormones (falling in love), central vasopressin and oxytocin (romantic love, orgasm, pair bonding, maternal love).

Anhedonia and Un-happiness

A pathological loss of positive feelings and the inability to enjoy life pleasures, to be happy, is called anhedonia. Anhedonia is present in affective disorders (depression) in schizophrenia, in autism, in addiction, in Parkinson's disease. These disorders primarily reflect dysfunction of dopamine and serotonine-related structures. For example, dopamine in Parkinson's disease is not decreased only in nigrostriatal pathway (a neural pathway important for generation of movement) but also in the mesocortical and mesolimbic 'hedonistic' pathways.

While anhedonia dos not necesserily imply un-happiness and active avoidance, lesions in the nucleus amygdala and related structures trigger active fear or withdrawal reaction. The amygdala_plays a central role in processing information about external events that signal threats or dangers triggering fear or withdrawal reactions. Patients who have bilateral amygdala damage rate strangers as more approachable and trustworthy than ordinary people would consider them (Balakrishnan and Ratcliff 1996). Patients with depression seem to have enlarged amygdala or amygdala with greater activation. Amygdala also seem to be involved in laying down long-term memories. Dysfunctional interaction between the amygdala and the cortex may lead to unhappiness and to a tendency to dwell on negative memories .

Happines and left-right hemispheric difference

Asymmetry of the hemispheres may also play a role on the spectrum of (un) happiness with left hemisphere being more active in processing of the positive (happiness) and the right hemisphere in processing of the negative (sadness, unhappiness, nostalgia). Some experiments demonstrated that the prefrontal cortex manages goals and the way we achieve them by balancing approach and withdrawal: enquiring, left-sided regions of the PFC seem to be involved in making us approach things to satisfy our goals—and seem to be implicated in a positive affect; vigilant, right-sided regions make us withdraw—and are more implicated in negative affect. There is some speculation that the OFC and VFC are involved in the management of rewards and punishments, the left-sided OFC responding to rewards and the right-sided OFC to punishments.

Conclusion

Happiness can be (also) described and explained as a brain process, an interplay between deep seated archaic brain regions and recently evolved superficial frontal regions which mediates a uniquely human and social dimension to our pleasures and desires. It is particularly through this, recently evolved brain that we can add a uniquely human, contemplative and social dimension to our pleasures and desires. As Dalai Lama said:

»The systematic training of the mind—the cultivation of happiness, the genuine inner transformation by deliberately selecting and focusing on positive mental states and challenging negative mental states—is possible because of the very

structure and function of the brain... But the wiring in our brains is not static, not irrevocably fixed. Our brains are also adaptable.« (Dalai Lama and Cutler 1998).

References and Bibliography

Alexander, GE.; DeLong, MR.; Strick, PL. 1986: *Parallel organization of functionally segregated circuits linking basal ganglia and cortex.* Ann Rev Neurosci 9, 357-81..

Balakrishnan, JD.; Ratcliff, R. 1996: *Testing model of decision making using confidence ratings in classification.* J Exp Psy: Human Perc. and Perf., 22 (3), 615-633.

Berridge K. 2009: *Liking' and 'wanting' food rewards: Brain substrates and roles in eating disorders.* Physiology & Behavior 97: 537–550.

Bevan, MD.; Smith, AD; Bolam, JP.1996: *The substantia nigra as a site of synaptic integration of functionally diverse information arising from the ventral pallidum and the globus pallidus in the rat.* Neuroscience 75, 5–12.

Blood, A.J. & Zatorre RJ. 2001: *Intensely pleasurable responses to music correlate with activity in brain regions implicated in reward and emotion.* Proc. Nat. Acad. Sci. U.S.A. 98: 11818–11823.

Blood, A.J. et al. 1999: *Emotional responses to pleasant and unpleasant music correlate with activity in paralimbic brain regions.* Nat. Neurosci. 2: 382–387.

Dalai Lama and Cutler HC. 1998: *The Art of Happiness*, Riverhead Books; 44-45.

Goldman-Rakic, PS; Leung, H. 2002: *Functional architecture of the dorsolateral prefrontal cortex in monkeys and humans.* In: D.T. Stuss, R.T. Knight (Eds.), Principles of Frontal Lobe Function, Oxford University Press, New York, 85–95.

Kringelbach ML, Berridge KC. 2009: *Towards a functional neuroanatomy of pleasure and happiness.* Trends Cogn Sci. 13 (11): 479-87.

Le Moal, M.; Koob, GF.2007: *Drug addiction: pathways to the disease and pathophysiological perspectives.* Eur. Neuropsychopharmacol. 17 (6–7), 377–393.

Mogenson, GJ.; Jones, DL.; Yim, CY. 1980: *From motivation to action: functional interface between the limbic system and the motor system.* Prog. Neurobiol. 14 (2–3), 69–97.

O'Doherty J. et al. 2003: *Beauty in a smile: The role of medial orbitofrontal cortex in facial attractiveness.* Neuropsychologia 41: 147–155.

PUNCTUATING LIFE'S MESSAGE: A GRAMMATICAL-PHILOSOPHICAL EXERCISE ON THE QUEST FOR MEANING

Marian F. Sia, Terenure College, Dublin, Santiago Sia, Milltown Institute, Dublin

The Quest for Meaning

In one form or another our human situation unsettles us, and it is this which leads to the desire, and even a quest, for meaningfulness. That desire is translated in the present context into the question as to whether life is after all 'a sentence' passed on us. Admittedly but regrettably, that would seem to be the case as experienced by some. But one could also claim that life's message could be compared to 'a series of sentences'.[1] For it to be properly read — drawing on grammar — it needs the correct punctuation marks. We need, as it were, to punctuate it properly for its meaning to become clearer to us.

The quest for meaning in life takes us in different directions. For some, religion provides the right context, and the answers that the different religious traditions teach enable them to appreciate their present situation and the goal ahead of them. For an increasing number of people, however, a more acceptable road is that mapped out by psychology, the human sciences or even science itself. Others find greater satisfaction, and hence some meaning, in the more immediate and tangible results of their desire for a better kind of life as they pursue wealth, health and fame. Despite these seemingly unconnected routes being taken, however, there is at least a certain common starting ground; namely, that all of us are *questing* for an answer. In fact, even the rather negative position adopted by those who reject any meaningfulness to life[2] or the attempt to discover it can be said to be itself some kind of answer—and that in turn implies a certain route taken.

1 We are using 'sentences' in the loose sense, and are therefore including questions, exclamations, imperatives and so on.

2 A particularly poignant image that has left a lasting impression on us regarding meaninglessness is that of a clock that has its numerals but had lost its hands and still keeps on ticking.

The Philosophical Route

Since the claim is that all of us, no matter what station in life we occupy, are in varying degrees engaged in this quest, what then has philosophy to contribute to our understanding of this human situation and of this human pursuit?

Centuries ago the Greek philosopher Aristotle had commented on a similar situation. In his *Nicomachean Ethics,* he raises the question as to what it is that every human being is aiming for (the object of life, as he calls it). He defines it as 'good', not in the ethical sense but more in a biological or psychological sense since he bases himself on his observations of the general behaviour of reality. Commenting more specifically on human beings, Aristotle observes that all human beings aim towards a common good, leading him to maintain that there is agreement on the universality of the human search for happiness, *eudaimonia.* He notes, on the other hand, that people differ on what they consider to be the form of happiness they want. Aristotle lists wealth, fame, pleasure, and virtue as goals that some people set for themselves. Critiquing these as being inadequate — for Aristotle, these are goods rather than the good — he argues that each of these is really a means rather than the ultimate goal or end that human beings desire for its own sake. His own standpoint leads him to consider *eudaimonia* to be the full development of human rationality: contemplation, not in the religious sense, but thinking for the sake of thinking.

There is of course a link between the quest for meaning in life and the desire for ultimate happiness. Not only do both arise from our human nature, but it can also be demonstrated that achievement, or even the recognition, of the meaningfulness of life can be so uplifting that it results in more than transitory satisfaction. It could also be argued that attainment of happiness is only possible when one not only derives complete satisfaction but also grasps its full sense. It should be added too that meaningfulness therefore should not be given a restricted intellectual interpretation. While the distinction between *eudaimonia* and meaningfulness is probably less crucial, it would be helpful nonetheless to point out that meaningfulness involves not just seeing sense *in* life but *of* life itself. It specifically focuses on more than just an appreciation of what life has to offer but more significantly that it matters.

To clarify the choice of a philosophical route, perhaps one should make the distinction between the study of philosophy and the act of philosophising. In some form or the other, it is actually the act of philosophising, that every human being engages in, rather than in philosophy itself. But it is that same act that leads to and is the basis of the study of philosophy. The more formal and structured form of this act — which is what concerns students and teachers of philosophy — is what is sometimes regarded as 'philosophy'. Needless to say, this is an essential development since the pursuit of the questions asked and the answers given needs to be carried out at a particular level that very few would have the luxury or the leisure to do so. Moreover, we can benefit from reading the works of those who have carried out the act of philosophising in great depth and to a large extent. Nonetheless, this more academic and formal pursuit should not ignore the basis of philosophical thinking itself.

Accordingly, in our quest for the meaningfulness of life, philosophy can be helpful, precisely because the desire for meaning needs to be pursued much more intensely and thoroughly if we are not to be satisfied with merely superficial answers. Admittedly, philosophers understand and practice philosophy differently — and this can result in much confusion — but philosophy, with its insistence on raising fundamental questions, analysing the issues and pursuing any answer to its logical conclusion, can prod us on towards a viewpoint that can stand the test of careful and rigorous scrutiny by human reason. While it cannot and should not guarantee indisputable conclusions, philosophy nevertheless can abet the task of arriving at a more consistent, coherent and adequate answer. After all, asking whether life is meaningful is more than just asking what one would like to do for the day. To give an answer to that fundamental question is definitely unlike merely enumerating the options that one can choose for the day's activity. Pursuing the meaning of life implies a thoroughness that befits our very humanity itself and challenges it. And for this task philosophy is particularly well suited.

Philosophy and Language

Just as philosophy has been associated with wisdom and truth, so has it also, particularly in contemporary times, been linked with language. In fact, at times philosophy is interpreted as the analysis of language. One hears of philosophy's function to be the clarification of issues that have become clouded — due to the misunderstanding of the meaning of terms or words — in the hope of dissolving, as it were, the problems that baffle philosophical minds. However, while this can be of invaluable assistance in arriving at truth or achieving wisdom, philosophy can and should go beyond — *pace* some philosophers — merely analysing language. Here we will try to do both.

In the present context, the connection between philosophy and language is particularly appropriate since the initial discussion in this essay focused on life as a series of sentences and the correct punctuations to enable one to read its meaning. The grammar of language — more particularly, punctuation marks — will therefore serve as a valuable metaphor for this exercise. Taking up once again what was asserted at the start, the claim that is being made here is that we need to insert the proper punctuating marks — that is to say, to engage in certain kinds of human acts in life — to allow life's meaning to come across to us as readers — that is to say, as participants of life. That meaning is lost if we do not make the effort; and it becomes distorted when we insert the wrong punctuation marks — meaning, neglect certain essential human activities.

To assume that life *has* meaning is not to ignore that this very fundamental issue should also be of concern to us here. However, what is implied by this assumption is that we will not know the answer to that *until* we are actually engaged in the very task of searching for it. In other words, it is *in and through* our efforts to discover meaning that we learn *that* life has meaning. This point is quite different from saying that we create meaning, as some existentialist philosophers were prone to assert, as if there is no other meaning except the ones of our subjectivist creation. Rather, just as a series can simply be a grouping of words with no coherent sense unless and until we punctuate them properly so that they become sentences, so does life present itself to us. It is of course possible that the grouping of words is merely that: words strung together, not even qualifying as clauses, much less sentences. But generally we will not know that to be the case until we take the trouble to place certain punctuation marks even if only tentatively. We could of course also be accused of reading meaning or sense into the assembled words. But that would in fact confirm the point that it is in and through our effort that meaning is discovered. In short, the attempt is in a way also a disclosure.

Turning to Grammar

Punctuation marks, an integral feature of the grammar of any language, enable us to read a group of words in ways that convey a definite sense and elicit a specific response from us.[3] Punctuation marks break up words, sentences and even paragraphs to facilitate our grasp of the message.[4] They are marks which we add to the words of the text to enable us to get the meaning. Without them the text would be merely a collection or even an undecipherable jumble of words.

For example, a particular grouping of words, which we would normally refer to as a sentence and which ends in a full stop (or period) indicates a statement of fact, a description, a declaration and other similar claims. A question mark elicits a different response, this time from the reader or, in conversation, from the other party. At times, it may be what is termed a rhetorical question and thus no specific answer is expected or given. What is common is that a message that is followed by this punctuation mark, unlike a full stop, raises a point or makes a query. It asks rather than states. In contrast, a message that ends in an exclamation point comes across more strongly: it is intended to express the speaker's feelings, or to alert the reader.

Other punctuating marks play other roles in eliciting grammatical sense. Quotation marks enclose the message and disclose a source; they can also show that a certain significance is being given to the quoted message in relation to the primary text. A colon (or a semi-colon) halts the message, thus indicating that there is more to come: a further explanation or an illustration. Commas, on the other hand, merely provide a pause in the message, a 'breather' as it were. They are essential in delineating the grouping of words, thus bringing out the sense not only of the group of words but also of the entire message. A dash is another kind of pause, more as an aside but one that is regarded as relevant to the point being made.

Punctuation marks can also be the basis of agreement or differences inasmuch as we can agree on their appropriateness or inappropriateness as we seek to interpret the sense of the sentences or the entire message itself. They can be said to set the parameters of how we read (or are meant to read) the text. For this reason, care must be exercised by whoever inserts these marks to forestall any misinter-

3 No attempt is made here to provide an exhaustive list of punctuation marks.

4 An interesting book in this regard is Truss's *Eats, Shoots & Leaves*. A particularly useful example which she provides on p. 9 is: 'A woman, without her man, is nothing.' and 'A woman: without her, man is nothing.'

pretation. The author or editor of a text needs to check the extent that a particular punctuation serves a purpose, and clarifies or confuses the meaning of the text.

Punctuating Life's Text

On a number of occasions life has been compared to a book — we even make references to the book of life. Similarly, but with a different focus, reading the meaning of life's message can be likened to the writing of the book. In the present context, instead of the composition of the book of life, it is the significance of the punctuation marks that we put on the text that we wish to stress. For it is also in the editing of our life's sentences and not just in the authoring of them, as it were, that life's message is communicated to us. Sometimes we compose the sentences, more often we receive them — and it is in the interaction between the active and the passive side of life, so to speak, that life's message can be read, interpreted and lived. At the same time, how we break the text of our lives into meaningful phrases, clauses and sentences is what enables us to discover the meaning of life itself.

Taking our cue then from grammar, one could say that we need to make the effort — just as much as we need to be given opportunities — to place the appropriate full stops, question marks, exclamation points as well as the colons, the commas and the dashes in the proper moments, stages and cycles of our lives. For only then can we understand and appreciate what life is to us. We need to insert punctuating moments to the sentences that we compose in life as we carry on with our daily routine, engage in specific activities or celebrate certain events. Those sentences may be our responses to what life offers to us, or they could be creations of ours as we make our own contributions to life itself as it moves on, affecting us and others. Just as in our use of language, there is a received as well as a composed side to the over-all communication.

Transliterated into the context of life, the full stops (or periods) of life are the moments when we do come to the end of one activity, event, or phase and then move on to the next. These moments spell decisions made, activities completed, or simply points accepted. To some extent, these are the general markers in our lives as we press on from day to day. Sometimes these are just routine; others are more significant but not sufficiently so for us to regard them as 'out of the ordinary' such that they are life-changing moments.

Life, too, has its ups and not just downs: when we are surprised, uplifted and even thrilled. These exclamation points of our lives are moments that enable us to see life as a gift, to see beyond the routine. They make us stand still — and it is a pause that is indeed pregnant. At times, these special situations make it all worthwhile for us to continue; and, since they stand out, they somehow throw light on our lives, enabling us to appreciate what we have been given or what we have achieved. Living is no longer merely 'existing' but 'ex-sisting'.

It will not come as a surprise that philosophical thinking would be associated with a particular punctuation mark — and that is the question mark. Philosophy is equated with the pursuit of wisdom; and it is generally held that the beginning of wisdom starts with the questions we raise regarding ourselves and our world (Sia, 1994, p. 19f). The question marks of life are the moments when we, just like the symbol of this punctuation, 'curl back' because we are reflecting (*reflexere)* on our experience of various aspects of life — both humdrum and profound. Daily life presents situations when we ask, query or challenge. Unlike full stop moments, these moments make us step back and not merely move on. There are even occasions when we raise fundamental questions about life itself: asking about its significance, its purpose and its destiny. These questioning moments are sometimes the result of terrible or tragic situations; in some cases, they come about because of our inability to see what is in store for us or whether there is any point in continuing.[5] At other times, because we wonder, we ponder.

Often, we pause, not because we are reflecting or questioning but because we expect further information, explanation or illustration of what we have just experienced. These colon moments of expectation stand between the past and the future, between what has just been or what is to come. And when what was expected has come to pass, we begin to appreciate what has happened because we have been provided further information, explanation or illustration. Sometimes these colon moments simply take place unexpectedly; at other times, we ought to make them happen.

But there is another punctuation mark that can be said to facilitate our search for meaning; namely, the comma. The association of philosophy with the comma is not obvious in the way that the question mark is. But there is something about reflection — integral to the philosophical activity — that invites the comparison.

5 The existence of evil and of suffering is one such occasion. Cf. *From Suffering to God*, where we develop this point and its challenge to our concept of God.

For just as in grammar where, to decipher the meaning of a sentence or a text, appropriate commas can be useful, so in life appropriate pauses — which create an atmosphere of reflection — do enable us to establish balance, maintain priorities and sharpen a focus. These comma moments can aid us in making sense of the seemingly endless series of activities that we are engaged in or the various pursuits that we are trying to fulfil — when we take the time to see how the particulars are to be understood in the context of the general, or when we 'take a moment' to view the details as they come together in the light of the overall scheme of things. These moments enable us to see connections, small enough (like the symbol of the comma) to enable us to continue with everyday life but important enough to leave an impression on us. Comma moments are not just inserted as 'breathers', as it were (although they can be useful in that way), but because they serve the important function of providing 'sense'. And as we see the sense of the various groupings, they can open up the bigger picture. It seems that as we take — and make — the time to add these comma moments in our lives, we provide ourselves with a greater opportunity to see not just the 'senses' of the various happenings in our lives but even more importantly, the 'sense of it all'.

In this respect, there is something quite instructive in the actual mark of the comma itself. The comma, unlike the period (or full stop), is a dot that curls downwards and towards the left. It does more than just bring out the meaning of the sentence. It does this by connecting us, as it were, with the past — the group of words that have been separated by the comma. In life too, we need to be reminded that the question of where we are heading is partly answered by considering where we have come from.[6]

Text and Context

So far, the claim that has been made is that to draw out the meaning of a series of sentences in a text, the proper punctuation marks have to be inserted. This is a task both for the writer if he or she wants to ensure that the meaning is correctly understood and — in the absence of such marks — for the reader to insert the

6 A particularly helpful way of understanding and defending this point is provided by Charles Hartshorne's metaphysical category of creative synthesis. Cf. his *Creative Synthesis and Philosophic Method.*

appropriate ones to elicit an intelligible interpretation. It should be added now that such a quest for meaning, particularly on the part of the reader — which is our point of comparison — is often aided by making use of various resources to complement one's individual efforts.

One such valuable resource to understanding the sentences in a text and their meaning is knowledge of the context of the sentences. In fact, a sentence that has been lifted from the paragraph or the section (or even a greater context like a chapter) does not always convey as full a sense as it is meant to. Awareness of the general theme of the text as well as of the background (including that of the writer), connotations, varying interpretations, culture and so on can heighten and deepen the reader's sensitivities to such an extent that the reader can confront not only the explicit but also the implicit meaning of the text and of the words which make up the text. The same claim can be made — if life is being likened to a text — about discovering the meaning of life. The quest for meaning can be greatly enhanced by taking life's contexts into account. This is because this task is not simply a matter of inserting punctuating moments, as it were, by the individual but also of interpreting the meaning of those moments and eventually appreciating them.

The task of interpreting a text — as is well illustrated in literature — is much more than merely providing one's own understanding of it. While this can be and often is done, one nonetheless risks arriving at subjective conclusions. This is also the case with our quest for meaning in life. It is important that our individual efforts should also avail of the collective wisdom of humankind and the extensive experiences of others. After all, if it is true that the quest for meaning is a common human activity, then there is something that we can learn from one another.

By 'context' we mean that the act of philosophising takes place in the concreteness of life. These are specific life-situations, but they are not completely subjective nor are they entirely particular instances, such that one does not see any resemblance to other situations. The concreteness of life serves as the starting points for our reflections. But 'context' as used here also refers to some kind of a unifying vision or at least the need to recognise its significance. The specific life-situations on which the act of philosophising is based serve as pointers because it is through these specific situations that we become somewhat aware of a larger picture. In fact, we can only recognise them as specific because there seems to be a broader background against which they are set. Whitehead's analogy of "seeing the wood by means of the trees" can be helpful here (Whitehead, 1967, p. 6). It is the trees that we initially encounter, but it is also they which enable us to become aware of the wood. In seeing the wood, we have gone beyond merely noticing the trees. We may even see them in a different light because we see them against the backdrop of the wood. Similarly, the larger picture or the vision, that are opened up by the various contexts in which we philosophise, can enlighten us when we look again at the specific situations, including those that have set us off initially on our philosophical pursuits.[7]

'Context', as used here, thus refers to two distinct but related meanings: (1) the concreteness of our human experience as the basis for our philosophical reflections; and (2) a unifying vision that underlies our response to that experience. The question that inevitably arises is how something concrete (or detailed) can be reconciled with what is essentially abstract (or general). In insisting that philosophising is always carried out in context, are we therefore claiming that this activity is at all times both concrete and abstract? That would be a correct conclusion, except that as these terms apply here, they refer to different dimensions of the philosophical act. Insofar as philosophical thinking emerges out of the concreteness of life, it is concrete. It is based on and grounded in the day-to-day questions which need to be addressed as we live our lives and carry on our daily routine. But philosophical thinking, if it is not to be a superficial or an ad hoc response, must address those questions against a more general framework that helps to provide a sharper focus. This is the abstract dimension since it is general and comprehensive. There is something about human nature that is not fully satisfied with mere instances or selected examples. The human desire for some continuity, comprehensiveness, and unity in our understanding of reality, and in our attempts to make sense of it, is what we believe drive us to this quest for a more general vision.

Concluding Comments

In this paper, we have been concerned with developing further the claim that if life is not to become a 'sentence' on us, we can regard it more as 'a series of sentences'. However, if we do not wish them to become disjointed or a mere collection of words, then we should make the effort to punctuate them properly. The use of punctuation marks in grammar is particularly useful in clarifying and

7 T.S. Eliot puts it even more succinctly: "...we arrive where we started/And know the place for the first time."

developing this claim. Moreover, again turning to the role of punctuation marks in grammar, we assert that it is only when we insert those 'punctuating moments' that we discover whether life has any meaning at all. In our quest for meaning, the various contexts in life, e.g. religion,[8] can be helpful just as knowledge of the context can facilitate the interpretation of a text — to which life is being likened.

References and Bibliography

Hartshorne, Charles. 1983. *Creative Synthesis and Philosophic Method* (University of America Press).

Sia, M.S. 1997. *The Fountain Arethuse: a Novel* (Lewes, UK: The Book Guild).

Sia, Marian F. and Santiago, 1994. *From Suffering to God: Exploring our Images of God in the Light of Suffering* (Macmillan).

Sia, Santiago. 2004. *Religion, Reason and God: Essays in the Philosophies of Charles Hartshorne and A.N. Whitehead* (Peter Lang).

Truss, Lynne. 2003. *Eats, Shoots & Leaves: The Zero Tolerance Approach to Punctuation* (Profile Books).

Whitehead, A.N. 1942. *Adventures of Ideas* (Cambridge University Press).

Whitehead, A.N. 1928. *Symbolism: Its Meaning and Effect* (Cambridge University Press).

Whitehead, A.N. 1978. *Process and Reality: an Essay in Cosmology* (corrected version, ed. by David Ray Griffin and Donald W. Sherburne) (N.Y.: The Free Press).

Whitehead, A.N. 1967. *The Aims of Education* (N.Y.: The Free Press).

8 Despite some valid criticisms as well as misinterpretations, religion can be regarded as providing one such valuable context in this instance, particularly since the various religions do concern themselves—in its scriptures, teachings and practices—with, among others, the human quest for meaning in life. Cf. 'The Function of Religion in Human Life and Thought: a Whiteheadian Exploration' in S. Sia, *Religion, Reason and God: Essays in the Philosophies of Charles Hartshorne and A.N. Whitehead.*

THE ART OF LIFE: KEKES AND BAUMAN ON ATTAINING THE GOOD LIFE

Vojko Strahovnik, Ljubljana

1. Introduction

In recent decades we are witnessing a renewal of interest in the topic of living a good life, what it is and how to achieve it. Before that ethics predominantly dealt with questions of moral rightness and wrongness of actions (moral status of actions) and after which there was a revival of virtue ethics, focusing on moral virtues and vices as characteristics of an agent. The questions about good life, how a worthwhile life is to be lived and pursuit of happiness seem a natural extension of interest, since besides answering the questions of "what we should do" and "what sort of persons we should be" there is a further basic question of "how should we live in order for our lives to be good". The philosophical endeavour of posing and answering this last question (and questions similar to it) was labelled as "the art of life" and its again becoming an important part of the practical philosophy. "*The truth is that philosophy* has become *a theoretical discipline over time and as a result of many complex historical developments.*" (Nehamas, 1998: 1) The art of life has in part regained its significance regarding questions of how one should shape their life and what sort of life is a good life.

This paper deals with two recent accounts of the art of life by two prominent thinkers, namely John Kekes (2002) and Zygmunt Bauman (2008). Both accounts share a lot of similarities, but are also importantly different form one another. Kekes uses a bottom-up approach and examines several examples of good lives in order to determine what constitutes the art of life and which conditions must be meet in order for us to attain a good life through it. His account of the art of live is pluralistic, eudemonistic and uses a broad virtue ethics frame for its development. It is a universal account and can surpass different historical circumstances and social conditions. Kekes uses a notion of a personal excellence as a formative element of our character to show how one can through practicing an art of life (developing personal excellences, following reasonable ideals and engaging in projects, developing well-integrated balanced dominant attitudes and avoiding aberrations) attain a life that is good. Such successful practice of the art of life results in a life that is "*personally satisfying and morally acceptable*". (Kekes, 2002: 3)

Bauman on the other hand starts with a lucid examination of the modern society and then tries to give us answers on how to practice the art of live in it in order to attain happiness. Attainting happiness proves to be a very difficult endeavour in our "liquid modernity" of consumerism and constant changes. Bauman therefore does not offer us a general account of the art of life; instead he examines what are the most important barriers for identifying meaning in our lives and living them well. It lucidly examines several relevant aspects of the modern pursuit of happiness. He uses the thoughts of Sartre, Nietzsche and Levinas to identify our will, choices and responsibility for those choice as central part of the art of life despite restrictions of fate and external conditions beyond our control that influence our life trajectories. Art of life is therefore for him something that everybody must practice since even to do nothing or decide nothing is to make a choice. In order to attain happiness we should be able to accept the uncertainty of our future and find our identity even though this means a lot of hard work.

2. Kekes, personal excellences and the art of life

In his book *The Art of Life* (2002) John Kekes offers us a detailed account of the art of live that can be situated inside the tradition of virtue ethics. *"The art of life is making a good life for oneself. It is an art because it requires individuals to make a lifelong creative effort that no one can make for them and for which no blueprints exists. For a good life has to be constructed out of one's character, circumstances, experiences, and ideal, which vary with individuals, societies, times, and places."* (Kekes, 2002: 1) One of central elements of practicing such art of life is reflection on other lives that were good. Kekes uses several concrete examples of such lives in order to demonstrate how personal excellences shape lives that are good. These lives feature self-direction (Michel de Montaigne and Thomas More), moral authority (*sophron*), decency (Newland Archer and Countess Olenska), depth (Oedipus) and honour (Lamoignon Malesherbes) as central ideals and personal excellences that enable their bearers to attain a good and satisfying life (at least at its end).

Montaigne and More both displayed the personal excellence of self-direction, since they stood firmly behind their core ideals and did not make compromises regarding their deepest, unconditional convictions. The *sophron* (a figure of a wise elder man in Cyprus villages that plays an important role in a community) presents a moral authority that consist of (i) thorough familiarity of a particular moral tradition, (i) a commitment to this tradition, (iii) reflectiveness, (iv) being articulate and (v) conduct of moral authority, which is exemplary in the area of life where her authority holds. Sophron exhibits moral authority and others go to him when they need advice on what to do and this is another possible form a good life may take. Newland Archer and Countess Olenska (characters in a novel *The Age of Innocence*) display in their lives the excellence of decency, since they surpass their love and passion for one another and accept compliance with the deep norms, standards in conventions of behaviour in their society, since they are an important part of their shared ideal of a good life. Oedipus exhibits depth since at the end of his life, he has leaned to accept the contingencies of life (e.g. bad things that have happened to him and were beyond his control). The life of Malesherbes demonstrates the excellence of honour, since he was loyal to what he believed to be the constituent goods of his ideal of a good life. These cases are of course not the only forms a good life may take nor are they the only ways of following the art of life. These are just illustrations of how living in accordance with a personal excellence and an ideal of a good life can bring about a good life. (Kekes, 2002: 123-125) This account of the art of life is therefore inherently pluralistic.

Kekes uses these examples to investigate what can make lives good and what are basic constituents of such lives. First he exposes two necessary (but not sufficient) conditions of a good life, namely moral acceptability and personal satisfaction. A good life must be a moral life (i.e. conform to universal, social, and individual requirements of morality), since *"all human beings have some physiological, psychological, and social needs that must be satisfied if they are to live good lives. Their satisfaction is a minimum requirement of all good lives, and one purpose of morality is to create the conditions in which they can be satisfied. Reasonable people pursuing personal excellence have good reasons, therefore, to conform to these requirements, since doing so protects the conditions on which their own pursuits depend."* (Kekes, 2002: 147) The art of life can therefore only be practiced within the limits of morality. In case of a conflict of personal excellences and ideals one pursuits and morality no general answers can be given about its resolution. Here Kekes account is particularistic; the resolution of such a conflict depends upon particular circumstances of the case and private reasons. Furthermore, the art of life is also prominently particularistic, given that it goes *"beyond the mechanical, or even the intelligent, applications of rules."* (Kekes, 2002: 203) Living according to the ideal of a given personal excellence must be adapted to a person and circumstances they find themselves in. And a good life is personally satisfying, meaning that individuals have lived as they reasonably thought they had to live (in accordance with a reasonable ideal) and have been engaged in projects, from which (either successfully achieving them or just pursuing them) personal satisfaction can be gained.

For Kekes personal excellences are essential formative elements of our characters, important for our identity and self-esteem.[1] They are intertwined with an indirect pursuit of worthy ideals, which people accept as their own. The art of life requires pursuing those in various projects people engage in during their lives. Those activates are predominantly goal-directed, but being successful in exemplifying a particular ideal of personal excellence is fully compatible with being unsuccessful in one's project. One can obtain such an core ideal inside their moral tradition as an implicit ideal or through the form of moral education where one is acquainted (through literature, history, religion, philosophy) with admirable lives (or kinds of lives) that can serve as ideals. One then needs practical wisdom to adapt those models to themselves and their context.

Next, one must form one's character according to individual ideals of personal excellence and then act in accordance with it. They must form an appropriate attitude towards it; an attitude that encompasses cognitive, emotive and motivational aspects of personality that must be well-integrated and balanced in order to minimize mistakes and errors one might do.

Kekes distinguishes between three generic kinds of such errors, namely moralism, sentimentalism, and romanticism, which stand for aberrations that occur when cognitive, emotive or motivational aspect of one's character constantly overrides the other two when they are in conflict, leading to fragmented attitude and ultimately to bad decisions. There are no general rules how conflict among these three elements should be resolved in each case and good judgment is always needed.

For Kekes, one way of making lives good is a successful practice of the art of life, which means successful pursuit of an ideal of personal excellence within morally acceptable limits. He therefore opt for the combination of traditional mod-

1 Kekes distinguishes his notion of personal excellence from moral virtues in Aristotelian sense. Moral virtue is according to the latter (a) a character trait that is (b) concerned with choosing actions, (c) based on reason, and (d) aiming at the mean between excess and deficiency. Personal excellences do not fulfill conditions (b) (c) and (d); they are connected with choice, reason and emotions, but the connection is not as close as in Aristotelian account of moral virtue. (Kekes, 2002: 164-169)

els of the art of life, namely moral one (Kant, Mill) which is based on practical reason, morality and universalism, and aesthetic one (Nietzsche) which centres on creative life, freedom and individualism. Both models have serious flaws, but Kekes combines them into a novel model, in a way the moral model contributes the basic moral framework to protect the requirements that all good lives share (e.g. protection of basic human needs, etc.) and the aesthetic model contributes the importance of freedom when choosing one's own ideals and personal excellences that constitute a good life for an individual.

3. Bauman and the modern pursuit of happiness

Bauman starts his inquiry on the art of life with investigation of happiness (being the goal of the art of life) and its quandaries. Firstly, it seems that happiness bears no connection with economic growth in developed societies and living standards of people in modern times despite a deeply rotted conviction that it does. Nonetheless, in a consumerist society the pursuit of happiness is closely connected with shopping for commodities and the hope that this will lead to happiness. In consumer-market society we are forced or persuaded to adopt this pursuit that can never end in a state of happiness. *"The secure* state *of happiness not being attainable, it is only the* chase *of that stubbornly elusive target that can keep the runners (however moderately) happy."* (Bauman, 2008: 9) The pursuit of happiness establishes itself as our right, duty[2] and purpose of life. We are happy as long as we haven't lost the hope of becoming happy.

Consumerist society constantly creates new desires and preserves them with the idea of one-upmanship, which is acquiring things that other people don't have chance or prospect of getting. Exclusivity of the offers is always pointed out. There is always something new on the market that promises happiness to us. The most horrible command of our society is not "you must..." but "you want ..., you wish ..., you deserve ...". Hence *"if 'to be free' means to be able to act on one's wishes and pursue one's chosen objectives, the liquid modern, consumerist ver-*

2 Here Bauman comes close to the thought of Pascal Bruckner (2004), who speaks about enforced or compulsory happiness and about the pursuit of the state of permanent ravishment as a substitute for happiness.

sion of the art of life may promises freedom to all, but it delivers it sparingly and selectively." (Bauman, 2008: 78)

Secondly, the modern society is a society of permanent change and the feeling of uncertainty. For Bauman younger generations see life as a series of unconnected moments, and every non-pleasurable moment is a waste of time. (Bauman, 2008: 56) The world is fragmented and discontinuous. (Bauman, 1994) The past no longer determines the present; the future – in the light of its uncertainty and the lack of resources to deal with it – is a source of anxiety. One sign of all this is the ever more obvious trend of our failing to form lasting and deep intimate relationships, since we see such deep intimate bond either as an obstacle for our "freedom" or a danger of becoming a hostage of the fate (uncertain future that we do not have control over and that leads to anxiety).

Thirdly, it is very difficult to form permanent identity in such a world. In the past the choice of the life project was the choice of all choices that determined all subsequent choices. In liquid modernity identity is flexible and in a state of permanent transformation, in which one perpetually redefines oneself through becoming someone other that one has been so far.[3] (Bauman, 2008: 73) Bauman claims that the product of the art of life is supposed to be the identity of the artist, but a stable identity is something not easily achievable.

Is then the hope for attaining good life empty and futile? Despite all mentioned quandaries Bauman's response is optimistic. The successful practice of the art of life can still lead us to good life. Three concepts are important part of this optimism, namely choice, will and responsibility. We must first realize that life is a work of art and that it can't not be a work of art; every person is an artist of life, not by choice but by decree of the fate. But inside this framework of fate it is still our choices that co-determine our life and these choices must be made despite of uncertainty. *"All that, however, only soon to find out that our choice of guiding star was in the last account* our *choice, pregnant with risks as all our choices have been and are bound to be – and* our *choice, made on* our *responsibility, it will remain to the end..."* (Bauman, 2008: 54) Taking responsibility for the

3 One prominent example of this are internet social networks (like MySpace or Facebook), where people can form its own identity and also in the next moment dismantle it, replace it with another, "improved" version, thus redefining themselves without any real effort.

outcomes of our choices is at the end this ultimate choice that is central for the art of life and which we confront in our pursuit of happiness. And we must be willing to form intimate relationships and deep friendships, since that is a possible safe passage through liquid modernity.

4. The art of life in modernity

We have seen that both accounts of the art of life struggle to provide guidance for its practice. There are also important differences between Kekes and Bauman. An important thing to note is the different focus of their work. Kekes focuses on universal elements of the art of life and tries to answer the question of how they are connected with attaining a good life. The stress is on the conditions internal to a person. Bauman, on the other hand, attempts to reveal crucial elements of our modern consumerist society that stand as obstacles to the successful practice of the art of life.

While Kekes still claims that tradition plays an important role in shaping individual's model or ideal of a good life, Bauman exposes that there is no such solid frame in the modern society that one could trust in.

Kekes is mostly silent on quandaries of modern society, but nevertheless notes that our society is neither stable nor simple; *"social mobility, moral ambiguity, rapid technological changes, and conflicts of responsibilities, loyalties, and roles are ever-present."* (Kekes, 2002: 174)

Both approaches see character as central for the art of life. Kekes understands cultivating personal excellences is deeply connected with good life, since personal excellences are character traits, lasting tendencies to think, feel, and act in certain ways are essential components of our psychological identity that enables us to attain personal satisfaction. Bauman offers a similar answer. *"All artists struggle with the resistance of the material on which they wish to engrave their visions. All works of art bear the traces of that struggle – of its victories, defeats, and the many enforced, though not less shameful for that reason, compromises. Artist of life and their works are no exceptions to that rule. The chisels used by the artist of life (knowingly or not, and with greater or less skill) in their engraving efforts are their* characters. ... *Fate and its guerrilla troops, accidents, decide the set of choices confronting the artist of life. But it is* character *that decides which choices are made."*(Bauman, 2008: 103)

Both accounts also understand uncertainty of our future and contingencies of life together with our strategies for dealing with both as an important part of the art of life (for Kekes depth is an appropriate attitude towards contingencies of life and for Bauman accepting risk and taking responsibility for one's choice are appropriate responses to uncertainty). This is also a point where we can fruitfully combine both accounts in order to obtain an insight in the present situation. In a liquid modernity it is extremely difficult to commit ourselves to a reasonable ideal of personal excellence or a good life (just as Bauman notes our about intimate relationships). Committing to it seems to give away a part of our freedom. It means taking risks, since our projects might be unsuccessful. Such a choice seems like a hindrance in our lives. It means making our destiny a hostage of fate. That is the crucial hindrance for the art of life and the consequences of such state are vividly described by Bauman. Hope however remains, since an art of life is possible, though difficult.

References and Bibliography

Bauman, Z. 1944: "Alone Again: Ethics After Certainty", London: Demos; available at http://www.demos.co.uk/publications/aloneagain.

Bauman, Z. 2008: *The Art of Life,* Cambridge: Polity Press.

Bruckner, P. 2004: *Nenehna vzhičenost* (*L'Euphorie perpétuelle*), Ljubljana: Študentska založba.

Frankfurt, H. G. 1988: *The Importance of What We Care About*, Cambridge: Cambridge University Press.

Haidt, J. 2006: *The Happiness Hypothesis*, New York: Basic Books.

Kekes, J. 2002: *The Art of Life,* New York: Cornell University Press.

Nehamas, A. 1998: *The Art of Living: Socratic Reflections from Plato to Foucault*, Berkeley: University of California Press.

MEANING OF LIFE

LIFE AND THE QUESTION OF MEANING. SOME PHENOMENOLOGICAL CONSIDERATIONS

Branko Klun, Ljubljana

Human life is characterized by the specific reflective ability to question and understand itself. In our everyday life we question what we are doing and ask ourselves about the meaning of our actions. We seek to understand not only the particular realms of our living, but also life as a whole. The ultimate question of meaning concerns life in its entirety, including its definite boundary of death. But, are we also in the position to find an answer to this question? What does it actually mean to find or have a meaning; what is meaning? Could it be that any meaning we might attribute to human life is only our invention, whereas life itself does not have any relation to meaning at all?

The question of meaning is a very complex one and in this paper I intend to offer only some preliminary reflections concerning the close connection between life and meaning. The phenomenological approach that will be used here is consistent with the early lectures of Heidegger. In contrast to the theoretical attitude of Husserl's phenomenology, Heidegger regards "factical" life in the immediacy of its experience as the origin of phenomenological analysis. Although Heidegger does not explicitly question the meaning of life, he offers some indispensable insights about meaning in general. Only if we succeed to clarify how life and meaning belong together in a very elementary way can we subsequently pose the question about the meaning of life on the whole.

1. Phenomenology as the original science of life in itself

Methodologically, life represents the origin for approaching any "object" or "realm" of knowledge. Human knowledge cannot be detached from life; it is in fact a specific modality of life itself. However, life should be taken in a methodological "purity", refraining from any previous *idea* of life. Biology, for example, deals with life and living beings (as distinguished from non-living nature), but in this case life is already interpreted ("objectified") in a specific way. The life, which can serve as an absolute origin, is the one that I am living in the immediacy of my experience. Although it belongs to me, it is associated with other people through its understanding and shared meanings. It is important to see that before I can create an "idea" of life, I am living this life (to "live" as a transitive verb!) and even the creating of an idea (understanding) of life remains within the "flow" of life; it remains one of its modalities. There is no possibility of stepping out from the stream of factical life and taking up a purely "objective" stance, called for by empirical sciences. The presumed objectivity of these sciences stems from some particular mode of life and is the result of a specific orientation towards reality. When a biologist examines life in his alleged role of uninvolved observer, he or she applies some specific "view" to nature, which determines what is understood as world. In other words: the objectivity which is supposed to be independent from ("subjective") life, is nothing but a specific mode of this very life; it is one of the possibilities of how life relates to the world. In this sense we can understand how, from the phenomenological viewpoint, everything "exists" only in relation to life and represents one of its modalities (possibilities).

We are confronted with a specific situation of "life" that needs to be analysed phenomenologically. Given the complexity of the phenomenon we shall focus only on some key aspects relevant to our question about meaning. Life in its concrete "course" has always had to do with interpreting and understanding what is being "lived". It is not that we first live, and then, *in addition,* interpret things and events of the world, but to live means to interpret and understand living in the world. Life and understanding cannot be separated. For this reason we speak about the fundamental "openness" of life. Husserl's idea about the intentional openness of our consciousness for the world (including our "inner world") becomes with Heidegger the openness of our life. In Husserl's language the correlation of this openness is the "intentional object", i.e. something that we understand in a specific sense, or laden with a certain meaning. Life cannot proceed but through interpreting the world, and everything that happens within life is charged with meaning. We can also use the word "sense", which at this stage seems more appropriate for a phenomenological analysis. Sense is correlative to our understanding – even if we don't understand something or consider it a "nonsense", this is possible only while a certain sense has already been presupposed. The sense of individual things and events is however never isolated, but constituted through a relation to a broader context of significance. A professor's podium – a favourite example of Husserl and Heidegger – becomes its sense or its meaning from the whole context of academic life. It is related to the classroom, students, lectures, discussion etc. While Husserl remains within a theoretical attitude when phenomenologically describing the "sense" or the intentional meaning of the podium, Heidegger emphasises the more original constitution of its meaning within concrete factical life. Heidegger would claim that when I take a theoretical stance towards the podium, I have already objectified it as a specific "object". In order to approach its original meaning I have to enter into the living experience of the podium within the factical stream of life. Prior to creating any theoretically reduced meaning we have to become aware of its practical, "living sense" (GA 58, 173; Petkovšek, 2004: 105). We can illustrate this point with a farmer who cultivates his field. He would probably never ask a theoretical question about what a field actually is (unless some natural catastrophe happens and the field looses its original function), but the field is meaningful for him by the way it "occurs" in his life. The farmer lives the meaning of the field in his everyday life and the whole nexus of significances which he lives (land, field, cultivating, nature, tools, etc.) is precisely what can be called his world. The world is not a sum of objects and events, but a nexus of intertwining significances. This sense-laden context is not a given in a theoretical fashion, but is a lived and continuously exercised experience. For this reason Heidegger would speak about the world as a "significant whole" (GA 2, §18) that is "happening" (and not staying "out there") within the human existence (which itself should be understood as "happening").

There is a frequent objection to this phenomenological analysis, in that it overemphasizes the subjective perception of the world while neglecting its objectivity, paving the way to scepticism and relativism. But the phenomenological position only wants to take seriously the fact that our knowledge is always mediated by how we approach the reality we want to understand. Any question concerning "what" something is, has to become aware of the way, or "how" we approach it. Our approach sets the frame (of meaning) for the understanding of that "something". There is no immediate and objective knowledge of "things in themselves" for us as humans. The question about the truth of a phenomenon thus shifts to the question of the most appropriate approach, through which the phenomenon can show itself as it genuinely or originally is. The question of meaning (understanding, truth) relocates from the "thing" to its constitution within the "openness" of human life, characterized by freedom and possibility.

2. Life and the context of significance

If we return to the example of the lecturer's podium we can trace its meaning back to factical life in the academic milieu. But let us suppose, Heidegger writes, that a tribal African would enter the lecture hall, what would he see? Certainly not the pure giveness of some unknown object, but perhaps "something to do with magic, or a defence against arrows, or simply something he does not know what to do with." (GA 56/57, 71-72). The immediate experience is not mute, but "meaningful", intentionally structured. This calls to mind the movie "The Gods Must Be Crazy" (1980), where a Coke bottle thrown from a passing plane lands near Bushmen in the middle of a Kalahari village. As a hitherto unknown phenomenon the bottle immediately enters into the life of the tribe and in its context of significance: it is used as a tool for various purposes. Desired by many, the bottle soon brings jealousy and hatred in the community and disrupt its order. The Coke bottle is as different an "intentional object" for Bushmen, as it is for the world acquainted with the American "way of life". It is precisely the way or mode of life which confers a meaning to things and events. Can we now ask the question of what (the true meaning of) the Coke bottle actually is? Is it a glass object shaped in a specific way? Can its "essence" be defined by the genus (bottle) and its specific difference? The meaning of a Coke bottle depends on our approach to it and, as we have seen in our example, its sense can change accordingly.

Heidegger tries to analyse the constitution of meaning (or sense) of a particular phenomenon within the lived experience (GA 58, 261; GA 59, 62; GA 60, 63). Firstly, he speaks about content-sense (*Gehaltssinn*, "containment sense" by Kisiel, 1993: 122). This is what a phenomenon signifies. For a tribal woman in the Kalahari the content-sense of the Coke bottle is a device for milling grain, while for a Western person it is a liquid container for a special drink. The meaning or sense of the Coke bottle is also related to a broader context of significance. The indigenous woman sees the bottle in relation to the activity of milling grain within the context of food supply. The approach to a phenomenon is oriented in some direction; it is taken in relation to something. This is called a "relational sense" (*Bezugssinn*), which precedes and determines the "content sense". The content depends on the perspective, "toward which" (*Woraufhin*) something is interpreted. But, there is a third dimension of meaning: the "enactment" or "actualisation sense" (*Vollzugssinn*). The meaning of the bottle is primarily determined by its use in the concrete experience of life. What a bottle "is" (its meaning) depends on how it is "happening" in a lived experience (how it "acts", how it "actualises" itself in life). If a tribal African put the bottle on the shelf and never used it, its meaning would be different even if the bottle were understood as a tool for grinding. Contrary to the theoretical (a-temporal) meaning and its presumed objectivity, Heidegger emphasises the "lived" meaning (temporality of "happening"). The Coke bottle would still have the same theoretical significance in the West even if it would no longer be produced and consumed. Yet its meaning would be profoundly changed because it would cease to "live" within factical life.

The original context of significance (horizon) of any phenomenon is life in its temporal "happening" (*Vollzug*), in its living, which occurs not as an impersonal process (*Vorgang*), but as *my* lived experience. We cannot generalize life to some universal and neutral concept, since life is "in each case mine". The understanding which life "exercises" or "lives" is characterized by some fundamental interest (life is "interested" in living) or concern (the understanding is an *issue* for the one who is living). This motivation and concern of life has an ultimate "orientation" which in its purely formal sense is no longer relative: life seeks for itself, for the true and authentic life, for the full "possession" of itself. Any context of significance within a lived experience is determined by this final orientation.

3. Existence and meaning

In traditional metaphysics meaning is closely linked to the notion of "essence". The essence (what something "is") largely determines what the specific use of a thing is; it reveals its particular purpose. The meaning of a knife is defined by its essence, but this essence has to be "actualised" in practice. It is essential for a knife to cut, and a one that never cuts would become meaningless. To know the essence, or the meaning, of something presupposes the intelligibility of that thing. Classical metaphysics believes in the intelligible structure of entities which can be discovered by human intellect. We can apply the same approach for a human being and his life as well. If there is a pre-given "essence", it determines the self-actualisation of man and thusly the meaning of his life. The meaning of human existence would therefore be objectively founded and would not be left to the free choice of an individual.

From the phenomenological point of view the metaphysical approach lacks radical reflexion concerning its presuppositions. It takes a presumably neutral stance toward reality and looks for immutable and timeless essences of entities. But this approach is not neutral at all. It is led by a certain orientation, or "relational meaning", which defines the horizon within which things or reality can show themselves. The problem of metaphysics is not so much the inadequacy of its approach, but its belief that it is the only possible approach. In *Nichomachean Ethics* Aristotle defines the highest good of human life as happiness (1095a), which would correspond to the phenomenological formal orientation of life towards its full possession. He is also aware of different conceptions about happiness which result in different modes of life. Some people see the highest good and the meaning of life in pleasure, others in the honours of public life. But, according to Aristotle, true life is a contemplative one: the lover of wisdom sees the highest good in the true understanding of logos which permeates life and reality, giving orientation to the "bios theoretikos" (1098a). To achieve a fulfilled life implies developing virtues, which are those modes of living that correspond to the insight of reason (logos).

Whereas Aristotle believes in a common human nature (essence), which can be discovered by reason and "actualised" in life conduct, Heidegger maintains that any understanding of life represents only one possible understanding, and that there is no metaphysical essence of man which would imply a pre-given and "objective" meaning of human life. Phenomenology, as understood by Heidegger, is about human finitude which always remains within some relative context of understanding, unable to reach out for absolute, immutable and eternal truth. Human life necessarily takes place within some meaningful context, but there is no ultimate and universally valid meaning of existence. But, Heidegger goes even further. Being fully immersed in life, we are also immersed in certain meanings (tendencies and motivations of life) which influence any subsequent reflexion about them. In other words: our judgments about meaning and sense are made in the light of already given and lived orientations (i.e. meanings). Heidegger concludes that life "always speaks to itself only in its own 'language'" (GA 58, 31). What a religious person experiences as sin may, in the context of another person, not be understandable that way at all. Achieving a fulfilled and meaningful life is conditioned by the aims (meanings) which have already been adopted by this life. Heidegger calls this characteristic the "self-sufficiency" of life (GA 58, 27). It should, however, not be thought of as the spontaneity of an individual to create meanings for one's own disposal, but, in a broader sense, of being embedded in a both tradition and historically conveyed meanings. The Bushmen live the self-sufficiency of their life and they eventually reject the Coke bottle, which fails to integrate into their intentional nexus. So even the meaning of "meaning" is not a general concept (presupposing the "essence" of meaning in general), but, according to Heidegger, only a "formal indication", open to different structures and contents.

Does this analysis result in a radical relativism about different life options and their concurrent conceptions of meaning? Given the self-sufficiency of life, can we refer to any external criterion which would enable us to compare and evaluate different ways of life? A similar problem emerges already at the stage of intentional meaning of some particular phenomenon. Heidegger, in accordance with Husserl, refers to the criterion of originality: a more adequate understanding and one, in which a phenomenon gives itself originally, genuinely, authentically (GA 59, 74). The approach which allows the phenomenon to show what it "genuinely" is, and this also includes our *genuine* experience of it, is therfore the most appropriate. We can interpret the phenomenon of love as a neuronal process in the brain or a particular mode of existence in relation to another person. In which case is the phenomenon given and experienced originally? Thus, Heidegger still remains within the "self-sufficiency" of life, which provides the criterion: when a phenomenon is genuinely given in a lived experience, it somehow "intensifies" life (GA 56/57, 110), while a phenomenon given in an inadequate way, impoverishes its sense and causes the fading, or "un-living" of life. This is especially true for the theoretical approach, which detaches phenomena from lived experience, treating them as pure objects, and causing impoverishment or even the suffocation of life.

4. Conclusion

The radical self-sufficiency of life is one of the major problems of Heidegger's position. There seems to be no possibility to overcome the finitude of life and attain a transcendent or absolute meaning. Western metaphysics beginning with Socrates is, however, driven by the desire to transcend factical and temporal life in order to find such a meaning (logos). By grasping the eternal logos a horizon of meaning is discovered, which serves as the basis for man's self-understanding, granting him infinite dignity (Juhant, 2006: 18). Heidegger is known for his critique of metaphysics, which he developed in his later writings. But, if we accept the criterion of life, the criticism cannot affect the possibility of an absolute meaning as such, only a meaning which "weakens" life (in the sense of Nietzsche's critique of metaphysics). The self-sufficiency of life could even be regarded as a way of living an "absolute" (i.e. self-sufficient) meaning. Heidegger himself undertook an analysis of the religiosity of the first Christians and their lived meaning (GA 60).

He would, however, still reject any absolute meaning in the sense of its universal or objective validity.

We should not underestimate the criterion of life-intensity. The meaning of life, which deserves this name, should make life truly "alive", bringing it to the full possession of itself (Žalec, 2006: 54). Such a meaning can never be grasped and conveyed purely theoretically, through general and objective concepts, but only through living. The convincing power of a life-meaning, in order to be accepted by others, is its ability to bring someone's life to fulfilment. But is this acceptance not the primordial sense of "objectivity"? Is its meaning not "stronger" than any theoretical validity?

References and Bibliography

Heidegger, M. 1977: *Sein und Zeit*. GA 2. Frankfurt/M: Klostermann.

Heidegger, M. 1987: *Zur Bestimmung der Philosophie*. GA 56/57. Frankfurt/M: Klostermann.

Heidegger, M. 1993: *Grundprobleme der Phänomenologie (1919/20)*. GA 58. Frankfurt/M: Klostermann.

Heidegger, M. 1993: *Phänomenologie der Anschauung und des Ausdrucks*. GA 59. Frankfurt/M: Klostermann.

Heidegger, M. 1995: *Phänomenologie des religiösen Lebens*. GA 60. Frankfurt/M: Klostermann.

Juhant, J. 2006: 'Autonomous person as the basis of ethics: Man between modern and postmodern morality', In J. Juhant, B. Žalec (eds.): *Person and Good*, 27-35. Münster: Lit.

Kisiel, Th. 1993: *The Genesis of Heidegger's Being and Time*. Berkeley: University of California Press.

Petkovšek, R. 2004: *Le statut existentiel du platonisme*: *Platon dans l'analytique existentiale de Heidegger*. Bern (et al.): Lang.

Žalec, B. 2006: 'Good life and morality: For virtuous particularism, against generalism', In J. Juhant, B. Žalec (eds.): *Person and Good*, 37-64. Münster: Lit.

ART OF LIFE FROM PENOMENOLOGICAL POINT OF VEW

Tomas Kačerauskas, Vilnius

Introduction

The antique concept of philosophy as love of wisdom presupposes a nurture of the art (*technē*) of life. Philosophy was not only an interpretation of texts, but also a spiritual training that guided one's inner development. If we believe Plato's version, Socrates did not write on principle in order to avoid a text as an interruption of the stream of communication. In *Phaedrus* Plato directs our attention to the ambiguity of a text: it heals as a *pharmakon*, inviting to take part in the spiritual context, and poisons by blocking memory, which opens the contemplation of divine *eidos* for Plato. True life for Plato is a return to the place, from where we have sailed being in the water of forgiveness and concealment[1]. Thus a question concerning the relation between a text, remembrance and life emerges. Life is to be treated as coexistence, participation in an existential interaction, which develops in our environment of the texts, i.e. in the spiritual context. My first thesis is the following: *the art of life has been nourished in the spiritual context where we live the text interpreted. In other words, interpretation of life as a text in spiritual context aalows the nourishing of the art of life.*

While interpreting a text we involve both ourselves into the co-existential context and the phenomena to be described into our life. In such a way these phenomena take part in the creation of this text. Herewith we create ourselves, our life story, which emerges in the environment of the spiritual co-existence. The art of life is inseparable from the creation of our history, which we are creating not by describing the facts of life, but interpreting phenomena as the factors of the coherent existential whole. The phenomena have been inscribing into the existential whole created by us, where we become heroes. Existence, being the whole of harmonic events created by us from birth till death, demands mastership, knowledge of

1 Let us remember Heidegger's existential truth as aletheia, i.e openness. According to Heidegger, this truth is to be sought in the thinking before Socrates, actually, before Plato.

technē, otherwise our life becomes a jumble of incoherent episodes, where only the supporting actors who do not become heroes participate.

While living we write our own existential story, the hero of which is forming us, the masterful writers. Thus the conception of the art of life (*technē ton bion*), that arose in the antique philosophy, covers Heidegger's existential project (Heidegger, 1993) and Bakhtin's author's and hero's conception (Бахтин, 2000). Herewith it can help to develop the model of culture as an existential creation. Here the life and the text are not to be contradistinguished, but considered as two poles of a human creative interaction. Existence develops between the flow of life and the text to be written: life becomes ours, after we have inscribed its events into the coherent whole of our aims, senses, and images. On the other hand, this whole has been expanded every time. Life provides not only mobility for the existential project created by us. Life also guarantees an existential cocreation: on the one hand, we are writing our history together with other participants of existence, on the other hand, the co-creation emerges in the environment, which is expanded by it. Following Husserl (1952), I call this environment spiritual. That is why our mastership (*technē*) is required not only by the existential story written by us, but also by the spiritual environment created by us.

M. Aurelius (1983) wrote for himself, but it was not the registration of the fights of the defensive wars of his empire against barbarians. Often episodically in a tent between the fights, writing was a part of existential becoming for him. Everything that threatened the borders of his existential empire had to be inscribed riskily into the life's story, in order to transfer its borders. Existential imperialism, as a topic of Levinas (1984) philosophizing as well, requires creative mastership. Otherwise the borders of our existential project will be abolished by barbarous components we encounter every day. The mastership of the author, who is creating a story, is analogous to heroics of its actor, with every new phenomenon barbarism becomes a part of a hero's life, which determines not only a further course of events, but also a new link with the past phenomena already inscribed into the story. Hero in this case becomes a factor of author's existential becoming. Herewith this factor changes his entire spiritual environment. The borders of the author's existential project, his/her spiritual environment and hero's story do not coincide, instead, they are defined every time anew when the territories limited by them are merging. Existential creation is a constant exit (*ex-sistus*) from the spiritual borders to be defined: during our life we are preparing ourselves for the great exit, after which our existential whole will be further inscribed into the empire of the spiritual environment. We should search the content of life's art in the technique (*technē*) of this great preparation.

Spirit (*psychē*, *spiritus*, *Geist*) is formed when we as the authors of our existential project are influenced by the heroes to be created and we become the heroes to environment's co-creators. The analogy allows applying of Bakhtin's model of author and hero in the description of social reality: we are taking part in the creation of the spiritual environment *ana ton logon,* i.e. thanks to the tension between the linguistic existence and the existential language. This tension, analyzed in other works (Kačerauskas, 2008a, 2008b), emerges from creative activity of existential participants as co-creators of the spiritual environment. We shall see how it could be linked with Arendt's conception of *vita activa*. Social interaction as a modus of the creative activity allows considering also God as a phenomenon of the coexistence: God emerges as a factor of interaction between the linguistic existence and the existential language, a line of contact between the spiritual environment and the existential whole, when the borders of the existential environment (*logos*) are transferring. The technique of our exit (*exsistus*) as life-art is being formed in the existential environment where we were born earlier than we emerge in a physical way. In this sense we are passive participants of our environment. Levinas connects passivity with suffering in the presence of social transition. Speaking in a metaphoric (*metaphoreo* means to transfer) and Christian (transferring Levinas's thought) way, we learn life-art in the environment of Christ's suffering, which is filled with tension between our birth and death, passivity and activity. We become heroes only by being involved into the movements and revolts, i.e. being born in the environments full of intranquility.

The ideas of Christianity in late antiquity are to be connected with theories of the Stoics and Epicure, while they are connected with Plato's thinking. While Christianity was spreading across the whole empire unimaginably fast, it turned Christians into the heroes, who expanded the borders of the spiritual empire that were to be transferred into barbarian territories. Baptism in a river used to mark the beginning, the birth for heroic life in new time. According to Habermas (1994), that is how modernity emerged: this concept was first mentioned in the late antiquity in order to mark Christian ideas. Baptism involves with modern Christian community which seeks for inspiration in the Script (*Logos*). This spiritualizing is connected with temporalization in a new time and embodiment, while describing new boundaries of social body. After baptism we are taking part in creation of new (modern) spiritual reality: the hero of Christian life, created by us, creates his author, who becomes a factor of a community's creation. Plato's doctrine of participation (*methexis*) coalesces here with the idea of the singularity (*Einmaligkeit*) of birth and death, while doctrine of embodiment (incarnation) has been transferred to a new spiritual environment, where it marks belonging to spiritual community (Christ's body), although it kept the rudiments of physical rebirth (Resurrection of the bodies).

Therefore the content of the notion "spirit" has been changing under the influence of Christian impulses of the divine creation. My second thesis is the following: *our activity emerges as the creativity in the spiritual environment, co-creators of which we are.* I shall illustrate this thesis by interpreting H. Arendt's conception of *vita activa.* The third one follows from the first two by expanding them: *philosophy as the art of life is a factor of cultural creativity.* Philosophy matures and forms our life during our living. In this sense it constantly moves as interaction between a thought and life, when we become ourselves. By creating the heroes of our life story, who form us, we are taking part in the creation of the spiritual environment, which is one of our births as well. The circle (mutual interaction) of becoming of us and the spiritual environment allows speaking about spiritual imperialism: the existential creativity as a conquest of new territories and transferring of empire's borders. My interpretation of *vita activa* will be based on this warlike conception[2] of creativity, which is related to the conception of realization as temporalization, naming and embodiment. However, first of all I shall analyze, referring to P. Hadot (1991), the antique attitudes of Plato, the Stoics and Epicure towards the interconnection between philosophy and life.

Art of life in antique philosophy

For Socrates, philosophy is *maieutikē technē*, i. e. it is an art of giving birth for the ideas, which were matured in the discussions of the participants of a dialogue. The role of a philosopher is here only to help interlocutors to formulate these ideas on their own. In Plato's dialogue *Meno* (1999), a young uneducated slave is able to divide the area of a square into two equal parts after being questioned by Socrates, who forced him to contradict himself. He succeeded after "these notions have just been stirred up in him, as in a dream." (1999: 85c) Furthermore, Plato asks:

2 Com. Aristotle's entelecheia as realization and dynamis as mobility in *Metaphysics* (1924).

"is this spontaneous recovery of knowledge in him recollection?" (1999: 85d) I would interpret it as the birth of a slave for a new community that is philosophical, where the knowledge emerges in crossfire of the questions, i.e. in the spiritual fight. Remembrance (recollection) of the ideas is not transference of them as constants[3]; on the contrary, it is their trial in the middle of the life's battlefield. This allows rising an assumption about interaction between philosophical ideas and life: the ideas gain their plane in the spiritual environment being influenced by a life story created by us and, vice versa, we follow them in order to reach our existential whole. I shall come back to this precondition after analyzing *Meno* in the standpoint of the author's and hero's interaction.

Like other early (and intermediate) Plato's dialogues *Meno* is doubtful because of its authority. There was a question in *Meno:* what is a virtue; and the ideas of remembrance and of interaction between wise spirit and virtue arouse. Who is the author of these ideas: Plato, Socrates or all the interlocutors (including Meno, his slave and Anytus, who later contributed to Socrate's death)? The above-mentioned Bakhtin's conception of interaction between author and hero presupposes that the question of idea's authorship is related to the question of a hero. The hero of the dialogue, Socrates is constantly ironic: contrary to the sophist Gorgias, he does not know what the virtue is. I shall come back to this irony later. What is important here is that Plato's theory of ideas, the part of which is doctrine of remembrance, was formed under the influence of the philosophical intranquility of his dialogue hero (Socrates); and this philosophical intranquility was embodied by Socrates' irony. On the other hand, the latter requires a spiritual environment, which consists of the considerations of other dialogue participants, who are inspired by Socrates' irony. Therefore, Plato's ideas were developed in dialectic coupling, which consisted of two circles. The big circle is that one of the dialogues of authors' and the main hero's ideas. The small circle is one of the hero's considerations. A dialogue in this case is an authored (as well heroic) text, with the help of which the spiritual context for the development of the philosophical ideas was created.

Let us get back to Socrates' irony. By stating that he does not know anything, Socrates presupposes an auxiliary role of a philosopher. Disregarding that, a phi-

3 Aristotle in *Metaphysics* interprets Plato's ideas as the static units.

losopher helps creating the environment of thought's intranquility, spiritual context (where the ideas have been remembered) which forms an individual soul. In this way an interlocutor was born for the philosophical dialogue. In other words, he emerges anew as a member of a thinking community, being anxious about the question of virtue (in *Meno*). Being born in the context of Socrates' questions, he has been inspired for new insights. *Meno* ends with an aporia: although the practice of virtue is related with the mental education[4], it is an idea that has been inspired by God ignoring the mind[5]. How is this aporia to be solved?

The inspiration or spiritual madness (*mania*) is mentioned as well in *Phaedrus*, where Socrates' "bosom is full" and interlocutors (Socrates and Phaedrus) call one another as demonic. The participants of the philosophical dialogue are united by inspiration, "condition of madness" (1996: 266a), which helps to concentrate on "all things in common" and trise towards "true being" (1996: 249c). Therefore the participants in the philosophical environment should acknowledge that they do not know anything, i. e. to be born anew in order to expand the borders of their intellectual empire herewith the spiritual environment after they had been inspired by a flight of thought. This happens after the great and small circles of the author and the hero merge. Although the author separates himself from his "sons" (written texts), this namely allows him to take part in the inspired dialogue with them. Madness as un-reason means spiritual intranquility as un-easiness, when the empire's borders fall down after barbaric madness, after which these borders transferred even further. This is how "all things in common" are born in the dialogue between the author and heroes. "All things in common" is the whole of ideas, which is maturing spiritual (inspired) environment for our existence, which again is *ex-sistus*, exit beyond borders inscribed sometime. Mastership is an ability to be the author of existential project to be inscribed into spiritual environment. This is a school of exit, repetition for the great exit, after it our story becomes integral ("all things in common") and as such it will be inscribed into spiritual environment, where it have to be reborn for new life. This "rebirth"

4 "All other things hang upon the soul and the things of the soul itself hang upon wisdom, if they are to be good." (Платон, 1999: 88e)

5 "Virtue is neither natural nor acquired but it is an instinct given by God to the virtuous. Nor is the instinct accompanied by reason." (Платон, 1999: 99e)

allows speaking about existential incarnation, which emerges in the boundaries between Platonic and Christian embodiment.

Christian embodiment and rebirth are inseparable from suffering, from the Passion. Birth in spiritual (inspired) environment, which appears earlier and continues longer than us, gives passive meaning to existence: we were born before our physical birth and we rebirth later than we die physically. On the other hand, the spiritual environment is the space of our creational activity, in which we are changing and which we change while inscribing our existential story within it. Therefore passivity and activity are two poles, and due to their anxious interaction our existential project emerges as a part of the spiritual whole. As Levinas notices, another side of passivity is suffering, although he tries to avoid Christian meaning of the Passion (bringing rebirth). Our participation in creation of our story from birth till death is full of such existentials as anxiety (*Angst*), fear (*Furcht*) (Kierkegaard, 1952), disposedness (*Befindlichkeit*) or de-distancy (*Entfernheit*) (Heidegger, 1993), all of which only push us towards the creational intranquility.

Philosophy for Socrates is giving the art of birth, which is full of tension and intranquility: during thinking, we are re-born and at the same time renew the spiritual environment, by which we are inspired. Therefore philosophy being passive is a factor, which activates environment and presupposes the mutual interaction between soul and spirit. Philosophizing as passive contemplation becomes an impulse of movement towards itself. This movement is possible only in the environment of the creative interaction between soul as a part and spirit as the whole. In other words, philosophizing allows us to be born anew, herewith giving birth to environment of our thought and action. It is environment of a spiritual fight, where our birth is determined by death. Thus life's art, *technē tōn bion* (*ars vitae*) is also a technique of the renewing of the whole of life, i. e. of the existential creation.

Existential creativity is inseparable from mortifying of the old living whole. Plato's thoughts, which have influenced Christian attitudes, had matured being influenced by the thinking of Pythagoreans. Pythagoreans raised the conception of body as a soul's grave (*sōma – sēma*) and were anxious about life's way (*bios pythagoreios*), which included also mortifying of the body. That was the preparation for the exit from the body, which was a significant, but temporary part (to be mortified), of a rebirth cycle. Having taken them from the Pythagoreans, Plato passed the conceptions of rebirth and embodiment together with a doctrine of participation (*methexis*) in a divine idea over to Christianity. But unlike Pythagoreans he did not propose to mortify the body, which is an important factor for remembrance of the divine idea (in other words, spiritualizing the environment), even though senses are deceptive. Aristotle in *Nicomachean ethics* (1990) propagated the middle way, which would wisely combine the sensitive cognition and the voice of mind. As mentioned above, it is a dynamic (*dynamis*) way of realization (*entelecheia*), which requires our creative attempts. Heidegger realized our mortality (*Sein zum Tode*) as a factor of existential creativity. In all cases philosophy as an art of life develops in the environment of interaction between passivity (mortifying) and activity (creativity) or of tension between spiritual embodiment and body's spiritualization.

Birth (as well as death) is a factor of our existential creation. The figure of a philosopher as a midwife brought up by Socrates means our constant rebirth in the spiritual environment, which we create together with a background (*Hintergrund*) of our private heroic narrative. Our existential story and its background make up "all things in common", i. e. the existential whole, which requires our *technē* of philosophical life. Birth and death in the background of the existential creation are analogical. We do experience neither birth nor death. Despite that, they emerge as phenomena which direct and give wholeness for our existential narrative. They appear *ana ton logon*, i. e. according to *logos* of spiritual background, which provides existence with structure of unit narrative from birth till death. Life does not match with existence as birth does not with death. Existence is harmonious (although full of tension) narrative, heroes of which become not all participants of life.

Analogy of birth and death is also possible because the creative renewing is inseparable from the learning to die in the teachings of Pythagoreans and the Stoics. We are born every time when we think about our existence to death, naming death a spiritual background. Although we do not experience death, the latter emerges as an imaged reality, analogical to fiction in the literature. Used in the development of philosophy as life's art, the conception of interaction between the author and a hero allows considering philosophical works as literature, although not all works are close to Plato's dialogues, which are to be interpreted in this way. Philosophy and literature are analogical not only because they both are the works of human creation (culture). Philosophy as an art of life is *technē* of phenomena's selection and grouping into "all things in common" between birth and death. In other words, it is *technē* of the turning of chaotic flowing life into existential narrative. Existential creation is more than inscribing of facts into a diary, it is inscribing of phenomena, which interact each other, into our spiritual background, where we constantly rebirth herewith renewing our environment.

Therefore analogy here means the participation of interactions in our spiritual environment, which we expand with the help of these phenomena. The vault of spiritual environment created (given birth) by us is based on the poles of embodied fiction and spiritualized body. Removing of the body would abolish the tension of phenomena's interaction, therefore would impoverish (despiritualize) our creative environment, which is always a field of fight. That is why neither Plato nor Aristotle or Epicureans[6] ever advised to mortify the body as an analogical participant of the spiritual environment.

The body is a component of creative life, of our spiritual environment. Both birth and death are inseparable from the body, although herewith they are the factors of our becoming in a spiritual background. We are born and reborn by changing the whole of spiritual background, which we inspire by new existential story. The act of baptism embodies renewal of spiritual Christ's body by its new participant. Baptism is the birth of a child as a participant of the environment to be renewed (inspired), as well as the rebirth of the parents as spiritual environment's participants. Herewith baptism is an inscribing into metrics, creation of a text. Without it, our story would not develop; during inscribing this story, we name, spiritualize and embody our spiritual environment, where we are constantly reborn. We create our story as an interaction between living and thinking in the spiritual background. That is the interaction between *vita activa* and *vita contemplativa*, where we are learning to die by living.

Vita activa: interaction between living and thinking

Time has come to talk about H. Arendt's conception, which I will interpret in the context of the existential creativity. H. Arendt's *vita activa* includes work, production and action (*Handeln*)[7]. Work emerges here as cultivation, falling into the spiritual environment. Production emerges as *Her-stellen,* exposition in the general environment. Therefore action as creative mobility is inseparable from passivity, being in the background of creation.

6 Body, for Plato, is a medium, in which an idea is recognized; for Aristotle is a factor of happiness; for Epicureans it is a factor of friendship.

7 „Mit dem Wort Vita activa sollen im Folgenden drei menschliche Grundtatigkeiten zusammengefast werden: Arbeiten, Herstellen und Handeln“ (1960: 14).

We are taking part in the political life, herewith we are creating it. Existential creativity has been supported by us as *animal laborans* and *politikon zōon*. Therefore we have a fight's world, which pulsates by interaction between the personal and the public life. Here K. Schmitt (1963) is to be remembered, for whom politics included the war state. Ch. Mouffe (1993) continued this thought: our political environment is a live background of a thought's fight. In the context of existential creation we talk about intensive spiritual environment, inspired by which we fight back our existential whole. Tension between private and public planes fills up the spiritual world created by us, where the inspirations are embodied and bodies are spiritualized. This happens as a fight between a part (our existential story) and the whole (spiritual background) when we fight back the new phenomena over and over, as well the territories, which pompose with previous "all things in common". This imperialism presupposes our existential rebirth as a challenge for the spiritual background, which borders are constantly being exploded.

H. Arendt speaks about impoverishing of polyphonic environment, when only one aspect dominates in mass society and variety of perspectives diminishes in political life[8]. Therefore, it is important to be anxious about the spirit of fight and environment full of tension in order for our constant to be reborn within it. It corresponds to Mouffe's anxiety about saving manifold and colorful public life, in which we are fighting for our identity, i.e. we are writing our story.

Therefore only private life robs the human's things as audible and visible reality in the common world of things, which differ and bind, i.e. it robs "all things in common"[9] to be created by us. Differences and bonds give a meaning to our *vita activa* as the creational existence, which unfolds in common spiritual world of a body and a thought, private and public spheres, things and God. *Vita activa* appear as intranquility (*Unruhe*), *nec-otium*, *a-scholia* (1960: 21), which stimu-

8 „Eine gemeinsame Welt verschwindet, wenn sie nur noch unter einem Aspekt gesehen wird; sie existiert uberhaupt nur in der Vielfalt ihrer Perspektiven" (1960: 57).

9 „Nur ein Privatleben fuhren heist in erster Linie, in einem Zustand leben, in dem man bestimmter, wesentlich menschlicher Dinge beraubt ist. Beraubt namlich der Wirklichkeit, die durch das Gesehen- und Gehortwerden entsteht, beraubt einer 'objektiven', d. h. gegenständlichen Beziehung zu anderen, die sich nur dort ergeben kann, wo Menschen durch die Vermittlung einer gemeinsamen Dingwelt von anderen zugleich getrennt und mit ihnen verbunden sind, beraubt schlieslich der Moglichket, etwas zu leisten, das bestandiger ist als das Leben." (1960: 57–58)

lates to search for a new harmony of spiritual world as the environment of our becoming. For a creative *homo faber* the world becomes a place for realization of phenomena, when we embody our goals and spiritualize the body's heroic movement towards death.

„Von solchen Heldentaten ist allerdings faktisch in dem taglichen Kleinkampf, den der menschliche Korper um die Erhaltung und Reinhaltung der Welt zu fuhren hat, wenig zu spuren; die Ausdauer, deren es bedarf, um jeden Tag von Neuem aufzuraumen, was der gestrige Tag in Unordnung gebracht hat, ist nicht Mut, und es ist nicht Gefahr, was diese Anstrengung so muhevoll macht, sondern ihre endlose Wiederholung. Die "Arbeiten" des Herkules haben mit allen Heldentaten gemein, das sie einmalig sind.“ (1960: 92)

Realization, embodiment and spiritualization occur here as cultivation, which requires our heroic endurance for fighting back a new spiritual environment. Arendt mentions infinite repetition for cultivation of yesterday's chaos. Our work is cherishing of life's technique in order to realize death. Arendt does not say anything about the coupling of life and death, which provides mobility[10] to our world. We prepare ourselves to die by inscribing death as a real phenomenon into our life's story, into bio-graphy[11], by means of our works we become ourselves. Existential analogy (coupling) between writing and life allows speaking about context of the spiritual world to be created by us, i. e. about the coexistence towards death.

Conclusions or Existence as Creation

Philosophy as the art of life presupposes existence as creation. We exist while we, with the help of philosophy, inscribe the phenomenon of life into the existential

10 „Geburt und Tod setzen die Welt voraus, namlich etwas, das nicht in stetiger Bewegung ist, etwas, dessen Dauerhaftigkeit und relative Bestandigkeit An-kunft und Aufbruch ermoglichen, das also jeweils schon da war und nach jedem jeweiligen Verschwinden fortbesetzen wird.“ (1960: 89)

11 „Das Hauptmerkmal des menschlichen Lebens, dessen Erscheinen und Verschwinden weltliche Ereignisse sind, besteht darin, das es selbst aus Ereignissen sich gleichsam zusammensetzt, die am Ende als eine Geschichte erzahlt werden konnen, die Lebensgeschichte, die jedem menschlichen Leben zukommt und die, wenn sie aufgezeichnet, also in eine Bio-graphie verdinglicht wird, als ein Weltding weiter bestehen kann. Von diesem Leben, von dem bios zum Unterschied vom zōē, hat Aristoteles gemeint, das es 'eine praxis ist'.“ (1960: 89–90)

story created by us from birth until death. Thus life's stream assumes an order, which is analogous to the spiritual background, where our existential project is being realized. Analogy here means mutual interaction in the whole of the linguistic existence and the existential language, in which we revive every time while herewith renewing it. Both birth and death are the factors of the existential creation: death provides the wholeness to our existential story and birth (revival) provides mobility and newness, when it is inscribed into the spiritual background of the coexistence.

References and Bibliography

Arendt, H. 1960: *Vita activa oder Vom tatigen Leben*, Stuttgart: W. Kohlhammer Verlag.

Aristotle 1924: *Metaphysics*, ed. W.D. Ross. Oxford: At the Clarendon Press.

Aristotelis 1990: 'Nikomacho etika', in: *Rinktiniai raštai*. Vilnius: Mintis, 61 - 273.

Aristotelis 1929: *Politika*, Hg. Otto Immisch, Leipzig–Berlin: Lipsiae in aedibus B.G. Teubneri.

Habermas, J. 1994: *Die Moderne – ein unvollendetes Projekt*, Leipzig: Reclam Verlag.

Hadot, P. 1991: *Philosophie als Lebensform*, Berlin: Verlag Mathias Gatza.

Heidegger, M. 1993: *Sein und Zeit*, Tübingen: Max Niemeyer Verlag.

Husserl, E. 1952: 'Ideen zu reinen Phanomenologie und phanomenologischen Philosophie' II, in: M. Biemel Hg., *Husserliana IV*. Haag: Martinus Nijhoff.

Kačerauskas, T. 2008a: 'Tikrovė ir išmonė kalbinės egzistencijos perspektyvoje', *Santalka* 16 (1), 4 – 12.

Kačerauskas, T. 2008b: *Tikrovė ir kūryba: kultūros fenomenologijos metmenys*, Vilnius: Technika.

Kierkegaard, S. 1952: *Der Begriff Angst*, Dusseldorf: Eugen Dietrichs Verlag.

Levinas, E. 1984: *Totalite et Infini. Essai sur l'Exteriorite*, Haag: Martinus Nijhoff.

Markas Aurelijus 2005: *Sau pačiam*, Vilnius: Alma littera. Mintis.

Mouffe, Ch. 1993: *The Return of the Political*, London: Verso.

Platonas 1996: *Saidras*, Vilnius: Aidai.

Schmitt, C. 1963: *Der Begriff des Politischen*, Berlin: Duncker & Humblot.

Бахтин, М. 2000: *Автор и герой*, СПб.: Азбука.

Платон 1999: 'Менон', in: *Апология Сократа, Критон, Ион, Протагор*, Москва: Мысль.

SEARCH FOR IDENTITY AS ART OF LIFE IN THE POLITICAL PHILOSOPHY OF HANNAH ARENDT

Gábor Kovács, Budapest

Hannah Arendt, the disciple of Martin Heidegger and Karl Jaspers, in her political philosophy as a starting point chose the notion of existence inherited from her masters. The point of gravitation of her doctoral dissertation entitled *Liebesbegriff bei Augustine* is the Augustinian question: 'Questio mihi factus sum', I became a question to myself. Is human existence capable to come out of his/her isolation and to find the way to the community of his/her fellow-men? This problem accompanied Arendt during her whole intellectual carrier. One of the central problems in her political philosophy is this searching for identity which in her theory is public or political identity. Private identity without political identity is a truncated mode of existence for human beings. Action which is one of the basic ontological characteristics for human beings is possible only if they enter the *space of appearance*. Arendt uses a metaphor: public realm constituted by the space of appearance is a stage of theatre on which the actors must wear mask to hide their naked private existence.

The fact, that Martin Heidegger and Karl Jaspers were her mentors and Jaspers was her dissertation director predetermined Arendt's starting point and the way she approached the life-work of Saint Augustine. Her reading was an existential one, which was a popular approach in that time at German universities. But it was only the starting-point which was predetermined; the way of interpretation of Augustine presented by Arendt was an autonomous achievement. Augustine for Arendt was interesting as a philosopher and not as a theologian.[1] According to her Augustine is a philosopher who was standing at crossroads. The traditions which he drew on, originated partly in Greek philosophy, first of all Neoplatonism and stoicism, partly in Christianity, first of all in the thought of Saint Paul. God, for Augustine was not impersonal Supreme Being but a personal Creator, the

1 Hannah Arendt: Love and Saint Augustine. Edited and with an Interpretative Essay by Joanna Vecchiarelly Scott and Judith Chelius Stark. Chicago–London: The University of Chicago Press, 1996, p. 122.

God who had revealed himself in the Bible, to whom man is attached by love. At the time of Augustine this double tradition was broken; the life-experience of the late Roman Empire was not approachable by it. Augustine is a paradigmatic thinker, who, similarly to his successors, Kierkegaard, Nietzsche and Marx, tried to interpret a new existential situation with the help of an old intellectual tool box.

The book of Augustine entitled *Confessions* is the most important Augustinian writing for Arendt. It naturally exposes itself to the existential reading. The story of the book is the Soul's lonely journey to God. During this existential wandering Soul tears itself from the earthly bounds and ascends to the Creator. But the Soul, using a bit profane metaphor, has bought a return ticket for this journey. After ascending to God the Soul returns to the human society. Neighborly love (dilectio proximi) is a basic virtue for the Christian believer. In a nutshell it is the core of Arendt's reading of Augustine. In the third part of her dissertation entitled *vita socialis* Arendt emphasizes that in Augustinian theory human existence is not a separated mode of being; it is historical and social existence. But at the same time she criticizes Augustine, because, in her opinion, neighborly love is an instrumental one; the believer can not love his/her neighbor for his/her own sake, but only for the God's sake:

"And just as I do not love the self I made in belonging to the world. I also do not love my neighbor in the concrete and worldly encounter with him. Rather, I love him in his createdness. I love something in him, that is the very thing which, of himself, he is not (...) It also means that for the neighbor as well love is merely a call to isolation, a summons into God's presence. The lover turns the beloved into his equal. He loves this equality in the other whether or not the beloved understands it. In self-denying love I deny the other person as well as myself, but I do not forget him."[2]

The Augustinian notion pair of *use – enjoyment* (usi – frui) and the hierarchical order of love (ordo dilectionis) involve this kind of instrumentality. For Augustine, man is the citizen of two worlds; that of *city of Earth* (civitas terrena) and that of *city of God* (civitas Dei). For Arendt the essential feature of Augustinian philosophy is that human person in it is not a lonely being isolated from his/her neighbors and in spite of the dual citizenship he/she is embedded

2 Ibid., pp. 95-96.

in human world created and maintained by him/her. So, emphasizes Arendt, the Christian believer's identity is obtainable only in the community of believers, his/her private existence is inseparable from his/her public existence. In other words, private identity and public identity are intertwined. That is why Augustine was a key figure for the young Arendt. Her critics accused her with a selective use of sources and a selective reading of Augustine (Noteworthy that this type of critics was accompanying her during her later intellectual carrier.) However Augustine gave a chance for the young scholar to detach from her mentors, first of all from Martin Heidegger and to break with the notion of separated human existence. In her dissertation appeared the well-known ideas of her later works: *natality* i.e. the fact that the birth of every human person brings the chance of a new beginning into the world; the human made *world* as the home of human species and the *plurality* of human beings as a basic fact of human existence.[3] Undeniably, Arendt secularizes the Augustinian thought. The three layered notion of Augustinian love – love as *cupiditas*, love as *dilectio* and love *caritas* – is merged by her into the love for the human made world. Love in her interpretation is the starting point of the world-constituting and world-maintaining deeds.

In her second book entitled '*Rahel Varnhagen. The Life of a Jewess*' Arendt investigated the same problem, i.e. the relation of private and public existence, but put it into another frame of reference. The choice of subject was predetermined by historical circumstances. When Arendt, after the Nazi takeover of power, left Germany the book, except for last two chapters, had been completed. The subject, the history of German Jewish identity certainly concerned her very deeply and very personally. The story about a Jewess of Berlin in the age of the Napoleonic wars is a very subjective biography. It's a story of an assimilated Jewess written in a historic moment when assimilation as a realizable life-strategy had been questioned. The book presents the story of the search for identity of Rahel Varnhagen in the age of Romanticism, as well as the personal struggle of Arendt for identity in the age of totalitarianism.

3 For the key notions of political philosophy of Hannah Arendt see: Margaret Canovan: *Hannah Arendt. A Reinterpretation of Her Political Thought*. Cambridge: Cambridge University Press, 1992, pp. 99-154.

In this biography Arendt consequently takes difference between private sphere and public sphere. The story of Rahel Varnhagen is the journey of lonely, separated human existence from her isolated existential situation to the public world. This not a smooth journey, but a painful odyssey burdened with obstacles and blind alleys. The life problem of Rahel Varnhagen is presented by Arendt in terms, which are familiar from Existential philosophy: "No human being can isolate himself completely; he will always be thrown back upon the world again if he has any hopes at all for the things that only the world can give..."[4]

For a time the salons of Berlin established in the late 18th century seemed to be an alternative public world in the maintaining of which the Jewish women played important role. In the opinion of one of the Arendt's feminist interpreters, Seyla Benhabib these salons represented a very important development; they gave a chance for emerging a new kind of public space, in which Jewish women were able to acquire public identity as Jewish persons and as women as well. The woman identity outlined by Arendt in the figure Rahel Varnhagen, argues Benhabib, was the historical prefiguration of the postmodern woman identity delineated by contemporaneous feminist movement.[5] Telling the truth, Arendt herself was more critical evaluating the historical role of the salons of Berlin in the age of Romanticism. In her opinion this type of public space provided for the illusions of a mixed society only for a short time. It was a transitional social constellation in which the Jews played the role of mediator among different social strata offering a neutral public space for them.[6] But, argues Arendt, this was not a real public realm because intimate and public was inseparably intertwined in it.[7] For right interpretation of this critical assessment we have to keep before our eyes that mingling private and public spheres in Arendtian political thought is the original sin, which involves the fall of public sphere.

4 Hannah Arendt: *Rahel Varnhagen. The Life of a Jewess.* Edited by Liliane Weissberg, translated by Richard and Clara Winston. Baltimore and London: The Johns Hopkins University Press, p. 93.

5 Seyla Benhabib: *The reluctant modernism of Hannah Arendt*, London–Delhi: Sage Publications, 1996, pp. 14-22.

6 Hannah Arendt: *Rahel Varnhagen*, p. 127.

7 Ibidem, pp. 176-177.

However, Rahel Varnhagen's salon in Berlin after a decade and a half (1806) ceased to exist because of the changing for socio-historical constellations. The possibility of an alternative public space never came back again for her, so she had to continue her odyssey from isolation into the community of human beings. Unfortunately, the odds were against her; she was a Jewess. Because of her Jewish origin she had only one way to society; it was the way of assimilation. Arriving at the end of this road she had to discard her Jewish identity and to assume the identity of a *parvenu*. The another chance offered by modernity for Jews, argues Arendt, is the *pariah* identity; i.e. to remain voluntary outside of the society which in exchange of admission requires giving up Jewish history and cultural traditions. Assimilation in Germany has proved to be a historical blind alley, summarizes Arendt her opinion in the shadow of Nazi regime:

"For the person who really wanted to assimilate could not pick and choose among the elements to which she would be willing to assimilate, could not decide what she liked and disliked. If one accepted Christianity, one had to accept the time's hatred of the Jews right along it. Both Chritianity and anti-Semitism were integrating components of the historical past of European man, and living elements in the society of Rahel's day. No assimilation could be achieved merely by surrendering one's own past, but ignoring the alien past. In a society on the whole hostile to the Jews – and that situation obtained in all countries in which Jews lived, down the twentieth century – it is possible to assimilate only by assimilating to anti-Semitism also. If one wishes to be a normal person precisely like everybody else, there is scarcely any alternative to exchanging old prejudices for new ones."[8]

In Arendt's conception the relation of private realm and public realm is paradoxical. On the one hand, individual existence is incomplete; the ontological wholeness of human being can be attained only in public realm. The term 'private' by Arendt is traced back to its original Latin meaning; to be stripped of something, to be stripped of the chance to enter the light of public realm. On the other hand, the nakedness of private human existence must be hidden entering the public scene; without this hiding private realm deforms and destroys public realm at last. Metaphors of *scene* or *stage* and *mask* appear again and again in the

8 Ibidem, p. 256.

writings of Hannah Arendt. They are served for illustrating of complicated relation of private and public identities. These metaphors are embedded in the context of political philosophy in her book entitled *On Revolution* (1963). The *space of appearance* constituted by human words and deeds is a stage, on which the actors must wear masks, like it was compulsory to wear masks for the actors who played their roles on the stage of Greek tragedy. It is not by chance, Arendt warns, that the figures of the French Revolution of 1789 used this metaphor for describing their own political activities borrowed from the language of theatre life conspicuously frequently. She, similarly her former mentor, Heidegger, regularly calls to help of etymology to deconstruct the notions, to strip them of the petrified layers of false interpretations and to reach the original contexts in which they gain their real meaning. She applies this fenomenological method borrowed from Heidegger as well in this case. The Greek term *proszópon* and its Latin translation *persona* originally meant the masks, behind which the actors entering the stage to hide their personal identities:

"At any rate, it was in this twofold understanding of a mask through which a voice sounds that the word *persona* became a metaphor and was carried from the language of the theatre into legal terminology. The distinction between a private individual in Rome and a Roman citizen was that the latter had a *persona*, a legal personality, as we would say; it was as though the law had affixed to him the part he was expected to play on the public scene, with the provision, however, that his own voice would be able to sound through. The point was that 'it is not the natural Ego which enters a court of law.' Without his *persona*, there would be an individual without rights and duties, perhaps a 'natural man' – that is a human being or *homo* in the original meaning of the word, indicating someone outside the range of the law and the body politic of the citizens, as for instance a slave – but certainly a politically irrelevant being."[9]

However, the using of the mask metaphor is associated with a philosophical anthropology. It is explained for the first time in her book on totalitarianism. Here Arendt distinguishes three layers of human person: those of juridical per-

9 Hannah Arendt: *On Revolution*, London: Penguin Books, 1990, pp. 106-107.

son, moral person and naked human individuality.[10] The extermination of human person in concentration camps was accomplished in three consequent steps. First step is the annihilation of juridical person, the tearing off his/her public mask; the victim ceases to be a citizen of any political community. Second step is the doing away with moral person. At the end of this process remains only the last residue, the naked human individuality, the *homo* which can physically be exterminated in gas chambers.

It is conspicuous that Arendt stubbornly returns to the problem of human nature in her writings. In her most philosophical book entitled *The Human Condition* (1958) which is frequently considered to be the opus magnum of her oeuvre she treated this question in a philosophical context, applying traditional philosophical notions instead of using metaphors. In the train of thought of the book Saint Augustine plays a main role again. We human beings, argues Arendt are able to determine the natural essences of the things surrounding us, but we are unable to do this concerning ourselves. It is impossible as it is impossible for us to jump over our shadows. Unlike to the things of the surrounding world human being does not have nature or essence. If we had such nature or essence only a god would be able to determine it. In the case of human being must be made a distinction between the question of *who* and that of *what.* Arendt here refers to the *Confessions* where Augustine turns to himself posing the question: 'Who am I'. The answer is a man. Then the Soul turns to God posing the question: 'What is then am I, my God? What is my nature?' (Quid ergo sum, Deus meus? Quae natura sum?) This proves that Augustine clearly recognizes that the latter question is answerable only by God, concludes Arendt.[11] Arendt in the *Human Condition* treating the problem of action resumes the basic difference between the question of *who* and that of *what. Who* presents itself implicitly in every speech and action is accomplished by a human person in the space of appearance. In contrast to it *what* is definable as the aggregate of personal human qualities, talents, gifts, shortcomings. These can be displayed or hidden – it depends on only his/her decision. On the contrary, *who* "can be hidden only in complete silence

10 Hannah Arendt: *The Origins of Totalitarianism*, Cleveland and New York: Meridian Books, 1967, pp. 447-453.

11 Hannah Arendt: *The Human Condition*. Chicago: 1958, The University of Chicago Press, p. 10, footnote 2.

and perfect passivity, but its disclosure can almost never be achieved as a willful purpose".[12] The *who* is an inter-subjective quality of human person which reveals itself in speech and action: "it is more than likely that the *who*, which appears so clearly and unmistakably to others, remains hidden from the person himself, like the *daimon* in Greek religion which accompanies each man throughout his life, always looking over his shoulder from behind and thus visible only to those he encounters."[13]

Conclusion

Richard Sennett, who had been Arendt's disciple, in his book entitled *The Fall of Public Man* developed a theory in which he applied his former professor's distinction between private and public realms. His starting-points are the metaphors of mask and theatre as well. In his train-thought the 18th century was the golden age of public realm which flourished in the public spaces of cities like London or Paris. In these cities the structure of public sphere was very similar both in the street and in the theatre. In both cases the place of appearances was constituted by conventional mode of communication including gestures, verbal communication and clothes. These means maintained the aura of formality and the individual was able to hide behind the conventions; hence the destroying forces of intimacy were not allowed to enter the stage of public realm. But this is true in reverse as well; the conventions protected the private sphere from the distorting influences of public sphere. Sennett – following the logic of Arendt's theory – here outlines a paradoxical thesis; the lasting sustenance of public realm based on inter-subjectivity requires some kind impersonality ensured by conventions. Putting this conclusion in another way; a flourishing public sphere demands a healthy balance between private and public identities:

"That history is of the erosion of a delicate balance which maintained society in the first flush of its secular and capitalist existence. It was a balance between public and private life, a balance between an impersonal realm in which men could invest one kind of passion and a personal realm in which they could invest another. This geography of society was governed by an image of human nature

12 Ibid., p. 179.
13 Ibid., pp. 179-180.

based on the idea of a natural human character; this character was not created by the experiences of a lifetime, but was revealed in them. It belonged to Nature and was reflected in man. As both secularity and capitalism arrived at new forms in the last century, this idea of a transcendent nature gradually lost its meaning. Men came to believe that they were the authors of their own characters, that every event in their lives must have a meaning in terms of defining themselves, but what this meaning was, the instabilities and contradictions of their lives made it difficult to say. Yet the sheer attention and involvement in matters of personality grew ever greater. Gradually this mysterious, dangerous force which was the self came to define social relations. It became a social principle. At that point, the public realm of impersonal meaning and impersonal action began to wither."[14]

14 Richard Sennet: *The Fall of Public Man*, London: Faber and Faber, 1993, pp. 338-339.

TRUTHS OF THE WORLD, TRUTHS OF THE LIFE

Robert Petkovšek, Ljubljana

The art of life is to *know how* to conduct one's life. This fundamental question appears in Michel Henry's work *I'm the Truth* and in the distinction he draws between the truths of the world and the truths of life. The question we ask here is about the characteristic of the truths by which the art of life can be properly directed?

Truth of the world

The twofold structure of truth: 'what is true' and the 'truth itself'

Henry draws attention to the twofold structure of the truth based on the difference between "*what is true*" and the "*truth itself*" (13, 16 [22, 26]). He sees a difference between the essence of the truth which consists of the "fact of self-showing" on one hand and on the other hand the effect of that self-showing as expressed in concepts, judgments, propositions, wisdom, sciences or mythology. The truth expressed in a judgment is deposited in *cognitive content* and in different *cognitive attitudes*; it takes place in some kind of *what* and *where*. In this sense, *what is true* is a derived mode of truth. But originally, the truth is not a content or an attitude; it is a phenomenological capacity of self-showing, "the fact of self-showing, considered in itself and as such" (13 [22]). The *essence of truth* is primarily a *phenomenological capacity of showing itself*, of *revealing itself*, of *manifesting itself*. This capacity has been attributed in the Western tradition to the world that is equivalent to the light that makes the phenomena possible. This capacity is the condition of the possibility of phenomena and the power which *makes* the things *appear*. There are no phenomena outside the light of the world. Like Heidegger, Henry claims, "The phenomena of the world are things inasmuch as they show themselves in the world, which is their proper manifestation" (14 [24]). Being reveals itself by appearing. "What is 'is' only inasmuch as it shows itself" (14 [24]).

The concepts of the world and of the world's truth are thus central to Henry's phenomenological analysis of life. The "world" is a transcendental category; it is "the horizon of light where things show themselves in their quality as phenomena." As a transcendental category, the world does not designate *what is true* but rather the *Truth itself* (14 [23]), the *capacity and the power of self-showing*.

Outsideness as alienation of a thing

What is the effect of the power of self-showing attributed to the things by the world? To appear means to come *into the world*; by coming into the world, the thing comes *out*, gets *out,* steps *out* into the light of the world. Apparition is hence only possible inasmuch as the thing becomes a "being-there-before-us", an object. Objectification is the effect proper to the apparition, i.e. to the truth of the world. In some way, the thing objectified, "being-there-before-us", is at our disposal, available, at hand, obtainable, consumable. By becoming a thing-for-us it somehow betrays itself, moves away from its original condition and gets deposited in expressions which convey its meaning. In the expression, meaning gets separated from the thing and becomes autonomous. Therewith, *what is true* gets separated from the *self-showing* of the thing. There is a dividing line between *what is true* and *self-showing* which alienates the expressions from the thing. The alienation is a consequence of the self-externalization of the thing, i.e. to the apparition. To become an object for us, the thing must externalize itself, it must manifest itself externally in the power of the light of the world and submit to the regime of the world. The regime of the world is essentially the regime of the "outsideness".

We now expose to view the basic structure of the world's truth. The essence of the world's truth is its *outsideness. What is true* – e.g. true judgments – is a kind of truth as reflected in the otherness; *what is true* is only possible because of the self-externalization of the thing in the world; the outsideness or externality is the truth of the world (15 [25]). And Henry sharpens this idea by stating that the world consists of the "self-externalization of the externality of the 'outside'" (17 [27]). Self-externalization as the basic structure of the world creates the horizon of visibility and as a result *makes* the things *manifest*, subordinating them to the regime of the world's truth. It makes them *appear* as objects, as beings-before-us. This structure establishes the relationship between the subject and the object by creating the necessary cognitive distance on which *what is true* is based.

Time as annihilation

Another essential feature of the world's nature is time. "Time and the world are identical; they designate that single process in which the 'outside' is constantly self-externalized" (17 [27]). The world is thus specified as a process of self-externalization conveyed by its temporality. The temporality is the way of the world's being. Finitude and temporality rule over the world. In the world everything goes to meet nothingness; sooner or later everything is annihilated. "Time is passage, a slipping away in the form of a slipping into nothingness"; it is "incessant annihilation" (18-19 [28-29]). The reality must void itself of its being in order to submit to the regime of the world's truth.

This passage from the original condition to the regime of the world's truth is destructive for the reality (19 [29]). Between the reality and its phenomenon, there is a fateful scission imposed by the regime of the world; the world makes appear but in a way of destroying and annihilating. Temporality of the world only allows the phenomena to subsist under the aspect of an apparition void of being.

The passage from reality to its appearance – externalization conveyed by the temporalization – is decisive. This passage is characterized as "presentation" because it converts reality into the image of the present which is homogenous with the image of the future as well as with the image of the past. Therewith, reality is destroyed and emptied of its being. The present, future and past are only modalities of an "Imaginary" put down in the outsideness of the world. Because of the outsideness which constitutes the world, the substance of the world can only be imaginary; in the world, everything is being mediated, nothing is given directly. Presentation is indeed a process of "principled derealization", a process that turns reality to its opposite, into "a state of original unreality" (20 [30]). The world is governed by the finitude, by the past into which everything disappears. Destruction and death are inherent to the world. "The form of this world is passing away" (1 Corinthians 7:31).

Indifference of the world

The appearance of reality in the world has as a consequence its subordination to the regime of the Imaginary of the world. Subordinated to the world, every appearance is temporal, destined and preordained to disappear. This is the fundamental law of the world. The world lets the appearances disappear, vanish, pass by. It doesn't keep them perduring; it doesn't make them safe. This attitude of the world vis-à-vis reality shows the neutrality and indifference of the world towards reality in itself. The "World's truth" is neutral and indifferent.

Therewith, we come to the essence of the world's truth: the indifference. The visibility granted by the world makes things appear indifferently, uninterestedly. Much as in daylight the things illuminated become visible but not the light itself; what appears in the world, i.e., *what is true*, becomes visible but not the self-showing itself. The self-showing withdraws itself. It remains hidden and indifferent towards the appearances. The only effect that the world has on things is to make appear their transitory being in the Imaginary of the world. For all the rest, it remains totally indifferent. Nothing is done by the world to sustain and to maintain the appearances. The world is powerless in regard to the annihilating power of the past (16 [26]).

The point of Henry's argumentation is as follows: 1) In the Western tradition, truth has been understood as the world's truth. 2) The visibility of the world in which the reality gets externalized remains indifferent towards the appearance and lets it succumb to the annihilating powers of the past.

Truth of life

Phenomenological failing of the Western thought

One of the conclusions made by Henry is that in the traditional thought based on Greek philosophy the idea of self-showing has been limited to the world as the horizon of being. For that reason, he resumes the traditional conception of truth under the expression "world's truth". Here we find what Henry calls the "phenomenological failing" of the traditional philosophy: the truth in itself – the self-showing – as considered in the traditional philosophy has been limited to the being as it appears in the world.

The expression of "phenomenological failing" designates the insufficiency of the traditional comprehension of truth. To explain that insufficiency, Henry introduces the concepts of phenomenality and phenomenalization. *Phenomenality* is the common quality and the totality of all manifestations in the world as seen from the viewpoint of their common denominator which is "*appearing*". The radical issue concerns the phenomenality itself, "How is the phenomenality being phenomenalized? How is the self-showing being phenomenalized?" These questions have not been approached in the traditional thought.

Truth is radically different from all other phenomena, yet it is also being phenomenalized. What is the specificity of the phenomenalization of the truth? Beings are phenomenalized as phenomena; truth is phenomenalized as phenomenalization of phenomenality itself, not as a particular phenomenon.

Radical phenomenology and phenomenological substance

The issue at hand concerns the truth of truth. The phenomenology characterized as a "radical phenomenology" tries to understand how truth *appears* in the truth; how it appears to itself. It is the phenomenalization of the truth itself which is being considered now. At this point, phenomenology deals with the truth revealing itself to itself, which is what Henry characterizes as an absolute self-revelation, revelation of the revelation to itself, revelation that is therefore neither derived nor mediated.

The "object" or the content of the absolute self-revelation is nothing else but revelation itself: it is revelation revealing itself in the revelation. We thus touch upon the question of the "phenomenological substance". It is the absolute self-revelation what Henry calls "phenomenological substance" or "phenomenological matter". The whole essence of the phenomenological substance is but to appear; it doesn't contain anything that is external or alien. In the absolute revelation, the revelation is affected by the revelation. It therefore has "no place" for the outsideness in it. Western thought has been wrongly convinced that "every form of experience borrows its phenomenality from that of the world" (42 [56]). Henry establishes two fundamental types of experience: *worldly experience* and *pre-worldly experience*. The former is based on the phenomenalization of phenomena; the latter concerns the phenomenalization of phenomenality, i.e. the advent of the truth itself. They both compose the totality of man's experience.

Worldly and pre-worldly experience

The difference between worldly and pre-worldly experience is due to the original concept of truth. The truth is originally an absolute self-revelation, a pure revelation of revelation, presupposed by all other worldly truths. The experience of the truth in its original state cannot be made in the world; it cannot be mediated. The absolute self-revelation is a pure immediacy previous to the outsideness of the world, preceding all cognitive distances between subject and object, placed outside the outsideness of the world, in the "interiority" (67 [88]) where no distance takes place.

The pre-worldly experience is not made by the *consciousness of the world* but by life. Worldly consciousness is an intentional, objectifying experience, expressed by representations. On the contrary, life's experience is neither intentional nor objectifying; it is accompanied by a kind of a "consciousness without world" (Henry 1990, 331). Life is not a "phenomenological milieu" like the world; it is reality prior to the outsideness of the world. To reveal itself, it doesn't need the world; it reveals itself immediately to itself in itself; it is revelation of the life revealed to the life itself (30 [42-43]). In the field of life, the logic of truth is different from the logic of truth revealed in the world. It is more original. Consequently, world's truths are not capable of expressing the truths of life. "... life is nothing other than that which reveals itself." It is "the self-revelation that owes nothing to the truth of the world" (27 [39-40]). Such immediate self-revelation of life to life results from its non-intentional character. Life is immediately given to itself because there is no outsideness and as a result there are no distances in it. "We do have access to Life itself. Where? In Life. How? Through Life. That it is only in Life and through it that we can accede to Life implies a decisive presupposition: it is Life itself that comes forth in itself." (55 [73]) Life is therefore irreducible to the being: "Life 'is' not. Rather, it occurs and does not cease occurring." (55 [74])

Being and life

We now come to the dividing line traced between "being" and "life". Life *is* not but it *occurs* in an endless process. It is characteristic of the being to make things appear in the framework of the outsideness and distances in the world. On the contrary, there is no distance or outsideness in life. This fundamental difference makes being and life incompatible. Life comes forth, gets self-generated and self-revealed without distancing from itself. "Life does not cast outside itself what it reveals but holds it inside itself ... Life embraces, experiences without distance or difference." (30 [43]) On the other hand, being exteriorizes by making things appear in the world, abandons things to what they are not, to the unreality of appearance, to the annihilating finitude of time.

Life is not under the regime of outsideness. It gets nothing from outside. The self-affectedness of life makes it intimate with itself, holding it back from alienation in the outsideness and enables it to form a pre-worldly interiority. In this intimacy of life, "it is Life itself that comes forth in itself," and accordingly, Truth is to be defined originally as Life: "Life is self-revelation. Within life, it is life itself that achieves revelation; and itself that is revealed. This is because it is life itself that originally comes forth by itself." (55 [73])

The essence of Life consists of a phenomenological substance, in pure appearance, which has not yet undergone the regime of outsideness. This is what makes the self-revelation possible. To characterize life as a phenomenological substance simply means that the possibility of self-revelation is not given to life from the outside, but it is its inmost capacity, the capacity of self-affectedness. The self-affectedness of life makes possible the self-revelation of the truths of life to life itself, not by means of cognition but as given by the self-affectedness.

Radical phenomenology is radical because its objects are not phenomena but phenomenological substance, i.e., phenomenalization of phenomenality, which is life. To the question, "What is the truth?" Henry answers in the sense of the Gospel according to St. John: "Life." Life experiences itself. It is the primordial capacity of self-experience and self-revelation because there is no outsideness, no distances in it. Life – because its substance itself is phenomenological – reveals itself immediately to itself. Henry thus concludes, "Life that speaks not a word knows everything" (50-51 [68]).

Conclusion: another Truth

The truth does not only make things thinkable, but it is also "the bread of life", "the water of life." Truth is life.

In the tradition of Western philosophy, Cartesian *ego* with its scientific reason has been increasingly prevailing over life. So, the main question of modern civilization has become: "For what reason? What is the purpose of …?" Whatever doesn't serve a purpose is superfluous. In the modern technocratic world, *humanity* of man, *naturality* of nature, *justice* of a state, *truthfulness* of truth are superfluous because they are not functional. But the crisis of the contemporary culture reveals that these values will have to regain their proper role, although they are not functional in the economic sense. If they are not functional, it does not mean that they are not values in themselves.

There are unpredictable phenomena, irreducible to a concept, which elude rationalist methodology and exceed scientific conceptuality. These phenomena challenge the modern subject and its instrumentalist rationality. One of the phenomena that cannot be subordinated to the instrumentalist rationality is the human body. It is more than an object which can be conceptually determined and defined by science. It bears life in itself. This is the reason for which Henry designates it as a "phenomenological embodiment", "phenomenological flesh" (62 [82]). Primarily, the body is life, it has interiority, it is "flesh of a pathos, pure affective material, in which any cleavage, any separation, finds itself radically excluded. It is uniquely because such is the phenomenological matter of which this revelation is made that we can say that in this revelation what reveals and what is revealed are one and the same" (30 [42]). The body bears in itself a kind of "cognition" that is much deeper and larger than the cognition of the modern Cartesian subject. As stated by Nietzsche (1891, I,4), "'Ego,' sayest thou, and art proud of that word. But the greater thing – in which thou art unwilling to believe – is thy body with its big sagacity «dein Leib und seine grosse Vernunft»; it saith not 'ego,' but doeth it." Basic truths cannot be found in the world but are being revealed in life and by life to life. These truths are not indifferent theoretical truths but truths "capable of assuring salvation" (1 [7]) which – as shown in the Gospels – is "the only thing that matters" (62 [82]).

Life and salvation are the purpose that truths of life serve. Life is the ultimate end of the truth; and truth – revelation – is the ultimate end of life which is phenomenological substance itself. This supreme permeation of life and truth exceeds every theoretic attitude and its indifference. In its supreme mode, Truth is neither affirmed nor thought but lived, embraced by life itself, adopted as revelation in believing which is beyond every cognitive distance. Revelation granted by Life involves and regenerates the whole human being. The salvation is not paved by "means of thought but by Life" (62 [82]).

References and Bibliography

Greisch, Jean. 2004. *Le buisson ardent et les lumières de la raison. L'invention de la philosophie de la religion. Vol. 3: Vers un paradigme herméneutique.* Paris: CERF.

Heidegger, Martin. 1950. *Holzwege*. Frankfurt: Vittorio Klostermann.

–––. 1956. *Was ist das – die Philosophie (1955)*. Pfullingen: Günter Neske.

Henry, Michel. 1990. *L'essence de la manifestation.* 2. ed. Paris: P.U.F.

–––. 2003. *I Am the Truth: Toward a Philosophy of Christianity.* Stanford: University Press. Originally, *C'est moi la vérité: Pour une philosophie du christianisme.* Paris: Editions du Seuil, 1996.

Jacob, François. 1970. *La Logique du vivant*. Paris: Gallimard.

Marion, Jean-Luc. 2005. Foi et raison. In: *Dialogue: Entre la foi chrétienne et la pensée contemporaine,* présenté par Jean-Marie Lustigier, 11-37. Paris: Parole et Silence.

Nietzsche, Friedrich. 1974. *Thus spoke Zarathustra: a book for all and none. Translated by Thomas Common.* New York: Gordon Press.

LIFE AS A DUTY FROM THE VIEWPOINT OF FRANKL'S LOGOTHERAPY

Zdenka Zalokar Divjak

Introduction

Today's way of life demands that we get to know it in all of its complexity, interconnectivity and integrity.

Logotherapy sees the essence of man's conduct in his ability to rise above the instinctive reduction and lust for winning and tends to meaning. Its tendency towards meaning signifies realization of tasks, recognizable in every situation, and are always directed towards some work or interpersonal relationship. Man's spiritual dimension includes his specific conscious and intuitive abilities.

In practical life, this means that we as individuals have at any given moment different possibilities, which we can then take into consideration and, of course, choose the one we believe to be the best in a given situation. Spiritual dimension also enables us to be able to surpass ourselves, defy tragedy and correct the wrong decisions. Thus, man is not mostly dependent on his genetic or behavioural patterns even though they can be of great significance to his development but more on the way he can use his spiritual dimension.

Freedom and responsibility

V. E. Frankl (1977) defines freedom and personal responsibility as the most common features of spiritual dimension. Freedom in the language of logotherapy means the ability to decide between more possibilities and our internal use of ourselves. Man has the freedom in the decision of choosing one of various possibilities that are at his disposal and attract him and leave the rest. The decision, however, has reflections and sacrifices. When we decide on one thing, we have to take leave of others and that hurts. This is always the case when we decide between things that attract us. Therefore, freedom and responsibility that is connected with it always weighs heavily on us. Freedom is inevitable. Even when we do not want to decide, we in a way do decide. He, who does not want to, wants not to want.

With deciding we can also see the human limitation and finality. Latin »decidere« means »to completely cut through«. The choice is connected with sacrifice. Man's personality can be developed especially with decisions. He who is free has the power over himself; in folk language you could say he is his own master.

With the correct use of freedom of decision comes that deeper freedom when man ever more coincides with what he really is. That is also seen with the correct choice. If it can be seen that the choice was good then we as individuals climb our personality ladder. When the choice was not good it means that we have to choose the other possibility. It is not about the absolute freedom but about the weighing of possibilities and freedom in formation of life's assets respectively. Every free decision has its own history. Previous decisions condition present possibilities in two ways – they either expand them or limit them. Therefore, our constant striving for successful and good decisions respectively is important.

The knowledge that an individual can make progress and improve only through choices and decisions is also important. He, who avoids decisions and responsibility, cannot develop personally; he can also fall ill or keeps turning in magic circle of his own dissatisfaction. Freedom is thus at the same time a gift as well as a burden. A gift since it shapes the space for personal forming of life and a burden because in constantly demands decisions from us. An individual must know how to and want to live from his self, especially from the recognition of his own freedom. In the face of meaning and values which demand something from a man, he must constantly decide between being and have to.

In today's time, individuals often give up freedom due to the burden of consciousness with responsibility. In the background is probably hidden the fear of failure while on the outside excuses and culprits for their (in)decisions are being sought. Excuses often refer to social, political, economical situations or simply give way to conformism – "there is no other way", "nowadays nobody wants to be any worse than others", "everyone else does it, so – no shame in doing it once" etc. Resting on objective reality can make the correct choice easier for us. Reality is actually a measure that in advance determines the correctness of choices and at the same time assesses them. Every act that we perform gives payment back to us. Therefore, an individual cannot be the one who determines the logicality of actions; it is the reality of life itself.

All reality is deeply meaningful (V. E. Frankl, 1975-1984). Things do not arise from us but are given to us, therefore we have to cooperate with them and take into consideration their order. Every thing consequently has its own logos, so we first have to find the explanation in the thing itself. And this is not possible without deeply engaging in it. Only thus can we realize its meaning, its regularities, its inner harmony and its charm.

The old saying: "It is natural for reason to establish order" does not only indicate only some possibilities of a human reason but expresses something incomparably more important: reason cannot live with order. Arranging is its necessity. If it cannot find order in reality, it tries to impose its own artificial order on it. This is also completely natural; the more the experiencing of natural order decreases the more the need for artificial – from man-given order increases. The need for creating artificial order grows increasingly, especially nowadays when certain goals want to be achieved quickly. That is the reason why there are so many disappointments in personal as well as occupational field nowadays. If we take only the example of a family in the personal field, we can quickly establish how much "work" in the spiritual area the relations in the family demand. It takes a lot of decisions for patience, consideration, good communication, physical presence, responsibility etc. Unfortunately, we usually only become aware of that when it is too late, when the family is already in crisis and its members filled with negative sensations, hurt feelings and tired of unsuccessful communication.

Likewise, every serious work demands to be performed conscientiously. It is not possible anywhere to succeed with irresponsible behaviour, poor knowledge, evading working obligations, looking for sick leave etc. Everything is interrelated in balance or instability. The universe operates according to laws of harmonious oscillation. And we call everything that is in harmony with it beautiful, kind, loving, and calm. Discordance, however, bereaves us of strength, will, joy, energy, clear thought, and benevolence. Balance means health, instability means sickness. It is our duty to learn how to use them in our interest.

The first logotherapeutic axiom says: man is a free being. If we were to remain at presumption that man's behaviour is determined by various stimuli then it would always be possible to determine it or at least foresee it according to the pattern stimulus – reaction. The responses to stimuli are thus one-track, clear and mean only one thing. Yet a part of man's behaviour is not determined by any stimulus neither from within nor from without, since man as a subject can add something either positive or negative, in view of "decision in me".

This freedom is enabled by precisely that spiritual dimension where with the help of his own consciousness in given reality he discovers the most optimal possibilities and thereby his duties. All objective circumstances are constants that motivate man for life. In spite of all that man is even within the limits (of objective circumstances) free since the decision in every situation occurs in him and not in conditions or motives.

Problems occur with reasonable decisions. They can be of physical nature, meaning that it is difficult for man to do what he decided for; they can be spiritual when there is primarily the desire to enjoy and other spiritual motives that draw towards momentary satisfaction. Behind every meaningful possibility there is a certain duty in the background that has to be performed. The bigger the value that determines such a duty the more effort it requires for the duty to be performed.

Inherently arises the question what is it in man on the basis of which he can decide what is right and what is not or what is reasonable and what not.

We call it conscience and it is immanent spiritual capability, which means that an individual intuitively comprehends unique and non-recurring meaning of every situation. In logotherapy, conscience is defined as a spiritual organ and can be compared to the magnetic needle of a compass that always points north or, metaphorically, in the right direction. All those that thought about some kind of intuition and inner voice were on the right track.

In man exists not only instinctive unconscious but also spiritual unconscious. A human being is in comparison to animals not an instinctive being but a deciding being. The criteria by which man decides about existentially important extends into the depth of unconscious. These are the spheres and decisions of consciousness which are not adopted by mind but by heart.

In truth it is about the forming of life with an abundance of prejudices that people persistently hold on to, use them as an excuse for not working, failures etc. Man's autonomy lies in his spiritual extension and is therefore not threatened by co-people (as they want to foist it upon them) or bad living conditions, but by mental and behavioural automatism in us.

Life as a duty

So in our objective reality life is conducted according to precise lawfulness and order that provide the framework of our everyday. So man does well only if he discovers his life duties in reality and degenerates if he sets his goals arbitrarily and separated from the whole reality. Objective reality puts duties in front of man and is a challenge to him, whereas his life has the character of recognizing duties and providing creative answers. Behind concrete duties are values that pull themselves with their worth, therefore man's energy is oriented outwards, not onto itself. Values are thus understood as clear points in the net of meaningful structure of reality. When man orients to some duty in his will for meaning that becomes his answer to meaningful totality. Logotherapy is based on assertions on values as facts and not on judgements of facts as values.

In logotherapy (Lukas, 1985-1988), personality is constituted from three layers: bodily or physical, psychic and spiritual dimension. The first two dimensions were described already by other authors; spiritual dimension in the sense of Frankl's logotherapy presents an area of responsible freedom of an individual. Spiritual dimension therefore illustrates the path that leads from freedom to responsibility and is at the same time the path of every personality's maturity. If we were to try and explain the area of spiritual dimension, we would first have to determine individual components comprising it.

The most important component of spiritual dimension is duties. He who takes over a duty also takes over the responsibility for what is imposed on him. Dedication to a certain duty belongs to essential factors that preserve life and strengthen it. As far as man has a duty that he likes, energy, existence of which man normally does not even imagine, flows from his hidden reserves. The researches have shown that, for example, taking over the social roles sets free endorphins that soothe pain. As we devote our attention to our co-person we forget about ourselves and our worries, and indirectly about an individual's metabolism, blood pressure etc.

It is specifically human to turn our focus to "more than ourselves" and every finished duty must have more value if done for someone else as it would have if it were done for us.

Individual's freedom is therefore always embraced with the responsibility of personal reactions. In many cases the freedom of an individual was replaced by impudent freedom that does not only lead into anarchy but into today's pathological phenomena as well: aggression, depression and various forms of addiction. If we swear by individuality of personality and its democratic development we at the same time have to swear by its responsible actions. Man can, of course, freely answer the questions that are provided by life. But that freedom must not be equated with self-will. It has to be interpreted responsibly. Man is responsible for the right answer to the question in order to find the real meaning of such a position. It has to be found with conscience.

Frankl (1985) in his works teaches that living is not only intentional but also transcendental. The essence of living is surpassing oneself. The essence of man's being is therefore obligation to realize meaningful possibilities that are out there in the world and not realizing his own possibilities first, if we put it nicely. Being human means being directed towards something else than oneself. Thereby the area of trans-subjective is created which is again tried to be blurred by excessive emphasis of subjectivity of being human. Being human means having a meaning in front of you, which has to be fulfilled and values that have to be realized. It means to live in the polar field of tension between reality and ideals which must be realized. Man lives according to ideals and values.

Logotherapy is based on meaning as man's primary motive, motivation and at the same time signifies a blow to all current motivational theories that are still based on the principle of homeostasis. Man is a being that cares only about fulfilling needs and all of that only in order to keep or restore balance. All co-beings he loves and all things serves they only see the tool that helps him to get rid of the tension caused by instincts or needs as soon as they are not met and satisfied. Surpassing oneself, which is logotherapy's essence of man's being, is not taken into consideration in modern motivational theories. And yet man is not only a being that only reacts to his instincts and does not only respond to stimuli, but is a being that functions in the world.

Due to essential self-transcendental (self-surpassing) characteristic of man's being he is a being that extends further than he himself. Buber with Ebner essentially explains man's being as an answer between ME and YOU. We establish that that dialogue overcomes itself if ME and YOU do not surpass themselves and do not reach the meaning outside themselves. Two human beings meet, whereby they line up towards each other with logos, that is to say with the meaning of being.

Musek (1977) similarly defines man's being. He states that man has potential for instinctive behaviour as well as for spiritual motives. That he strives for self-actualization, realization of his higher potential and talents; that he wishes to give meaning to his existence and gives it meaning with experiencing (which means value by itself, value in absolute indelible meaning) for example, experiencing love, creativity, cognition, hope and faith, all that is also part of his specific and perhaps the most decisive nature.

Man therefore realizes himself only if he is directed towards someone or something which his conscience discovered as meaning. When he is devoted to it, he surpasses himself and thereby realizes himself as man and culturally completes reality. Only in man's capability to overlook himself, to forget about oneself, give himself up to a certain duty or person, only then is he himself. After that he realizes himself – not in a sense of anxiety for his own self-realization but forgetting about himself. Therefore self-realization can happen only as a side effect, as consequence of unselfishness. Phenomenological analysis of a simple man with the street experience of the process of evaluation shows, however, that you can find meaning in life if you create work or perform activities or experience nature and culture and, not least if you meet some other unique being, if you love them.

The duty of logotherapy is also how to change education into "education for responsibility". It offers us some elements that can be condensed into:

- considering the notion of person as something unique, multi-complex, exceptional;
- considering the notion of person that is not directed towards searching for their own affirmation and pleasures but in discovering life's duties;
- considering the belief that man's person is in spite of all limitations, conditions and defeats free (that it can distance itself from conditionality and defeats);
- considering the belief that man is personality that has the possibility for realization in every day as well as in borderline situations such as suffering and death.

Today's man experiences severe residential emptiness and disorientation of value in material prosperity. Sudden deviation from nature into concrete, from basic human society into nameless mass, from a dialogue with oneself into swarm of stimuli; all that has confused him and he cannot experience correctly neither himself, co-people, society, culture nor being on the whole. In such state his spirit cannot obtain proper food. On personal, interpersonal level the next alarm in our civilization will probably be "ecology of man's being and interpersonal relationships", for ethical and moral actions.

Conclusion

More and more young people suffer from feelings of absurdity and emptiness. They have the means for life but do not have a goal in life that is worth living for, to carry on living. The main manifestations of residential deprivation – boredom and apathy, have become a challenge for both, education and psychiatry. Boredom can be defined as a lost of interest. Young people lose the interest in world, to change something in this very world, to improve it while it is still possible. Apathy means lack of initiative. Today's education warns us not to dare demand anything from the young, to burden them, at last arouse tension in them. But this pedagogy swears by long ago exceeded motivational theory that wants to avoid tension by satisfying the needs. But man requires tension. Mostly one that is the most accessible to him and arises between man on one side and goal and duty on the other. If one thing can help overcome problems, that thing is the consciousness of a certain meaning that, so to speak, is waiting to be fulfilled.

Without the direction towards ideal man cannot survive; and it is that which creates tension, we have to be capable of fighting, waiting, we need tolerance, resistance to deprivation. We should persist in that as well since nowadays holds true that children are not prepared to give up anything in the interest of some far-reaching goals; that they are not capable of waiting, they want everything here and now, there is no tolerance, let alone compassion and sacrifice. They are only capable of compassion for themselves. Therefore education that cares about he least amount of tension, burden directly educates for psychic non-resistance. We can expect a great deal from children only when we demand a great deal from them. Of course, it also implies the other way round as well.

By working with children (Z. Zalokar Divjak, 1993) we should build especially on experiencing values as indirect pointers towards the meaning of life. If you can conjure up the beauty and mystery of the world to a child at a very early age, if a child falls in love with life, than that is the best foundation from which he will draw all the rest of meaningful content and take care of values such as love, beauty, truthfulness etc.

Instead of that education adds in a negative sense to the residential emptiness. The symptoms of this new neurosis are the following: living from one day to another, without planning and goals, without meaning and future that creates the so-called prosaic relationship towards the world. We can also add other forms to that: excessive yearning for stimuli, morbid infatuation and love for oneself (American sociologists speak of "me generation" and psychoanalytics of "age of narcissism"), too big a haste, illnesses of addictions, suicidalness etc.

Teachers and parents as the primary holders of education cannot, of course, teach values. Values must be lived. Just as the meaning cannot be given. What teachers can pass on to their students is not meaning but an example, their own paragon, their own dedication to questions of truth, beauty, goodness, science etc. Today, the question of education is presented as duty that lies in front of us. Every duty is also a problem, demand. Yet the meaning of life is not in avoiding all commitments, obligations, demands but to make something meaningful from our life. Experiencing meaning is about spiritual benefit, the biggest fulfilment of being in sense of not having lived in vain.

References and Bibliography

Frankl, V. E. (1977) *The Doctor and the Soul: From Psychotherapy to Logotherapy*. New York, Vintage Books.

Frankl, V. E. (1985) *Man's Search for Meaning: An Introduction to Logotherapy*. New York [etc.], Washington Square Press.

Frankl, V. E. (1981) *The Will to Meaning: Foundations and Applications of Logotherapy*. New York, New American Library.

Frankl, V. E. (1975-1984) *Der Leidende Mensch. Antropologische Grundladen der Psychotherapy*. Bern, Verlag Hans Huber.

Lukas, E. (1985-1988) *Psychologische Seelsorge. Logotherapie - die Wende zu einer menschenwürdigen Psychologie*. Freiburg, Verlag Herder.

Musek, J. (1977) *Psihologija osebnosti*. Ljubljana, Dopisna delavska univerza Univerzum.

Zalokar Divjak, Z. (1993) *Osebnost vzgojitelja z vidika logoterapije* (doctoral dissertasion), Ljubljana.

SURVIVAL AND SOCIETY

THE BEATITUDE OF SOULS AMONGST THE THINGS INDIFFERENT. ADIAPHORA IN THE STOICAL ETHICS AND IN THE CHRISTIAN THINKING

Béla Mester, Budapest

Adiaphora-debates as Forms of Political Thinking; from the Stoa through the Reformation to the Early Modern Political Philosophy

The word *adiaphora* was a part of the terminology of Stoical ethics. However, Scriptures are lacking in it — its opposite, *diaphora* was used by Paul the Apostle —, Christian thinking used it from the early times; with two important changes of its meaning. *Adiaphora* in Stoical ethics were *things* and *circumstances*, especially *physical things and circumstances*, ethically indifferent *for individuals*. Then it was always used for human activities in Christian thought, for instance: meat offered for an idol, is an *adiaphoron* – this statement refers to an activity of Christian people, eating this meal, not to a physical object, to a piece of meal. It was used as a collective concept: *adiaphora* are theoretically the same for every Christian individual, their *Christian freedom* is a collective phenomenon. It is an important consequence of this Christianized *adiaphora*-concept that it created possibilities to calculate with other minds' opinions in ethical affairs: it is an ethical obligation to avoid causing scandals, confusions in the minds of the "weak believers".

Political consequence of the use of this concept is a possibility of a new connection between power and individuals. The biggest part of the possible human activities are *adiaphora*, but every Christian person is characterized by the obligatory civic obedience in *adiaphora*, as an affair of Christian conscience. It means that ethically indifferent things become objects of ethics in the political space. The most often used scriptural topic in the time of the Reformation in *adiaphora-debates* was Paul the Apostle's *Epistle to the Romans*. This writing discusses the questions of original sin, Christian freedom, and earthly power on neighbouring places, and those problems were linked in the interpretations: the need for the earthly power is a consequence of our corrupted human nature after the fall of Adam, and our Christian freedom is an inner liberty, coexisting with our external civic obedience. We can understand that every possible interpretation depends on the natures of the *original sin* and the *earthly power*.

Let us see the system of Protestant political ideas derived from Paul the Apostle's *Epistle* on the basis of Calvin's interpretation. He initiates the word *adiaphora* to his system of ideas in the following way: In external things, which are *adiaphora*, we should not feel any religious obligation to God. We can use or avoid them by our will (Calvinus 1863–1892a, column 198.).[1] He wrote about connections between original sin and the need of earthly power in his argumentation against Anabaptists: We wouldn't need any earthly power, if God's kingdom made the end of our earthly life now (Calvinus 1863–1892a, column 229).[2] His statements on power in his *Institutio*: (A) civic obedience is an affair of conscience for Christians; (B) the limits of this obedience are only the laws of God, all things, which are not *adiaphora*; (C) an important duty of the earthly power is the provision for external circumstances of the religious worship, that are *adiaphora*; (D) limits of Christian freedom —it is free human activity with *adiaphora* — is the prohibition of scandalising the "weak believers"; (E) our earthly connections with our fellowmen are under the rule of earthly power. One can derive from these points that all the sphere of *adiaphora* is under the rule of earthly power, at least because its right is to define and verify what is a scandal and what is not. One can easily understand that the main question of the early modern debates on *adiaphora* was the collision of ecclesiastical and earthly rule over individual conscience, despite their *motto*: *Christian freedom*. There is no place for individual freedom in this network of concepts, where is no vacuum between earthly

1 The *locus* in Latin: "nulla rerum externarum, quae per se sunt *adiaphorai* [this word written with Greek letters in the original text], religione coram Deo teneamur, qui eas nunc usurpare, nunc amittere *indifferenter* liceat." I have used the Latin text of Calvin's writings, ignoring the French version and the early English translations of his *Institutio*, because I have focused especially on his Latin terminology. In the following in the main text I will summarise his opinions, completing it with the relevant direct Latin quotations in the footnotes.

2 "Quae omnia supervacua esse fateor, si praesentem vitam exstinguit regnum Dei, quale nunc intra nos est."

and ecclesiastical powers: all human affairs must be ruled either by the former, or by the later, the question is just the border between them. One can understand only from this point of view the rigorous opinions of Calvinist puritans in these debates. *Tertium non datur* in this logic: a human activity is either prohibited, or obligatory, but it cannot be free. I have mentioned that solutions of this problem depend on the scriptural interpreter's opinions of the nature of earthly power on one hand, and the natures of men after Adam's fall on the other. Let us see at first the problem of power. Paul the Apostle's *Epistle to the Romans*, talks about earthly power, says *exousia hyperechousa*. It is a general expression, but the word *exousia* (power) was used as an element of the names and titles of concrete offices and their representatives in Paul's lifetime, so, we can regard the expression *exousia hyperechousa* as a juristic term. We can think the same of the ancient Latin version, *potestas supereminens*, too. Martin Luther's translation, *Oberkeit* is a linguistically genial expression of his conceptual incertitude: only a specialist of the law of state could answer the question about the nature of power, with mere juristic fictions, only, in his lifetime and in his country. Calvin, as a well-educated lawyer, could not solve the problem by this way in his clear, humanist Latin. In his *Commentarius in Epistolam Pauli ad Romanos* (1539) he speaks about the concept of power in details: Higher powers called all the people higher than others, not only the owners of sovereignty (*imperium*) (Calvinus 1863–1892, column 249)[3]. We can see in this text that Calvin does not regard the earthly power as a monolithic whole. In his *Institutio* he has explained the consequences for Christian individuals that he has derived from it. He writes on the civic obedience a lot, but in the end he turns his chain of ideas: I am always talking about ordinary men. If there are *higher powers from the people* for controlling the king, like nowadays the three states [actually: the representatives of the states in the Parliament] in some countries, I agree, if they *act* by their *calling [pro officio]* against the tyrannical rule (Calvinus 1863–1892a, column 248).[4] Our second problem

3 "*Potestates supereminentes* vocat, non supremas quae summum imperium obtineant: sed quae excellant supra reliquos homines."

4 "De *privatis hominibus* semper loquor. Nam siqui nunc sint *populares magistratus*, ad moderandum regum libidinem constituti [. . .], funguntur in singulis regnis tres ordines, cum primarios conventus peragunt, adeo illos ferocienti regum licentiae, *pro officio* intercedere non veto".

was the human nature after Adam's fall. By Calvin's solution, despite corrupted human nature, every person has a faculty for *iustitia civilis*. Calvin wrote that the civil government has a destiny to conduct our earthly life amongst people to peace by *civic justice* (Calvinus 1863–1892a, column 248).[5] It must be mentioned some philological peculiarity connected to this piece of text. This *locus* is on the ending pages of *Institutio minor*, so one can read it as a conclusion of the whole work or as a clause of resistance; all the before quoted *loci* of *Institutio* are parts of a continuous chain of ideas in *Institutio minor*, and they appear in the same form in later editions, too; but the connections between them are less clear: editions were becoming larger and larger, and in the last edition, in his *Institutio maior* (Calvinus 1863–1892b), Calvin reorganised his text, using a method similar to our "copy and paste" technique. The later quoted *locus* in *Institutio maior* was moved to the book II, near the *locus* discussing Adam's fall from the last chapter, discussing the civil government. It is known that Calvin's teaching on *iustitia civilis* later had an important role in debates between Luther's and Calvin's followers, and it had an almost larger influence in Protestant Europe then Calvinism itself.

Reconstruction of Calvin's network of political concepts can show that there was created an interesting, semi-secular space for political activity of Protestant people. One could and must think about the most of ruler's activities as secularised, rationally disputable affairs, and sometimes choose a loyalty from the colluded loyalties of different legal powers. One could be an obedient subject of a ruler with different religion on the basis of the teaching on earthly power, but could be resistant to a ruler with the same faith on the basis of the teaching on *iustitia civilis*; and both of these possibilities could be in accordance with his conscience.

This Calvinist place for political thinking and acting has depended on actual diversity of legal, colluded earthly powers and in it one could calculate only with already existing powers. Our faculties for *iustitia civilis* are enough to make rational choices in given circumstances, but are not enough to create other circumstances. We have discussed the Continental *adiaphora*-debates above. Eng-

5 "At huic destinatum est, quamdiu inter homines agemus, vitam nostram ad hominum societatem componere, ad *civilem iustitiam* mores nostros formare, nos inter nos conciliare, communem pacem ac tranquilitatem alere ac tueri." (my italics)

lish debates on this problem have some important peculiarities, which will be analysed in Locke's writings in the next part of my paper.

Locke on Adiaphora

Locke's writings, that are nearest to the problems of the *adiaphora*-debates are his *Two Tracts on Government* (Locke 1967),[6] typical works of those debates, but his *A Letter Concerning Toleration* can be recognised as a part of this debates, too. The first two were written as an Erastian answer for the work of his colleague, Edward Bagshawe: *The Great Question Concerning Things Indifferent in Religious Worship* (1660). Locke's texts have two peculiarities, one of a philosopher and another one of an Englishman. We can realise, reading his texts, his always ironical style, when speaking about *adiaphora*. Later, in *A Letter* he changed his judgement, but did not change his ironic attitude. It is clear, that his irony doesn't refer only to those who prohibit *adiaphora, but* to those who regard it as an important thing. This style is derived from his attitude as an educated man. Every religious opinion, which is explained in written in conceptual form, is enough serious for him to be answered theoretically, but rites and gestures could not be important things, their seriousness is only a product of the superstitions and unskilled thinking of uneducated people. Locke defines the power in his *Tracts* in the network of Calvinian concepts, but contrary to Calvin's concept itself. His description of power in this work is almost a direct quotation of Calvin's *Institutio*, with two important differences: Locke's text lacks all statements on *populares magistratus* or on the *clause of resistance*, and he defines contrary to Calvin's quoted opinion: *magistratus* is who rules as a sovereign over all others (Locke, 1967, p. 187).[7] Remember Calvin's descriptions above. The question is clear: whether Paul's *exousia hyperechousa* is an *imperium*, or not. It is interesting, that later, in his *Paraphrase and notes on St. Paul's Epistles* he followed in this part Calvin's interpretation: "But who it was, to whom any of these, or any other dues of right belonged, he decides not, for that he leaves them be determined by the laws and

6 It was not published in Locke's lifetime.

7 "Per magistratum hic intelligimus illum qui curam gerit communitatis qui summum in reliquos omnes obtinet imperium, et cui denique condendarum abrograrumque legum delegata est potestas."

constitutions of their country" (Locke 1824, p. 405; for a newer edition see Locke 1987); but it was more then three decades later, when Locke was after a religious and anthropological change, and this statement on details of power in the new context has almost no weight. (Otherwise, Locke in his *Paraphrase* translated Paul's *exousia hyperechousa* as *over-ruling powers of the government*, which is a very strong interpretation in harmony with his former concept of power.) Locke's image of power in this writing mirrors a typical attitude to the power of English *adiaphora*-debates of sixteenth and seventeenth century. Earthly power in these discussions means always the king or queen of England, because of the strong royal power and the special history of English local authorities. Calvin's above discussed Continental solution, on basis of the actual difficulty of powers, did not work in England, where one could not choose the adequate one from difficult loyalties because of the actual unity of power. An Englishman could choose in this situation either the tyranny, or he had to find a solution to create a free space for political activity, contrary to Calvin.

We could see above the connection between Calvin's anthropology and his concept of power: he thought that our faculties for *iustitia civilis* are not enough to create a new, legal power, but they are enough to use it for navigation in the labyrinth of the existing ones. England's system of power had no place for this navigation; may be it was the cause of the different, central role and strictness of the *adiaphora*-debates in England, compared with that of the Continent. A useful solution of the English *adiaphora*-debates needed a new anthropological basis instead of fruitless strictness of English puritan option, and Locke found it by a radical enlargement of Calvin's teaching on human faculties for *iustitia civilis*.

Escape from the Network of Concepts of Classical Adiaphora-debates—Adam's Sin and the Theory of Contract

We can realise in Locke's *A Letter Concerning Toleration* a hidden transgression of Calvinist limits of human faculties. As it was explained above, Calvin thought in a social world of various, but static factors and human social faculties fitted for it. It was impossible, that human beings had faculties to establish new denominations and states freely; as in Locke's world. There must be a larger, theologically demonstrated anthropological background behind it, which was found by Locke in the Unitarian teaching on rejecting the dogma of original sin. There is no place here to discuss in details the many different interpretations of changes of Locke's religious opinions. Here I can only make some notes about the connection between Locke's opinions on original sin and his opinions on epistemology and politics. In the first paragraph of his *Reasonableness* Locke wrote: "For whilst some men would have all Adam's posterity doomed to eternal infinite punishment, for the transgression of Adam, whom millions had never heard of, and no one had authorised to transact for him, or be his representative" (Locke 1824a, p. 4; for a newer edition see Locke 2000). We can see a similar statement in his *Second treatise* in the argumentation against Filmer's opinions on an everlasting power and subjection, both are Adam's inheritances connecting his fall (*peccatum originale originans*), with original sin (*peccatum originale originatum*). "[A] ny act of the Father can no more give away the liberty of the Son than it can of any body else" (Locke 1960, p. 364). However, he did not explain in these writings religious consequences of his statement, connections are clear: Adam's sin is a part of "any act of the father", and we are his sons. It must be mentioned, that there is an interesting *locus* for our present aim in his *Essay*. His arguments against *ideae innatae* use an instance of the ideas of virtue and sin: "And, therefore, I imagine, it will scarcely seem possible that God should engrave principles in men's minds, in words of uncertain signification, *such as virtues and sins*, which amongst different men stand for different things" (book 1, chapter 2, § 19). There is another interesting peculiarity of Locke's and Unitarians' argumentation, that they did not reject the possibility of inheritance of Adam's fall only, but made some cautious mentions about rejecting of the theory of all the people's origin from Adam, but I cannot penetrate into the jungle of early modern theories of *prae-Adamitae* in here.

Details of Locke's theory of contract are not a topic of this essay. However, I wanted to add some notes on presumable theological and anthropological basis of our faculties to make contract, which are much larger, than our faculties for *iustitia civilis* in Calvin's theory. Let me put it quite simple: What did it mean in Locke`s lifetime (in a deeper sense than it is meant in political thinking) that we were born free? It means: we were born free *from the original sin.*

* * *

We have seen the history of the concept of *adiaphora* in a nutshell. It was a narrative rooted in the Stoical ethics, which was very individual phenomenon, very far from any form of the community and the public sphere. After that I have tried to show the transition of this concept to the ideas of community in the Christian thought, and after that to the political ideas in the early modern political philosophy. The term *adiaphora* was always a framework of the human liberty, concerning the individual human activity within the physical universe; or the common human activity within the social world. Philosophy can merely describe these frameworks. However, only living happily within those frameworks is the art of life.

Refereneces

Calvinus, I. 1863–1892: Commentarius in Epistolam Pauli ad Romanos, in: Baum, G. – Cunitz, E. – Reuss, E. (eds.): *Ioannis Calvini Opera quae Supersunt Omnia*, Vol. 49. Brunswig: Schwetschke [*Corpus Reformatorum*, Vol. 77.]

Calvinus, I. 1863–1892a: Institutio Religionis Christianae [Institutio minor], in: Baum, G. – Cunitz, E. – Reuss, E. (eds.): *Ioannis Calvini Opera quae Supersunt Omnia*, Vol. 1. Brunswig: Schwetschke [*Corpus Reformatorum*, Vol. 29.]

Calvinus, I. 1863–1892b: Institutio Religionis Christianae [Institutio maior], in: Baum, G. – Cunitz, E. – Reuss, E. (eds.): *Ioannis Calvini Opera quae Supersunt Omnia*, Vol. 2. Brunswig: Schwetschke [*Corpus Reformatorum*, Vol. 30.]

Locke, J. 1824: A Paraphrase and Notes on St. Paul's Epistle to the Romans, in: *The Works of John Locke*, 12th ed. London: Rivington, Vol. 7, pp. 271-428.

Locke, J. 1824a: The Reasonableness of Christianity as delivered in the Scriptures, in: *The Works of John Locke*, 12th ed. London: Rivington, Vol. 6, pp. 1-158.

Locke, J. 1960: *Two Treatises of Government*, Cambridge: Cambridge University Press, a critical edition with an introduction and apparatus criticus by Laslett, P.

Locke, J. 1967. *Two Tracts on Government*, Cambridge: Cambridge University Press, ed. by Abrams, Ph.

Locke, J. 1987: *A Paraphrase and Notes on the Epistles of St. Paul*, Volume I-II, Oxford: Oxford University Press, ed. by Wainwright, A. W. (*Clarendon Edition of the Works of John Locke*).

Locke, J. 2000: *The Reasonableness of Christianity. As Delivered In the Scriptures*, Oxford: Oxford University Press, ed. by Higgins-Biddle, J. C. (*Clarendon Edition of the Works of John Locke*).

This paper was supported by the Hungarian Scientific Fund, within the framework of the research project titled *Early Enlightenment on the Threshold of 18th Century* (OTKA-67798).

THE MEANING OF HUMAN LIFE

Tadej Strehovec, Ljubljana

Introduction

A thorough understanding of technology and the inner logic of modern society is key to finding new ways to understand the meaning of human life. Technology has become the leading force of transformation of the human person and society where one lives. For example, the Internet, airplanes, and genetic tests present new opportunities as well as challenge the way we see ourselves and understand the place of the human person and the relations between society, state, education and religion. The main aim of this paper is to present a paradigm of understanding of the meaning of human life in this new world. Attention will be given especially to the influence of biotechnology and technological society to the understanding of human life. The perspective where human life is the main aim of biotechnology and, at the same time, its principal victim, is the paradigm where the bio-techno-theological process will be revealed as a source of new bioethics.

It is not possible to understand the meaning of human life within the past philosophical and sociological systems. It is necessary to include the meaning of new technologies and their influence on human relations and the functioning of modern society. Modern people live in a world that is the result of not only natural and coincidental evolution but also technological evolution, where new technologies influence the inner structure of human life and body. The Human Genome Project and *in vitro* fertilization are the best examples of such human transformations where new knowledge and new desires were created. Therefore, modern society aims to technologically transform the human body, for example, through gene enrichments and the use of stem cells. Its ultimate aim is to create a new type of human body through the use of genetic engineering and cloning, which will lead to the creation of a new human techno-race that will be healthier, more capable and more profitable.

Today's technology can be seen as products such as machines and electronics, or as knowledge space for active production of new discoveries and comprehension. Some thinkers understand technology as a source of symbolic force and space of untouchable ethical freedom (Reiser 2004: 2499). It could also be seen as a machine for the production of non-symbolic and non-religious truth, which breeds new fear that replaces the natural fear of the past, such as the fear of lightning (Mitcham 2004: 2505; Heidegger 1977: 52). All these views of technology influence the meaning of technologically transformed human life and become part of the demythologization process where new meanings could be revealed.

1. Demythologization as a source of the new knowledge

To understand technological science such as biotechnology and the influence of new technologies on the perception of human life it is necessary to demythologize it (Ellul 1970: 85). The special process of thinking that is bio-techno-demythologization of technology implies the use of the paradigm of the Scripture and its force to connect, disconnect and reconnect different symbolic images to discover new logic and understanding of human life and society as a whole. The use of metaphors and symbolic stories is present in many works of art (*e.g.*, Pablo Coelho, The Matrix, Critical Art Ensemble). The starting point for the demythologization of biotechnology could be the Book of Genesis.

The story of Genesis 1 is about the creation of the human person and the original sin; in order to use it to analyze technological science, it is important to reflect on the symbolic fact that human nature was affected through the original sin. Every newborn child is contaminated with this symbolic malediction, which, according to Christian teaching, opens our nature to sin and evil. This curse is transmitted from generation to generation. Before their fall and eviction from Eden, Adam and Eve possessed a nature that was immortal, immune against suffering, without sin and of perfect dignity. Therefore, the constant human yearning to return to Eden and to regain the pristine nature that was lost is a consequence of this symbolic biblical event. Today's technological science, especially biotechnology, is well aware of this symbolic reality in human nature. Indeed, biotechnology has its roots in the Greco-Roman foundations and the Judeo-Christian revelation about the nature of God, world and man. Therefore, technological science fully accepts this symbolic statement about the fall of human nature and, consequently, seeks to detect and repair the affected points of human nature. Deconstruction and reconstruction are the main methods of biotechnology, an understanding that leads to the imperative: "To detect all infected points of our nature and to remove their consequences." That such an imperative underlies biotechnology is clear from such practices as the sequencing of the human genome and research into the uses of stem cells. The malediction of the fall to earth can be seen in the Human Genome Project, where the atomic structure of nucleotides (adenine, guanine, cytosine and thymine) is seen as the source of not only human health, but also of disease, suffering, aging, and eventually death. Both the Human Genome Project and stem cell research probe the entire human, both with respect to the whole genome and the human organism from the very beginning. Therefore, today's biotechnology sees in the human genome the empirical medium of this fundamental malediction, *i.e.*, the original sin. Every human person is affected with the sin-structure at the time of conception, and this connects him or her to an unredeemed world. Biotechnology is very aware of this reality and accepts it as its main challenge.

2. New messianic religion – biotechnology and technological science

Technological science, including biotechnology, reveals itself without symbolic and religious convictions. Nevertheless, the concepts of new age messianism are many times included in public presentations of new achievements of biological and technological sciences. Science as a redeeming force that aims to defeat human suffering and ultimately remove death from society could be seen as a new kind of religion with special theological concepts. DNA could be understood as a new form of immortal human soul and forbidden space for ordinary citizens. Only scientists as a new type of techno-priests have access to knowledge and could reveal the face of a new type of techno-holiness. According to this interpretation, laboratories become the new type of churches where new hopes for humanity are generated and new human bodies and lives are created. The similarity with Christianity could be evident for many people and the interpretation of technological science as a new type of para-Christian religion could be understandable.

The anonymity group Critical Art Ensemble speaks about the new golden age where capital, knowledge and the concept of the new human body will dominate (Critical Arte Ensamble 2003). The human body will be created according to the criteria of capitalism and new techno-messianism (Critical Arte Ensamble 2004). Incredible progress in the field of medicine opens the door for the production of human body through *in vitro* fertilization, abortion, eugenics, human embryo experimentation and genetic enrichments. For technological sciences, especially for biotechnology, sciences such as genetics, proteomics, molecular biology, cytology and biochemistry become the new golden door to this new Jerusalem.

3. Biotechnology as a seed for new forms of cannibalism

The French philosopher René Girard said that religion is not the phenomenon of society. In reality, society is the phenomenon of religion. Through his famous description of mimetic rivalry and mimetic violence every human society is a place of different tensions and innocent victims (Girard 1977: 214). His works present many excellent accounts where rituals, victims and myths are connected and incarnated in different types of societies. His explanation that innocent victims could become the most powerful source of establishing peace within a society is most interesting. The story of the Passion of Jesus and unfriendly relations between King Herod and Pilate is a good example of how the condemnation of the innocent man could bring peace in personal and social relations (Girard 2001: 85). According to Girard, every society knows the processes of mimetic imitation, the founding murder and different kinds of violence-generating tensions (Girard 1987: 32). The modern type of founding murder could be recognized in the use of atomic weapons in Hiroshima and Nagasaki in 1945. The use of these weapons resolved the conflict between Japan and the USA through the unselective destruction of thousands of innocent human lives. This event of an instant mass killing of innocent people could be seen as a new type of founding murder as it was well known to old civilizations. As a consequence of this event, sciences such as genetics and molecular biology received huge financial and political support, which ultimately led to the famous Human Genome Project and new types of therapies (Danchin 2000: 31). The technological society created through this type of founding murder, like mythic societies, generates different types of tensions, which are resolved through the process of selection of innocent victims. The mainstream media and sciences today instill new tensions as a consequence of the slow pace of research, the limits of knowledge and impatient investment capital. In the past the solution for this kind of social tensions was the sacrifice of millions of healthy adult human lives (soldiers), where peace was established by war. In a biotechnological society peace is established by the killing of people who live at the fringes of society, such as unborn human embryos (abortion, embryo stem cell research) and unconscious terminal patients in hospitals (euthanasia). Their death is a source of new kind of techno-peace where the tensions between capital, research and desire for immortal and suffering-free life are confronted. This kind of biotechnotheological paradigm sees laboratories, scientific institutions and hospitals as new forms of Jerusalem, where silent human sacrifices and crucifixions could be performed.

Conclusion

In order to understand the meaning of human life it is necessary to be aware of the world and society, both of which strive to generate and transform the human body. The biotechnological society seeks to exert influence upon the look of the human body, its physical ability, freedom and perhaps political convictions. At the same time human life itself is the ultimate aim of the new technologies and proof of their messianic nature. Nevertheless, such a non-mythical technological society could in principle become trapped in its limits and negative tensions, which would open the way to chaos and destruction. To prevent such an outcome technological society unconsciously starts with the process of selection of innocent victims and projection of the collective blame upon them. In a world where the ideology of human rights and idea of freedom are both present and praised, the best innocent victims could be found in the sphere comprising the unborn and those near death. Human embryos and terminal (near death) patients become excellent victims for the resolution of intense negative tensions stemming from competition, profit seeking, supremacy and destruction. Much like Jesus Christ, the Christian prototype of an innocent victim, these new techno-victims are silent and many times deprived of any rights, including the right to life and protection from harm. Such a paradigm understands human life as a potential price to pay through crucifixions, peace offerings, and solution for different kind of conflicts. Biotechnotheology together with the process of demythologization reveals the hidden mechanisms of modern biotechnology and technological society where human life is understood as a means toward the realization and incarnation of a mythical para-Christian techno-religion. Human life in such a kind of para-religion is not only sacred; many times it is sacrificed to reach temporal social peace as well. Biotechnotheology as a new kind of "postmodern peacemaking" is the starting point to protect biotechnology and technological science from the so-called techno-cannibalism.

References and Bibliography

Critical Art Ensamble. 2003. Flesh Machine. In: www.critical-art.net. (accessed 9.8.2009).

Critical Art Ensamble. 2004. Molecular Invasion. In: www.critical-art.net. (Accessed 14. 07. 2009.)

Danchin, A. 2000: "Une Histoire Intense Presque Violente", La Recherche 332, 27-34.

Ellul, J. 1970: The Technological Society, New York: Vintage Books.

Girard, R. 1977: Violence and the Sacred, Baltimore: Johns Hopkins University Press.

Girard, R. 1987: Things Hidden since the Foundation of the World, Stanford, Calif.: Stanford University Press.

Girard, R. 2001: I See Satan Fall Like Lightning, New York: Orbis Books.

Heidegger, M. 1977: The Question Concerning Technology, and Other Essays, New York; London: Harper and Row.

Mitcham, C. 2004: "Technology: Philosophy of Medical Technology." In Encyclopedia of Bioethics, edited by Stephen Garrard Post, 2503-11, New York: Macmillan Reference USA Thomson/Gale.

Reiser, J. 2004: "Technology: History of Medical Technology." In Encyclopedia of Bioethics, edited by Stephen Garrard Post, 2497-503, New York: Macmillan Reference USA Thomson/Gale.

POSTHUMAN EXISTENCE IN THE CONTEXT OF THE END OF HISTORY: SOME THEOLOGICAL CONSIDERATIONS

Tonči Matulić, Zagreb

Status Quaestionis

The modern ideologies of the end of history, the last man and the approaching posthuman future rest upon two main premises. The first concerns a specific understanding of history, i.e., time. The second concerns a specific understanding of man, i.e., the social organization of human life.

The modern ideology of the end of history is based upon a specific understanding of history with roots in the historical millenarianisms and apocalypticisms derived from secularized concepts of the Judeo-Christian history of salvation and eschatology (Moltmann 2004: 192-235). Such a concept of history rests upon the concept of modern times, the roots of which extend back to the millenaristic messianism of Joachim de Fiore (1135-1202), based upon a vision of history in three stages (De Lubac 1981). The most influential secular version of such a vision of history was developed by Auguste Comte in the Law of Three Stages of Social Development (Comte 1998). The final stage of the development of a society was scientific, i.e., positivist, that only acknowledges sensory experience for the evaluation of human knowledge, discarding all theology and metaphysics as superfluous fantasies. With the establishment of science appeared the reign of the third or final stage of social development, where alternatives no longer exist. The present can be considered as modern times in relation to the overcome past and the "end of time" in relation to the future (Moltmann, 1971: 155-160). The place of a providential God, as the creator and lord of the world and history has, nonetheless, not been assumed by man because he must disappear. This place has been assumed by science, not any kind but applied science or technology that will bring about the end of history and create the prerequisites for life in the posthuman future. Economics and politics have formed an alliance with knowledge as power, thereby facilitating the building of a social system of total control. Here history (*Geschichte*) is no longer possible because history has come to an end under social conditions of total control. Only mere events (*Geschehen*) are still possible, because freedom, work, thought and activity are strictly controlled by a bureaucratically regulated world (Morra [2]1996: 95-96).

Modern anthropology, among other things, has begotten a specific concept of man that starts from a negative and defeatist interpretation. It was most eloquently inaugurated by Nietzsche ("man is an animal with red cheeks" or "man as a still undefined being") (Nietzsche 2007), and Arnold Gehlen developed the idea of man as a "deficient being" (*Mängelwesen*) who compensates for his natural shortcomings with solid social structures and institutions (Gehlen 2004). Social structures must function in order for man to become what he should be. Social structures create a specific form of civilization that provides the foundations for the so-called "second nature" of man, who by his nature is a chaotic being (Moltmann 2004: 221-222). Without or outside structured civilization, man remains an undefined animal.

The idea of the end of history is one of the old apocalyptic themes. The end of history symbolizes the end of the world, whereby history is understood to mean the reality of the world. The end of the world is in God's hands. By contrast, the modern ideology of the end of history, in the sense of post-historical thinking, began in 1933 with the ironic and often whimsical lectures by Alexandre Kojève in Paris on Hegel's phenomenology of the spirit (Kojève 1980). Kojève unhesitatingly embraced Hegel's assertion that history had reached its end in 1806, the year of Napoleon's victory over the Prussian army and triumphant entry into Jena (Fukuyama 1992: 65-67/143-147). Critical theological inquiry into the ideology of the end of history reveals that it is encumbered by secularized messianism and apocalypticism that have constantly been reiterated throughout the entire modern age, down to the present (Fukuyama) in constantly new conceptual variants (Moltmann 2004: 219). The idea of the end of history contains the French neologism *post-histoire* (Cournot 1911: 22; Niethammer 1989: 16) which designates the time after the end of history, i.e., the post-historical period. This is a time of mere events, a time of a continuous series of unrelated events, a time of individual events but not a historical time. During the time after the end of history, man is no longer a historical but rather a post-historical being, who no longer needs to be a person because the "controlling world," i.e., the world of developed bureaucracy and stable structures, controls all his shortcomings. Human contingency is placed under strict administrative control that leaves no room for alternatives. Under such conditions, it is no longer possible to differentiate between the truth and falsehood, life and death, because the "controlling world" controls human beings without history or memory. Memory, as the historical memory of experiences, is locked in the "museum of history," which has no influence upon real life, whatsoever. Thus, the post-historical human being can be compared to the pre-historical human being. The relatively brief historical period (modern age) is placed between the pre-historical, i.e., instinctive, and the final post-historical, i.e., controlled, ages. It was a relatively brief episode in the struggle between instinct and reason. It has now come to an end, and the end is marked by instincts that have been elevated to the level of an organized and totally controlled society. The firmly organized global society becomes similar to the organization of life among sociable animals, such as termites, ants and bees (Seidenberg 1950: 179). A type of animalization of man indisputably occurs. This refers to the degradation of man to the instinctual level, who is now strictly socially controlled. While the temporarily historical human being (modern age) was free and could choose among various alternatives, among various ideological matrices of social systems, the post-historical human being is chained by necessity under the conditions of a strictly controlled institutionalized and bureaucratized world and, as such, no longer has alternatives, except those that are predefined and predetermined. There remains the possibility of individual caprices but they occur under the conditions of the predetermined framework of a strictly controlled life. The completely organized, strictly controlled and entirely bureaucratized world represents the "end of history," i.e., the post-historical reality in which the human being is nothing more than a totally culturally conditioned animal. The human being in the post-historical world, therefore, is no longer a genuine human being but an animal who lives in a cultural atmosphere of strictly controlled instincts, although without history, without memory, without subjectivity and, consequently, without responsibility. This is Nietzsche's last man. This is the meaning of the "dehumanized man" from Huxley, the very Brave New World in which technology based upon biological manipulation rules the world and controls human destinies. This is the meaning of man deprived of his privacy by Big Brother in Orwell's *Nineteen Eighty-Four*, where networked informatics technologies rule the world and control human destinies (Huxley 1998; Orwell 2003).

The post-historical period abolishes the linear concept of history based upon the Judeo-Christian revelation of the history of salvation and eschatology, and revives the old concept of history as a closed system (Moltmann 2004: 218-223). Such a concept of history is cloaked in the ideology of secular eschatology, which in place of belief in a personal God and in place of faith in a God involved in the world affords privilege to belief in the death of God and concomitantly belief in the end of history and the last man. From such spiritual humus emerge postmodern existential nihilism and polytheism.

The ideas of the end of history, last man and the beginning of the post-historical age have their origins in radicalized interpretations of the world, history, man, freedom, society, science, technology and progress, and which throughout the entire modern age from Hobbes (Leviathan) through Hegel, Marx and Nietzsche to the new postmodern re-interpretations (i.e., deconstructionism and structuralism) have been occupied with the establishment of an immanent metaphysics with its own secular eschatology. When all the accounts are added up at the end and the line is drawn beneath the historical balance of all these explorations, which are not waning even today, then the price to pay is not only too high but, above all, too dangerous. Man has taken his ultimate fate in his own hands and, as a result, instead of authentic divine liberation and salvation, he has obtained new forms of slavery and fear, which in recent times have begun to emigrate from the imaginary dystopias of science fiction (Huxley, Orwell) into reality. Moreover, the real threats of nuclear holocaust, the ever-present ecological crisis, the growing gap between the rich and poor, the absolute rule of instrumental rationality, the cybernetization of life and the distortion of reality by the mass media represent the general situation of the contemporary industry of fear and enslavement. In an atmosphere of profound spiritual crisis, there is daily growth in the procession of unbearable contradictions to which the person of the so-called post-historical age is exposed and which increasingly push him toward the chasm of existential nihilism.

Another End of History after the End of History

Twenty years ago, the American political economist Francis Fukuyama published a text under the intriguing but already familiar title of "The End of History" (Fukuyama 1989: 3-18). As others before him, he invokes the end of history, the end point of which is always shifting. Three years later, the same author published a book entitled "The End of History and the Last Man" (Fukuyama 1992) in which he expands the main thesis presented in the article and, amidst new historical circumstances, provides original interpretations of Hegel, Marx and Nietzsche, as well as the rest of the tradition of post-historical thinking.

Fukuyama's main thesis is based upon the most recent trend of Western liberal democracy, as the latest sign of socio-cultural evolution. Fukuyama views the end of history, in his judgment, as the culmination of the specific Western socio-cultural evolution, i.e., the liberal-democratic government. The end of history is actually the beginning of the global rule of liberal democracy, in the sense that in addition to the current majority, all the remaining countries of the world will accept liberal democracy as a model of human government. After the fall of the rival ideologies of monarchism, fascism and communism, liberal democracy has emerged as the winning option. Liberal democracy is "the end point of mankind's ideological evolution" and "the final form of human government," and as such represents the "end of history" (Fukuyama 1992: XI). History is actually an evolutionary process that has come to an end. "The end of history would mean the end of wars and bloody revolutions. Agreeing on ends, men would have no large causes for which to fight. (...) They would, in other words, become animals again, as they were before the bloody battle that began history. (...) If man reaches a society in which he has succeeded in abolishing injustice, his life will come to resemble that of the dog" (Fukuyama 1992: 311). The end of history is not merely the establishment of the universal rule of liberal democracy and the end of wars, revolutions and injustice, as well as the cessation of their causes, but it is also a feature of the last man. The life of the last man is that of "physical security and material plenty" (Fukuyama 1992: 312) provided by the post-historical state government that administrates a democratically and technologically arranged world which has no alternative.

Ten years after the thesis of the end of history and the last man, Fukuyama felt the need to revise some of his optimistic and triumphalistic views. Some of his revised views were first presented in his book "The Great Disruption" (Fukuyama 1999). During the past thirty years, the most highly developed countries of the world experienced major transformations, from industrial to informatics societies. These great social transformations had an impact on an increase in crime, a decline in the birth rate, destabilization of the family structure and a drastic decline in confidence, facts which are simultaneously the cause and effect of the victory of individualism over communitarianism (Fukuyama 1999: 21-149). Fukuyama finds a response to the destabilizing factors in society in a revised evaluation of human nature and social norms of behavior, in light of an evolutionistic paradigm (Fukuyama 1999: 143-247). This is a prerequisite for the major reconstruction of society on the basis of new social and moral values that respond to the need for major changes in postindustrial societies (Fukuyama 1999: 249-280).

The story does not stop here. Fukuyama again tackles the question of the end of history, i.e., the last man (Fukuyama 1999: 16-33). The concluding thesis relies on the assessment of the possibilities of the natural sciences, i.e., their technological applications. "The open-ended character of modern natural science suggests that within the next couple of generations we will have knowledge and technologies that will allow us to accomplish what social engineers of the past failed to do. At that point, we will have definitively finished human history because we will have abolished human beings as such. And then, a new, posthuman history will begin" (Fukuyama 1999: 33). The possibilities of biotechnology, such as cloning, genetically modified organisms, stem cell research, preimplentation genetic screening, nanotechnology, neuropharmacological manipulation of human behavior and clinical prolongation of life, speak eloquently about the real dangers to which mankind has become exposed. Fukuyama takes this fact into serious consideration in the context of a discussion on the possibilities of the biotechnological revolutionizing of life, especially human, which has forced him to revise his optimistic thesis on the end of history and the last man. In biotechnological possibilities, Fukuyama sees the presence of a "devil's bargain: longer life, but with reduced mental capacity, freedom from depression, together with freedom from creativity or spirit; therapies that blur the line between what we achieve on our own and what we achieve because of the levels of various chemicals in our brains" (Fukuyama 2002: 8). Many biotechnological possibilities have become reality, justifying such dystopic authors of science fiction as Huxley and Orwell. Huxley foresaw modern biotechnology as the greatest danger, capable of altering human nature and thus taking us into the posthuman level of the development of history (Fukuyama 2002: 7). It is true that the biological species *Homo sapiens* will not disappear in the coming posthuman future, concedes Fukuyama, but will certainly undergo changes of many properties that we consider essential for human beings. "Human genetic engineering raises most directly the prospect of a new kind of eugenics, with all the moral implications with which that word is fraught, and ultimately the ability to change human nature" (Fukuyama 2002: 72). Biotechnological possibilities for interventions in humans require a reassessment of the concepts of human rights, human dignity and human nature, although now no longer on theological grounds but instead on alternative grounds of secular argumentation (Fukuyama 2002: 105-177). "While religion provides the most clear-cut grounds for opposing certain types of biotechnology, religious arguments will not be persuasive to many who do not accept religion's starting premises. We need to examine other, more secular, types of arguments" (Fukuyama 2002: 91). Thus, Fukuyama embarks upon a double undertaking. From one side, he philosophically questions and establishes the value and significance of human rights, human nature and human dignity, as a precondition for their general validity under the conditions of the prevailing liberal-secular democracy. On the other side, he politically (opportunistically) changes his own position on non-interventionism by the state in biological research and its biotechnological applications. Fukuyama is dissatisfied with the dominant but conflicting attitudes in the society, liberal and conservative, that offer solutions to various biotechnological challenges. The conditions and possibilities for the regulation of the application and development of biotechnology are, in his opinion, somewhere in the middle of these mutually exclusive positions (Fukuyama 2002: 182-183). What we could call Fukuyama's middle path is determined by the commingling of the good and bad consequences inherent in biotechnological activity. Therefore, he is simultaneously a fervent advocate of biotechnological progress, from the one side, and the necessary restriction of biotechnological progress, on the other. Consequently, following the secular establishment of human rights, dignity and nature, Fukuyama sees the ultimate resolution of the biotechnological challenges, i.e., the limitation of biotechnological progress, as the task of the state. "In the face of the challenge from a technology like this, where good and bad are intimately connected, it seems to me that there can be only one possible response: countries must regulate the development and use of technology politically, setting up institutions that will discriminate between those technological advances that promote human flourishing, and those that pose a threat to human dignity and well-being" (Fukuyama 2002: 182). Thus, Fukuyama, as a member of the Policy Planning Staff of the U.S. Department of State, arrived at a conclusion, which he certainly knew before entering the discussion of contemporary biotechnological challenges. The state, led according to the principles of liberal democracy and the free market, can and must control the development of the sciences and biotechnologies by legally curbing those undertakings that threaten survival and security. Nonetheless, the post-historical state is not quite the same as yesterdays. Fukuyama only speculates about what it could be like (Fukuyama 2002: 216-218). Such conjecture is inevitable because post-historical thinking is imbued with the secularized understanding of the history of salvation that in Fukuyama's analyses reveals the countenance of a biotechnological utopia, in which he attempts to anticipate the future using the bio-techno-political imperative. Fictional dystopia describes the world and man as they could be but still are not. Utopian fiction describes the world and man as they already are but would not have to be. What is the solution? It is necessary to abandon the secular ideology of post-historical thinking (Liessmann 2007).

Posthuman Existence or Conditio Humana

The ideologies of post-historical thinking turn the meaning of history upside down. The contradictions of contemporary scientific-technological civilization are mounting and the ideologies of post-historical thinking do not have suitable solutions for them. They merely provide new secular interpretations of the end of history and the last man. Thus, the end of history is constantly extended, i.e., postponed, because there is no history here. Nonetheless, it is not necessary to be deceived. The contradictory nature of contemporary society proves that it has no precedents in the history of mankind. In the light of their radical critique appear what could be considered as the features of posthuman existence, not the features of a posthuman future in the sense of the ideology of the end of history and post-historical man, but the features of post-human existence in the context of the future endangered by man (*exterminism*) (Moltmann 2004: 204-216). Vulnerability stems from the accumulated contradictions of the contemporary world that the ideology of post-historical thinking cannot and does not know how to solve. Somewhat more will be said later about some contradictions, the radical critique of which brings to light several features of posthuman existence, i.e., existence under conditions of the fear of self-destruction, new (biotechnological) forms of slavery and nihilism.

Our concept of posthuman existence covers the meaning of human existence based upon the spiritual and intellectual humus of the postmodern degradation of man from a being in the image of God to a state without transcendental meaning and purpose, i.e., in the *conditio humana* (Sanna 2005: 282-291). In this context, a judgment by the Second Vatican Council has acquired prophetic value: "For without the Creator, the creature would disappear. (...) When God is forgotten, however, the creature itself grows unintelligible" (GS, No. 36). Postmodern man has severed his relationship with a personal God (Sanna ^{3}2004: 337). Therefore, he remains alone in his humanity (Gauchet 1985: 240-260). Thereby, he has lost his transcendental footing. The identity of "being a man" has become irrelevant and, therefore, threatened at its foundation (Metz 2004: 134). The postmodern cultural matrix dramatically affects the pulsation of the consciousness and conscience of the individual, particularly in the manner that he accepts his own unintelligibility as an essential prerequisite for a life worthy of man in a plural and democratic society. The characteristics of this unintelligibility are evident in the following phenomena.

First, there is the growing phenomenon of an *exclusive humanism*, which neither recognizes nor accepts purposes beyond that of human (earthly) wellbeing. This is an essential characteristic of the secular age "in which the eclipse of all goals beyond human flourishing becomes conceivable; or better, it falls within the range of an imaginable life for masses of people. This is the crucial link between secularity and a self-sufficing humanism" (Taylor 2007: 19-20). Exclusive humanism attempts to fill the void that occurred with the rejection of God through the disenchantment of the world and the search for an alternative to God.

Second, there is the growing phenomenon of *postmodern polytheism*, which allegedly, after the death of God, would represent the only healthy myth. Only the polytheism of Olympic deities or postmodern disenchantment and playful polymythism can compensate for the unique story of the monotheistic myth (Marquard 1981: 91-116). It can be said that modern culture has still rested on the metaphysical triad of God, man and the world as "strong" (*forte*) subjects and, viewed from the theological perspective, has still understood them as the Creator, creature and creation. Postmodern culture is the triad of God, man and the world transformed into "weak" (*debole*) subjects (Sanna ^{3}2004: 254-255). Modern culture has acknowledged strong ideas such as individuals, history, science, progress, together with God, as myths. Postmodern culture has proclaimed the death of man on the site of the execution of God. Religion, philosophy and science no longer have anything to say to the postmodern man, who still lives solely from art or ambiguous aesthetics as a substitute for interred principles. Man, of course, cannot live without myths. Therefore, it is necessary to select the right myths. However, as long as the myth of the monotheistic God and the Promethean myth of man who wanted to replace God are rejected, only the myth of the death of God remains, which makes the resurrection of many gods possible. Man, of course, after the death of the one God, did not become a master because polytheism is chance and a polytheistic man is conscious of the contingent life, i.e., life in the embrace of sheer chance. Chance is thus imposed as the only true god in the pantheon of postmodern culture. The cosmos is not a reflection of beauty, order and intelligibility, but is a reflection of sheer chance. The universe is the kingdom of chance (Morra^{2} 1996: 114-117).

Third, during the past twenty years or so, there has been a systematic *depersonalization of man*. Postmodern anthropology on the execution site of the dead God is being transformed into a defective and, above all, negative anthropology. Indeed, the rejection of the personal God, a God engaged with man in the world, has resulted in a faded, New Age deity, and thus exerted a retroactive effect upon the creation of a faded and vague concept of the human being (Sanna 2005: 291-303). The concept of the person in the postmodern age has been subjected to total relativization (Mondin 1997). This relativization is most evident in the negation of the personal identity of some human beings, particularly during vulnerable stages of their existence, from conception to natural death (Singer [2]1997). Postmodern culture erases the equal sign between the human person and human being, because man as a person, i.e., a unique spiritual-physical being, is wrenched from the safe anchor of transcendence and extradited to the mercy of superficial socioeconomic assessments of the quality of life. The concept of the quality of life is acquiring exclusively materialistic connotations that evince open contempt for God and the idea of the God-based sanctity of life (Dworkin 1993; Singer 1995).

Analyses thus far have at least somewhat substantiated our understanding of posthuman existence as a linguistic variant of human existence degraded to the *conditio humana*, i.e., without reliance upon the strong subjects of God, man and the world. *Conditio humana* indicates a state of open opposition to any kind of metaphysical interpretation and, of course, theological interpretation and understanding of the meaning and purpose of human life in light of transcendence and a personal God. Consequently, the humus of *conditio humana* is sprinkled with epochal value reversals, which in the consciousness and conscience of postmodern man sometimes provoke anxiety and fear, and sometimes naive optimism and frivolous faith in self-deliverance. One and the other are commingled. The commingling of disparate feelings and expectations foster a state of profound spiritual crisis.

(Post)modern value reversals occur at various levels of human thought and activity, which we shall merely touch upon below, since they have been discussed at length in another place (Matulić 2008). Theological investigation of the dominant spiritual, intellectual and moral features of the *conditio humana* bring to light a whole series of value reversals that provide insight into the state of the consciousness and conscience of modern man.

First, the *conditio humana* conceals the cause of all problems, i.e., the enthronement of man in the place of God as a "superfluous hypothesis," "private matter" or "a purely subjective sentiment." Consequently, there has been a shift in consciousness from a theocentric vision of the world toward an anthropocentric vision. Anthropocentrism has taken precedence over theocentrism.

Second, the world as creation, i.e., the place for the realization of the history of salvation, has been replaced by nature as viewed by the positive sciences. This fact has caused a shift in consciousness from an anthropocentric to a biocentric understanding of nature. The evolutionary paradigm based upon necessity and chance has superseded the theological paradigm of creation with its essential dimensions of purpose and meaning. Evolutionist biocentrism has assumed primacy over theological and ethical anthropocentrism.

Third, history has assumed the place of ontology, causing a shift in awareness from a value-based world toward a world of man-made values. Historicism has totally hegemonized human understanding of the world.

Fourth, instead of metaphysics, natural sciences have the last word. This fact has caused a shift in consciousness from transcendental to an immanent, materialistic understanding of the foundations of the world. Positivism has infected all the intellectual pores of modern man, crowding out the idea of transcendence whenever and wherever it can.

Fifth, the ontological understanding of the human person (*imago Dei*) has been subjected to relativization, and the positivistic understanding of the concept of the biological species (*Homo sapiens*) has the last word. Human consciousness has been diverted from the divine origin of the human person, as a unique spiritual-physical being, toward the natural origin of the human being as one of many species of animals that occurred through natural selection within the battle for survival. Biologism has taken precedence over personalism, which is yet another variant of the precedence of biocentrism over anthropocentrism.

Sixth, the body has entirely hegemonized the human spirit, a fact reflected in the shift from understanding man as a spiritual and personal substance to that of man as a bodily substance composed of physical laws and biochemical compounds. Materialism has not only taken precedence over spirituality but the dominant contemporary New Age spirituality is essentially revealed as materialistic and pantheistic.

Seventh, technology is regularly concealed behind the concept of ethics, i.e., the logic of cost/benefit calculation. The dominant ethic in the postmodern society is actually camouflaged technology. Everything that is technologially feasible and economically profitably is also considered to be ethically permissible. Consequently, ethical awareness distances itself from moral good and approaches the instrumental calculations of efficiency and profitability, for which the end justifies the means. Utilitarianism, i.e., economy, profit and technology, has taken precedence over moral good as the bearer of moral values.

Eighth, the establishment and spread of cybernetics and cybernetic systems have made possible the creation of artificial intelligence and controlled parallel virtual worlds. Human consciousness is under the constant pressure of artificially created time, space, relations, communication and experience, and therefore becomes transformed into an artificial creation that falls easy prey to consumeristic and hedonistic offers. Fantasy is no longer an object of human imagination but is transformed into a mode of everyday life and interpersonal communication.

The above only draws attention to some of the cultural dynamics and value dimensions of the postmodern unintelligibility of man degraded to the *conditio humana*, in consequence of having rejected God as the only lord of life and history.

Instead of a Conclusion

At the end, it should be clearly repeated that the (post)modern ideology of post-historical thinking, in all its old and new variants, is the successor to Christian theology based upon the biblical concept of the history of salvation. It is also the heir to the secular millenarianism based on the concept of modern times. While the older variants of post-historical thinking still believed in historical progress to the final realization of the "golden age," new variants have turned to apocalyptic belief in the end of history, achieved through the abolition of the human being. The replacement of divine providence with the idea of biological evolution, the abolition of the historical human being (*imago Dei*) and the establishment of totalitarian power that ensures the end of history have nothing in common with the Christian understanding of history (Moltmann 2004: 225-226) and the strong subjects of God, man and the world. The historical process of secularization in the system of post-historical thinking has become transformed into a malignant and dangerous ideology. Theological analyses of the so-called posthuman existence (*conditio humana*) reveal the scale of the postmodern metastases that have occurred in the tissue of the ideology of post-historical thinking, i.e., the end of history and the abolished human being. The full complexity of this problem can be expressed by a single concept: ideology of secularism.

References and Bibliography

Comte, A. 1998: *Cours de philosophie positive.* [Paris: Bachelier, 1830-1842]. Paris: Éditeurs des sciences et des arts, Éditions Hermann.

Cournot, A. A. [[1]1861] 1911: *Traité de l'enchaîbement des idées fondamentales dans les sciences et dans l'histoire*. Paris: Hachette.

De Lubac, H. 1981: *La Postérité spirituelle de Joachim de Fiore*, Vol. 1-2. Paris: Lethielleux.

Dworkin, R. 1993: *Life's Dominion: An Argument About Abortion, Euthanasia, and Freedom*. New York: Alfred A. Knopf.

Fukuyama, F. 1989: The End of History, in: *The National Interest*, 18: 3-18.

Fukuyama, F. 1992: *The End of History and the Last Man*. New York: Avon Books, Inc. – The Free Press.

Fukuyama, F. 1999: *The Great Disruption: Human Nature and the Reconstitution of Social Order*. New York: The Free Press.

Fukuyama F. 1999: Second Thoughts: The Last Man in a Bottle, in: *The National Interest*, No. 56: 16-33.

Fukuyama, F. 2002: *Our Posthuman Future: Consequences of the Biotechnology Revolution*. New York: Farrar, Straus and Giroux.

Gauchet, M. 1985: *Le Désenchantement du mond. Une histoire politique de religion*. Paris: Éditions Gallimard.

Gehlen, A. [11956] 2004: *Urmensch und Spätkultur. Philosophische Ergebnisse und Aussagen*. 6. erweiterte Edition. Frankfurt a./M.: Vittorio Klostermann Verlag.

Huxley, A. [11932] 1998: *Brave New World*. New York: Perennial Classics.

Kojève, A. 1980: *Introduction à la lecture de Hegel: leçons sur la Phénoménologie de l'Esprit professées de 1933 à 1939 à l'École des Hautes Études*. Paris: Les Éditions Gallimard.

Liessmann, K. P. 2007: *Zukunft kommt! Über sekularisierte Heilserwartungen und ihre Enttäuschung. Essays*. Wien: Styria Verlag.

Marquard, O. 1981: *Abschied vom Prinzipiellen. Philosophische Studien*. Ditzingen [Stuttgart]: Philipp Reclam Verlag.

Matulić, T. 2008: *Metamorfoze kulture. Teološko prepoznavanje znakova vremena u ozračju znanstveno-tehničke civilizacije*, ["Metamorphoses of Culture: Theological Recognition of the Signs of the Times in the Atmosphere of the Scientific-Technological Civilization"]. Zagreb: Glas Koncila.

Metz, J. B. 1997: *Zum Begriff der neuen Politischen Theologie*. Mainz: Matthias Grünewald Verlag.

Metz, J. B. 2004: *Politička teologija 1967.-1997.* Zagreb: Kršćanska sadašnjost.

Moltmann, J. 1971: *Hope and Planning*. New York: Harper & Row.

Moltmann, J. 2004: *The Coming of God: Christian Eschatology*. Minneapolis: Fortress Press.

Mondin, B. (Ed.) 1997: *Antropologia e bioetica. Ricerca interdisciplinare sull'enigma uomo*. Milano: Massimo Editore.

Morra, G. [2]1996: *Il quarto uomo. Postmodernità o crisi della modernità?* Roma: Armando Armando.

Nietzsche, F. 2007: *Also sprach Zarathustra. Ein Buch für Alle und Keinen* [1883-1885]. München: Deutschen Taschenbuch Verlag, 11. Auflage.

Niethammer, L. 1989: *Post-histoire: Ist die Geschichte zu Ende?* Leipzig: Rowohlt Verlag.

Seidenberg, R. 1950: *Post-historic Man: An Inquiry.* Chapel Hill: University of North Carolina Press.

Orwell, G. 2003: *Nineteen Eighty-Four* [Harcourt Brace and Company, 1949.]. Orlando (Fl.): Plume.

Sanna, I. 2005: "Dal crepuscolo degli dei al crepuscolo dell 'uomo," in: Ignazio Sanna (ed.), *La sfida del post-umano. Verso nuovi modelli di esistenza?* Roma: Edizioni Studium, pp. 282-291.

Sanna, I. [3]2004: *L'antropologia cristiana tra modernità e postmodernità.* Brescia: Editrice Queriniana.

Taylor, Ch. 2007: *A Secular Age.* Cambridge (Mass.) – London: The Belknap Press of Harvard University Press.

Singer, P. 1995: *Rethinking Life & Death. The Collapse of Our Traditional Ethic.* Oxford – New York: Oxford University Press.

Singer, P. 21997: *Practical Ethics.* Cambridge (UK) – New York: Cambridge University Press.

Singer, P. 2003: *Praktična etika.* Zagreb: KruZak.

THE VICTIMS OF GLOBALIZATION AND THE ETHICS OF LIFE. NOTES ON RECENT LATIN AMERICAN ETHICS OF LIBERATION

Gunter Prüller-Jagenteufel, Vienna

Three years ago at the first worldwide conference on Theological Ethics in Padua, one question was raised frequently: how could humankind achieve a good life for all? In particular, the problems caused by economic globalization were presented and put under criticism (cf. Keenan, 2007; Hogan, 2008). And currently, more than ever before, we can immediately see the still unresolved problems of globalization: financial crisis, ecological crisis, food crisis, human-made global warming and the consequential natural disasters. But to fully understand the complex problem we have to look at it from the perspective of the poor: meaning, those who are marginalized and excluded from welfare, education, social and political participation, and ultimately from justice. After a brief consideration of some facts, I would like to present the Latin-American concept of an "ethics of life" which has been developed by a number of philosophers and theologians. And finally, I want to ask who could be the subject of such a new concept of ethics.

1. Globalization from the perspective of the poor: the marginalized and excluded

1.1 Globalization is a political project

Globalization is clearly a multi-dimensional process. Nevertheless, economics and economical interests are the very heart of that process. Therefore the human person is regarded mainly as "homo oeconomicus" and consequently the "good life" as good economical conditions. The world is reduced into a world market, countries into markets, people into consumers. The goal seems to be a total market with total efficiency – everything else is subsumed under this perspective, seeking unlimited growth through unlimited competition (cf. Hinkelammert, 2001: 553).

The ongoing competitive dynamics between countries is the reason why politicians and companies alike strive for more competition and less regulations. Laws that should protect workers, children, families, our environment, etc. are seen as mere "hindrances" for the free market. Maximum efficiency needs maximum reduction of costs (for work, taxes, etc.) and maximum use of "free" resources (environment, infrastructure, etc.). The costs are socialized while the profits are privatized. And all of that seems so be a natural law, nothing to be done about it.

However, that process is not at all "natural" or "inevitable"; rather; it is a political project driven by political agents. As the Latin American Jesuit *Xabier Gorostiaga* puts it: 'Neoliberalism … is not an economic project but a project of society, of state, of international relations and of social relations within each society.' (Gorostiaga, 1999: 83) But more than that: this project is rooted in a philosophical concept, an individualistic anthropology deduced from an evolutionary point of view, reducing all relationships to the concept of competition and survival of the fittest. Following this concept the only task of politics is to set optimal conditions for the market which consequently means that politics loses more and more of its influence to shape the world. That is why Nobel Prize laureate *Joseph Stiglitz* strongly demands the democratization of globalization, which means the re-entry of politics into the field of economy (cf. Stiglitz, 2006: 335-362).

Of course, this position stands strongly against neoliberal ideas, but it is a must if we consider the consequences of globalization. Free competition leads to structures that exclude the majority of the world's population from our society, the struggle for the "survival of the fittest" leaves the not-so-fit behind and the old idea of the "common good" is lost. This affects not only our economic and political life, but also personal and social relations. As Hinkelammert observed,

'The clearer it becomes that we exclude ever larger parts of our society from its welfare, the lesser will we be able to avoid inhuman attitudes against the marginalized. So competition and exclusion become more and more the standard of the day-to-day relationships among those who live within that system.' (Hinkelammert, 2001: 551).

1.2 Totalization of the market and annihilation of the human subject

We have to bear in mind that those effects are not merely consequences of bad practice, while the theory is flawless. On the contrary, it is the theory of the "total market" that has to be revised. The problematic of the "totalization of the market" is that the market serves the interests of individuals by the laws of supply and demand. The subjects that interact in the market are in theory abstract ones: the "individual calculator of his benefit". But that is precisely the problem: the real subjects are not abstract like Platonist ideas without body and needs, but they suffer from concrete physical needs. Thus, Hinkelammert argues that it is of no use to me to know that rising food prices will lead to a decrease of demand and the prices will fall again if I need my food right now – for consumption, not for speculation (cf. Hinkelammert, 2004). So it may be true that the market distributes all goods most efficiently, yet, not according to the needs of human beings, but only according to the inherent rules of the economic system. That is why Hinkelammert, et. al. state strongly that the answer to the basic needs of the people cannot be left to the market alone. The plain physical life cannot be traded for anything else; there is no measure for it because its alternative is simply death. And life and death cannot be considered as mere interests, they are fundamental absolutes. That is why a number of Latin American philosophers and theologians – most prominent *Franz Hinkelammert* and *Enrique Dussel* – urge us to a different view on the human person: They focus on the concrete human being who is in need of the means of survival; a bodily subject where the physical condition is to be regarded as transcendental (in the Kantian sense), because the bodily life is the *conditio sine qua non* for all other interests.

1.3 Human rights or market rights?

This leads to a special problem of globalization: the question of human rights. In our system of globalized world economy, the rights of the free market are often considered as more valid than the rights of human beings as individuals and as groups. The freedom of enterprise is regarded as a higher value than the rights of workers, consumers, and environment. *Hinkelammert* therefore remarks,

'The strategy of globalization has turned the concept of human rights upside down. ... Since competition is regarded as the highest, maybe even the one and only value, in the name of the rules of the market ... we liquidate all human rights. Market rights instead of human rights.' (Hinkelammert, 2001: 557-558).

Nowadays it is no longer those in positions of political power but those having economic ones that are acting subjects. We understand this when we listen to the news: the market "wants" something, the market "reacts", "is getting nervous" and so on. Finally and fundamentally, "the market is always right". Thus, the market is seen as super-subject, the crown of a different kind of evolution. In the theories of *Friedrich A. Hayek* we find this evolutionary idea very openly: the market is seen as a self-organizing and self-developing system evolving with utmost efficiency. Therefore any interference would be only disturbing the system, disturbing the efficiency (Hayek, 1984). A problematic aspect of this theory is the basic idea that a self-organizing system inevitably reaches a state of balance. But that is an ideology. We can see this in reality where the totalization of the market is disastrous for society and nature as well. Consequently, it is self-destructive. If we look at it from the perspective of the poor, the ones who are marginalized and excluded by market rules and economic effects, we can observe this even more clearly. And it is these two topics, the poor and the environment, that are the main fields of the actual ethical discourse in Latin America. It is an ethics from the perspective of those who have to be included in the economic system (cf. Hinkelammert, 2007; 404-407; Mo Sung, 2005: 86-92).

2. Ethics of life (ética de la vida)

A discourse has been going on in Latin America during the last fifteen years to consider a new ethical approach from the perspective of the victims, the marginalized and the excluded; not so much an option *for* the poor, but an option *of* the poor – a different option for the world. *Enrique Dussel* and other scholar theologians and intellectuals have been working on this approach which they call "ethics of life" (*ética de la vida*) or "ethics of the subject" (*ética del sujeto*). The main idea in this concept, its starting point and ultimate goal, is the human person within the context of concrete conditions: physical, psychical, social, etc. And from the experience of mass poverty and early deaths the focus is simple, but fundamental: it is life, starting with the plain physical survival to the fullness of life in good personal, communal, social, and spiritual relationships (cf. Dussel, 2000: 495-500). Always, the point of reference is the concrete human being, especially the victim, the poor, the marginalized, the excluded.

When talking about the human person as subject, we need to understand that in this concept the human person is seen mainly as a subject for and within human relationships – relationships that induce responsibility. To be a subject means to live in a net of relationships, which implies being responsible. If a human person takes responsibility for others he/she becomes truly a subject. This is especially true if we take responsibility for persons who are denied their original status as persons. And in acting for the other out of love we find our true self.

Viewed from a structural perspective we see that the goal of interpersonal responsibility is the common good – a traditional term taken from Catholic social teaching. Linked to the basic idea of the ethics of life we come to the overall principle: the basic survival towards a decent life for all is the core of the common good. All other values are not absolutes but relatives – valued in relation to that core. Indeed, this critical ethical approach is not anti-market at all. In fact, it is in favour of working with the market, as long as the market is truly serving human life. The criticism focuses on the ideology of the total market and its fatal effects (cf. Mo Sung, 2004: 110-113).

3. Subjects of ethical praxis vis-a-vis globalization

The ultimate goal of this ethics of life is 'a society, where there is place for all and which is in harmony with nature' (Richard, 2001: 327). Therefore the ethics of life has a twofold view of itself: 1) as a *universal* concept of ethics, but without deducing concrete norms from universal criteria; it starts from the experiences of concrete life instead and goes on inductively, and 2) as a *critical* concept of ethics, which focuses on critique in the first place and only then tries to bring up new concepts of society, yet always open for critique and improvements. The Brazilian Theologian *Jung Mo Sung* explains:

'To struggle for a society, where there is place for all, does not mean pursuing a political and economic concept a priori. It means applying this principle as a criterion for distinguishing various possible global and local projects.' (Mo Sung, 2004: 112).

3.1 A new understanding of the preferential option for the poor

Granted that we accept the main idea presented above, how do we put it into action? How could an ethics of life work out? According to the aforementioned Latin American theologians and philosophers, three characteristic elements are to be considered.

3.1.1 Ethical indignation

The origin of ethics, according to *Dussel*, *Hinkelammert*, et. al., is not to actively turn one's attention to another person. They rather follow the concept of *Emmanuel Lévinas* stating that the original ethical experience is the encounter with the "other" who is approaching me. More specifically, the encounter with the oppressed, marginalized, excluded and victimized other:

'The human subject reveals itself in the victim, who is oppressed and excluded by the system. It reveals itself as a concrete and living subject. In an extreme case it reveals itself as "interruption": the subject, that cannot live, screaming with pain.' (Dussel, 2000: 524).

The scream is experienced as the utmost revelation of humanity – theologically the image of *ecce homo*. More than 25 years ago the Spanish moral theologian *Marciano Vidal* called the encounter with the poor and the oppressed the preferential *'locus ethicus'* (Vidal, 1982: 291-293) of Christian theology. *Nota bene*: "locus" means the place, not the origin. The poor and marginalized are not the origin of ethics but the preferential place, where we encounter the challenges of our time.

The first response to that experience is called "ethical indignation" (*indignación ética*). Indignation is the fitting answer in situations where we see that others are denied their dignity.

'Ethical indignation, recognition of the dignity of the victim, and recognition of his/her vulnerability … are the bases of the new conceptualization of the subject that has been developed by a recent theology of liberation. That is at the same time the basic condition for any effective action towards liberation.' (Gutiérrez, 2005: 6)

So the ethical indignation is not just passive observation, it is always linked to concrete fields of praxis: living out the preferential option for the poor in concrete action.

3.1.2 Recognition of the other as an experience of grace

Following the basic principles of *Emmanuel Lévinas* this new Latin American ethics of the subject focuses on the asymmetry in this intersubjective relationship. It is the other who is obliging me to act according to his/her needs. In the encounter with the other, face to face, we experience the "epiphany" of the subject. Theologically speaking, this epiphany is to be considered as an experience of grace:

'In an extreme case: if we encounter a woman who is either poor and/or black, lesbian, prostitute, suffering from AIDS, handicapped, ugly, old, and if we are able to perceive her as a human being with basic and inalienable dignity, that encounter is a spiritual experience of grace (in realizing the pure gratuity beyond all social convention) and of faith (in seeing what is concealed from the "eyes of this world").' (Mo Sung, 2005: 44).

Recognizing the other in this way is by no means a neutral experience, it is always partial, because we are responsible for the vulnerable other and we act according to this reality in opposing the annihilation of the other as subject and in supporting him/her to fully become the subject of his/her own life.

3.1.3 Step-by-step ethics

To do this rightly we have to avoid any form of paternalism:

'Solidarity realizes the dignity of the poor in asymmetric relationships, and rather than suppressing it seeks to promote this dignity by involving the poor as protagonists on the way to their own social and personal liberation.' (Yáñez, 2008: 18).

In that light it becomes clear that the ethics of life seeking a society where there is place for all cannot act according to a top-down model to set its goal into reality. That would only lead to a totalitarian system. The ethics of life is rather following a bottom-up concept similar to the one we know from Ignatian spirituality: we seek 'a society which is *more* just, *more* human, *more* brotherly …' (Mo Sung, 2005: 49) and we set it into motion step by step.

3.2 The role of the churches

Finally, one more crucial point to mention. The main agents of this ethics of life or ethics of the subject are not individuals but communities. This seems logical because the key issue is precisely that it is not the individual, but the person related to other persons that makes the ethical subject. More concretely, it is the "social movements" (NGOs, civil society, and also religious groups and churches) who are called upon to take up responsibility. *Enrique Dussel* calls them 'moments of a micro-structure of power' (Dussel, 2000, 525) that are able to put this ethics to praxis. Accordingly, I think this might be the call for Christians and churches to realize it. This might even be more acceptable to us when we understand that this concept is not following an ideology that should somehow be applied to reality. On the contrary it is a step-by-step process of looking for concrete solutions to concrete problems, following the basic idea that everybody should be able to participate in society and nobody should be excluded. It is, in other words, another model of being church, a model following the concept of civil society rather than a governmental role.

In that concept the first step would be to become fully aware of the victims of globalization, to perceive the ethical indignation and to speak up prophetically against unjust and fatal structures. But more than that we have to go on from ethical indignation to an option for life which means a preferential option for the poor and oppressed, the marginalized and the excluded. This option is not to be considered as just one possible option among others but an option for justice, and therefore, not just deliberately chosen but the fundamental and universal obligation of everyone, especially Christians (cf. Vigil, 2004).

For the churches this means to take up and live out the option for the poor not only by working *for* them but rather *with* them by truly including them into their communities and empowering them to become true subjects. For, as A. C. Grayling puts it, 'possession of the amenities of life – which includes not just objects like houses and motorcars, but also powers … – is equivalent to status, to full membership of the community, to having a place and a voice.' (Grayling, 2002: 142-143).

References and Bibliography

N.B.: All quotations from the following references have been freely translated from German and Spanish by the author.

Dussel, E. 2000: *Ética de la liberacion en la edad de la globalización y de la exclusión*, Barcelona: Editorial Trotta.

Gorostiaga, X. 1999: Is the Answer in the South? A Latin American View, in: Amaladoss, M. (ed.), *Globalization and its Victims. As Seen by the Victims*, Delhi: Vidyajyoti Education & Welfare Society, 77-102.

Grayling, A.C. 2002: *The Meaning of Things. Applying Philosophy to Life*, London: Phoenix.

Gutiérrez, G. 2005: Vulnerabilidad, corporalidad, sujeto y política popular, in: *Pasos* No. 121, 1-12.

Hayek, F. A. 1984: Die Ursprünge und Wirkungen unserer Moral: Ein Problem für die Wissenschaft, in: *Conturen* Vol. 5, No.15A/16A, 61-72.

Hinkelammert, F. J. 2007: *Das Subjekt und das Gesetz. Die Wiederkehr des verdrängten Subjekts*, Münster: Edition ITP-Kompass.

Hinkelammert, F. J. 2001: Globalisierung als verschleiernde Ideologie zur Verdrehung und Rechtfertigung der Missstände in der gegenwärtigen Wirklichkeit, in: *Conc(D)* Vol. 37, 549-559.

Hinkelammert, F. J. 2004: La vida es más que el capital. La deomcracia de ciudadanos y el proyecto de la sociadad en la que quepan todos los seres humanos, in: *Pasos* No. 113, 12-16.

Hogan, L. (ed.) 2008: *Applied Ethics in a World Church. The Padua Conference*, Maryknoll: Orbis.

Keenan, J. (ed.) 2007: *Catholic Theological Ethics in the World Church. The Plenary Papers from the First Cross-cultural Conference on Catholic Theological Ethics*, New York: Continuum.

Mo Sung, J. 2004: Exclusión social: Un tema teológico?, in: Duque Zúñiga, J. (ed.): *Perfiles teológicos para un nuevo milenio*, San José/C.R.: DEI, 89-113

Mo Sung, J. 2005: *Sujeto y sociedades complejas. Para repensar los horizontes utopicos*, San José/C.R.: DEI.

Richard, P. 2001: El grito del sujeto. Un aporte radical de Franz J. Hinkelammert a la Teología de la Liberación, in: Duque, J./Guiérrez, G. (eds.): *Itinerarios de la razon crítica. Homenaje a Franz Hinkelammert en sus 70 Años*, San José/C.R.: DEI, 315-327.

Stiglitz, J. 2006: *Die Chancen der Globalisierung*, München: Siedler.

Vidal García, M. 1982: La preferencia por el pobre, criterio de moral, in: *StudMor* Vol. 20, 277-305.

Vigil, J. M. 2004: La Opción por los Pobres es Opción por la Justicia, y No es Preferencial. Para un reencuadramiento teológico-sistemático de la OP, in: *Revista Latinoamericana de Teología* Vol. 63, 255-266.

Yáñez, H. M. 2008: Opting for the Poor in the Face of Growing Poverty, in: Hogan, L. (ed.): *Applied Ethics in a World Church. The Padua Conference*, Maryknoll: Orbis, 13-20.

THE PILGRAMIGE AS A WAY OF LIFE

Anton Jamnik, Ljubljana

Introduction

The modern way of life is governed by individualism and quest for agreeable life based on a certain measure of tolerance or justice. It is characterized by a limited and minimalist morality. The tradition considered the whole life as a Divine creation. Man's free will primarily consisted in discovering what God was expecting from him, the basis of his decision-making was the Divine indicative. Such views keep slowly disappearing together with a gradual break with the tradition and a growing emphasis on man as a rational, free and autonomous being with equal rights.

When making ethical decisions, the modern man is at a crossroads: should he lock himself in a world of liberalist self-sufficieny, arbitrariness and calculating pragmatism or should he search for his identity within a community, a system of values and a closeness to others and open himself to the Transcendent while experiencing the mystery of existence?

1. Ethical relativism

When speaking about the challenges of time problem of ethical relativism should be mentioned, which has a strong impact on modern culture, public opinion and the way of life of the modern man. The roots of ethical relativism lie in the growing radicalness of anthropocentrism being characteristic of modern thinking. The scientific intellect applying itself to external objective phenomena and based on a very narrow empiricist-analytical conception of science contains man's desire for emancipation. In contrast to external objective phenomena, the world of subjective morality is inaccessible to any kind of observation. This results in the world of moral principles and values being pushed into an area of arbitrary subjectivity. Thus, moral values cannot be a topic for discussion but are completely left up to the free choice of the individual.

Empirical-analytical science forming one of the bases of liberalism has abolished the normative role of moral values, which have become practically absent or a private matter of the individual. Man's existence dwindled to immanence where man himself (anthropocentrism) became the master of his history. No room exists in liberalism for transcendent and more than just historical norms and values.

It is a paradoxical and worrying fact that parallelly to asserting and distinguishing itself in the field of mathematics, natural sciences and technology, human mind has been feeling more and more powerless in the field of ethics. Whereas theoretical reason has been expanding to all areas of knowledge about the world, practical reason has been withdrawing from its own area of man's aims and values. The decisive theoretical move occurred quite imperceptibly and in a rather marginal region of Europe during the Scottish Enlightenment at the turn of the 17th century. Important names in this respect are Lord Shaftesbury and his pupil Francis Hutcheson, these ideas having been widely received via the works of David Hume.

This search for a source of morality that would be independent of reason was given a final form by David Hume, who emphasized that man's practical reason only worked on command of irrational, instinctive or interested endeavours. He went even further. He maintained that our reason was just a slave of our desires and instincts. According to his opinion the reason does not have any initial influence upon actions and is incapable of setting off or preventing any action or of judging different endeavours and irrational intentions. Thus, for Hume the reason remains a slave to passion, which is its permanent role, and sticks to it all the time. The basis of moral approval or disapproval cannot be found in any other kind of distinction or relation reason could comprehend. Morality cannot be based on rational understanding, it is a matter of feeling and not of judging.

This meant a complete break with Aristotelian and scholastic traditions conferring the decisive role in man's actions to his practical reason, to his »cleverness«. »... in accordance with Aristotle's views the reason is meant to lead and educate endeavours, whereas Hume understands reason as a servant of these endeavours.« This, however, had fatal consequences because it led to the acceptance of the momentous idea that man's actions do not come from his reason, but from completely extra-rational, spontaneous motives. And this could then lead to the conclusion that man cannot find any predetermined aims and values but sets them himself at will. There is simply no generally valid morality. Concerning the generally valid morality a universal doubt and scepticism prevailed, morality became a matter of individual choice and taste. This relativism trying to give a reliable judgement concerning the basic human intellectual wealth was opposed by the teaching of natural law. Yet this form of searching firm foundations was severely shaken by the loss of the rational basis. It is quite interesting that recently the interest in natural law has been revived because man has not been able any more to find his way in the »easy-going« pluralism and does not know what to lean his life upon.

Such a negation of values is very convenient for liberalism because it enables the individual to decide only impulsively and pragmatically and to keep adapting his decision-making to the situation. In relation to man, however, it is questionable and degrading in at least two points: according to such logic man is not a source of moral acts because liberalism denies any possibility of knowing or leaning on the basic values of existence; since just instinctive and interested decision-making would be dangerous for the man himself, liberalism produces certain agreed rules of procedure, which, however, lack any foundation as to contents and values. So man has to follow something that is a matter of agreement and not what is a matter of his inner convictions. This is an important degradation of human dignity because moral actions turn into fulfilling certain rules. The lack of a substantial view of man and the negation of values i.e. the contents of man's moral actions are a decadence of man himself and of mutual relations.

2. Individualism

The second characteristic determining the time and culture we live in is the problem of individualism and man's withdrawal into his shell. By emphasizing freedom often turning into abitrariness, by man's fateful withdrawal into self-sufficiency and individualism, whereby he shuts himself off from his neighbours as well as from God. When speaking about man and his relation to other persons, there are, broadly speaking, two characteristic views and traditions:

a) Man is is predominantly a being of relations and of community

Aristotle gave us the known definition of man as a »political animal«. By his nature man is a social being. Therefore he forms a family, several families join into a village and villages join into a *polis*, a state. In Aristotle's case this is a Greek city-state resembling more a larger municipality with a city in the middle and the countryside around it than a state in the modern sense of the word. Man is a social being by nature, which is expressed in the most basic form of human association, in the community of husband and wife, in the family. Yet this community cannot exist independently of others as it is not self-sufficient. Therefore families join together into villages and these join together into the *polis*. Since man's biological nature required family as the basic cell of association, this finally led to the state. This is the basic meaning of Aristotle's saying of *zoon politikon*.

This view of man accepting Aristotle's point of view about the social nature of man was also the prevailing one during the Middle Ages. This means that man's solidarity with others is so deep that the search for what is good for an individual cannot, as a rule, be in conflict with the search for what is good for the community. Man can only reach his aim together with others. Medieval philosophy and theology found enough support for this Aristotelian view of man as a social being in the Jewish-Christian biblical teaching. The biblical view of man contains the thought that it is not good that the man should be alone. His being the image of God requires of him to live together with others because God by creating man in his image created him male and female. Hence all Jewish and Christian religious truths particularly emphasize community and solidarity.

b) Modern individualism

At the beginning of the modern era man discarded these views. Thomas Hobbes was the first one to explicitly reject the Aristotelian-scholastic standpoint that man is a social being by nature. Instead, he maintained that man was an individual by nature. By nature i.e. in a natural, original, pre-civilisation state man is not a social being oriented towards others but an individual. His primary endeavour is self-preservation. Thus, man is devised as a special case of the physical law of inertia: he wants to preserve himself and has every right to do so. All people have this basic tendency. So it necessarily follows from the teaching of man as individual that man endeavouring to preserve himself collides with the same endeavours of others. This self-assertion is unlimited by nature. Therefore man constantly feels threatened by others.

Man's natural state is similar to that of an animal: without society, without common production and culture. Everyone lives in a constant fear for himself. Therefore man is interested in living at peace with his neighbours. Hence a kind of non-aggression pact and peace treaty comes into being. According to this contract citizens, freely and to their own benefit, give up their unlimited rights and assign them to the sovereign. He guarantees the compliance with the contract on mutual non-aggression, co-operation and peaceful co-existence.

The basic characteristic of Hobbes' view is that he understands liberty as itself requiring to be limited. Outside the state and its laws limiting the liberty, liberty turns against itself. This already suggests the modern liberal thought seeing liberty as the highest criterion of man's existence. And in connection therewith the theory of the social contract develops with T. Hobbes, Locke, Rousseau and Kant as its best-known representatives. The basic emphasis of this theory is that man as an individual is an absolute subject deciding about himself also when decisions are taken by a political authority. The latter decides about him since he himself wanted it, by his consent. This is also one of the key elements of the liberalist view of man and society emphasizing the importance of the freedom and autonomy of the individual.

The first and central question of liberalism is the fundamental emphasis on individualism and liberty. Certainly the modern emphasis on man as an individual also has positive consequences: the importance of the freedom of the individual, human rights etc. We live in a world where people have the right to choose their own life pattern, to decide to their best knowledge and belief which convictions to support, to define their way of life in a multitude of ways their ancestors could not control. But in liberalism such man is left to himself, separated from his neighbours and denying any possibility of transcendence of his existence because he wants to be autonomous.

In antiquity and in the Middle Ages men usually saw themselves as a part of a bigger order. In some cases this was cosmic order, a »great chain of existence« where they were discovering their position. This hierarchic order in the universe was reflected in the hierarchies of human society. Men lost this broader view because they were predominantly concentrating upon themselves. With other words, the dark side of individualism is a concentration upon oneself which makes man's life more shallow and narrow, impoverishes its meaning and takes away his interest in others or in society.

It is a consequence thereof that today we speak of the »permissive society«, of the phenomenon of the »ego-generation« or of the preponderance of »narcissism« to mention just the best-known phenomena expressing individualism.

It is interesting that also Pope John Paul II drew attention to the problem of ethical relativism and individualism when paying his first visit to Slovenia:

»Your people go through a period of radical changes. While trying to gradually free themselves from the negative consequences of totalitarian ideology by which they were strongly marked in the past, they also try with all their strength to shape a more fraternal and democratic society. Special attention must be paid to these happenings. This is the only way to prevent that the space emptied by the former ideology will be taken by some other, no less dangerous one: the ideology of UNSCRUPULOUS LIBERALISM. You now live in a period of transition and your word accompanied by your example is of vital necessity like Moses' leadership was once« (John Paul II 1996).

And when speaking to representatives of culture, science and art in Maribor, the pope drew attention to the decisive crossroads at which the modern man stands:

»This hour is thus an hour of truth for Europe. Walls have fallen, so have iron curtains, and the question about the meaning of life and the value of FREEDOM arises in human consciousness stronger than ever before. How could one fail to see that the core of this problem is the question about God? Does man understand himself as a being created by God and given a FREEDOM OPENING A WORLD OF ENDLESS POSSIBILITIES before him and at the same time giving him precisely defined duties or does he elevate himself TO AN ABSOLUTE LEVEL, WITH FREEDOM WITHOUT LAW that exposes him to different impulses and shuts him into self-indulgence and self-love« (John Paul II 1996b).

In the continuation the pope explained what man's elevating himself to an absolute level and deciding on freedom without law may lead to:

»It is well-known how the fall of ideologies affected a certain lay humanism that has been prevailing on the cultural scene for a long time. Nowadays man's main temptation does not lie in trying to base everything on his reason, but in GIVING UP THE SEARCH FOR ANY FOUNDATIONS AT ALL and abandoning himself to dangerous currents of scepticism« (John Paul II 1996b).

3. Metaphors of nomad, vagabond and tourist as symbols of a modern seeker

The search of modern man in the fields of religion and ethics (as well as in other areas) could be illustrated by metaphors describing man as a nomad, vagabond and tourist. Modern man likes to compare himself to a nomad. This comparison shows an interesting similarity to the pilgrim. Is this a transition from the modern pilgrim to the post-modern nomad? Nomads are constantly on the move. They move within well-orderdered structures having a long tradition and an established order. If nomads are compared with pilgrims, one can say that the nomads' journey has neither a final aim nor special places where they could rest during their journey. Neverthless, they move from one place to another in a certain order. The metaphor of nomadic way of life very aptly characterizes the post-modern man.

A more radical metaphor is the one of a vagabond. The vagabond does not know how long he will stay where he is. There is no rule when and how he will decide to move on. His journey is very indefinite and unforeseeable. The vagabond moves because he has been disappointed at a certain point and he believes that the next place he visits will be without mistakes and failures he has experienced at the places where he has already been. An undefined kind of hope makes him move on ... One could say that a vagabond is a pilgrim without aim and a nomad without plan. The vagabond travels through an unstructured space like someone wandering in the desert who only knows the track made by his own feet, which get filled up by sand as soon as he travels on. The vagabond uses a structure (trail) only to destroy and leave it again. He sees each following place just as a local and momentary adventure.

A further metaphor characterizing the post-modern man is the one of a tourist. Probably only both metaphors together, the one of the tourist and the one of the vagabond, give a good characterization of the post-modern man. The vagabond and the tourist know well that they will not stay long in the place where they have arrived. The tourist accepts certain limitations, he must pay for his freedom. The freedom is based on an agreement that has its price. The tourist is extraterritorial as the vagabond is, but his extraterritorial life is a privilege. Independence, the right to be free and have the freedom of choice, he has the licence to restructure the world. The world waits just for the tourist, everything is made so as to move him and to fill him with enthusiasm, from restaurants and important monuments up to religion and ethics. It is meant to catch his attention, but the tourist also has to pay for it. The world is a kind of a tourist oyster. It is intended to give pleasure and this also gives it its meaning.

Another feature is common to the vagabond and the tourist. Both wander through a space where other people live. These people are determined by their space and work, but neither the vagabond nor the tourist are interested in the results of their work. They only briefly and superficially encounter the local space and the concrete situation. Physically close and spiritually distant is the formula used by both the tourist and the vagabond. The attractive charm of such kind of life lies in the solemn promise that physical proximity will not turn into a moral one. When the tourist is in question, this is very clear because he has guarantees in this respect. The freedom from moral duty was prepaid (certain agreements, limitation, obligations aceppted with the aim to guarantee one's own security). Neither the vagabond nor the tourist are prepared to accept any moral responsibility in their lives. They see it as something troublesome and annoying, which would spoil their fictitious happiness. The tourist is full of numbers, everything is measured, the mutual obligations are defined, everything it depersonalized. »This is what everybody does« becomes also a criterion of my actions.

In the post-modern world the vagabond and the tourist are not just some marginal figures or just a marginal phenomenon. They become a model that growingly encompasses and shapes the whole life and represent a basis of everyday activity and also of reviewing this activity. And this way of life is ideal for marketing and the media. Tourism is not just something taking place in the holiday period. If the normal life is to be pleasant and good, it should become a never-ending vacation. From an ideal point of view, one can be a tourist anywhere and at any time. Physically close and spiritually far. Completely free, all exemptions from contractual duties have been prepaid. All these contracts give the tourist a sufficiently strong sleeping drug to put his moral conscience to sleep.

Thus, the post-modern society is becoming fragmentary and individualistic and the social security is diminishing. From a philosophic point of view thist means a decline of the large systems and the metaphors of the tourist and the vagabond give a good illustration of the uncertainty of the individual and of the search for momentary satisfactions. The basic difficulty is how a spiritually empty man educated in passivity and indifference could tread a demanding path requiring a strong and responsible personality. This transition contains the crisis of the modern man, the difficulties, but also a hope for the future.

4. To become a pilgrim

Will this post-modern nomad, often also a vagabond and a calculating tourist, have enough strength and courage to tread a more demanding path, to accept responsibility, to accept himself as a gift and the environment in which he live as a possibility of realizing his vocation, his freedom and his uniqueness? Will he be prepared to tread a path of risk and hope that is not based on »to have« but on »to be«, on pure generosity and gratuity of existence?

Will he be prepared to make a step further and stop being a nomad and a vagabond in order to become a PILGRIM? The pilgrim receives the strength for his risks and hope as an attitude of life just from his vocation where the aim of his way already starts to show. »Sometime somebody stands up and goes because some church is out there in the east«, says Rilke in one of his poems speaking about Russia. Thus, to be a pilgrim means to keep standing up, beginning, transcending everyday life and setting on a journey with a clear aim. To be a pilgrim means that one keeps leaving everyday life for a sacred place, where the heaven is open in a special manner, where God's closeness whispers to man in a new manner. To be a pilgrim is a life decision, it means to believe and to hope into the aim of the way changing already the present moment of my existence; to be a pilgrim means to hope together with others, to meet other people as gifts and signs, it means to enjoy our existence and the world we live in and to be simultaneously also aware of the fragility characterizing everything in this world. The pilgrim is grateful for everything he receives while travelling, for the gifts and crosses he encounters, but his hope finds strength in the aim of the way, in the gift of redemption, of a fully harmonious existence. The pilgrim is open for the unexpected, he knows that his God is a God of surprises who can do much more than man think and hope. This gives him the strength to keep setting on the journey, to risk, to hope against hope, to have tthe courage to despair of the illusions and lies behind which he had felt safe at a certain moment.

References and Bibliography

Brown, A. 1990: *Modern Political Philosophy*, London, Penguin Books.

Freeman, S.1994: 'Utilitarianism, Deontology, and the Priority of Right', *Philosophy & Public Affairs* 23, 313-349.

Hubin, D.C. 1979: 'The Scope of Justice', *Philosophy & Public Affairs* 9, 3-24.

Hudson, W.D. 1983: *Modern Moral Philosophy,* London, Macmillan.

John Paul II 1996a Speech in the cathedral of Ljubljana, May 17 1996. In: Janez Pavel II. *Govori v Sloveniji*, Cerkveni dokumenti 64, Ljubljana, Družina.

John Paul II 1996b Address to representatives of culture, science and art in Maribor on May 19 1996. In: Janez Pavel II., *Govori v Sloveniji*, Cerkveni dokumenti 64, Ljubljana, Družina.

Larmore, C. 1996: *The Morals of Modernity*, Cambridge, Cambridge University Press.

Lyons, D. 1989: 'Nature and Soundness of the Contract and Coherence Arguments', *Reading Rawls,* Stanford, California, Stanford University Press, 141-168.

MacIntyre, A. 1981: *After Virtue: a study in moral theory,* London, Duckworth.

McClennen, E.F. 1989: 'Justice and the Problem of Stability', *Philosophy & Public Affairs* 18, 9-15.

Macpherson, C.B. 1962: *The Political Theory of Possesive Individualism*, Oxford & New York, Oxford University Press.

Murdoch, I. 1970: *The Sovereignty of Good,* London & New York, Routledge.

Parfit, D. 1984: *Reasons and Persons*, Oxford, Oxford University Press.

Rawls, J. 1971: *Theory of Justice,* Cambridge, Ma, Harvard University Press.

Scanlon, T.M. 1989: 'Rawl's Theory of Justice', *Reading Rawls,* Stanford, California, Stanford University Press, 169-205.

Taylor, C. 1989: *Sources of the Self, The Making of the Modern Identity*, Cambridge, Cambridge University Press.
Tillich, P. 1960: *Love, Power and Justice – Ontological analyses and ethical applications*, London-Oxford-New York, Oxford University Press.

POSTMODERN HUMAN IN THE PRIME OF LIFE; LIVING WITH OR WITHOUT VIRTUES

Mateja Pevec Rozman, Ljubljana

In this moment of history, in this postmodern moment of our civilisation, we all are artists of life, whether we know it or not. In postmodern individualized society we find out that different lifestyles are popular and acceptable. The following essay consists of three parts: At first, we shall see a short outline of some characteristics of postmodern times, some of those outstanding characteristics, which denote us and our life. In the second part we shall try to find out what kind of lifestyle is more flourishing; is there something that can give us a hand to make our life more fruitful and make us the unique artists of life. In the third part, we shall try to find out if life according to virtues for the human in the prime of life of this postmodern times is still reasonable and what kind of life is worth living (what good life is). We shall see some ideas of the topics from the perspective of some Slovenian philosophers.

The main characteristics of contemporary time

Modern thinkers define time or culture in which we live as the time of postmodernism and the culture of postmodernism. It is a sort of culture shift, which is in many aspects indeterminate, indefinite. However, its characteristics can be joined in few points: individualism, relativism and plurality.

1. Individualism (as a postmodern lifestyle)

Individualism advocates the standpoint that everyone has the right to develop their own forms of expression and their specific styles of life. The decision for choice is not the result of rational reflection (intellectual decision) but momentary feelings, personal inspirations and desires. In this sense an individual appears as a value; or is a value »self-actualization« of an individual. An individual is nowadays liable to himself and to what realizes his self-fulfilment. Postmodern individual is independent, liable only to himself and to what realizes his »peculiarity«. Individualism stimulate heterogeneity as opposed to average, originality and innovation as opposed to uniformity; individualism is also the achievement of contemporary civilization; people have the right to choose their way of life, religion, political beliefs and other beliefs.

However, Ch. Taylor in his work *The Malaise of Modernity* warns us of a trap: the dark side of individualism is in the excessive focus on oneself. Consequently, that makes life narrower and poor (Taylor 2000, 8-9). If an individual focuses only on himself, he does not see anything else beside himself. Contemporary individual is not interested in issues about society, political issues, issues about common good of wider society. Those things lead to even greater alienation, passivity, indifference.

Slovenian philosopher Janez Juhant establishes that the postmodern human is eager to solve his own problems, yet he is not prepared to share his own life and participate in the community. This is the one of the greatest problems of postmodern society (Juhant 2007, 34). Individualism on one hand liberates, unbinds us from narrow-mindness and determination, and on the other hand raises feelings of being lost and uncertainty.

2. Relativism as a consequence of individualism

Relativism appears as the next characteristic of contemporary postmodern time. The standpoint of relativism is that every knowledge and value is relative: everything depends on the relationship between a subject that is being recognized and an object that is recognized by the subject. Relativism argues that ethical standpoints are right or wrong in relationship to these or those standards. There is nothing that is right or wrong itself (unconditional – simpliciter). In postmodern society there are norms, such as truth, kindness and beauty understood as a result of some process and they depend on it, thus they are immanent to it. That means that no universal values exist, that there is no absolute truth, which could serve as an examination for everything else. Values as such do not exist. They are domain of interpretation of certain place and time. We could say also that we live in the time of equalizing criteria.

If we want to define relativism more precisely, we could say that it is all about the "extinction of human desire" to find the truth. The extinction is nowadays general phenomenon, which is present in all fields (Senegačnik 1998, 14-15). Under the influence of relativistic patterns of thinking and evaluating the fundamental shifts on the level of human sense have occurred. Human identity has been shaken and even started to melt.

3. Pluralism – the companion of relativism

Pluralism, in short, is opened to several different concepts of good; everything is equally »right«. The characteristic of modern societies is that common and universal values are not given beforehand and are not structurally anchored. It is possible that at the same time plenty orders of values exist. Coexistence of different orders of values and fragments of order of values in the same society is a great basis for development of the condition, which we call pluralism (Berger and Luckmann 1999, 24-27). When it develops to the superior value, it soon becomes the excuse for inconsistence, indefinitions and avoidances. There is no need to search for common universal values, no one truthfulness, which would be identical for all.

Such conditions stimulate the expansion of subjective and inter-subjective crises. However, vaguely formed values of contemporary pluralism have also some useful effects. For example, they stimulate peaceful coexistence of different life forms and orders of values (Berger and Luckmann 1999, 29). One of principal characteristics of postmodernism is in acknowledgement of legitimacy of particular parts and denial of possible existence of the integrity. As opposed to the totality is in postmodernism set pluralism. Plurality becomes also the basis of an individual. A person is not a simple unit, hierarchically formed and self-controlled, but he is a variety of impacts, powers and different elements.

How to be a successful artist of life?

How should we live in such world or how can we be the artists of life in such cultural conditions? We are artists of life in this "postmodern" cultural moment whether we like it or not. In our liquid modern society as Zygmunt Bauman describes contemporaneity, we are all expected to give our lives a purpose and form it by using our own skills and resources. According to effort we invest and results we are able to achieve, we are more or less successful "artists" of life. Our postmodern society of consumers, influences the way we construct and narrate our lifestyle. So how should we live, how to be the best artists of life? Solutions by different philosophies are offered. I think that virtue ethics in connection with the ethics of responsibility could suitably answer to the question.

The key topic of virtue ethics is searching for a concept of correct managing and justifying behaviour principles. The virtue is a disposition or a kind of inclination to acting correctly. Aristotle in his *Nicomachean Ethics*, where he gives an excellent discussion of the virtue, issues a warning at an early time that

»discussion should not be theoretical...because we are not discussing something to establish what the virtue is but to become good... which is why we have to pay all our attention to actions, especially focusing on how actions should be carried out« (Aristotle 1103b, 77). Aristotle gives a clear answer: actions have to be delivered in line with common sense. We have to act as a wise man would act. That is in accordance with the intellect, which is right. The more we practices the virtue the more likely it is that our deeds will be virtuous and right. Aristotle believes that the polis is the one and only political form where human life virtues can be fully expressed. McCabe says that polis is actually the reason for the existence of rational animals and the purpose of polis is that those animals succeed and live the life, which is suitable for them, or in other words, to live simply fully live in polis (McCabe 2008, 50). Polis thus needs virtuous people and it is at the same time the instrument, which enables people to become virtuous.

Searching for the good (life)

Every single activity and exploration strives to achieve something good, whereas good or something good is what is characteristic of human beings to strive for. What is specific in the human nature is that man is always inclined to a certain *telos* (goal). Aristotle sets forth to show good, which is at the same time local and special and cosmic and universal. He believes that the highest goal that the entire human will and all his actions are directed to, the supreme good, that man can achieve in his actions is *eudaimonia* (happiness, prosperity). In fact happiness is a kind of reasonable participation, which is in accordance with the perfect value and lasts throughout one's lifetime. Happy life is considered only the life led in accordance with the virtue. And virtues are the very distinctions that will help a person to achieve *eudaimonia*.

Why, anyway, it is so important to be the best artist of life than one can? Because we believe that the art of life has its purpose. And the purpose of the art of life should be and can be happiness. Every human being is longing for happiness and for good life. Alasdair MacIntyre is convinced that the only criterion for being successful or not being successful in the whole human life is in searching for good. The man is »presented« with human nature but at the same time is invited to fulfil this nature by his activity. In this part realization of human essence is comprehended as good.[1]. MacIntyre says that »...*the virtues therefore are to be understood as those dispositions which will not only sustain practises and enable us to achieve the goods internal to practises, but which will also sustain us in the relevant kind of quest for the good, by enabling us to overcome the harms, dangers, temptations and distractions which we encounter, and which will furnish us with increasing self-knowledge and increasing knowledge of the good"...* MacIntyre describe a provisional conclusion about the good life for man: *the good life for man is the life spent in seeking for the good life for men, and the virtues necessary for the seeking are those which will enable us to understand what more and what else the good life for man is* (MacIntyre 1985, 219).

Good life includes membership of community

However, MacIntyre warns that striving for good and *practising* virtues an individual himself cannot achieve (MacIntyre, 220). Individuals live in different social circumstances as well as within the same time frames or social frames, in which we are the carriers of certain social identity. An individual is always determined: he is a resident of certain town, member of certain community, has political or religious beliefs, is a member of certain tribe or nation. As such he is the carrier of inheritance of his family, tribe or nation and also the heir of debts and obligations, law and duties. Everything that was given to him and he could not choose composes his moral starting point (or background) and gives his life some ethical speciality.

MacIntyre is aware that such comprehension is opposed to the standpoints of modern individualism. Individualism argues in favour of the definition that I am what I choose to be. However, tearing self from the context or from certain history story does not lead to good life. The consequences can be terrible if an individual is faithful only to his nature and originality and ignores his history as well as others. Frequently happens that an individual devotes his attention only to himself and does not care for the external laws. This does not lead him to good life but decreases the quality of life of an individual. It leads him to even greater

1 Aristoteles define good as a goal (purpose, gr. telos) to which everything is oriented (Klun 1997, 24).

remoteness from other as well as from himself, even to the loss of himself or even to the loss of sense of living.

We can say that art of life includes tradition and personal history. MacIntyre claims that the story of life of an individual is always *woven* into the stories of other people and communities, on which we build our identity. An individual is born within history, every attempt to separate ourselves form history as individualism attempts to do, means deformation of present relationships. The possession of historical identity and social identity is supplementary. MacIntyre emphasises that "self" has to search for its ethical identity through the membership of communities such as family, neighbourhoods, towns, tribes, thus in some tradition. In modern individualism there is no space for tradition because it limits individual in his self-actualization (history becomes the burden if we do not clarify things, which means to clarify things with ourselves) (Pevec Rozman 2009, 94). Searching for good expands from generation to generation within certain tradition. Therefore also the history of our life is a part of the broader and longer history, greater number of traditions, and is understood only in the relationship to the set of those realities.

It is the fact that through history civilizations have been decaying, changing and some disappearing. What sustains and strengthens traditions that do not decay? What weakens them and what ruins them? MacIntyre offers the clear answer: performing or not performing relevant virtues. According to MacIntyre, the sense and purpose of virtues is that virtues support those relationships, which are necessary for achieving various *forms* of good in individual practices.[2]

Personal satisfaction and good life

The art of life is to live according to the personally satisfying and morally acceptable ideal of personal excellence. It is obvious that the successful practise of the art of life depends on goal-directed activities (Kekes 2002, 158). Kekes claims that there are two sources of personal satisfaction in one's life (Kekes 2002, Žalec 2005, 74-75). The first involves aiming at a reasonable ideal and having good

2 1. Virtues support the form of individual life, in which an individual can find his good and good of his entire life; and 2. virtues support those traditions, which form necessary historical context of all practices of every individual life (MacIntyre, 223).

reasons to believe that one has done tolerably well in approximating it. The ideal is to become the one who exemplifies some particular personal excellence such as altruism, creativity, justice, purity, sensitivity, wholeheartedness, wisdom etc. The possession of the personal excellence is shown by how the activities are performed and not by what those activities are or by state of mind that leads on to be engaged in them.

Another source of personal satisfaction has to do with one's projects. Bojan Žalec claims that good life includes personal projects, which can be athletic, scientific, etc. People consider good life differently and want to live in accordance with it. There are always internal[3] and external[4] barriers on this way (Žalec 2005, 27). In order to be able to handle the external barriers and to remove internal barriers we need to transform our character. Therefore we have to develop traditional moral virtues and personal excellences. Thus, the character transformation has to do with cultivation of values and personal excellences. Personal excellences are the characteristics of character, constant tendencies to live and to act in certain ways. Moderateness, courage and fairness are the virtues that were within the traditional comprehension understood as necessary for all sensible comprehension of good life (Žalec 2005, 27-28).

Žalec claims that to live good life means also to accept sensible decisions about which alternative to take for oneself. Therefore the art of life is necessary in order to make right decision and to perform our decision successfully.

For making the right decisions, it is vital to know the motive of our acting. We have to be aware why we act precisely the way we do; we have to see the background of our acting. McCabe says that we also have to reconcile ourselves with the fact that we can always make a false step or we are uncertain. If we know ethics (moral principles), we are more successful at avoiding mistakes and indistinctness. This means that moral principles are never solid and we have to find out what is progress in our comprehension and what is decline (McCabe 2008, 17).

At this point we can see that even in this postmodern moment we cannot deny the importance of moral philosophy. Moral philosophy is the examination of the most important of all human activities. Ethics should be a hypothesis about good

3 One's own deficiencies, their opposite actions and bad judgements.

4 Accident, poverty, lack of stimulation, sickness, injustice etc..

conduct and about how it can be achieved (Murdoch 2006, 91-92). We realise that lives of personal excellence are good not only because they are satisfying but also because they are morally acceptable.

The art of life is making of the good life for oneself

Why is this an art, should we ask. It is an art because it requires individuals to make a creative effort that no one can make for other (Kekes 2002, xi). For a good life has to be constructed out of one's character, circumstances, experiences, and ideals which vary from individual to individual, tradition and society, times and places. An essential element of this art involves reflecting on admirable lives and adapting the ideals they represent to one's personal context. For art of life it is important to be personally engaged and devoted to our life task(s).

The art of life is to live good and fruitful life. If we live in accordance with virtues, in accordance with ourselves, if we do the best we can, our life can be good and happy. The art of life is also the ability to live in the present moment; we can make the best of our lives if we are active agents. We should not just wait for what life can bring to us but what can we make and get from life.

We could claim that the art of life is also in man's ability to exceed himself. Likewise, Anton Stres claims that sensible existence is not in self-realization but in exceeding oneself (Stres 1994, 317). Virtues can assist us at achieving this. The art of life includes also others: the fullness of human existence is realised in a dialogic relationship. Man is open for real values, for truth and for love, only when he withdraws from the centre with the intention to admit the other, values, truth, and to cede them the place they merit (Petkovšek 2007, 125, 136). Edvard Kovač says that the "other" is the one who enable me to resign out of "myself". This is possible under condition of my ethical ability to listen to the other and to see his distress and to respond to this call (Kovač 1998, 13).

It is clear that harmonious co-existence in certain (every) community is possible only if it consists of the individuals, which are aware of their responsibility to each other and try to live in accordance with virtues. Living (with) according to virtues is still or even more reasonable in this postmodern moment because without sharing some common virtues harmonious life in no human society is possible.

References and Bibliography

Aristoteles. 1994. *Nikomahova etika*. Ljubljana: Slovenska matica.

Berger, Peter L., & Thomas Luckmann. 1999. *Modernost, pluralizem in kriza smisla; Orientacija modernega človeka*. Ljubljana: Nova revija, Zbirka Paradigme.

Juhant, Janez. 2003. *Človek v iskanju svoje podobe: Filozofska antropologija*. Ljubljana: Študentska založba, Claritas.

Juhant, Janez. 2007. Anthropological Foundation of Dialogue. In: Peter Hünermann, Janez Juhant, Bojan Žalec eds. *Dialogue and Virtue; Ways to Overcome Clashes of Our Civilizations*. 33-47. Műnster: Lit Verlag.

Kekes, John. 2002. *The Art of Life*. New York: Cornell University Press.

Klun, Branko. Etična misel pri Aristotelu, Kantu in Levinasu; Poskus primerjave. In: *Filozofija na maturi* 1/97: 23-31.

Kovač, Edvard. 1998. Vznemirjujoča neskončnost. In: *Etika in neskončno,* 7-19. Ljubljana: Zbirka Tretji dan.

MacIntyre, Alasdair. 1985. *After Virtue; A study in Moral Theory*. London: Duckworth.

McCabe, Herbert. 2008. *Dobro življenje: Etika in iskanje sreče*. Ljubljana: Študentska založba, Claritas.

Murdoch, Iris. 2006. *Suverenost dobrega* (The Sovereignty of Good). Ljubljana: Študentska založba, Claritas.

Pevec Rozman, Mateja. 2009. *Etika in sodobna družba*. Ljubljana: Nova revija.

Petkovšek, Robert. 2007. Dialogical Being: Religion, Philosophy, Culture. In: Peter Hűnermann, Janez Juhant, Bojan Žalec eds. *Dialogue and Virtue; Ways to Overcome Clashes of Our Civilizations*. 121-139. Műnster: Lit Verlag.

Senegačnik, Brane. 1998. *V iskanju izgubljene mere*. Ljubljana: ŠOU, Študentska založba.

Stres, Anton. 1994. *Človek in njegov Bog*. Celje: Mohorjeva družba.

Taylor, Charles. 2000. *Nelagodna sodobnost*. Ljubljana: Študentska založba, Claritas.

Žalec, Bojan. 2005. *Doseganje dobrega*. Ljubljana: Študentska založba, Claritas.

WHOSE LIFE IS THIS? ART OF HEALING TRAUMA AND SEARCH FOR DISOWNED SELF IN RELATIONSHIPS

Tomaž Erzar & Katarina K. Erzar, Ljubljana

The antique concept of philosophy as love of wisdom presupposes a nurture of the art of life (*téchne tonb íon, ars vitae*). For Greek thinkers philosophy was not only an interpretation of texts or an exercise in dialogue, but also a spiritual training that guided one's inner development. The knowledge of oneself, the ultimate goal of Greek philosophy, is a fundamentally practical, social and experiential acquisition. Here we must place a caveat: Greeks did not ask the question how to unite thinking and living that bothered modern times. They rather asked the question of how to guide one's life and gave an answer to this question in the figure of Socrates. So when the idea of bridging theory and praxis reached its climax in the work of Marx and Engels, the idea did not imply any more a goal of leading or changing one's life, but the goal of transforming society, leaving the personality of those who transform society out of focus. Either in the ancient or modern form, the notion that philosophizing needs a spiritual or practical complement in order to obtain credibility points to a danger: the risk that thinking, speculating or dialoguing may easily turn into a manipulative and ineffective exercise. In fact, that was the accusation raised by the Sophists and citizens of Athens against Socrates and his way of living (Erzar, 2006). From that time on humanity attempts in vain to answer the enigma posed by Socrates' death: Did his death silence the Sophists'critical voices?

Today the question of the art of living takes a new form. Philosophers appear to have given up the battle to demonstrate the validity and relevance of their profession in the eyes of public. Instead of opening up to objections, thinkers of today seem to protect themselves by a sort of postmodern disdain for empirical facts and demands of practical life. Price for this attitude is an ever growing irrelevance of philosophy to society and an ever growing isolation of philosophers. The idea of art of life sounds today more as an appeal to lead life as an aesthetic creation, as an artifact set up for admiration or as a process which absorbs its own creator and leaves nothing behind or outside. This idea brings with it a solitary, uprooted and individualistic vision of human existence, in which people are supposed to pull themselves by hair out of the mud of life. This vision prevails in many twentieth century trends in thought like psychoanalysis, structuralism, and heideggerianism (Juhant, 2005).

In opposition to this vision, religious thinkers and ethically oriented philosophers of all times stressed the importance of living for others. If one leads life according to this ethical injunction, his life will not be lost, they claim, but gained and given its full meaning. In this perspective the art of life consists in living a life of interpersonal and moral excellence. Whereas this vision may have filled the gaps left by Greek philosophy, it opened new questions regarding the way in which this selfless or sacrificial living should be led. Despite the obligatory form in which it is announced, life for others should not be felt as a burden or a sacrificial martyrdom imbued with self-reproaches. By this change of focus on personality, the traditional philosophical and ethical themes became the object of psychological and psychoanalytic interest.

Today the theory of attachment developed by British psychoanalyst John Bowlby (1907-1990) is a dominant approach to understanding early social development and intimate relationships. Bowlby postulated that human beings do not seek satisfaction of innate drives, but proximity to figures who offer a child care, emotional contact and attunement. In this article we follow the path of attachment theory and propose that the question of art of living today cannot be tackled relevantly without considering the quality of interpersonal relationships and emotional attunement.

Experiencing adult life through the eyes of a child

The study of the effects of childhood traumas on adult lives of victims revealed that the traumatized person continues to be acutely sensitized to any subsequent experience that could be interpreted or felt as an actual or impending repetition of the original trauma (Stolorow, 2007). In a more radical way, retraumatization could be said to occur whenever there is a loss of an emotional bond that could have been a source of alternative ways of organizing experience, without which the learned reactions and defensive behavior are pulled back into the fore. This especially holds for childhood traumas that may imprison people in long term abusive relationships where insecure attachment patterns inhibit their personal growth and development of potentials (Van der Kolk & Fisler, 1994). Despite obvious functionality of their professional, social, and even familial life, emotional life of these people is characterized by re-experiencing feelings of emptiness, abandonment, betrayal, helplessness, despair, and rejection. These feelings gain their prevailing influence due to the fact that once they fully determined child's experience of self and others and that at that time they were perceived by the child as overwhelming, uncontrollable, frightening, incomprehensible and unpredictable. To these feelings the child reacts with anxiety, intense fear and arousal, dread, despair and detachment, and later learns to avoid them. Either felt or avoided, these feelings and reactions associated with them continue to govern his emotional life and patterns of building intimacy.

In his writing Bowlby insisted that infants' internal life is not determined by fantasy and biological needs, but rather by real life events and emotional experiences with the caregivers. Since he laid emphasis on actual experiences, he opened door to a renewed interest in traumatic childhood experience and actual familial situation. Thus he explained child's phobic behavior in Freud's classical case of Little Hans as provoked by actual threats by his mother to desert the family (Bowlby, 1973). The child's fear of being bitten by a horse was shown by Bowlby to be closely linked to the idea of departure. In fact, Hans feared that if he left the house, on his return he would not find his parents at home because they would have gone away. Reinterpreted in this light, the case of Little Hans clearly shows how traumatic experiences are absorbed by the child and expressed in dysfunctional behavior.

In general, children react to new experiences according to how people to whom they were attached reacted to them. If child's parents treated him in a consistent, predictable and affectionate manner, it is most probable that the child's relationship experiences will be organized around secure bonding. On the other hand, if parents either acted as a source of traumatic experience or failed to protect the child against such experience, the child may end up not only harboring doubts about the actuality of this experience and the validity of his emotional experience in general, but also about the possibility of stopping and making sense of the abuse that befell him. Once internalized, such doubts (about oneself and one's own emotional experience) may undermine permanently the capacity to seek help and reorganize past and present experience.

Intergenerational transmission of traumatic experience

It is believed today that trauma is remembered and re-experienced on four different, mutually unintegrated and unrelated, levels: through bodily sensations, conscious recall, representation of self and others, and regulation of affect. While the traditional conception of trauma, still reflected in the DSM-IV definition, defines trauma as an intrusion through defenses into individual psyche or a shattering of one's experiential world, modern conceptions underline the interpersonal context of traumatic experience, defining trauma as an interpersonal disruption and dysregulation of affects of fear, violence and horror. Defining trauma through interpersonal context, regulation of affect and the processes of representation has the advantage of better explaining the prevailing force of retraumatization in adult life of victims and the intergenerational transmission of traumatization. Indeed, if it is true that trauma reinforces and brings to the fore some deep seated attachment and representational processes, the healing of trauma will require much more than just putting together pieces of experience. It will require a long-term commitment to secure attachment relationships in which all the insecure aspects of past experience will be given a new regulation.

Ironically or happily, nature has provided its own way of healing trauma, exactly in the way described above: the parenting. Bowlby clearly demonstrated how parents' insecure attachment style can result in a propensity to unconsciously triangulate their children into helping them manage their own attachment problems (1969). This was the situation he identified as 'reversed attachment'. While it serves to establish secure bonding for the parents, reversed attachment deeply hampers children's development as autonomous beings and predisposes them towards yet another type of insecure attachment, avoidant attachment style. It also deeply affects child's representation of himself or herself, because the child's self-image is likely to develop in ways that justify parents' behaviour. The child will come to feel that she or he deserves what she gets from her parents, and that she provokes their reactions (Pietromonaco & Feldman Barrett, 2000). Moreover, she may come to learn that her security in the relationship depends on this particular way of being in the relationship, and any information that contradicts this learned belief will be discounted.

Expelling negative content from conscious awareness thus goes hand in hand with its distortion or alteration, which serves the purpose of maintaining contact with the attachment figure (Crittenden, 1999). From a different perspective, although not from a different tradition, this point was approached by Robert Firestone with the concept of fantasy bond (1985, 2000) which explains how the child, in order to preserve the contact with her parents, tries to fulfill their unconscious needs, thereby sacrifying her own need and desires. Firestone claims that the motivation for the child to establish a fantasy bond with the parents does not arise solely from developmental needs neither solely from the need to ease the pain caused by this relationship, but also from the need to maintain an ideal image of the parents and an image of herself as a worthy and thankful child. It is the child's deepest interest and longing to be able to provide a solution for the way her parents feel about themselves and to help them repair the negative self-image they have about themselves as parents. Fantasy bonding could thus be seen as a perpetuating force of false connectedness and avoidant attachment.

The idea of transgenerational transmission of traumatic affective states has also been confirmed by research. The research by Hesse and Main (1999) demonstrated the existence of unsecure attachment in the generation of children whose parents exhibited no direct maltreating behaviors, but suffered from unresolved traumas and losses. The authors stress that the secondary traumatization is transmitted to children not only through direct behavioral enactment, but through the indirect, subtle behavioral and affective cues that pass unnoticed. They also remark that such behaviors are difficult to recognize and classify because they are often fleeting and momentary, but clearly revealed in linguistic slippages in parental narratives about their own childhood. This finding was somehow prefigured already by Firestone who claimed that by means of fantasy bonding the child not only takes care of her own traumatic experiences, but also of parental traumatic experiences, because they offer the safest and the deepest contact with the parents.

Living one's own life

Given the central motivational importance of affective experience as it develops relationally within child-caregiver system, one grasps how parenthood can act as a selfregulative and selfhealing outlet for the traumatizing affects and how these affects are internalized by the child in an effort to establish a bond with the parents (George and Solomon, 1999). Through these efforts, the child disconnects from his own feelings and needs in hope to connect with the parental side of her parents, but actually succeeds to connect with their childish side. It is therefore not unwarranted to say that, by becoming the caregivers of their own parents, children of traumatized parents live through the lives of their parents as children.

Many children of Holocaust survivors later in their adult lives described how their parents, while trying to live a normal life in post-war America, actually transpired a sense of imminent danger, insecurity and horror. They described their parents as people who lived outside the world they actually lived in and whose future never began. The astonishing part of this transmission is that it was only very late in life that the children of Holocaust survivors realized that the world they lived in was actually a traumatized one, filled with catastrophic expectations, disproportionate rage, unjustified fearfulness, bitterness and pessimism, lack of empathy and humour, and unexplicably long periods of silence or passivity. A hidden child of the Holocaust Sophia Richman in her wonderful autobiography *A Wolf in the Attic* (2002) describes how her parents, either implicitly or explicitly, pictured the world for her: "The world is not a safe place; people are capable of anything; so, be careful whom you trust. Don't expect much, and you won't be disappointed. Life is tenuous and uncertain, tragedy may be lurking just around the corner. At its best, life is difficult; it is up to us to overcome obstacles we find in our path. Some people may try to help, but ultimately we are responsible for ourselves and cannot rely on others to rescue us" (p. 217). She also describes with great sensitivity how slowly and painfully this predestination for catastrophy disappeared from her life, one occurrence after another, the last occurrence being the tragic health problems of her only child. Her personal narrative brings to the fore the ultimate question of all children who were either traumatized themselves or lived with parents who were traumatized: when do we get to live our own lives and when do we come to terms with our traumatic past.

Kellermann (2001) found that the children of parents Holocaust survivors tended to over identify with their parents, felt they needed to be super-achievers to compensate for parental losses, and experienced the burden of being "replacements" for lost relatives. His findings indicate exaggerated family attachments and dependency or exaggerated independence and difficulties in entering intimate relationships and in handling interpersonal conflicts. Some had parents who smothered them with care, solicitude, and their ever present and all encompassing anxiety. Others had cold distant parents unable to demonstrate their love for fear of losing their loved ones all over again. Thus an important step toward overcoming secondary traumatization and starting to live one's own life for these individuals seems be to see and experience parents through the eyes of an adult, and not through the eyes of a child they used to be. To see the parents as helpless adults who can hardly cope with life's demands and who do not feel comfortable among their peers, may actually help their children put their feet emotionally back to the ground.

In her book, Sophia Richman relates an event which gave her a better perspective on her father. After many years of working in the field of psychotherapy, she started to concentrate on her own story as a child of Holocaust survivors and meet other people with the same family background. At that time she met someone who, like her father, survived several concentration camps and had written a memoir about his wartime experiences, much like her father, but unlike her father, he could smile, laugh and listen. "I had always wondered", she writes, "if my father would have been a more loving individual if he had not been exposed to such dehumanization in the concentration camp. Was he irreparably damaged by his wartime experiences, or did his suffering merely exacerabate his natural tendencies. Franek's capacity to love seemed intact. His daughter, born shortly after the war, was the fortunate recipient of that love. To me, Franek was living proof that one could suffer the indignities and torment of concentration camp life and still emerge a vital, caring, loving person" (p. 216). By realizing that her father was just one victim among many others and that he could have coped with the trauma differently, she was not only able to see him in a more objective light, but to re-experience her relationship with him as saying more about him than about her. In this brief and unexpected realization, the father appeared as an adult among other adults with whom he shared the same fate and who were able to choose how they lived in the aftermath of Holocaust. By this change of perspective, she ceased to try to undo the trauma she had no control over and could start to live her own life.

For Sophia, as well as many other children of traumatized parents, living beyong childhood trauma requires an insight into intergenerational sorces of traumatization. It means no less than that they mourn the lost safety of the parental world and no longer define themselves and their lives in terms of the parental trauma (Kompan Erzar, 2006). Since the answer provided by the lives of their parents is no longer the only possible answer to traumatization, the children can start believing that the life they live is rooted in an unconditional Love that resurrects from death. For some of them, this may be a lifelong endeavour, a true art of living.

References and Bibliography

Bowlby, J. (1969). *Attachment and Loss: Vol. 1. Attachment*. London: Hogarth.

Bowlby, J. (1973). *Attachment and Loss: Vol. 2. Separation: Anger and Anxiety*. London: Hogarth.

Erzar, T. (2006). Krepost in izpostavljenost zlorabi v Platonovih dialogih [Virtue and exposure to abuse in Plato's dialogues], *Anthropos*, 1–2 (201–202), 41–48.

Firestone, R. W. (1985). *The fantasy bond: Structure of psychological defenses*. New York: Human Sciences Press.

Firestone, R. W. (1990). *Compassionate child-rearing: An in-depth approach to optimal parenting*. New York: Plenum Press.

Hesse, E., and Main, M. (1999). Second-Generation Effects of Unresolved Trauma in Nonmaltreating Parents: Dissociated, Frightened and Threatening Perental Behavior. *Psychoanalytic Inquiry*, 4, 481-540.

Juhant, J. (2005). *Globalisierung, Kirche und postmoderner Mensch*. Münster: LIT.

Kellermann, N. P.F. (2001). Transmission of Holocaust Trauma - An Integrative View. *Psychiatry - Interpersonal and Biological Processes*, 64 (3) Fall, 256-267.

Kompan Erzar, K. (2006). *Ljubezen umije spomin* [Love heals memory]. Ljubljana: Brat Frančišek in Frančiškanski družinski inštitut.

Pietromonaco, P. R., & Barrett, L. F. (2000b). Internal working models: What do we know about knowing about the self in relation to others? *Review of General Psychology*, 4, 155-175.

Richman, S. (2002). *A Wolf in the Attic. The Legacy of the Hidden Child of the Holocaust*. The Haworth Press: Binghamton.

Solomon, J., George, C. (eds.) (1999). *Attachment disorganization*. New York: Guilford Press.

Stolorow, R. (2007). *Trauma and Human Existence. Autobiographical, Psychoanalytic, and Philosophical Reflections*. The Analytic Press: New York.

Van der Kolk, B. A. and Fisler, R. E. (1994). Childhood abuse and neglect and loss of self-regulation. *Bulletin of the Menninger Clinic*, 58 (2), 145-168.

LIFE AS A PILGRIMAGE, RELIGIOUS MESSAGES OF THE POST-SOVIET RUSSIAN CINEMA

Inna Naletova, Vienna

At the time of global migration, fluidity of territorial identities and dissolution of stable communities, a view on life as a pilgrimage can provide a framework of meanings and orientations restoring the wholeness of human life and rebuilding one's connections with other people. Combining a literary-philosophical approach to life of Santiago Sia (this volume) with Viktor Turner's anthropological views on pilgrimage, I would like to look at pilgrimages not only as the traditional Christian practices, which are often accociated with religious instituions, but rather as personal ways of (re)structuring one's life by 'punctuating' important life messages as the steps in an (imaginable) pilgrim journey toward a centre that is 'out there.'

When viewed as a pilgrimage, human life acquires a certain 'punctuation structure' in which important events, such as the rites of the passage and religious turning points, can be marked in accordance with their meaning on the journey to a holy place. One could also view this journey as a text consisting of a series of 'sentences', starting at home (with a 'capital letter') and going through cities, fields and villages, as if through a certain 'text', requiring efforts to properly 'read' and understand it. Like a pilgrim on a road to a holy place one could stop at some areas and have a 'pause' or a break, a religious enlightenment ('exclamation mark') or a request ('question mark'). Some moments of the life-pilgrimage can be marked with a prayer and concentration ('ellipsis'), with forgiveness and reconciliation, also marked in a certain way. After a culminating moment, the reader-pilgrim turns back, finishing one's walk with a 'dot' or a 'period' marking the end of the journey and (possibly) the beginning of another one: a new phase of life, a new start.

Life without punctuation does not have structure and looses its meaning. Life punctuated as pilgrimage acquires a special structure and, in a Christian context, a special set of meanings: suffering, sacrifice, and loss are certainly parts of it, but also joy in encountering with the holy, and hope for resurrection and a new beginning. The idea of life started anew, offered uniquely by Christianity, might have a healing effect on modern individuals burdened by traumatic experiences. To live beyond trauma, as Thomaž Erzar pointed out (this volume), requires an ability to break through the circle of the past events and to renew one's personal attachments, thus finding one's true self in relations with others. In this context, the practice of punctuating one's life as a pilgrimage might serve as a valuable resource of meaning helping to elevate the burden of a traumatic past.

I chose to analyse three Russian films made after the break of the Soviet system and directly or indirectly using the symbolic resources of pilgrimage/exodus in application to the individual life situations typical for the post-Soviet society. These films are *Nebesa Obetovannye* ("The Promised Heaven") by Eldar Riazanov, the best film of the year 1991; *Vosvraschenie* ("The Return") by Andrej Zvyagintzev, the best film of the year 2003; and *Ostrov* ("The Island") by Pavel Lungin, the best film of the year 2006. The films also received a number of international awards including a Kingfisher award granted to the film *Ostrov* in Ljubljana in 2003. What unites these films together is, first of all, a creative cinematic approach to religious resources -- such as symbols, ideas, images, fantasies, and prayer-songs -- as 'punctuation' marks leading the film characters towards a religious turning point, to a moment of enlightenment, when religious healing or religious solution of the life problems become possible. These films also reflect on the post-Soviet experience of social transition resulted with the situation of meaninglessness, poverty, and devaluation of values experienced by the whole generation of Russians searching, personally and collectively, for a ground to build their new lives on. Following the tradition of the Russian cinema, established by Tarkovskiy, Paradzhanov and Kozinskij, these films reflect on the very essence of religious experience, but, contrary to the famous works of their predecessors, they go far beyond the 'elit culture' appealing to a larger circle of viewers. It would be sufficient at this point to mention an unexpected development that happened after the film *Ostrov* was shown on the Russian TV before Christmas 2003. A forum was created on the film's website, in which many people began to express not only their opinions about the film, but also shear their life stories, deepest confessions, and guilt acknowledgements. Although this forum was not initiated by the Church, it was impossible for the clergy not to get involved in these discussions as well. Considering the magnifying effect of the mass media, it would not be an exaggeration to say that *Ostrov* (as well as the other two films) represent not only the talented works of art but also noticeable social events of the modern Russian culture.

Another important feature common to these films is the fact that the Church did neither sponsored nor gave an official approval to any of them, nor did the filmmakers state any personal affiliation with any religious organisations. I suppose, the remarkable success of the films could be attributed to their fresh, neophyte-like approach to religion, which is similar to the ways in which religion has been re-discovered by the Russian society in general. There is also a development in the film's approach to religion: In the "Promised Heaven" (1991) a religious transformation took place only at the very end of the film which was also the last moment in the lives of the film's characters. In the "Return" (2003) a transformation (a rite of the passage) happened in the lives of two teenagers triggered by the return of their father. And in the "Island" (2006) the whole life of an individual was interpreted as an uninterrupted religious self-transformation going on from the beginning of one's life to its end. Without being supported by the Church, these films carried a religious energy and a religious message that have been understood and appreciated by their viewers.

An anthropological view on pilgrimage

I would like to start my analysis from Viktor Turner's view of pilgrimage as a transition from *structure* to *anti-structure* (Turner 1978). During a pilgrimage, according to Turner, pilgrims became separated from the normal, institutionaly defined way of living in which their roles and interactions are determined by the 'structure' of their society, and enter a world of totally different meanings and relations. Pilgrimage, for Turner, is a process leading individuals away from and beyond the normality of the home-world. Stripped from their socially determined identities pilgrims become transformed into a community of equals which Turner called *communitas*, or a state of the *essential We*. While walking together toward a holy place, a center which is 'out there', pilgrims are freed from everything they have became accustomed with. In an extreme form, this new state of being can be called *liminality*: being, at least temporarily, nobody and nowhere. Turner supposes that *communitas* and *liminality*, when esperienced in their fullness, condition the feeling of absolute freedom and might have a turning effect in the lives of pilgrims, described as a revelation, enlightenment, or healing. Such turning points can be experienced not only by individual pilgrims but also by the whole societies undergoing a dramatic social change, such was, for instance in Europe, when the Medieval social order changed into a new order based on the capitalist economy. At that period, pilgrimages became particulalrly popular in Europe: people felt need to move from place to place seeking a connection with the holy but also establishing new moral codes and new roads for commercial activities (Turner 1973, 1974). It taked only one step further to suggest, following Turner, that the rise of pilgrimages in the post-Soviet Europe echoes the process of social change there (Naletova 2009). Both processes, pilgrimage and social change, are based on the experiences of *liminality*, *communitas*, and tension between *structure* and *anti-structure*, as well as the feeling that a centre is not here, but *out there*. It seems to me these punctuation moments mark important events in the lives of pilgrims and societies at large. And as such they could be helpful in structuring our thinking about human life in general.

"The Promised Heaven" (1991)

For the first time after the state atheism, Biblical references were given a central role to play in the film "The Promised Heaven." The title of this film and a prayer-song played at the culminating moment hint at the overall interpretation of poverty, humiliation und helplessness experienced by millions of people in Russia at the time of the post-Soviet economic breakdown as that of an exodus, with the end open to transcendence. The film tells us about a group of homeless people living on the edge of the Moscow city. The main characters were formerly an intellectual, an artist, an army officer, and a housewife. Each suffers a life crisis and finds himself/herself on the fringes of the society, having no social status, no home, no security, and no material means for living. Desperation brings these people together, and they begin to live as a community, making a home in an old train carriage abandoned by the railways. Like pilgrims on a road to the unknown they separate themselves, or rather are forced to separate, from the things familiar to them. The "essential We" begins to dominate in their relations as they continue to help each other. The community gives them moments of happiness and hope to build a new life on. But the city authorities decide to clean up the area and remove the cast-off carriage, leaving the desperate people without any shelter. At this moment, the old train miraculously takes off and with all its inhabitants inside rises above the tracks and departs above the railways – to the Heaven.

The miraculous end of the film is also a fantasy spread among the community members believing that aliens would come from an extra-terrestrial civilisation to take them to a better world. In the desperate situation, the people believe that the miracle will happen at the day when the first winter snow will fall on the city. Indeed, by falling, the first snow flakes, like the Biblical manna, smoothed people's departure to the Heaven, their death.

Although placed outside of an institutional religion, the film story refered to a universe of recognisable religious symbols, such as snow-manna and prayer-song. Also the old wagon departing to the Heaven looked similar to the real wagons, which some contemporary monasteries have made into their pilgrim quarters. *Liminality*, *communitas* and a religious turning point punctuate the stages in the lives of the characters as if those were the stages of a journey to another world, an exodus. Not without some irony the film offered a religious solution to the life situation which could not – as it seemed particularly true at the beginning of the 1990s – be solved by any other social means.

"The Return" (2003)

This film articulates a religious message by using the allegory God-Father unfolded through a story about two teenagers living with their mother and grandmother in a small Russian city and knowing of the father only from a faded photograph. One day the father mysteriously returns and takes the boys to a fishing trip to a remote island. As the story develops, we see the children being more and more disappointed with their father, as well as puzzled and scared. While the oldest Andrei is willing to accept the father's authority, the youngest Ivan views the father with a growing suspicion. The father himself does not seem to be interested in spending time with the children. His strictness makes them wonder, if he actually loves them: Why did he come? Where he was? Is he really their father? "What if he takes the knife and kills us?" – asks the anxious Ivan. Made in a style of a psycho-thriller or a road-movie, the story tells us about the fears of the children – the fear of the height and the deep water, the fear of being excluded and ridiculed, the fear of death and uncertain future. These fears take a particulalrly acute form in the youngest Ivan, who experiences the father's return as a separation from his close attachment to his mother and the older brother.

Like in "Promissed Heaven" the transformation in the life of the characters goes hand in hand with a religious transformation presented in the film as a background story indirectly connected to the main narrative. Becoming aware of their weakness and dependency on the father, the children, unconciously, begin to search for a way out, for a solution. Symbolically, such a solution (as a sterway to the Heaven) is found above, on the top of a watch-tower, where Ivan is trying to escape by risking his life. Trying to save his son, the father follows him and accidentally falls from the tower. At this culminating moment, the father finally 'returns' to the children, through death giving a way to their new life.

By depicting tense relations between the father and the sons, the film tells us a story of suffering caused by the loss of trust and family connections. It also shows us a way of rebuilding the trust and connections by taking a special trip (a pilgrimage) from the home-world to a remote place where the tensions between the characters became extremely intensified, thus opening a space for a final confrontation. It is there, on the island, the previously established world of meanings collapses and the boys are prepared to enter into a new world, which they will do not as dependent and confused children, but as thoughtful and responsible individuals.

The symbol of the father's death/return obviously refers to a Christian context toward which the viewers are lead through a series of religious symbols punctuating the texture of the story. For instance, the father dies/returns on Sunday: in the Russian, "Sunday" (*voskresenie*) means resurrection. When the children see the father for the first time, he is at home, sleeping: the image of the sleeping father undoubtedly refers to the Andrey Montenya's the "Dead Christ". There are other guiding symbols, such as the leaves under the father's car which remain the palm leaves thrown under the Christ's feet at the day of his arrival to Jerusalem. One could also recognise the Trinity in the position of the characters when they are shown together on the way to the island. The way Andrey turns toward the father looks like an iconic Orthodox image of an angel. As well as many other guiding symbols, such as the watch-tower, the fish caught by the brothers, the family's patriarchal dinner on the eve before the departure remained the viewers about a religious layer of the film being there without directly entering into the story. Also at the last minutes of the film we see a series of black-and-white photographs, made by the children during the trip and shown slowly, one after another, as the evidence of the father's presence in their memory, as the icons. These photographs indeed are recognisable reference to the icons appeared at the end of Tarkovsky's "Andrey Rublev." Through such symbols, images, and associations, religious tradition opens itself up, offering resources for deeper understanding of the events in human life.

"Island" (2006)

A transformative power of pilgrimage is also shown in the film "Island" which story, like that of the "Return," is located on an island. This film was the first in the post-Soviet Russian cinema to approach religion directly, by showing the life of a small monastery in the Russian North.

The film begins with an episod of betrayal happened at the time of the war: a young man killed, or rather was forced to kill an innocent person, his friend. Since that moment, the life of that young man (the future Father Anatoly) fully changed turning toward monastic seclusion and prayer. Yet, the life of the monastery, in which Father Anatoly lives, is not absolutely secluded. In fact, it is constantly interrupted by visitors, coming there to consult with the Father Anatoly, known for his ability to heal wounds and thicknesses. Each visitor brings with oneself a heavy load of personal sufferings, questions, and problems unsolved in the world. Among the pilgrims we see a mother, bringing to the monastery her hopelessly sick child, a girl, terrified by her unwanted pregnancy, and an old woman having strange dreams about her though-to-be dead husband. Each story, including that of Father Anatoly himself, is unique and typical at the same time. As a character, Father Anatoly resembles Father Zosima, one of the elders of the Monastery Optina Pustyn' described in Dostoyevsky's "The Brothers Karamazov." Father Zosima is a spiritual authority of a particular kind, the one bridging the world of the Church as an institution with the rest of the world. One could also see in Father Anatoly a peasant-traveller depicted in a story written by an unknown author in the 19th century and entitled (in some publications) as "The Way of a Pilgrim." This well-known story describes the life of a peasant who, like an eternal pilgrim, devoted his whole life to travelling from place to place seeking to learn the right way of Jesus prayer and looking for a spiritual authority out there, in the world, but finding it within one's own heart and in relations with people he met on his way.

Like the 19th century peasant-pilgrim, Father Anatoly seeks forgiveness through prayer, hard work and ascetic limitations. Like Father Zosima, he seeks solutions to people's problems beyond the prescriptions of the Church. The island, where he lives, is also a place with many layers. It is a place for reconciliation and final departure, like that in the "Promised Heaven". It is also a place for other people's pilgrimage, like that in the "Return." And it is a place where Father Anatoly's inner life-long pilgrimage toward himself begins and ends.

Conclusion

The three films that I choose for this article can be seen as progressive steps made in the Russian cinema from the early 1990s to the present time in reflecting about the ways for modern people's coping with the traumatic experience of modernity. Each film can be seen as a (mental) journey, a pilgrimage, or exodus toward a centre located somewhere 'out there,' beyond the given material realities, but also within human life and human relations. A transition from the world of *structure* to that of *anti-structure* through *liminality* and *communitas* are the recognisable moments structuring the stories of these films along the lines of the Christian message: the message of resurrection and a new life. It seems to me, through such a mental journey or a pilgrimage, religious language become interwoven into the language of human life, reflecting and echoing each other. This bi-lingual echo has been convincingly captured by the post-Soviet Russian cinema.

References and Bibliography

The Way of a Pilgrim, trans. by Gleb Pokrovsky, Skylight Paths, 2001. This work is written by an anonymous Russian writer in the 19th century and is re-published 2003 under the title *Otkrovennye rasskazy strannika dychovnomy otzy svoemy* (The Sincere Stories of a Wanderer Told to His Spiritual Father) Moscow: Lestvitsa.

Naletova, Inna. 2009. "Pilgrimages as Kenotic Communities beyond the Walls of the Church", in Chris Hann and Herman Goltz, eds, *Eastern Christians in Anthropological Perspectives.* Columbia University Press, pp. 203-227.

Turner, Victor. 1974. "Pilgrimage and Communitas" *Studia Missionalia* 23: 305-328.

______. 1978. *Image and Pilgrimage in Christian Culture. Anthropological Perspectives.*

New York.

______. 1973. "The Center Out There: Pilgrim's Goal" *History of Religions* 12: 202-223.

Trailers of the films and reviews:

"The Island": http://www.ostrov-film.ru/

"The Return": http://www.kino.com/thereturn/mainframe.html

"The Promised Heaven": http://www.afisha.ru/movie/photo/186640/168031/

REVERENCE FOR LIFE: THE CURRENCY OF SCHWEITZER'S ETHICS

Roman Globokar, Ljubljana

In the twentieth century, the Enlightenment belief in scientific and technical progress increasingly diminished. The ambivalence of progress became more and more apparent. The abuse of modern technology against man was obvious not only in phenomena such as Auschwitz and Hiroshima. The entirely peaceful and, at first sight, philanthropic use of the means of modern civilization also started to turn against human beings. The ecological crisis demonstrates that scientific and technical progress has its limits and its negative aspects. Towards the end of the twentieth century, a common awareness arose that the question of progress is at its core an ethical question. By the end of the First World War, Albert Schweitzer prophetically drew attention to this matter. This well-known doctor working in the African primeval forest was also a great theologian, a very talented musician and music critic, and a cultural philosopher, which he felt was his primary intellectual task.

At the beginning of the twenty-first century, an increasing number of thinkers searching for an appropriate answer to the challenges of the present age are referring to Schweitzer's ethics of reverence for life. It seems that it is only now, nearly one hundred years later, that the depth of Schweitzer's thought is understood. He is considered by many to be a pioneer of ecological ethics, a seeker after common moral principles in great human civilizations, and an architect of a new moral attitude of man towards life. This article outlines his ethics of reverence for life, critically assesses it, and ascertains its current value in the modern social context.

The Decay of Western Civilization

The absurdity and atrocities of the First World War led Schweitzer to think about what had happened in the western world to allow such a tragedy to take place. According to him, the war was only an external sign of the earlier internal collapse of western civilization. "The disastrous feature of our civilization is that it is far more developed materially than spiritually" (Schweitzer 1987: 86). Science and technology led to inconceivable progress. Modern man gained extreme power to control and change life, but the fact is that morally he is not equal to this power. According to Schweitzer, material development that ignores moral and spiritual development is "like a ship with defective steering gear that goes out of control at a constantly accelerating pace, thereby heading for catastrophe" (Schweitzer 1987: 86). When sailing, the speed is not really important, nor is the type of propulsion – what really matters is the correct course of the vessel. The same holds true for culture. Faster and more powerful propulsion also demands better control and faster navigation.

It is not material development that is essential for culture, but, above all, the spiritual state of people that encourage perfection of the individual and the community:

"The essential nature of civilization does not lie in its material achievements, but in the fact that individuals keep in mind the ideals of perfecting man, and improving the social and political conditions of peoples, and of mankind as a whole, and that their habit of thought is determined in living and constant fashion by such ideals" (Schweitzer 1987: 86).

The decay of western civilization may have started in the mid-nineteenth century because consciousness of responsibility and morality were no longer capable of directing technological development. Belief in development liberated itself from ethical guidance, and development started to function according to its own laws. Moreover, ethics even became a disturbing element for scientific and technical progress. Schweitzer said that "we regard this renunciation of consistent ethical judgment as an advance in practicality" (Schweitzer 1987: 92).

Restoration of Civilization through the Ethics of Reverence for Life

This was Schweitzer's basic diagnosis on the ailing and decaying western culture. However, as an outstanding physician, Schweitzer did not merely content himself with the diagnosis, but also prescribed the therapy because he was convinced that western civilization is not fated to collapse entirely.

At the beginning of the modern period, philosophy took a wrong direction: it reduced man to its "cogito" and laid aside everything that was physical, material, emotional, and sensuous. Schweitzer searched for an alternative. He found Descartes' principle "cogito, ergo sum" abstract and illogical. Thinking is not a vain act in and of itself. "When I think, I always think about something. The question is the following: what is the content of that thinking in which I always render myself an account of my existence" (Schweitzer 1999: 426)? In his central work *The Philosophy of Civilisation*, Schweitzer attributed the following basic content to human thought:

"True philosophy must start from the most immediate and comprehensive fact of consciousness, which says: 'I am life that wills to live, in the midst of life that wills to live.' This is not an ingenious dogmatic formula. Day by day, hour by hour, I live and move in it" (Schweitzer 1987: 309).

This is the basic experience of life for each man. Due to his fear of nullification, man longs for the fulfilment of his existence. Life-affirmation is embedded in human nature. His natural will-to-live leads man through the process of thinking about himself and the world to universal world-affirmation. A person that thinks about himself and the world realizes that everything around him – plants, animals, and people – wants to live as he himself does. Man recognizes that all living creatures are some kind of mysterious universal will-to-live. Thus, the basic experience of a human being is not his absence from the world (as with Descartes), but his experience of affinity and connectedness with the life surrounding him.

A human being is thus part of nature and his life is essentially connected with other living organisms. Nonetheless, he was assigned a special role in nature. However, nature is far from being an ideal harmonious system. Each will-to-live strives for affirmation and the best realization of its being. This leads to a conflict of interests and a struggle between the living creatures of the natural world. Events in nature are ambivalent: beauty and logic intertwine with horrors and illogicality. Therefore, man cannot establish clear guidelines for his life based on his knowledge of nature. The natural world around him does not behave ethically, and so he must find the guidelines for his life in his internal will-to-live.

According to Schweitzer, the ethical will-to-live is an innate element of each man that commands him to show equal respect to all wills-to-live as to his own. "Ethics therefore consists of my experiencing the compulsion to show all wills-to-live the same reverence as I to my own" (Schweitzer 1987: 309). Ethics is not a closed system of obligations and virtues used to determine in detail how should a man function. Its task is to provide individuals with a basic moral principle that serves as a compass, pointing out the direction in every concrete case, but not making the decision in advance at all. "Ethics is not a park with precisely arranged and well maintained paths, but a wilderness in which everyone should find and travel his own route. What is determined is the direction that one has to follow" (Schweitzer 2000: 154).

The Radical Nature of the Ethics of Reverence for Life

The philosopher of the African primeval forest is convinced that, through his basic principle of "devotion to life inspired by reverence for life" (Schweitzer 1987: 311), he provided a general material content to the formal ethical imperative. The basic ethical principle shall read: "It is good to maintain and encourage life; it is bad to destroy life or obstruct it" (Schweitzer 1987: 309). Through his ethical demand, Schweitzer extended moral responsibility to encompass all living creatures. If man acknowledges his connectedness with all living creatures, if he is aware of his basic experience that man is "life in the midst of all life," then he is not permitted to set up a limit up to which he will respect life. No matter wherever and for what purpose man harms or destroys a life – any form of it – he acts unethically and is guilty. The radical nature of Schweitzer's ethics was even more apparent when he did not allow any scale of values for living creatures.

"A man is truly ethical only when he obeys the compulsion to help all life that he is able to assist, and shrinks from injuring anything that lives. He does not ask how firmly this or that life deserves one's sympathy as being valuable, nor, beyond that, whether and to what degree it is capable of feeling. Life as such is sacred to him" (Schweitzer 1987: 310).

Ethics is defined as "responsibility without limit towards all that lives" (Schweitzer 1987: 311). In the long run, every human action should be directed toward the preservation and promotion of one's own life and the life of the creatures that are part of one's environment.

It is obvious that man inevitably intervenes in the life of other living creatures. Schweitzer was a realist in this respect. Man is forced to kill other living creatures to survive. On the one hand, the ethics of reverence for life is totally consistent on a theoretical basis and allows no ranking of beings as more or less worthy of living. On the other hand, at the practical level people have to face reality. The demand "Preserve and promote life" puts man in a paradoxical situation. To save one life, a man is obliged to destroy another one. Schweitzer presented the following example: "In order to keep a heron from starving if it has broken its wing, we must condemn that many fish to death. We can show mercy only if we act without mercy at the same time" (Schweitzer 2000: 153). For such conflict situations, Schweitzer created the following guideline: "Whenever I injure life of any sort, I must be quite clear whether it is necessary. Beyond the unavoidable I must never go, not even with what seems insignificant" (Schweitzer 1987: 318). The ethics of reverence for life does not reveal where the limits of inevitability are and which basic criteria man shall apply when choosing between different forms of life. They require the individual to respect the fundamental principle "to maintain and promote life," whereby the concrete realization of this principle is up to the individual.

Evaluation of the Ethics of Reverence for Life

Schweitzer's ethical acts touch the reader profoundly. His texts enriched by clear examples seem provocative and force people to think. Basic moral questions are discussed in a new and broader way. Readers have to reconsider the viability of their ethical positions. Schweitzer's radical positions compel readers to verify the validity of the existing ethical positions and make them willing to act in accordance with the basic moral principle of reverence for life.

The ethics of reverence for life was largely criticized by philosophers for lacking terminological precision, which could easily result in misunderstanding. Schweitzer proceeded with ease from the argumentation level to the personal level in his writing and tried to directly evoke readers' emotions. Notions such as "resignation," "a necessity of thought," "rationalism," and "guilt" are not used entirely uniformly. The central notion of "will-to-live," which in fact denotes a conscious and targeted orientation, is used uncritically for all living creatures (Lenk 1993). The reason for this could also be attributed to the very difficult situation in which the author worked. His essays on ethics were not primarily designed for academic circles, but for a large number of people in order to stimulate cultural reform through change in each individual. "I intentionally avoided technical philosophical terminology. I wanted to appeal to thinking men and women, and to motivate them to think in a basic sense about the questions of existence that are in the minds of every human being" (Schweitzer 1998: 202).

The most harshly criticized part of Schweitzer's philosophy was definitely his refusal to rank life forms. In this regard, Schweitzer is reproached for "pantheism, anthropomorphism, excessive subjectivity and guilt mongering" (Martin 2002: 166). Schweitzer advocated that all life is sacred. His support for the intrinsic value of all living beings originates in his metaphysics, which suggests there is a cosmic, creative, and mysterious will-to-live, "in which all Being is grounded" (Schweitzer 1987: 283). He did not permit ranking of life forms even though he did not de facto attribute the same value to all living creatures. There arises the question of whether it is the task of ethics to distinguish between different life forms at the theoretical level and to help individuals make their decision. It is definitely true that man as "a life in the midst of life" discovers fundamental connectedness with all living things as well as dissimilarities between our will-to-live and other living beings. Human life undoubtedly possesses higher inherent worth than that of other living creatures. As a doctor in the African jungle, Schweitzer implemented this approach every day. However, it is certainly necessary to overcome Schweitzer's dichotomy between "ethical and necessary," such that taking life is unethical even when necessary to protect other life. If human beings were accorded a special role within the living world, the ethics of reverence for life would not lose its value. Moreover, they would gain in its applicability and practicality.

The real downside of Schweitzer's ethics is its limitation to individual ethics. The socio-ethical aspect is disregarded and underestimated. Due to the Enlightenment belief in human reason and the Protestant inclination to individualism, Schweitzer undervalued the power of social structures. He could be partly understood if one considers his historical background. At the beginning of the twentieth century, ideologies – be these socialist and communist, or biologistic and nationalistic – subjected the individual to society. Schweitzer's response to this was therefore sound, but one should consider it to be immoderate. It is not possible to solve great social problems (environmental protection, world justice, etc.) within modern complex society through only individual ethics.

The Currency of the Ethics of Reverence for Life

At the beginning of the twenty-first century, Schweitzer's philosophical ethics pose a unique challenge. Its currency mainly lies in setting a man in his living environment and in emphasizing his fundamental connectedness with all living creatures. Schweitzer laid the foundations of biocentric environmental ethics half a century before other thinkers. The content of Hans Jonas' ethics of responsibility nearly summarizes Schweitzer's criticism of culture and his ethics of reverence for life. Jonas searched for new ethics for the new situation (Jonas 1984), but he overlooked the fact that Schweitzer had pointed to the fundamental discrepancy between material and spiritual development, between human (technical) power and internal responsibility, some time before him and thus laid the foundations for the new ethics. Jonas' originality somehow fades when compared to Schweitzer's ethical thought. From the philosophical point of view, Jonas' ethics is undoubtedly more perfected; however, Schweitzer's is more profound and original. They both provide solid foundations for the creation of a contemporary ethics of life

(Globokar 2002: 528–544). The understanding of man as a "life that wills to live in the midst of life that wills to live" constitutes an excellent starting point for the creation of ecological ethics, which is of primary importance today if people also want to ensure the existence of mankind on this planet in the future.

Man is fundamentally incorporated in the kingdom of all living things and, through his connectedness with all living things, is aware of his moral responsibility to encourage and promote life in all its forms. Through the notion of "life," ethical demand gains universal material content. A person as a living individual can never live out of himself and for himself; there exists no solipsistic existence in the world. His life is maintained and thrives only through harmonious connectedness with other living creatures. Unfortunately, man still often acts as the absolute master of the entire universe. This is why Steiner purposed that reverence for life should serve as a basis for all "political, economic, and scientific debates and decisions" because it is highly possible that, by "adopting the concept of reverence for life and accepting responsibility for every living thing on Earth, we will determine the future of life on Earth in general as well as the future of each of us, or at least the not-so-distant future of future generations" (Steiner 2006: 240–241).

The ethics of reverence for life definitely provides a very good basis for the education of environmentally responsible behaviour. It is based on the immediate experience of life, which is of major importance for today's lifestyle. Schweitzer was convinced that a person is capable of accepting responsibility for life only if he internally experiences the responsibility for life. Therefore, it is very important to establish a direct contact with the environment and living creatures in children's education as well as to promote the perception of man's connectedness with the living world. This will encourage the development of responsible behavior within the natural environment. Isolated rules without immediate experience will not achieve their goal.

Only when man experiences connection with another life, when he tastes the oneness of life, when he feels connected to all beings – only then he is motivated to take upon himself the responsibility for all living things. Aesthetic experience, immediate enthusiasm for nature, is an indispensable complement to cognitive knowledge in education for environmental responsibility. The ethics of reverence for life provides a good educational basis because it does not separate the head from the heart, or separate demands of reason from everyday experience (Günzler 1988: 171–202). Schweitzer did not idealize nature, nor did he sacralize it. He was aware of the tension and cruelty in the natural world. One of the fundamental elements is the synthesis of the emotional and rational level, which is still topical today.

Promotion of readiness for personal asceticism is another contribution to the education of ecological consciousness. Ecological ethics undoubtedly need structural approaches, and individual ethics as proposed by Schweitzer does not suffice on its own. However, the individual sphere is far from being negligible in education. Solutions at the systems level cannot be efficient unless an individual is ready to change his way of life. In this context, Schweitzer's concept of resignation, which is an indispensable presumption for truly ethical behaviour, remains topical. The word "resignation" may sound pessimistic, passive, and inactive; however, it possesses a specific meaning in Schweitzer's system. In his autobiography he provides the following explanation:

"True resignation consists of this: that man, feeling his subordination to the course of world events, makes his way toward inward freedom from the fate that shapes his external existence. Inward freedom gives him the strength to triumph over the difficulties of everyday life and to become a deeper and more inward person, calm, and peaceful. Resignation, therefore, is the spiritual and ethical affirmation of one's own existence. Only he that has gone through the trial of resignation is capable of accepting the world" (Schweitzer 1998: 233).

True resignation denotes the ability to adopt critical distance towards the world; it represents true freedom, which creates in an individual the disposition to renounce and to sacrifice. Ecological crisis forces man to change his way of life. The return to plainer living and the renunciation of consumerism that goes with this are the first steps toward a more responsible attitude to the environment.

Refereneces and Bibilography

Globokar, R. 2002: *Verantwortung für alles, was lebt. Von Albert Schweitzer und Hans Jonas zu einer theologischen Ethik des Lebens*, Roma: Pontificia università Gregoriana.

Günzler, C. 1998: 'Ehrfurcht vor dem Leben. Albert Schweitzers Ethik als Grundimpuls für die Umwelterziehung', in: Günzler, C. (ed.). *Ethik und Erziehung,* Stuttgart: Kohlhammer, 171–202.

Jonas, H. 1984: *Das Prinzip Verantwortung. Versuch einer Ethik für die technologische Zivilisation*, Frankfurt: Suhrkamp Taschenbuch.

Lenk, H. 1993: 'Lebensethik', *Zeitschrift für Medizinische Ethik* 39, 343–353.

Martin, M. W. 2002: 'Rethinking Reverence for Life', in: Meyer, M. and Bergel, K. (ed.), *Reverence for Life, The Ethics of Albert Schweitzer for the Twenty-first Century*, New York. Syracuse, 166-183.

Schweitzer, A. 1998: *Out of My Life and Thought*, Baltimore: Johns Hopkins University.

—. 1987: *The Philosophy of Civilisation*, New York: Prometheus Books.

—. 1999: *Die Weltanschauung der Ehrfurcht vor dem Leben. Kulturphilosophie III. Erster und zweiter Teil*, München: C. H. Beck.

—. 2000: *Die Weltanschauung der Ehrfurcht vor dem Leben. Kulturphilosophie III. Dritter und vierter Teil*, München: C. H. Beck.

Steiner, A. 2006: *Das Leben, unser höchstes Gut. Albert Schweitzers Ethik im 21. Jahrhundert*, Freiburg: Herder.

THE RIGHT TO A GOOD NAME

Stanislav Slatinek

The importance of media in our postmodern world is becoming greater every day. The postmodern man has in this world many opportunities »to see and to hear« (Juhant 2005, 22). He can also read much more than he was once able to. This is made possible by different forms of public media. Printed media, such as daily papers, newspapers and magazines, deserve special attention. Printed media are a penetrating force whose information »decisively mark man's consciousness and his unconscious« (Juhant 2009, 26). Printed reports strongly influence individuals and the society. Journalistic articles can have a very positive role in the fields of economy, politics, culture, ecology, education, morality and religion. Yet they can also become a means of humiliating and manipulating human beings, they can jeopardise freedom and cause great moral damage.

With the discussion on the right to a good name I wish to highlight the important role journalistic articles in newspapers have today in regard to respect of the basic human right to a good name.

Reports in daily newspapers follow two basic goals: to inform the society and respect human rights. The society has the right to be informed, while the individuals about whom newspapers write have the right to privacy and a good name. When reading daily newspapers one often gets the impression that journalistic articles follow primarily the first goal, they inform the public, while they neglect basic human rights, especially the right of individuals to a good name. Journalistic articles thus have only two possibilities. They either report fairly and decently (Segbers 2007) or they turn into a symbolic speech (Juhant 2007, 18) and become destructive forces which obstruct the wellbeing of people.

1. Journalistic ethics

The first fundamental lodestar of newspaper journalist is to ensure the public has the right to be informed as best as possible, at the same time ensuring the right of individuals to privacy.

Informing the public is the foundation of modern societies' functioning and a condition for functioning of democratic systems (McQuail 2005). Journalistic work is based on freedom of reporting, on the free flow of information and the openness of printed media to different opinions (Dulles 1987). Journalists are

»autonomous in creating contents« (ibid.), collecting and publishing of information, and expressing opinions. Journalistic ethics, however, obliges journalists to carry out their work »accurately, conscientiously and truthfully« (ibid.). Only such work can be the foundation of credible informing of the public (Lampe 2009, 56), since the right of the public to be informed requires that the contents of what is written are real and in line with equity and love. This means that journalistic articles avoid any »manipulation with truth« (John Paul II 1987/a, 535).

Respecting a person (Paul VI 1977, 2) is the second fundamental lodestar of journalists. Whenever journalists report, they are obliged to ensure individuals' »right to privacy« (McQuail 2005). Since journalistic articles are to a great extent prone to various abuses, they frequently cause damage to individuals and the common good. Journalists are not always aware that by publishing their information they can cause damage to an individual »who is not accustomed to the attention of media and the public« (ibid.). Journalists are therefore in their work obliged to observe professional and ethical standards, which require from them to respect truth and report correctly (Segbers 2007). Journalistic reporting in principle passes the boundaries of what is correct and becomes offensive or even hostile when it is no longer decent and fair (White 1987, 1555). It is thus of utmost importance that articles in daily newspapers are »considerate, professional and ethical« (Real 1989). Journalists' work is regulated by different legal norms, ethical and deontological codes (in Slovenia: the Code of Journalists, the *Slovenian Journalists' Court of Honour*, the Media Act from 2006), by the civil and the criminal law, as well as by international documents (in Europe: the European Convention for the Protection of Human Rights and Basic Liberties – ECtHR 1994; the European Declaration on Mass Communication Media and Human Rights from 1970, the European Court for Human Rights – ECtHR, and the European Ombudsman). Legal instruments are numerous, they are well accepted by journalists, yet they prove efficient only when they are strictly acknowledged. They contain moral sanctions and are considered competent to judge journalistic ethics (Lampe 2009, 58).

2. The right to privacy

When journalists publish articles in newspapers, they often infringe the right to privacy. This specifics can be in a particular way noticed in political scandals (for example those involving Berlusconi, Sarkozy, Putin) and the scandals of priests (scandals in connection with sex offences of priests). Europe has lately experienced strong anti-religious atmosphere (scandals in connection with religious symbols – banning the crucifix from public schools). It seems that printed media in particular contributes to the gradual disappearance of Christianity from Europe (Juhant 2009, 161). The European Convention for the Protection of Human Rights and Basic Liberties thus states that »everybody has the right to respect for his private and family life«. Suspending of these rights is in a democratic society allowed in three cases: 1) when it is in accordance with laws; 2) when protecting the rights and freedoms of others, and 3) when justified by the public interest (ECHR 1994, Article 8, paragraph 2).

The right to privacy is one of the basic personal rights of an individual. The right to privacy protects physical and personal integrity and dignity of an individual as a human being. The right to privacy is connected to a person and his/her goods, such as good name, honour and reputation. It is a right to which man is entitled as an individual, and it is inviolate except in cases sanctioned by law (Maite 2006).

»The right to privacy« is in Slovenia a special right protected by the Constitution of the Republic of Slovenia (Article 35). It has the nature of a universal right, which means that every man has the right to confidentiality of personal data, such as one's name and image. The right to privacy is a good and entails the right to inner peace, mental integrity and personal dignity. Due to its particularity, it is among the most vulnerable rights.

The Slovenian Constitutional Court points out that infringing the right to privacy is possible and legally permissible only when this serves »the general interest« and »a justifiable public interest« (Lampe 2009, 60). This is also confirmed by the practice of the Slovenian Supreme Court, as each separate case is deliberated to establish whether »the right of privacy« prevails over »the right of the public to know«, and vice versa. Slovenian judicial practice distinguishes between violations of the right to privacy »under public law« (police invasion of the right to privacy) and violations of the right to privacy »under civil law« (media – journalists' – invasion of the right to privacy).

The European Court for Human Rights in Strasbourg explains that police invasion (arrest, personal search, house search, confiscation of personal belongings etc.) or media invasion of the right to privacy is invasion of individuals' inner circle. The European Court for Human Rights understands privacy as the protection of people in their dwellings against any form of invading their personal sphere, personality and dignity. Invading privacy means invading one's personal life, one's right to physical and mental inviolability. When events from people's personal lives are revealed, this in a wider sense constitutes offences against their honour and good name. The concept of »privacy« is supposed to protect primarily the personal (physical and mental) sphere of an individual (White 1987, 1560).

3. The right to a good name

The right to privacy includes also the right to a good name. Depriving someone of his/her good name means infringing the right to privacy and inviolability of personal life. It means interfering with a personal good, one's peace of mind, honour and dignity. Robbing someone of his/her good name primarily threatens his/her peace of mind (1565).

The good name and reputation of an individual are most often destroyed by insulting behaviour. Offensive statements constitute insulting behaviour. If they appear in press, they represent aggravated insults. Insulting behaviour violates the right to privacy. Sharp statements, criticisms and judgments are in principle always allowed in printed media, yet they should not be contemptuous and humiliating. If the contemptuous intent of a journalist is recognised in statements, then they constitute criminal offences. Insults are criminal offences under the condition that insults display objective signs of insulting behaviour. Merely subjective evaluating of an individual does not constitute a criminal offence. An objective insult means that a journalist by a brutally written statement degrades, undervalues, shames and despises a person (Lampe 2009, 58) – it contains a negative evaluation of an individual. Objective signs of insulting behaviour are pondered over by a court of jurisdiction.

Good name and reputation of individuals may be exposed only in special cases when some general interest is protected or when it is required by the legitimate right of the public to be informed about an action or an event. Courts are compelled to decide which principle will prevail – the right to a good name or the right of the public to be informed – in cases of controversial articles which contain signs of violation of the right to a good name. Controversial articles in daily newspapers supposedly express criticism which is warranted by the public interest or the right of the public to be informed (Einspieler 2009, 212).

4. The image right

Among the rights to privacy is also the image right (Lampe 2009, 80). One's image is a good which should be protected and maintained (Juhant 2003). Consequently, publishing one's image or photography can sometimes be also controversial and offensive.

According to European legal practice, it is permissible to publishing photographs of »public personalities« and photographs »in connection with criminal offences«. Photographs of »public personalities« can be published because the right of the public to be informed is wider than the right to privacy. Despite this, this principle is not applicable without restraint (Einspieler 2009, 220).

Publishing one's photograph can insult the good name of an individual. In a broader perspective, it can threaten an individual's peace of mind. An individual can lose his/her peace of mind if the publication of his photograph exposes him/her to the public. It is frequently the case that publishing one's photograph, especially if it is offensive, spurs readers of daily newspapers to mock and despise a person. Thus, many questions remain open. As an example – deciding when to publish one's photography and grant the public »the right to be informed«, and when to protect the personal »right to image«? Is it permissible to publish a photograph which may offend religious feelings (e.g. pictures of Jesus, Mary, Allah)? Is it possible that publishing a controversial photograph can instigate intolerance and violence? (ibid.)

The European Convention for the Protection of Human Rights and Basic Liberties as a rule rejects such appeals due to the article 10 of the Human Rights Convention, which protects freedom of expression as a special value (ECHR 1994). The American Supreme Court and the German Constitutional Court have in similar cases judged that even the highest symbols of state can be used in very provocative way (e.g. burning a flag). Jurists are of the opinion that »religious symbols« (e.g. images of Jesus, Mary, Allah) cannot be exempt from public criticism (Lampe 2009, 81).

It is different, however, when it comes to publishing photographs of suspects and perpetrators of criminal offences. Presumed perpetrators of criminal offences in principle do not enjoy the right to privacy. This means that publishing their images and name in media is justified. Particularly in case of suspicion of a criminal offence which has the status of a »public event« (e.g. suspicion of a sexual offence against minors). Some photographs are nevertheless inappropriate – those depicting persons in a state of affect: handcuffed, among policemen, in a courtroom, while grieving and crying. Publishing such photographs is not an ethical act by which the right of the public to be informed is exercised (Einspieler 2009).

5. Diagnosis of the state and the proposed solutions

From what has been said so far, we can conclude that as European Christians we are responsible for the state of our society (Juhant 2009, 161). In the secularised Europe of today we can observe: 1) profound influence of printed media on political and social order of individual states; 2) strong influence of printed media on education; and 3) »hostile« influence of printed media on the religious and moral attitude of people (John Paul II 1987/b, 532). Printed media are becoming »an attractive market« or »a battlefield« where »readers«, »buyers of various commodities« and »voters of political parties« are fought over. Printed media (daily newspapers) are thus frequently nothing but an extended arm of leading political parties, state bosses, religious leaders, economists and banks. Behind every big newspaper house there is »a director« manipulating journalists in order to dominate economic markets and advance his ideological or political interests. However, the means to achieve these goals (e.g. political, economic or religious) are not always ethical or legitimate. Lies, deception and exciting events are used for no other reason than to provoke astonishment and draw attention, this often also instills blind obedience (in readers, buyers, voters). The diagnosis of the state of printed media is far from »media freedom« which respects human rights, for example the right to a good name. The fact is that news is a commodity which is marketed at the expense of human rights (534).

The troubles caused by neglecting the right to a good name, as seen in daily newspapers, put to trial the Catholic Church and other religious communities in Europe. It poses a challenge both to Christians and the members of other religions. Religions play a very important role in searching for ways to protect the good name of people, personal faith in particular. A question arises: what are in this case solutions which Christian culture can offer to Europe?

When protecting »the right to a good name«, the Catholic Church has a special task of spreading the »Gospel« in the field of printed media. This means that printed media (daily newspapers) become, wherever possible, a tool for the evangelisation of modern culture (Bacon 2009). Catholic journalists should set an example among European journalists and discuss a person's right to a good name respectfully, truthfully and benevolently, understanding the interests and needs of others. Europe for this reason needs pious men and women who will in the journalistic profession manage to write their journalistic reports in line with Christian culture, which highly values the principles of equality, freedom and tolerance, as well as human values, such as freedom of expression, respect for human rights, respect for personal and family life, freedom of thought, conscience and religion, and the right to a good name (Dulles 1987, 1520).

The solution is a new »info-ethics« or »information ethics« of printed media. We already know »bio-ethics«, which introduced a new (ethical) perspective of man. We thus need also »info-ethics« which can introduce a new (ethical) perspective of printed media (daily newspapers). We should consider »humane-info-ethics« of writing, advertising and reporting, as well as »humane-info-ethics« of listening and reading. The word should be protected. We are already familiar with »human ecology« and »environmental ecology«. Humanity thus urgently requires »word ecology« (John Paul II 1996, 5).

The solution is the »sanitation« or »recovery« of printed media. Printed media (daily newspapers) are »the creative field of culture« where ideas are exchanged, new habits formed and new values created. Daily newspapers literally create and mediate culture. It is important that printed media is »healed at the root« (canon law terms it as »sanatio in radice«), so they will not merely inform but also co-create modern culture. Journalistic articles are the best way to create »tolerant« culture (John Paul II 1997, 2). This, however, requires good laws. The law can enable printed media to blossom and stimulate them towards truth. Catholic MPs and catholic officials are for this reason morally obliged to vote for the laws which will help media work for the benefit of all.

The solution lies in »cultivated dialogue« (Juhant 2007). The discord concerning the protection of human rights will then vanish (especially in regard to the right to a good name). This is the way to solve the crisis of the modern world. We should be aware of our dignity and write letters to editors, call managers of media organisations and express protest against any abuse of one's good name and any unjust interpretation of the concept that democratic society provides »freedom of speech« while »the right to a good name« is neglected. It would benefit not only ourselves, but the entire society. Nowadays only well-grounded, dignified and peaceful protest is effective. Dialogue with »the media of words« should be undertaken self-confidently, with a proper dose of patience and love for truth.

These are but a few of possible solutions. There are many others. In order to find them, we should think in a well-intentioned and optimistic manner. We are all obliged to search the best solutions for upholding »the right of the public to be informed« and preserve »the right to a good name«. This is the task of all people, whether religious or not. It is necessary that jurists, statesmen and politicians are involved in the process of solving this problem since the right to a good name is a universal value which makes it possible that as few as possible people are hurt and all are satisfied. This endeavour is »the Art of Life«.

References and Bibliography

Bacon, Jono. 2009. *The Art of Community: Building, Managing, and Supporting Cooperation. Over the Internet*: USA: O'Reilly Media.

Dulles, Avery. 1987. Il Vaticano II e le communicazioni. In: Latourelle, R. (eds.), *Vaticano II., Bilancio e prospettive. Venticinque anni dopo (1962-1987)*. Assisi: Cittadella Editrice, 1507 – 1524.

Einspieler, Vili. 2009. Novinarska etika v praksi in novinarsko častno razsodišče. In: Lampe, R. (eds.), *Medijsko pravo*. Ljubljana: Planet GV, 210 – 249.

Janez Pavel II. 1987/a. Agli operatori dei mass-media nel «Registry Hotel» (Los Angeles). Esercitare il vostro ruolo come collaboratori della verità al servizio della giustizia, dell'onestà e dell'amore (15.9.1987). In: *Insegnamenti di Giovanni Paolo II*, X/3, 534 – 541.

Janez Pavel II. 1987/b. Teleconferenza con i giovani nell'«Universal Amphiteatre» (Los Angeles). Senza la fede in Dio non può esistere nessuna autentica duratura speranza (15.9.1987). In: *Insegnamenti di Giovanni Paolo II*, X/3, 530 – 534.

Janez Pavel II. 1996. Messaggio di Giovanni Paolo II. per la XXX. Giornata mondiale delle comunicazioni sociali. I media: moderno areopago per la promozione della donna nella società. In: *L'Osservatore Romano* (25.1.1996), 1 – 6.

Janez Pavel II. 1997. Messaggio di Giovanni Paolo II. per la XXXI. Giornata mondiale delle comunicazioni sociali. Comunicare Gesù: Via, Verità e Vita. In: *L'Osservatore Romano* (13.5.1997), 1 – 2.

Juhant, Janez. 2003. *Človek v iskanju svoje podobe. Filozofska antropologija*. Ljubljana: Claritas.

Juhant, Janez. 2005. *Globalisierung. Kirche und postmoderner Mensch*. Münster: Lit.

Juhant, Janez. 2007. Ethical dialogue as a link between philosophy, science, and religion. In: Juhant, J. in Žalec, B. (eds.). *On Cultivating Faith and Science. Reflection on Two Key Topics of Modern Ethics*, Münster: Lit, 13 – 33.

Juhant, Janez. 2009. *Občutek pripadnosti*. Celje: Celjska Mohorjeva družba.

Lampe, Rok. 2009. Varovanje osebnostnih pravic proti medijem. In: Lampe, R. (eds.), *Medijsko pravo*. Ljubljana: Planet GV, 56 – 92.

Maite, Melendo. 2006. *La comunicazione: base di relazioni comunitarie profonde*. Bologna: Edizioni Dehoniane.

McQuail, Denis. 2005. *Mass Communication Theory*. London New Delhi: Sage Publications.

Pavel VI. 1977. Messaggio del Santo Padre per la XI. Giornata mondiale delle comunicazioni sociali. La pubblicità nelle comunicazioni sociali: vantaggi, pericoli, responsabilità. In: *L'Osservatore Romano* (13.5.1977), 1 – 2.

Real, M. Michael. 1989. *Super Media: A Cultural Studies Approach. (Communication and Human Values)*. London New Delhi: Sage Publications.

Segbers, Michael. 2007. *Die Ware Nachricht: Wie Nachrichtenagenturen ticken*. Konstanz: UVK.

White, Robert. 1987. I mass media e la cultura nel catolicesimo contemporaneo. In: Latourelle, R. (eds.), *Vaticano II., Bilancio e prospettive. Venticinque anni dopo (1962-1987)*. Assisi: Cittadella Editrice, 1550 – 1577.

RELIGIONS

THE ART OF LIVING AS PROPOSED BY CATHOLIC CHRISTIANITY AND SUNNI ISLAM

Drago Karl Ocvirk , Ljubljana

Among the components of cultural patterns that complete human functionality are religions. They are carriers of meaning through their doctrines, of values through their ethics, of purpose through their eschatologies and soteriologies. Here we present the Catholic and Sunni propositions of the art of living.

1. Jesus' school of living and dying

If any want to become my followers, let them deny themselves and take up their cross daily and follow me. For those who want to save their life will lose it, and those who lose their life for my sake will save it. What does it profit them if they gain the whole world, but lose or forfeit themselves? (Luke 9:23-25).

In the Catholic doctrinal interpretation of Jesus' good news, the human person becomes the centre of attention and this is not only human but also divine attention. God himself, indeed, chose to become a human among humans in Jesus of Nazareth. He who emerged out of common people, showed a special concern for socially and religiously marginalized people. He exercised and preached love for them and invited them by simple parables to become his disciples. "I am the gate. Whoever enters by me will be saved, and will come in and go out and find pasture. The thief comes only to steal and kill and destroy. I came that they may have life, and have it abundantly" (John 10:9-11).

Such a conception of life inspires and requires a new set of values for performing Jesus' art of living. The universal ethics' claims are an essential correlation of the belief that humanity is one and indivisible because all humans are children of a loving God. "Charity gives real substance to the personal relationship with God and with neighbour; it is the principle not only of micro-relationships (with friends, with family members or within small groups) but also of macro-relationships (social, economic and political ones). For the Church, instructed by the Gospel, charity is everything because" (Benedict XVI. 2009, n. 2).

Driven by love Jesus does not impose, but only proposes his way of living. Because of it human freedom and free will are greatly emphasized. At the same time, by his attention to the most marginalized, Jesus promotes the equal dignity of humans regardless of any particular characteristics. The central role of the human person dethrones a collectivity of absolute domination over its members. This is a total inversion because "the whole man and all men is also the criterion for evaluating cultures and religions. Christianity, the religion of the 'God who has a human face', contains this very criterion within itself" (Benedict XVI. 2009, n. 55).

All foundations of traditional society came under the scrutiny of Jesus: family, religion, societal power, status of women, etc. Nowhere is the contrast between Jesus and Muhammad greater and more revealing of the gap between the foundations and spirit of their respective ethics than in the case of the adulterous woman. While Jesus at the risk of his life saves such a woman, even against a clear prescription of God's law (Jn 8:3-11), Muhammad, on the contrary, asked to arbitrate in the case of an adultery (*zina*), gave a verdict according to the Holy Book. The adulterous man had to get a hundred lashes and be exiled for a year, and the woman, if she acknowledged her crime, had to be stoned. This hadith reported by the very authoritative al-Bukhari ends: "Onais went to her and after she admitted the adultery, he had her stoned" (Gouguenheim 2008, 254). The third aspect of Jesus' good news concerns a human being's final destiny. Strikingly different from materialist, animist or pantheist doctrines, Catholic eschatology and soteriology affirm a resurrection of the flesh. This means both an integral personal survival, even though transformed, and a community with all loved ones, who have already passed away. The Apostles' Creed proclaims: "I believe in … the communion of saints, the forgiveness of sins, the resurrection of the body, and life everlasting." Clearly, there is no blind destiny but a loving personal God, who provides a special "economy" of salvation of his entire creation. God's love manifested through Jesus Christ saves each human person if s/he is willing to accept it, co-operate with it, and share it with other fellows. Through this love-dynamics a human person is saved from evil and death. A great intellectual and a convert to the Catholic faith, John Henry Newman (1801-1890), who all his life endeavoured to make a masterpiece of himself, expressed his total love for God both through the art of living and poetically through a hymn.

And I trust and hope most fully
In that manhood crucified;
And each thought and deed unruly
Do to death, as he has died.
Simply to his grace and wholly
Light and life and strength belong;
And I love supremely, solely,
Him the holy, him the strong (1974, 769).

2. Art of living in obedience to Allah's word in Sunni community

God is great (4x)
I testify that there is no god but God (2x)
I testify that Muhammad is the Prophet of God
Hasten to prayer (2x)
Hasten to success (2x)
Prayer is better than sleep (morning only)
God is great (2x)
There is no god but God.
The adhan – The call to prayer

The call to prayer, *adhan*, performed several times during a day in Islamic countries rhythmicizes the everyday life of all people there, even though some of them may not be Muslims. In any case, all of them are obliged, like it or not, to follow during the *adhan* some rules imposed by Muslim community. Similar things happen at many other religious occasions. For example last summer the holy month of Ramadan began on the same day in Iraq for both Sunnis and Shiites. For a country driven by sectarian strife that was a welcome omen. But that portent of a religious reconciliation did not make everyone happy because of the prescriptions imposed on all by the State. "Christians are exempt from many of the laws imposing Ramadan strictures, but not the ban on alcohol sales. Many of Iraq's secular-minded citizens were also alarmed, however. 'Why can't I practise my freedom in this country?' said Ahmed Abd, 42. 'If I smoke in the streets, whose fast does it hurt? Why shouldn't I drink water when I'm thirsty in such weather? Why should I hide like a criminal if I want to have a sandwich?'" (Nordland 2009). In any case, at this point an individual person, Muslim or not, has no other choice in public but to obey the way of life imposed by the Muslim community.

These examples reveal that Islam has created a specific societal environment, within which its members perform and realize theire life. Furthermore, the case of Iraq averts us that there are notable differences between Sunni and Shia Islam and that there are therefore at least two possible Muslim arts of living. To catch their inner driving force and consequently their respective art of living, we turn to their origins. We do it by following the recent historical findings.

"The opponents of Umayyad absolutism had two courses of action open to them. On the one hand, they could oppose the ruling dynasty in the belief that government would cease to be oppressive if there was a change of personnel. This was the course adopted by various followers of the *ahl al-bayt* such as *shi'a* (…) Alternatively, the opponents of caliphal absolutism could limit the area affected by it by withdrawing from caliphal control all matters of religious significance, above all the definition of God's law. This was the solution adopted by the future Sunnis. (…)

From the point of view of the political development of the Islamic world, the victory of the *'ulama'* was thus a costly one. (…) The fact that all aspects of life were rolled together in a single God-given packet in the Islamic view of things was of crucial importance for the formation of a new civilization (…); the same fact lies behind the ideological intransigence of Islam *vis-à-vis* the Western world today. It is a fact which throughout history has given Islam extraordinary powers of survival; but at the same time it has always interfered with the capacity of Muslims to organize themselves" (Crone and Martins, 2003, 108-109).

The victory of the *ulama*, the Muslim scholars, over political power, was not only determinant for the relationship between religion and state but also for the religious affairs too. The Sunnism, religion "of the people of tradition" (*Ahl al-Sunna*), which emerged through a long-term formation solely in the 9th century, started as and remained an anti-Shiism. Scholars especially despised and fought the Shia concept of *bida*: innovation, change, which consequently came to mean a departure from Sunna (Gozlan 2008). The brilliant jurist al-Shafi'i (d. 822) was with his work *Origins of the religious law* the first theoretician of what would become known as Sunnism. His "logic was simple and compelling: who is better than the Prophet to explain the meaning and practical application of revelation? If we know what the Prophet did or said on a particular occasion, it must reflect God's will (…). This elevation of prophetic Sunna and identification of Sunna with authentic *hadith* reports is the chief mark of Islamic legal theory in its mature form" (Brown 2009, 167). In the 11th century al-Ghazali established in his work *Refutation of the Philosophers* that only the *Qur'an* and the Prophet's Sunna allow people to know something of God's wisdom and teaching.

From those distant times onwards, the free examination and creative interpretation, the *ijtihad*, are no more allowed; the so called "door of *ijtihad*" is closed by the *ulama*. These real masters of Islam and legal craftsmen had then already finished a magnificent structure of law called *Sharia*. It is based on a convenient five-point scale against which any human action can be measured. Every action must fall into one of five categories: obligatory, recommended, neutral, discouraged or prohibited. The task of the *ulama* is to determine where particular actions fall and Muslims have to obey their decision because they are deemed to express God's will. The word *islam* itself means, indeed, submission and a *muslim* is one who submits him/herself ... to God's will. "From the outset, Islamic law has been an ethics of duty. (…) Questions of ethics were settled not by recourse to conscience, but by referral to tradition, the word of God, and the model of the Prophet. (…) Naturally, Muslims have never doubted, nor do they have any doubt now, that there is such a thing as a conscience. (…) What does not exist for Muslims is conscience as an autonomous authority, because conscience can only appeal to God or be touched by him. But God is also the originator of those laws that one would refuse to obey for reasons of conscience. Muslims follow not their conscience but the will of God" (Küng, van Ess 1996, 45-46).

The *ulama* in spite of their authority have always met some critics, opposition or dissidence. Generally they have not been disturbed by it because Muhammad already predicted that there had to be 73 sects in his community and all of them will perish save one. Today's dissenting voices among Sunnis span from one extreme to another: Let us linger just over one moderate modernist, Fazlur Rahman, because he is much respected among leading Muslims in Slovenia and his book *Islam* was translated into Bosniac by a mufti Nedžad Grabus (2005).

Rahman pleads strongly for skipping a medieval Islamic theology and ethics and returning to the *Qur'an* and the model of the Prophet. Only an ethics built on these two foundations "will represent the essence of the *Qur'an*, for the *Qur'an* is primarily an ethical teaching (with theological base) and not a book of law" (1979, 257). Such a return is much needed not because of the *ulama* monopoly over Islam but because of the Sufism. "To the masses, the Sufi spiritual ideal offered an escape from the uninviting realities of life (…). But this it did at the expense of the Islamic ideal of a social order. Instead of this social-moral order it taught people certain techniques of auto-suggestion and hypnotism and an excessive indulgence in an altogether emotionalized religion which can only be described as mass-hysteria. It is this phenomenon (…) that we have described above as the moral and spiritual debris from which Muslim society has to be reclaimed for Islam" (1981,

246). By this severe judgment on Sufism, Rahman sticks to the Sunnism of *ulama* as the authentic Islam … even though in need of some "fashionable make-up".

One may doubt that the return to the *Qur'an* and to the example of Muhammad advocated by Rahman could improve Sunnism, because the same claim is made by adversaries of the *ulama*. Obviously, all of them have their own preconceived idea on the one hand about the meaning and the requirements of the *Qur'an* and the example of Muhammad and on the other hand how their view about these matters is the only true one. That a struggle for power is involved here is evident, but there could also be a less obvious reason. It can be hidden in the most elemental creedal statement, the *Shahada*, contained in the *adhan*. The expression "*I testify that*" suggests indeed that a Muslim deals with obvious and certain things, namely, the oneness of God and the uniqueness of Muhammad. A Muslim possesses a knowledge of the divine message (*din*) transmitted by Muhammad and gives testimony (*iman*) of it. "The concept of Islam has a double meaning for a specific Islamic thought. As a fulfilment of God's law Islam is one of the components of *din*, as a community, *umma*, Islam contains on the one hand the *din* that is the obedience to the Sharia, and on the other the *dawla*, the politics, which is no more than a secular expression of requirements either coming from *Sharia* or being under its control" (Gardet 2002, 32).

In spite of all the above-mentioned points it is not justifiable to pretend that the large majority of Sunnis do not internalize the *ulama*'s proposition and submit themselves freely, out of a deep personal piety, to God's Word, which sovereignly decided to come to them through the Sunna. They pray the Opening, the first *sura* of the *Qur'an*, as a part of their answer to the *adhan* in the spirit of a complete abandonment and a total submission of all their being to Allah.

> All praise is due to Allah, the Lord of the Worlds.
> The Beneficent, the Merciful.
> Master of the Day of Judgment.
> Thee do we serve and Thee do we beseech for help.
> Keep us on the right path.

The path of those upon whom Thou hast bestowed favours. Not (the path) of those upon whom Thy wrath is brought down, nor of those who go astray.

Our narrative of the Catholic and the Sunni art of living already displayed some irreconcilable differences between them. Let us finish with one quite basic one. It is interesting to note indeed that Christians had much more difficulty than Muslims in expressing the newness of their relationship to God and had to be creative in order to do so. They achieved this by breaking valid grammatical rules and coining a new grammatical construction *credo in Deum* (*I believe in God*), which expresses a movement, involvement of a believer in a relationship of covenant with God in Jesus Christ. Already existing correct expressions *credo Deo* (*I believe to God*) and *credo ut Deus …* (*I believe that God …*) were not sufficient even though their meanings are included in the new Christian technical term. While a covenant with God in Jesus Christ presupposes a free and voluntary engagement in it, in Islam there is neither a covenant nor a similar type of engagement. On the contrary, a Muslim owes a total submission to the massive evidence of the reality of the one God and his unique Messenger. It only may be made on the one hand, by a Muslim's unshakable allegiance to the Sunni community, and, on the other hand, by the public testimony of this evidence through a kind of interpretation and action that is legitimated and approved by the Sunni community.

Despite of practicing very different arts living, mutual understanding, dialogue and cooperation are possible between the Catholics and the Sunnis. However, the establishment of authentic fraternity demands both openness to the other and readiness to listen to the wisdom of the people like Thomas Merton. Without falling into a trap of "syncretism, indifferentism, the vapid and careless friendliness that accepts everything by thinking nothing", he acquired indeed a skilful art of crossing borders between the different arts of living. "There is much that one cannot 'affirm' and 'accept,' but first one must say 'yes' where one really can. If I affirm myself as a Catholic merely by denying all that is Muslim, Jewish, Protestant, Hindu, Buddhist etc., in the end I will find there is not much left for me to affirm as a Catholic and certainly no breath of the Spirit with which to affirm it" (1989, 144).

References and Bibiography

Benedict XVI. *Encyclical letter Caritas in Veritate*, 2009.

Brown, W. Daniel. 2009. *A New Introduction to Islam*. Oxford: Wiley-Blackwell.

Crone, Patricia and Hinds, Martin. 2003. *God's Caliph. Religious authority in the first centuries of Islam*. Cambridge: University Press.

Gardet, Louis. 2002. *L'Islam. Religion et communauté*. Paris: DDB.

Gouguenheim, Sylvan. 2008. *Aristote au Mont Saint-Michel*. Paris: Seuil.

Gozlan, Martine. 2008. *Sunnites, chiites. Pourquoi ils s'entretuent*. Paris: Seuil.

The Harper Collins Study Bible. New Revised Standard Version. 1989. London: HarperCollins.

Küng H., van Ess J. et al. 1996. *Christianity and World Religions. Paths to Dialogue*. Maryknoll: Orbis Books.

Merton, Thomas. 1989. *Conjectures of a Guilty Bystander*. New York: Doubleday.

Newman, Henry John. 1974. Firmly I believe and truly. In: *The Divine Office*. 1974. London: Collins. 769.

Nordland, Rod. 2009. Sunnis and Shiites See an Omen for Reconciliation in Iraq. In: *New York Times*, August 23, 2009.

Qur'an. http://quod.lib.umich.edu/k/koran/browse.html (20.08.09).

Rahman, Fazlur. 1979. *Islam*. Chicago: University Press.

Rahman, Fazlur. 2005. *Islam* (trans. by Grabus Nedžad; Cerić Mustafa, reisu-l-ulema, a leader of Bosniac Muslims, author of supplementary text). Sarajevo: Tugra.

1981 (1952). *Avicena's Psychology. An English Translation of Kitab al-Najat, Book II, chapter VI.* New York: Oxford University.

TO BE SAVED IN RELATIONSHIP

Mari Jože Osredkar, Ljubljana

The art of life constitutes a question concerning the purpose and significance of human existence. This concept can be expressed through a variety of related questions, such as *Why are we here?* or *What's life all about?* Neither biology nor science in general can address these questions, thus they are not central to this discussion. However, world religions, philosophies, and theologies speak directly to issues of life and death. In theology, in particular, this topic is expressed by the doctrine of salvation.

The principal idea to develop in this paper is a religious "art of life" or more precisely a "Christian art of life." The expression "art of life" could well be translated into theological language by the "art of salvation", or by the question: *"How can my life be saved?"* Our concern is to look at how different philosophers and religions have answered this question through a historical perspective, and how theology today continues to define the essential parameters of "our life," as a stage in the passage to death and beyond.

How can my life be saved?

In today's religions, the doctrines of salvation vary and touch on many other related issues, such as, ideas of God, the soul, and the afterlife. World religions share the notion that humanity needs salvation from its present condition since humanity does not manifest its purpose of existence and therefore in some sense is "lost." So, let us review the most important lines of different doctrines of salvation in the history of philosophies and religions.

The old Chinese philosophy is expressed by Confucianism and by Daoism. The former recognizes that human nature needs discipline and education. Since mankind is driven by both positive and negative influences, those who follow Confucianism see a goal in achieving a better nature through strong relationships and reasoning as well as through minimizing negative energy. On the other hand, Daoism emphasizes the need for all people to return to the primordial, that is, to rejoin with the Oneness of the Universe by way of self-cultivation and self-realization. All adherents should understand and be in tune with the ultimate truth. The meaning of life for Daoists is to realize the temporal nature of existence. Only introspection can help find the innermost reasons for living.

Hinduism shares traits similar to Chinese philosophy. In India, the philosophies are intertwined with religion. In all schools of Hinduism, the meaning of life is tied up in the concepts of karma (causal action), samsara (the cycle of birth and rebirth), and moksha (liberation). Life is perceived as the progression of the atman (similar to the western concept of soul) across numerous lifetimes, and its ultimate attainment of liberation. The final salvation is the atman's liberation from samsara. It is the ultimate goal of Hinduism, where even hell and heaven are temporary. This salvation is called moksha, achieved when the individual atman unites with the ground of all being through the practice of yoga.

In another Indian religion, Jainism, the purpose of life also is to attain moksa, that is, release from the cycle of rebirth. Jains believe all living beings have an eternal soul, jīva, and all souls are equal because they all possess the potential of being liberated and attaining moksha. The most fundamental value of Jainism is nonviolence, or ahimsa. This word is usually found on the Jain symbol of the open palm (which means "stop"). Ahimsa is the first of the vows taken by both Jain householders and monks and is the most important way of salvation. The meaning of life may then be said to be: to use the physical body to achieve self-realization and bliss.

We find also in Buddhism, as is the case in Hinduism, that karma is the natural moral law of the universe, in which every good and every bad action has a corresponding effect on the doer. Buddhists believe that life is a matter of suffering, caused by attachment to objects material or non-material; this attachment in turn causes one to be born again and again in the cycle of existence. The Buddhist religious texts do not speak about "the meaning of life" or "the purpose of life", but about the potential of human life to end suffering by eliminating all attachments. Suffering can be overcome through human activity, simply by removing the cause of suffering. Attaining and perfecting dispassion is a process of many levels that ultimately results in the state of nirvana that is called salvation. Nirvana is seen as an end to suffering, rebirth, and ignorance.

In turn, we will continue by reviewing Greek ideas of salvation that we find in their philosophies. Some of the earliest theories of life were materialist, holding that all that exists is matter, and that all life is merely a complex form or arrangement of matter. Empedokles for example argued that every thing in the universe is made up of a combination of four eternal elements: earth, water, air, and fire. All change is explained by the arrangement and rearrangement of these four elements. The idea of salvation, even just earthly, was achieved by an appropriate mixture of elements. But finally, at the end of material existence, life finishes; it cannot be saved. This way of thinking is present also today in Western society. One of the Greeks, Democritus, introduced the idea of soul that would become the pillar of the doctrine of salvation in the thinking of the most important Greek philosophers. Plato considered the soul as the essence of a person, being that which decides how we behave. In Platonism, the art of living in the material body is in attaining the highest form of knowledge, which is about the Idea (Form) of the Good, from which all good and just things derive utility and value. Human beings are duty-bound to pursue the good, but no one can succeed in that pursuit without philosophical reasoning, which allows for true knowledge. He considered the soul as incorporeal, not needing a material body. Thus, the soul is a prisoner in the body, and salvation is its liberation brought about by the death of the body.

Aristotle argued that ethical knowledge is not a theoretical discipline, so a man has to study and practice, he has to be virtuous, practicing virtuous activities in order to become good. According to Aristotle, all things in the material universe have both matter and form, and the form of a living thing is its soul. Aristotle, following Plato, defined the soul as the core or "essence" of a living being, but argued against its having a separate existence in its entirety. He believed that while matter can exist without form, form cannot exist without matter, and therefore the soul cannot exist without the body. Unlike Plato, Aristotle did not consider the soul in its entirety as a separate, spiritual occupant of the body. The soul is an actuality of a living body and (in full) cannot be immortal (Polansky, 2007). These moments of his psychology rather don't support the idea of eternal salvation.

Up to this point, this paper has spoken about the idea of salvation in the philosophical and religious traditions of the East and Greece. It is not difficult to recognize that the common element of these viewpoints is the notion of soul. It is the object of salvation. Salvation for them is the liberation of the soul (as a separate disjointed entity). Although the soul is often considered in the same way in the monotheistic religions, the doctrine of salvation for them is more complex. Judaism, Christianity, and Islam recognize salvation as liberation of the whole person from the bondage of sin and the re-establishing of a personal communion with God. Let us present the most important aspects of their doctrines of salvation.

Judaism did not develop a system of salvation teaching as found in Christianity. Atonement is accomplished by sacrifices, penitence, good deeds, and a little of God's grace. No concept of substitutionary atonement as in Christianity in the person of Jesus Christ exists. In Judaism, God established a covenant with the Jewish people at Mount Sinai, revealing his laws and commandments in the

Torah. Judaism posits collective salvation for the whole people of Israel. In the Judaic world view, the purpose of life is to serve the one true God.

In Christianity Jesus is the source of salvation, and faith in his saving power is the focus. Life's purpose in Christianity is to seek divine salvation through the grace of God and the intercession of Christ. The New Testament speaks of God wanting to have a relationship with humans both in this life and in the life to come, which can happen only if one's sins are forgiven. In the Christian view, the main purpose in life is to live as Christ did: to love God with all one's heart, soul, and mind, and to love fellow human beings as oneself would be loved.

In Islam, man's ultimate life objective is to seek the pleasure of Allah, by abiding by the Divine guidelines revealed in the Qur'an and the Tradition of the Prophet. Earthly life is merely a test, determining one's afterlife, either in paradise or in hell. A person must both believe in one God and do well to get salvation.

Two doctrines of salvation

We can divide these different doctrines of salvation into two groups. In the first group, we put old Chinese philosophy, Hinduism, also Jainism, Buddhism and old Greek philosophy; in these we find the idea of self-salvation. Adherents of Hinduism, Buddhism and Jainism do not believe in salvation in the sense understood by most Westerners; they do not focus on Hell or Heaven as the end result of life. They believe in reincarnation after death. According to this belief, one's actions allow one to be reborn as a higher or lower being. Eventually, one is able to escape from samsara by attaining the highest spiritual state. Thus one is able to save himself. In the second group linked to the doctrine of salvation, we put the three monotheistic religions. Belief in One God is connected to the idea of being saved by someone other than the self; and this other is God the Savior.

We thus have two different schools of teaching about salvation. In the first a man can by himself alone find out the purpose and the goal of his life. The teaching of the second group is based on the dependence on God's mercy. But also in the monotheistic religions man participates in his salvation: he receives divine revelation, which instructs him how to live, and faithfully following this revelation enables him to be saved by God. In fact, the basic difference from the first group is man's inability to discover by himself the correct way of life. Monotheistic believers need God's revelation, and they willingly accept it as the instructions needed for saving their lives.

Ideologically these two doctrines of salvation give rise to a tension between self-sufficiency and dependence. But this tension is in fact a reflection of the tension between the "I" and the "other" in human society. They are competing and they are in conflict with each other. This tension could be relieved by paying attention to the already existing relationship between the "I" and the "other". That is the proper business of life, let us say the art of life. This fight between the "I" and the "other" is in fact the fight between man and God that has endured since mankind's fall from grace. Man makes God culpable for his own suffering and death and attempts to avoid them. At the same time man attempts to avenge himself by pleading ignorance of God's will. Man searches for God and at the same time he hides himself from Him, much like the first man in the Bible. Once again this tension could be relieved by paying attention to the already existing relationship between God and man.

Saved in communication with (O)other

The function of art is to inspire admiration and happiness in the beholder. The highest kind of art is a human life; human life is constituted by relationships, and what could inspire us more than that? So, to live means to be with others. We will try to show how modern Christian theology considers human salvation in relationship as the art of life.

What then is a relationship? First of all, it is a situation in which different subjects are found whether they want to be there or not. I can only become aware that I am already there. For example, I cannot decide to enter life, I can only become aware that I am alive. We all find ourselves in a life situation. I was not asked if I wanted to live or not. At one moment I realized that I was alive. I recognized my belonging to someone. These relationships are not something that we deserve. So I can say that the relationship was offered to me. It is a gift.

A human being cannot live outside of this situation. It is only in it that one can understand himself, because by belonging to others one becomes "himself". To be in relationship involves especially talking "with somebody". To say it in a simple way, it means to pronounce the word "you". The pronounced word "you" is the guarantee of the existence of the "I". Yet I can only pronounce it when I find myself in relation with you. It should not be said "until I form a relation with you", but "when I find myself in relation with you", or even better, when I become aware that I am already in relation with you. We can say that relationship saves man from nonexistence and brings him to existence. This is the first step of man's salvation in terms of relationship. And as long as he stays in it, he will be saved, he will be alive.

Being in relationship, one realizes that this dynamic works according to certain rules. One of these rules is that one is simultaneously present and absent to the other. But this presence and absence alternate in intensity. This is a basic condition of relationship and how it works. The difference between "I" and "you" assures the separate identity of each person; the similarity between subjects assures their closeness. Given this, when they are together they are still apart, yet when they are apart, they are nevertheless still together. Ordinarily, presence and absence are experienced partially; it is only in the case of death that absence is experienced in its totality and there is no presence. In the case of faith, on the other hand, we find the extraordinary situation that God and even those who have died are totally absent and totally present to the man at the same time even though he is still alive.

It is in the simultaneous alternating of presence and of absence where we can understand the relationship between man and God, called faith. Faith is often imagined by people as "conviction about God's existence", but it is more rightly a relation. Many have an idea about God, many philosophers and wise men speak about God, yet this is not yet faith, because to believe in God means to address God with a personal "you". Faith is the situation wherein I can address God with a personal "you". Faith creates a believer in me. And this faith is a gift since I can claim no credit for it. Saint Augustine wrote in his Confessions: "I would not have sought you if you had not found me before." What does that mean? Man would not seek God if he did not already believe in Him. It is only when one feels that he believes that one starts seeking God. And as long as one seeks God, one believes. Once one stops seeking or one believes that he has found Him, he does not believe any more. When he comes to the awareness of living in faith, he starts seeking God and starts to call Him "you, my God". Actually, faith is a relation with a 'someone' a man does not know, but he addresses Him with a personal "you" nevertheless. And when a believer calls him "you", 'god' becomes 'God'. Because God is present in his absence, one can believe also that those persons who are departed can be present while they are absent. So Christians believe that life after death continues but in a different way. This is the second step of man's salvation in relationship.

The third act of salvation occurs when a believer recognizes God's face in each human person–there is the recognition that relationship with the person includes relationship with God. Each relationship consists of two sides, a theological one and a human one. Like a sheet of paper with its two sides, the recto is inseparable from its verso. Just as it is impossible to divide them, it is also impossible to separate one's relation with God from one's relation with people.[1] This union of relation with God and people can be designated by (O)other. Faith then means seeking the (O)other and since we are all in relation, we all need and long for seeking the (O)other and desire to realize the relation with the (O)other. Since relation with people is inseparable from relation with God, the longing for 'other' is essentially a longing for God.

As was pointed out above, faith is a relation with a 'someone' we do not know. Neither is there a need for knowing him. The objective of believing is to maintain the relation with the Unknowable; therefore, we can now ask ourselves: Does to believe mean to maintain the relation only with Him? And the answer is: not just with Him; to believe means to maintain the relation with 'any other'. The believer is close to the (O)other.

References and Bibliography

Osredkar, M. J., *Il est important d'etre ensemble,* Paris: Editions franciscaines, 2008.

Polansky, Ronald M., *Aristotle's De anima,* New York: Cambridge University Press, 2007.

1 See Mt 25, 31-46

TO LIVE WITH GOD IN A WORLD WITHOUT GOD

Avguštin Lah, Ljubljana

Introduction

Speaking or arguing against God or denying the existence of God has been known to man since the beginning of modern times, starting with rationalism in the seventeenth and eighteenth centuries, continuing with the ideologies of the 19th and the 20th centuries and lasting into today's existentialism, nihilism, postmodern technicism, naturalism with emergence of the so called »godless mystics« (Dawkins 2007, 23). Even older than the theoretical discussions and rationalizations of the nonexistence of God is people living their lives as if God really did not exist.

The title of this discussion – to live with God in a world without God – is a paradox which cannot withstand theological criticism. A world without God does not exist. There is not a place, time, or circumstance in this world where God is not present. His omnipresence is a demonstration of his transcendence. God's absolute presence in all things around us makes it impossible for us to perceive him with our senses or knowledge. The only way to perceive and know God is through faith, we cannot feel or taste him like we feel other things. Therefore, a person who relies only on his senses cannot know, reach or understand God. For him God simply does not exist since he cannot perceive Him with his senses. This does not mean that God does not exist; people do not have the sense for all that is God. It is hard to say why God makes our lives richer and why life without God is poor. Declarative atheism is becoming increasingly common. It is therefore vital to address the matter of living the faith in God.

Atheistic understanding of nature: matter is everything

Contemporary radical sensualists and naturalists base their assertions on discoveries of modern science, especially brain research. Based on scientific research on brain activity, psychological activities and social interactions supporters of atheism conclude two things. First, that everything is based on matter, which embraces an infinite variety of phenomena, and that everything functions as matter.

The second conclusion is that all things function by themselves. Nature is about a self-rousing, self-organized, and self-regulated evolution with no aim and no control whatsoever. In addition to scientifically provable facts, there is the principle of coincidence which is in contradiction with the first part of the sentence. In its absolute determinism this kind of materialism replaces freedom with the term coincidence. Modern materialism also does not acknowledge any transcendental reality.

Dawkins defines philosophical materialism and naturalism as belief that »there is nothing beyond the natural, physical world, no *supernatural* creative intelligence lurking behind the observable universe, no soul that outlasts the body and no miracles - except in the sense of natural phenomena that we don't yet understand. If there is something that appears to lie beyond the natural world as it is now imperfectly understood, we hope eventually to understand it and embrace it within the natural. As ever when we unweave a rainbow, it will not become less wonderful« (Dawkins 2007, 14).

In nature as portrayed by materialistic naturalists who interpret all scientific efforts and achievements in atheistic fashion, there is no place for God. To live with God in such a world is difficult. The new atheists never impose their beliefs physically on other people but do it by portraying atheism as a kind of »privileged belief« supported by science, and as an exceeding of faith, since they argue that belief in God is »organized ignorance« (Mohler 2009, 15). To do this they have all modern communication tools at their disposal together with electronic media and money.

Nature, according to naturalists, is desacralized and demythologized, rid of all deities and spirits that old religions once believed in. By profaning nature naturalistic atheism sacralizes and mythologizes it all over again. Naturalists attribute nature divine characteristics by taking it away the slightest chance of relating to God and the other way around. Thus, nature is absolutized and becomes a deity spelled in small letters but is now completely subject to man who becomes its absolute master.

The world man is constructing is godless

Parallel to establishing a profane view on nature in the last couple of centuries a process of secularizing social cultural and other spheres of life took place. Rationalism put subject in the center of social history. This process is first and foremost a battle for autonomy. Abandoning religion and all its rituals has, primarily in western cultures, led to exclusion of God from all spheres of life. Today, personal, social, cultural, and scientific areas of life happen completely autonomously according to man and without the influence of God. Social climate has become atheistic or simply indifferent to religion.

Such a state is a result of emphasizing human capacity of comprehension which developed from rationalism. The human reason is regarded as an instrument for recognizing subjects in order to control and use them. Thus, everything becomes subjected to reason and reason itself becomes self-sufficient. Nothing is greater than reason, nothing is as real as reason unless it can be controlled or explained by reason. The human reason is the absolute criterion for everything, even for itself and as such leaves no place for God.

In addition to glorifying reason, pointing out human freedom has also become significant. The subject is the source of its own freedom which allows it to act according to its own wishes and desires. All obstacles hindering man from carrying out his will must be removed. Freedom means to be »free from« and at the same time it is an enclosed entity focused only on the subject and with no consideration for the freedom of others. Such subjectivistic freedom builds a concept of a self-oriented, self-centered and selfish subject whose only concern is to carry out its will and achieve its goals.

»From this perspective, freedom is achieved by possession and the main trait of such an individuum is to own everything that can be owned« (Vilanova 1996, 444). »My endeavour should be that of expressing my unique individuality without allowing myself to be enslaved or hampered by any alleged higher power such as God or the state or by any abstraction such as Humanity or the Universal Moral Law« (Copleston 1978, 237). On social level, this kind of freedom leads to a bitter competitive struggle in which every subject (company) claims their interests in the cost of destroying other subjects. Individuals act as instruments serving the collective purpose.

In a world where such a state has become global, where all subjects are absolutized and self-oriented, and are based on their freedom and reason there is no place for God.

With its characteristics the modern subject makes spontaneous choices and sets its goals instinctively. It must not, however, avoid certain questions that some sciences raise. Psychoanalysis in particular questions the solid core of autonomy. According to both socio-analytical and Marxist theories the individual is deprived from his freedom by being integrated into mutually dependent conditions or into a dialectical necessity of historic and economic processes. Despite severe restriction of an individual's freedom verging on determinism all these theories leave some room for possible change man can achieve to free himself from personal mechanisms or social conditionalities so that »the kingdom of freedom« can be established (Miggelbrink 2009, 166-167). No one ever relies upon God, God is a redundant hypothesis.

A world of technology without God

Technology plays an important role in dismissing God from the world we live in. Technological and industrial advances have led humans to perceive the world as something that can be built. With the help of technology humans are able to reshape nature and the whole world on every level according to their own image. By accumulating his own products man builds a world (cities) where he encounters only products of his hands. Money makes all this possible.

Man does not perceive himself as being dependent on God or being rewarded by Him and thinks that God is useless. In the world ruled by highly efficient (almighty) and flawless technical products God never appears. Experiencing God in the way the pre-industrious man did is completely alien to the modern man. His dealing with technical objects has influenced the way man handles other, non-technical things. Man treats another man like a machine in a strictly mechanical fashion. Where machinelike mentality has taken over a culture and people's way of comprehending reality, the sense of God has been lost. It is a world without God

Religiousness and faith differ from each other

What is it like to live in this world? What is the quality of a man's life in a world where God is forgotten and rejected and man no longer cares about Him? It almost appears as if man is freed from God. His life is more relaxed, rich, and fuller. But is this true? Furthermore, how can a believer live in a faithless world? Dietrich Bonhoeffer was one of the first people to study the secularized world before and during World War II. He named the secularized world »adult«, »mature« (mündig). This positive aspect originated from the protestant understanding of religion which is the work of man and is in contrast with faith.

It is possible to deduce the following without further analyzing religiousness and faith: Religiousness stands for a broad spectrum of human sensations and conduct which can be found in even the most ordinary chores and activities, such as sports, pleasure, and even technics (Mutscheler 1998/1999). Therefore it is necessary to distinguish between religiousness and faithfulness and to adopt the following claim: Religiousness and faithfulness are not the same thing and differ from each other. A religious person is not automatically faithful and a non-religious person is also not necessarily faithless. A religious person can also be faithful and vice versa. Latest research shows that in the postmodern world religiousness in all kinds of forms is on the increase with little or no faith in it, especially in cultures that were always prevailingly Christian.

Is it possible to believe in a non-religious way in a godless world? Or put this way: Can faith be found in modern atheism? It is clear that religiousness can be godless, yet it is uncertain if there is a godless, atheistic faithfulness. Were it possible to prove that atheism is a religion and that an atheist is faithful, though atheism in its core definition denies the existence of God, theists would have to fundamentally change their attitude toward atheists. The same applies to atheists and their opinion of theists.

Needless to say that foundations of faith in the modern world stand on trembling ground and that faith is in a way absent from this world which is not unexpected. Consider Jesus' question: »However, when the Son of Man comes, will he find faith on the earth?« (Lk 18,8).

To live with God

How does one live with God or think of God's presence in a godless word? Most people found it easy to accept God's presence when the world was still full of it; nowadays it almost requires certain skills. Man has banished God from the world but that does not suggest that God is subjected to man. It is absurd to think that God would submit to man's demands. »No one has ever seen God« (John 1, 18; 4, 12; 6, 46), therefore his presence cannot be proven the same way as other material objects and events. He is invisible and withdrawn from this world. His presence can only be understood in the sense that He is secluded from the world. God's presence in His seclusion from the world allows man to live and create freely.

God's absolute creative freedom exists in every created freedom in such manner that it moves away from it and in doing so enables it to make free choices. Man meets God either on conscious or unconscious level when he makes his choices. When he deliberates and decides freely he always deals with God (Rahner 1980, 42-46). The relationship between man and God is strengthened when man makes choices for he answers to God. Even if he tried to run he could never escape God whom he answers to without suffering severe consequences.

In a particular way, God's seclusion from the world is manifested in the cross and in suffering. When people suffer, either religious or nonreligious, they inquire about God. Faithful people turn to God in the hope of finding help and comfort or inquire about God in knowing that He has forsaken them (Mt 27,46), atheists on the other hand accuse God in their rage and demand that he be tried before a human tribunal. Every man turns to God either in hope or despair, in devotion or protest, in trust or rage but the ways it is done and the outcome are different. In doing this, believers consolidate their trust and devotion to God, and atheists grow stronger in their distaste and denial of God (Bonhoeffer 1951, 11-12).

In borderline situations in particular, God has to be comprehended as completely different, the absolute Other who should never be regarded as a human, an earthly being. He is the Other who is not at man's disposal, a Secret evading human control and desire to turn Him into a tool. Living in today's consumer and hedonistic society is possible only with a different God that is completely useless.

The dissimilarity of God cannot be observed and experienced other than by experiencing man's other self which is *you* at the same time. To actually live with God is to live with one's neighbour, to respect his uniqueness and inviolability, and to discover and acknowledge the mysteriousness that constantly evades control and dominance. At his level of relationship with his neighbour, man's virtues are revealed that surpass the bare subjectivity.

Modern society understands the self-confident and free subject as a »center of action« (Aktzentrum) that defines, acknowledges and gives sense to its own existence and to the existence of others, that needs nobody else, not even God, therefore a subject can never find itself, can never become what it should be – a person. Only in relationship with another human and in relationship with God as »God being spoken to and human speaking to God« can a human become a person. »Man simply does not exist; he does not live until he becomes the spoken-to and the speaker« (Miggelbrink 2009, 170).

An individual that sees himself and expresses himself in terms of »selfhood« and »subjecthood« does not take his originality and distinctiveness seriously but emphasizes his formal sameness with others in terms of deciding and acting freely (Dalferth 1994, 31). The *self* cannot be described as the supposedly stable and identical self from which acknowledgement and action follow but as the self which becomes the *self* in the state of acknowledging and taking action (Dalferth 2003, 416). Man does not find fulfilment in the subject-object relations nor in choosing objects and people and shaping them according to his ideas. Man as a person lives his life fully when he accepts from others and when he gives back. That is how he is able to live fully his relations to others and his relation to God.

In the modern world where there is a lot of religiousness but no transcendence man can never be fulfilled or content because he can choose according to his own wishes and needs (Reif 2009, 23). The variety of choices of things, people, environments, jobs, and beliefs causes man to lose stability and certainty and with that the knowledge of who he belongs to and who belongs to him. In the end, he becomes his own purpose, a servant of himself, his own hostage. Finally, this can only lead to emptiness.

On the other hand, a situation like that can become a starting point into something new, a door that opens for other people who form relationships with that subject and in doing this shape him into a person. Only in man's readiness to encounter his neighbor, to share his trust and affection, accept his attention, compassion and mercy, and to give and receive love and help can man find his personal fulfilment. Living in accordance with these values is living that what God is, God who is with us and for us (Mt 1,23; Is 7,14).

In modern society, this is true of poverty. According to the Evangelism the poor are a sign of God. The glorified Christ identifies himself with the poor: »Whatever you did for one of the least of these brothers of mine, you did for me« (Mt 25,40). In this godless world full of poor people, only those who give care to the poor live with God. In caring for others self-giving becomes serving, symbolized by objects (e.g. money) that one gives to those in need.

An extremely important, although not particularly valued or devalued throughout the entire human history, is love expressed through sexuality. It is characteristic of mature love that it calls into play all man's potentialities; it engages the whole man, so to speak (CD 112, 17). Love embraces the whole of existence in each of its dimensions, thus mature love is a way of knowing and embracing God's salvation love. Love is a path towards knowing the living God and the other way around: »Acknowledgment of the living God is a path towards love« (CD 112, 17). In a close personal relationship between a husband and a wife God himself is present. That kind of relationship signifies that God is love (1 Jn 4,16). A wholesome love between two sexually different beings is a way of to live with God in a world without God.

References and Bibliography

Bonhoeffer, Dietrich. 1951. *Widerstand und Ergebung: Briefe und Aufzeichnungen aus der Haft*. München: Kaiser Verlag.

Copleston, Frederick. 1978. *Historia de la filosofía* VII. Barcelona.

Dalferth, U. Ingolf. 2008. "Subjektivität und Glaube: zur Problematik der theologischen Verwendung einer philosophischen Kategorie". *Neue Zeitschrift für Systematische Theologie und Religionsphilosophie* 36, 18–58.

Dawkins, Richard. 2007. *Bog kot zabloda*. Ljubljana: Modrijan.

Miggelbrink, Ralf. 2009. *Lebensfülle: für die Wiederentdeckung einer theologischen Kategorie*. Freiburg-Basel-Wien: Herder.

Mohler, Alber. "Novodobni ateizem". *Tretji dan* 1-2, 15–23.

Mutschler, Hans-Dieter. 1998/99. "Technik als Religionsersatz". *Scheidewege. Jahresschrift für skeptisches Denken*, 28.

Papež Benedikt XVI. 2006. *Okrožnica Bog je ljubezen*. Ljubljana: Družina (CD 112).

Rahner, Karl. 1980. *Grundkurs des Glaubens: Einführung in den Begriff des Christentums*. Freiburg in Br: Herder.

Reif, Albert. 2009. "Es braucht nicht das grosse Gegenüber". *Publik-Forum* 21 (6. 11. 2009), 23–25.

Vilanova, Evangelista. 1996. *Histoire des Théologies Chrétiennes* III. Paris: Cerf.

ASIA AND THE ART OF LIVING AND DYING

Maja Milčinski, Ljubljana

> Driven by the forces of love, the fragments of the world seek each other so that the world may come into being.
>
> Teilhard de Chardin

I.

This paper elaborates on the contrastive dimension between Asian and European arts of living and dying and the notion of universal love and what (Karl) Robert (Eduard von) Hartmann (1842-1906), philosopher and axiologist, the founder of formal axiological science, the study of values, called intrinsic intelligence or our ability to love and be intuitive. We access this kind of value intelligence through "listening to our hearts." When we are connected to this dimension of value intelligence, we feel a direct connection, no boundaries, nor separation of our knowing into parts. We experience this intelligence directly; no objective analysis is required. It cannot even be described using words. Intrinsic values allow us to recognize the individual or situation as a whole, unique, one of a kind. It is the dimension of unconditional loving. How can modern world learn and benefit from such philosophy? We are born with value intelligence capacities which are operative throughout all living contexts; in all cultures, races, ages, genders, and perhaps even species. From this inner intelligence we develop our inner assumptions about reality. Can this be one of the founding pillars for building a harmonious world today by accepting the death and by living the full life?

European thought came very close to taking the step which places *thanatos* beside *eros*, not as a terrifying elimination but as the expected, inevitable and sometimes welcome counterpole. It is precisely this step, however, which created the notion of impermanence (Chinese: *wuchang*[1]; Japanese: *mujō*) as a meta-

1 The Pinyin transcription for Chinese characters has been used, therefore Daoism instead of the older transcription Taoism, Dao instead of Tao etc.

physical notion, one which supports the Buddhist idea that all material things are considered to have come into existence through some cause and are subjected to the process of creation, abiding, transformation and extinction. This process, moreover, is cyclical: all things are born and die over and over again. The cycle of rebirth can be avoided only by eliminating all desire and thus attaining *nirvāna* or enlightenment, the only stable, non-transient state. Such an attitude can also show us how to understand works like *The Tales of Ise*, and it also makes it possible to find beauty in its vanishing and to accept the fact that the impermanence and evanescence of all things makes everything even more beautiful.

It is important though not to cover one's eyes from the reality of death, but to enjoy the world as it is presented to us in all its aspects, to respect and develop the full human condition and incorporate it into our art of living. Such procedure, together with an authentic and satisfactory attention for the life-death continuum, is almost alien to mainstream European philosophy and psychology, or at least they are lacking in this respect, although it is sometimes found in lyrical writing and other arts.

Problems of diversity, wisdom and liberation became also the main concerns of the classical Chinese philosophical school of Mohism. Whereas Confucius stressed the importance of benevolence (*ren*) in relation to ritual and rules of propriety *(li),* in Confucianism the self-realization can be achieved and the wishes should be fulfilled in the specific ethical context. Daoism, famous for its use of paradox, which should bring the adept to a higher level of understanding and experiencing the reality, understood the Truth as *purity and sincerity of the highest degree*. The Superior man is able to reach the Dao and one's own liberation through meditation, intuition and congeniality with the feminine. The notion of reality in Daoism therefore brings into consideration new paradigms of understanding life and new sensibilities of the regenerated consciousness, which can be expressed only through paradox as a necessary tool for dealing with diversity, enriching us with it. It teaches us better ways to live our lives and points at the limits of exclusively rational approach to life and death.

Socrates's judgment that the unexamined life is not worth living can be applied to death as well. In the context of one's own ephemerality, the Chinese philosopher would instruct us in the following manner:

"Look at things from the point of view of things, and you will see (their nature); look at things from your own point of view, and you will see (only your own) feelings; for nature is neutral and clear, while feelings are prejudiced and dark" (Needham, 1956: II. 456).

Paradox and various other arts of debate can serve as the basis for putting into contrast various Chinese and European ways of living the truth and achieving freedom through these philosophical methods. The aim is to raise questions decisive for anyone dealing with different cultures in any way. On that way, Mo Zi (Mo Zi, 1954) can show us multiple ways of the construction of a coherent sense of one's own Selfhood through a possible dialogue and point at the necessary limits of the overall love and tolerance and the acceptance of one's death and impermanence. Through transcending the Self for the sake of creative living and an attitude of love to others and to oneself, special emphasis is given to the mind/body continuum which does not leave any room for the devaluation of emotional (bodily) aspects. The topics is particularly important for the possible construction of the multicultural societies and can provide us with some self-knowledge methods which might be helpful for practicing love, respect, autonomy and dignity together with various self-empowering methods.

When the differences among the ontological categories (being, non-being etc.) are denied, in regard to certainty new problems arise, as well as original solutions to the old problems. Therefore the demand for a radical negation as the basis for the achievement of certainty, Absolute Truth, which is beyond the beginning and the end, Being and non-being, something and nothing. Being and non-being are just two aspects of the inexpressible Truth. Such methodology and the paradox demand an intuitive structure of understanding which assures meaning in the combination of concepts which would otherwise be understood as logically inconsistent. Metaphorical thinking in Chinese philosophical tradition is not understood as something inferior to conceptual thinking, which is itself put into question, especially in the undertakings, such as the path to certainty. The demand for deontologisation has been strong. The notion of voidness is precisely the one which tests the nature of various attachments (to the Ego etc.). Therefore the demand for discovery of the nature of non-attachment, which forms the basis of certainty, is posed. Certainty, acquired in such a way, opens up new perspectives of existence. When the enlightened one, the one who has reached the basis of certainty, sees everything in the light of voidness, protection against the appearance of ontological entities is established, which then opens up this astonishing realm of suchness of Being. Although this means a temptation, the concept of voidness can never be brought to the metaphysical level or reduced to ontology. The voidness therefore is not the antithesis to Being, neither it is the position between nothingness and Being. Voidness is transcendence of all standpoints and positions. It provides the certainty which leads to the liberation from thinking, and from substantiating the Self and the imprisonment in the Ego and the limits of life and death.

Love as philosophical concept is interesting when treating the problems of life, death and certainty. The obsession of having one's life and death under complete control reached its peak later with a new genre of descriptions of the people who were certain to have had a good death, i.e. have gone to the Pure Land of Amida to be reborn there. In the imaginative geography, one reaches the model death by passing over the sea of uncertainty, landing in the Pure Land, which is conceptually beyond both hell and heaven. It is an illusion created and transferred beyond one's own death, a dream of a certainty reached in a paradise far away in the West. The moment of death becomes the sole possibility of attainment of the certainty and love sought for during the entire lifetime.

When analyzing the Mohist theories of Heaven, we see that in most of them the transcendental moment is present. The situation, described in the texts as Heaven, is the state of undifferentiated consciousness. Since the language is rooted in the differences, here the void space comes into play. The unusual vision, which might be a product of mystical experience, appears in the spiritual eyes as a vast, limitless space, where things exist in an amorphous, dreamlike mode of existence, always changing and flowing into each other. The Heaven can therefore be named as the highest point of uncertainty, where everything flows in a dreamlike insecurity and indetermination. The borders and limits are fluid. It is only the veil of illusion which constitutes the form of language. The primal function of the intellect is that it holds to these mobile and flowing borders, and fixes them into quiet entities. As a result, clearly defined and rigidly fixed distinctions are formed, however these do not correspond to the paradisiacal absence of the formation of meaning. The veil of illusion forms the totality of being and meaning by which, in our minds, the image of so-called reality is formed. This reality, however, is just a surface reality, just a phenomenon, an appearance, a distorted reality of a real unity of reality, which lies at the deepest level, hidden from the eyes of a common human being. Love and cultivation of knowledge as the means to liberation are instructive, since they do not deny the efficacy of knowledge and can tehrefore help us to advance by several ancillary techniques (Chapple, 1990: 62-63).[2] Such standpoint is therefore connected with altering the state of consciousness through the use of various physical techniques. It is the state that transcends the citta-vrtti-nirodha and is therefore indescribable.

II.

Such theory gives rise to a problem of language and the mind-body theory. The absence of Ego, the selflessness and the problem of the inexpressible are the effects of the absolute love and the transition to the level of citta-vrtti-nirodha. This is the level of the art of discourse (pian), mantra and of some of the concepts that slip through the clutches of silence and language - the situation which originates and derives from the voidness, as the basis of certainty and *prajñā* or supreme wisdom.

In the moment of loss of philosophical centrality, we are facing a radical critique of the long lived dream to attain a foundation of knowledge, certainty and an absolute basis for Truth. The topics discussed above call the rational argumentation itself into question. The obsession about whether or not something could be subsumed under the concept of Truth becomes irrelevant. One of the challenges that we face when approaching the notions of life and death in Asian philosophical traditions is the problem of language, of the status of words, and of the spheres of silent language and the language of silence in the process of attaining universal love and liberation. Language as the indispensable tool of intellect helps to create the distinctions of everything and the borders among the myriad things, which from the viewpoint of the citta-vrtti-nirodha are inseparatebly connected in the One. The word, by contrast, is a symbol, a sign of something that has been in the thoughts. The meaning itself is, on the other hand, the symbol of something which is beyond the grasp of logos and is indescribable, inexpressible, certain, since it manifests itself in everything. Here we are dealing with two levels: The surface

2 While the author presents the five fluctuations (vrtti) of the mind (citta) as described in the Yoga Sūtra, he comes to the conclusion that "for the yogi, the goal is to transcend all five by entering the state of citta-vrtti-nirodha. Hence, by definition, the practitioner of meditation is entering into a state of being that cannot be described in the same way one would describe conventional sensory or mental experience."

one, in which reality manifests itself in the form of the ten thousand, myriad things; and the other one, beyond it, the certain one, which is spoken of (or kept silent about) in the sense of the first chapter of the Dao de jing.[3]

The mind-body concept is based on radical transformation of subjectivity, and with it the notion of rationality and approach to love. The notion of Heaven, as understood and described in the way of transformation of consciousness, demands the opening up of the established governing positions of European metaphysics to deeper dimensions of truth, often related to the trans-rational and trans-linguistic experiences upon which any kind of certainty is grounded. This has implications for the philosopher's interest. Namely, how should one read the autonomous philosophical productions of Asia from the standpoint of the European tradition which has been called *philosophia,* the *love of wisdom*, a discipline that in its development sought in the name of Truth a "pure" starting point, a foundation of Absolute Truth, the ground of certainty. Such undertakings have been brought close to the reflections of Zhuang Zi:

"The Great Way is not named; Great Discriminations are not spoken; Great Benevolence is not benevolence; Great Modesty is not humble; Great Daring does not attack. If the Way is made clear, it is not the Way. If discriminations are put into words, they do not suffice. If benevolence has a constant object, it cannot be universal. If modesty is fastidious, it cannot be trusted. If daring attacks, it cannot be complete. These five are all round, but they tend toward the square. (All are originally perfect, but may become "squared", i.e., impaired, by the misuses mentioned.)

Therefore understanding that rests in what it does not understand is the finest. Who can understand discriminations that are not spoken, the Way that is not a way? If he can understand this, he may be called the Reservoir of Heaven. Pour into it and it is never full, dip from it and it never runs dry, and yet it does not know where the supply comes from. This is called the Precious Light." (Zhuang Zi, 1968: 44-45)

3 "As for the Way, the Way that can be spoken of is not the constant Way." Lao Zi, *Dao de jing*.

III.

In relation to human impermanence and death we might find in various Asian philosophical traditions mature attitudes, related to the pattern of meditative and mystical dimensions in the cognitive process, which has always formed a part of philosophical undertakings. In Europe, however, such an approach has often been labeled "unscientific" and unsuitable, although in the recent years the situation has changed, especially in the field of the explorations of consciousness related to the sleeping, dreaming and dying processes and their influence to the quality of life. By presenting the Sino-Japanese ways in contrast with some of the theories grown from the Graeco-Judaeo-Christian context, we may test two models of philosophical and wider spiritual reaction in encountering human ephemerality. The "Asian" and "European" are not taken here as geographical terms, but as two alternatives. Traditionally, Asian philosophical traditions have often included the meditative and mystical patterns as relevant, whereas the European philosophical discipline has often been limited to the logically discursive way of reasoning.

The negation of the ontological doctrine is one of the liberation techniques in the vast tradition of Asian philosophies. The way of achieving liberation through universal love can teach us about the illusion of the often supposed superiority of philosophical speculation as understood in the Judeo-Christian-Greek heritage. The techniques and practices mentioned in the text are directed to the development and transformation of the mind and personality aiming at the achievement of wisdom (*prajñā*). Unlike European philosophy which has in its history sought even mathematical models of philosophical thinking, the Asian philosophical schools have not put the demands of mathematical proofs in their philosophy. Instead of rigid intellectual and logical approach, they have employed direct intuitive experience, which is without doubt much richer than rationalizations based on a discipline of analysis and separation. The one-dimensionality of rationality is put into question and can therefore not be used as the sole tool for the »analysis« or »comparison« of these traditions under investigation with those of the Euro-American stream of thought. The soteriological project of the Asian traditions becomes evident, since knowing also in its trans-rational dimension, necessarily interconnects with becoming. This can lead to a certain challenge to the philosophical schools based on the Judeo-Christian-Greek tradition, which have separated the fields of ontology and epistemology, which have in the traditions discussed been cultivated together, inseparably. The metaphysics of subject and the ontological reductions so well established in modern European and American philosophical history can prove to be unsuitable for the approaches used in Asian philosophies and therefore also call for the re-examination of the foundations of rationality. The questions of reality and universal love encroach upon the realm of the ineffable which remains the source of the great creativity in any philosophical tradition and its way into liberation. To reach this stage, we have to yield our "given" spirit, and in accordance with this fasten the spirit, sit and forget, forget ourselves and lose ourselves in love, which is egoless, selfless, without desires and expectations, ideas about ourselves. That is why it is completely free. The unification with the universal love therefore means giving up our Ego, Selfhood, which does not mean a kind of self-repression but rather forgetting the Self where nothing is left which could still be subjected to any kind of repression.

IV.

Notions of the all-encompassing power of language and word have been ubiquitous in the history and philosophy of religions. So too, has been a recognition of the inability of language and word to give full expression to the realities that constitute and engage human beings and the world in which they live. (Reynolds, 1993: IX)

Let us say that the prospect of solving questions of life, death, love and spirituality lies in combining the logically discursive style of Uroboros with the meditative mystical style that is with the open circle, while dwelling on the subject. In this case, we must stop hoping that we will find a redeeming word for the final experience. Instead, we can hope for the indescribable experience, the enlightenment, as a quality of mysticism. If the Uroboros science and philosophy resist such tendencies, we can to some extent understand this as something characteristic for them and a possibility (on both sides) for useful, purifying dialectics. »Mysticism« in particular may be resisted by well established science and its philosophy, whether it is explained as uncontrolled fantasy or accepted only as a monopoly of the encapsulated and »the only true« Church. If we continue with our vision of approaching authentic spirituality, the prospect of gradual merging of philosophies and religions is revealed. Moreover, the sense for the »mystical« in literature and art and glimpses of »mysticism« on various occasions of our everyday life will grow sharper. Shall we still wait for the arrival of *mysterii tremendi et fascinosi*, for something so dramatic as the experience of Apostole Paul during his conversion on the road to Damascus? Such experiences, although much subtler and less noticeable, are not reserved only for people who dedicated themselves to a monastic lifestyle. It is impossible here to start a discussion worthy of attention on the science and method of searching for one's essence, meaning of life and death, such as has been developed in Asian philosophies, but this paper represents only a glimpse of its worth and challenge for philosophical and wider social undertakings today.

References and Bibliography

Chapple, C. 1990: "The Unseen Seer and the Field: Consciousness in Saamkhya and Yoga," *The Problem of Pure Consciousness*, ed. Robert K. C. Forman, Oxford: Oxford University Press.

Mo Zi. 1954: *Mo Zi jian gu*, Beijing: Zhonghua shuju.

Needham, J. 1956: *Science and Civilization in China*, Cambridge: Cambridge University Press.

Reynolds, F. E. 1993: "Foreword: Ineffability", *The Failure of Words in Philosophy and Religion*, ed. Ben-Ami Sharfstein, New York: SUNY.

Zhuang Zi. 1968: *The Complete Works of Chuang Tzu*, trans. Burton Watson, New York: Columbia University Press.

"DRIFTING AS THE SEA" – THE ART OF LIFE IN THE DAOIST TRADITION

Romualdas Dulskis, Kaunas

Various cultural lifestyles naturally interweave in today's world which is embraced in globalization processes. These enhance each other but, at the same time, they challenge us to examine the values in our own lives and to delve deeper into an understanding of our own identities. The Daoist philosophy and religious tradition presents exceptionally interesting and valuable insights into a person's vocation and life's purpose. Such insights may appear paradoxical at first glance; however, by taking a more astute observation, we notice their proximity to Christian values.

In Daoism the art of living relates closely with the idea of freedom. The Daoist purpose in life is to have no purpose, to be as free as the wind and sea and, along with that, to open completely to what inspires all life's processes—Dao. To what extent does the Daoist idea of freedom confront the Christian idea? Furthermore, what point of contact can be found between the Daoist view of a person's life and the teachings of Jesus?

The first step on the way of Dao towards true wisdom is to comprehend the interconnectedness between all things and to overstep the stereotypes of one's own thinking. According to Zhuangzi, ch. 26, "The fish trap exists because of the fish; once you've gotten the fish, you can forget the trap. The rabbit snare exists because of the rabbit; once you've gotten the rabbit, you can forget the snare. Words exist because of meaning; once you've gotten the meaning, you can forget the words. Where can I find a man who has forgotten words so I can have a word with him?"

1. "To build up power"

"Leading people" and "serving heaven" are the two concepts expressing the most important, authentic human purposes: public obligations and responsibility before the Divine. Laozi highlights that *being frugal* is what best helps to achieve both of these ends.

> "In leading people and serving heaven
> it is best to be frugal.
> Being frugal is to be prepared from the start.

> Being prepared from the start is to build up power [i.e. virtue, *de*].
> By building up power nothing is impossible.
> If nothing is impossible, then there are no limits." (*Laozi* 59) [1]

However, about what sort of frugality is Laozi talking? The next lines in the text say that *being frugal* directly relates to *building up power*. *Power*, in this position of the text, does not mean external physical power; it is the translation of the Chinese *de* concept. Certain translations use the word *virtue* for this same concept. However, the translators selecting the word *power* to express the *de* concept emphasize that *de* means not only a certain quality (value) but a quality containing power within itself. In order for a person to acquire this power, he/she must proceed on the way of Dao very seriously. Frugality (*se*), in this same chapter, is distinguished as a special characteristic of a Dao follower. First and foremost, this is frugality with one's own vital powers, a modest way of life and self-restraint to avoid squandering spiritual powers. As one's own powers are conserved, nature is being conserved by the same. Therefore frugality, by forming the conditions for a person to designate all his/her strength to Dao and acquire *power* (*de*), prepares a person for true and fruitful action. Such action corresponds with the *wuwei* principle; thus it creates harmony and peace in a community. The potential of a person who has acquired *power* is described by Laozi in very strong words: "nothing is impossible" and "there are no limits". These words talk, first of all, about the strength of the action by a person upholding the *wuwei* principle (A. Fox, p. 59-72). Here the purported inaction forms the conditions to accumulate forces for actions that are notable for exceptional strength and ability in overcoming all obstacles.

Nevertheless there is another aspect to "nothing is impossible" and "there are no limits" as well. That constitutes the characteristic of a Daoist sage spoken about in Laozi's chapter 20: to be as free and unrestrained as the wind and „seeming aimless, drifting as the sea". Generally this Daoist freedom contradicts the teachings of Confucianism which urge developing commitments to the community and responsibility to Heaven (J. Ching, 122-132). It is specifically because Confucianism emphasizes ethical responsibility that the teachings of Laozi on freedom are not-so-rarely explained as an ethically and religiously unrestrained

1 All citations from *Laozi* are taken from Sanderson Beck's translation.

lifestyle. In truth the teachings of Laozi are exactly that. But in which sense are they so? Is it that ethical standards and religious truths should be considered relative and refutable? Or should these teachings of Laozi be understood in the sense that ethics and religion are no longer comprehended as screw-bolts but as landmarks indicating the way towards the quality of life? The tendency today is specifically to explain the teachings of Laozi on freedom and superior and inferior virtues. An effort to merely "learn" how to behave ethically with respect to other people, to nature or to the Divine, as Laozi says – never brings the expected results. A person must not "learn" ethics or religion but comprehend the self as an integral part of nature, the community and Dao. Although, on the one hand, Christian theology does not accept the pantheistic identification of a human with God, it does, on the other hand, strongly accent the union, of a human with God as essential to the entire purpose of an ascetic and mystical Christian life. Nature also has its place in this union of the human with God because, just as sin does not injure only human nature but all creation as well, so the union of the human with God oes not only open the way for overcoming sin but reestablishes the harmony of nature as well.

In this context, it becomes clearer that Laozi's chapter 59 speaks not about the relativity of ethical and religious principles but about the rigidity of human thought. Specifically because people's thought processes are often constrained and restricted within narrow frames, they prevent the discovery of doctrines on ethics and religion in the broader sphere. Laozi does not urge crossing over religious or moral boundaries but becoming liberated from one's own limitedness and ignorance. A person must break free from the religion and ethics of his/her own making to be capable of opening up to the objective, divine Truth which surpasses the thinking of any human. For this reason, "nothing is impossible" for the Daoist sage, because he/she has understood that many matters become impossible simply because people decide within their hearts that it cannot be. Furthermore, according to Laozi, "there are no limits" for a Daoist sage, specifically because the sage has become a person "without limits"; i.e., the sage has learned to refrain from placing limits, within the heart, on truth and goodness. Upon becoming liberated from numerous internal and external restrictions, the Daoist sage becomes capable of intertwining a deep connection with Dao that encompasses the sage's entire existence. It is about this connection that Laozi speaks with such simplicity that it appears to be an entirely natural reality. It is natural for a person to be "deeply rooted in a firm foundation" (chapter 59). Upon taking root, this gives birth to a specifically Daoist process of action distinguished by exceptional positivism and success, because its basis is "maternal leadership" – i.e. Dao leadership.

2. Daoist leadership

The sages of ancient China paid a lot of attention to the teaching of rulers to believe that the wellbeing of the entire country depended on the morality of sovereigns. Laozi emphasized that a ruler who is learning to understand the harmony of nature, to live according to the principles of Dao and to rule people temperately will be led by success. The foundation for the success of such sovereigns lies in their not harming the natural processes of nature, not raising artificial and unnecessary demands on their citizens and their personal concern to allow Dao to occupy the fundamental place in their lives.

Therefore Laozi invites rulers along with all people seeking Dao to abandon wisdom and cleverness, humanity and morality and skill and profit. He asserts, "These three things [1) wisdom and cleverness, 2) humanity and morality, 3) skill and profit] relate to externals and are inadequate" (ch. 19). To uphold some matter as the highest life's purpose when it should only be secondary means to disrupt the harmony of the internal life of an individual as much as of public life. Wisdom, cleverness, humanity, morality, skill and profit are, without a doubt, important values in human life. However, Laozi asserts that the first and foremost place in personal and public life belongs to Dao alone. If Dao ceases to be the foundation of life in its entirety, the other, inferior values lose their foundation of support. Therefore there is no sense in contributing all one's forces to pursue inferior values, because they are impossible to achieve if Dao is rejected. To add strength to his phrase, Laozi expresses himself very sharply accentuating the necessity to abandon and discard inferior values. Laozi is convinced that, if Dao were to be selected as the most significant purpose in life, all other values will thrive as well. However, if Dao were to be rejected, the inferior values will depreciate despite their being accented and, in the end, they will remain as nothing more than empty words. Once the inferior values depreciate, the order in public life will fall apart as will the harmony between the human and nature. Thereby people are obliged to turn towards Dao with their entire beings and to stifle their external cravings in order to pursue the most important purpose with all their might.

Laozi submits his own view on the motives for human action by analyzing the features which should characterize good rulers. His words are designated firstly to rulers; however, he also dedicates them to all people. The excerpt below from chapter 17 reveals the scale of the worthiness of human action. This speaks about every individual's chosen position in life and manner of action which, by their own accord, influences the environment: persons nearby, nature and the quality of that same individual's own life.

> "The best leaders the people barely know.
> The next best they love and praise.
> The next they fear.
> And the next they hate".

Laozi knows from life's experience that there are leaders whom people hate or fear. The claim in the second line, that a good leader the one that people "love and praise", is familiar and understandable to us. Seemingly the leader who is respected and loved by people is worth being considered the best. However, Laozi does not consider such a leader the very best one. At first glance, Laozi's claim that the best is the one "the people barely know" seems incomprehensible and mysterious. In order to more readily understand him, we can compare him with analogies of this type in Christianity. Laozi's phrase about individuals the people barely know reminds us of the vocation for a contemplative life in Christianity and, as the Church accents, the importance of such a vocation. The monastic orders of contemplative monks and nuns are considered the lifeblood of the Church and their life of prayer – the foundation of the Church's pastoral activities. Furthermore theology considers meditation and contemplative prayer as the most important components of everyone's Christian life, because contemplativeness not only leads to a mystical union with Christ but it is also the basis of mature and successful activity. Thus, the claim by Laozi acquires a new light in the perspective of Christian contemplativeness. On the other side of the coin, the popular culture of today, on its own accord, seemingly confirms Laozi's claim by "loving" and adoring pseudo-leaders – the various stars of popular culture. Meanwhile the persons who truly have earned merit in the community usually remain much less noticed.

Nonetheless, Laozi does not limit himself to an assessment of popularity. He goes further and raises the question about the value of the good deeds for which people "love and praise" their leaders. Unquestionably here the text by Laozi speaks about positive deeds which merit a positive assessment and about leaders who are notable for such deeds. Nonetheless, Laozi assures that such activity, albeit being positive, is, by no means, the superior value. According to Laozi, the best leaders consciously avoid popularity and engage in activities that remain unknown or little known to the community-at-large and, for this reason, never receive any adulation from the broader public. Regardless, such activity is exceptionally valuable and bears the ripest fruits for the public. "As fish stay in the deep water" (*Laozi* 36), so the Daoist sage is inclined to remain unknown. The person who has known Dao and lives according to Dao attains exceptional knowledge about life and people. Such a person sees right through people and understands the true motives behind their behaviors and their goals. Nevertheless a Daoist sage usually does not display wisdom but remains simple and still, asserts Zhang Yi. Such a sage comprehends that the true pivotal point in the history of humankind does not consist of engaging in noisy action or advertising one's own talents but of a calm and ceaseless endeavor in line with Daoist principles, similar to the flowing of a river. By flowing peacefully and gently, water overcomes all obstacles in its way and moistens the earth, thereby providing it with the power to raise a crop.

3. Colors which blind the eyes

Certain of Laozi's teachings appear, at first glance, to be on a purely ethical plane. However, they actually attempt to achieve a somewhat more essential matter – to assist an individual in establishing the correct course throughout life. By turning around towards Dao, a person thereby acquires the correct relationship with other people and nature as well. Wanting to safeguard from unhealthy competition Laozi urges, "Do not exalt the worthy, so that people will not compete" (ch. 3). Such restraint from lauding the talents and merits of a person does not mean that Laozi is promoting not to recognize and not to appreciate people's talents and merits. However, when talents and merits are overly accented, it seemingly emphasizes that the true value of a human being lies within them. That way, people are being inspired to seek only external, "inferior" values and forget the true purpose – Dao. Laozi does not deny the need to appreciate people's talents and to be pleased with them; however, he notes that the essential worth of a person does not lie in them. Talents and merits supplement and enrich the life of an individual, but the most important purpose in life is one – to live according to Dao.

Another entreaty from Laozi has a similar purpose: "Withdraw as soon as your work is done" (ch. 9). This is highly reminiscent of the saying by Jesus: "So with you: when you have done all you have been told to do, say, 'We are useless servants: we have done no more than our duty'" (Luke 17:10). It is characteristic for a person to evaluate his/her own talents overly well and provide too great a prominence to the self. In the same way, we are inclined not only to rejoice with a job performed but also to have an exaggerated amount of pride in it. A successfully performed job, as per Laozi, can become an inducement for the "person of an inferior morality" to consider him/her self superior to others. Even more so, success can awaken aggression in a person and a desire to dominate by pushing others aside. This is why Laozi encourages not giving into the illusion regarding the meaningfulness of our activities to avoid losing our own identity. By becoming enraptured with the success of an external activity and concentrating only upon it, a person distances from the fundamental and most important purpose of life because an individual can only grow and mature as a persona by walking the way of Dao. Upon leaving the way of Dao due to an external fortune, a person experiences the essential misfortune of his/her life and that person becomes socially destructive.

While talking about the obstacles involved in getting to know Dao which arise from a surplus of material goods and life's pleasures, Laozi employs the images of five colors (traditional Chinese views regard black, red, blue-green, white and yellow as standard colors), five notes of the Chinese musical scale and five flavors (sweet, salty, sour, bitter and spicy):

> "The five colors blind the eyes;
> the five musical tones deafen the ears;
> the five flavors dull the taste." (*Laozi* 12)

By these images, Laozi speaks about the danger of a luxurious life. If a person consumes overly many material goods or pleasures, these overwhelm Dao in his/her life and, thereby, depreciate the true quality of life. Opulence not only overpowers true values but it pulls a person into a circle of pleasures and wastes the vital energy of that person. The conviction that luxury and gratifications are the only sources of joy in a person's life impedes that individual from experiencing the true joy in everyday life. The pursuit of external satisfaction from sensations alone leaves the essential needs of a person unsatisfied. Therefore the Daoist sages "satisfy the inner self rather than external senses; they accept the one and reject the other" (ch. 12).

According to Laozi, there is nothing stable in the world, excepting – Dao and following Dao. Thus Daoist sages try to have as few longings as possible that are not related with Dao. By rejecting the empty ambitions prompting intemperate consumption, so usual for many people, the Daoist sage lives a life that is peaceful and calm to the brim while, and at the same time, is a most directed life.

Conclusions

The analysis on the Daoist art of living reveals one of humankind's most important and enriching legacies of philosophy of religion. From many perspectives, this is an entirely different world than the one we find in the Bible. Nonetheless certain aspects of the teachings in Daoism by the classics are very near to those in Evangelical texts.

The insights of Laozi and Zhuangzi teach a discovery of deeper reasons for universal phenomena and the recognition of a person's true vocation. As per the stances of Catholic theology, discussions on divine inspiration regarding Daoist texts are out-of-the ordinary. Nonetheless, it would probably be difficult to deny the authenticity and subtlety of their wisdom. The context of Christian experience especially amazingly reveals the depth and harmony of Daoist teachings.

The Daoist life without purpose teaches one not to be limited to narrow and temporary endeavors alone. Although no person can live without any temporary goals, nevertheless, great damage comes to the personality concentrating on such matters alone. It is in this sense that Laozi encourages living without purpose—to be as fetter-free as the wind and as carefree as the sea. This telling is as similarly challenging as the phrase Jesus spoke about tearing out an eye and cutting off a hand (Mark 9:43-47). Both these phrases, it would seem, have the same objective—to free a person for a life according to the divine Principle.

References and Bibliography

Ching J. 1989: *Konfuzianismus und Christentum*, Mainz: Matthias-Grünewald-Verlag.

Dulskis, R. 2009: 'The Purpose of Human Existence and the Meaning of Immortality in Daoism', *The Philosophical Basis of Inter-Religious Dialogue*: The Process Perspective, Cambridge Scholars Publishing, 109-120.

Fox, A. 1996: 'Reflex and Reflectivity: Wuwei in the Zhuangzi', *Asian Philosophy*, Volume 6/1, 59-72.

Watson, B. (transl.) 1968: *The Complete Works of Chuang Tzu*, New York: Columbia University Press.

Zhang, Yi. 2005: 'Komentarai', *Laozi*, Vilnius: Vaga, 199-232.

EDUCATION

CHURCH RELATED HIGHER EDUCATION IN EASTERN AND CENTRAL EUROPE

Gabriella Pusztai, Debrecen

Effect of political transition on higher education

To study the current situation of church related higher education, we must review the circumstances in which the years of transition affected the higher educational systems of post-socialist countries, denominations, academic bodies, and the relationship of higher education and labour market. Before the transition, the special socialist model of higher education was characteristic to this region. When the promotion of higher education tutors was adjudged, scientific achievement (researches, publications) was effaced by political reliability. Higher educational supplies and limits were not influenced by student or labour market demands, as labour force-production was planned and controlled by the state with closed limits and multiple applications over college/university quota (Hrubos, 2002: 25). Denominations played double roles. They represented the interest of culturally consented people, even if this happened enclosed within the walls of churches. The official organizations of denominations had to find the modus vivendi with current governments. As a result of this compromise, the educational activities of denominations were strongly limited and strictly controlled (Pusztai, 2008: 122).

After the transition states in the region abandoned the restrictive higher educational policies. Higher educational institutions perceived the market demands directly through the number of students applied (Clark 1983: 142, Kozma 2008: 30) and by recognizing the logic of thc financing system, tried to admit as many students as possible. Academic values were free of ideological control and the receding states focused on accountability and checked the right to utilize supplies with the help of accreditation and other interim organizations (Kozma 2008: 35). In the academic sector, personnel were not radically changed – except for East-German territories –, so the view that religious ideology was not an equal partner remained characteristic to state-maintained universities. The socialist model of higher education was slowly transformed into a democratic, law-regulated model, which abolished the institutionalizing monopoly of the state. There is a difference between post-socialist countries in point of the extended range of potential school-maintainers, as in orthodox countries, denominations cannot establish schools but their foundations (Szolár 2008: 8, Murvai 2008: 107, Molnár 2008: 85). Those churches that had these historical conventions – by disposing their political restrictions – helped out the inefficient state-maintained systems to provide educational, social and healthcare services. Churches had a vision of their higher educational tasks, therefore denominational tertiary education affected areas that were most controlled ideologically or were most closed socially before (teacher- or lawyer-training) as well as areas that suit the traditional public responsibilities and roles (social, educational, healthcare professions) of denominations. The rapid expansion of higher education could not satisfy student demands; certain student groups in particular regions have still not found the higher educational options that are available and appropriate for them (Altbach 1999: 163). Such student groups include ethnic and religious minorities in different countries. These groups emerged as definite demands for church related higher educational institutions.

Concept of Church related higher education

Church related higher education is defined in a variety of ways by specialized literature. It is confusing that according to international statistics and the special literature based upon them (Slantcheva - Levy 2007), church related higher education institutions are labelled as private establishments, because all higher educational institutions are labelled as private establishments if they are not operated by governmental bodies. To be able to separate sectors, Levy (1992: 1183) suggests more aspects – finance, control, mission, social function, social-contextual categorization – to be examined. Our research is characterized by the comparative approach. In the first session of the research, we collected and analyzed case studies about the church related higher education systems of Central- and Eastern-Europe. The studies included five countries: Hungary, Slovakia, the Czech Republic, Romania and Estonia.

After the nationalization during the socialist era, churches have no substantive income. The church related HE institutions of the area are operated usually from state support. Students at church related higher education institutions have typical motivations for choosing profit-oriented or the church related institutions, so they satisfy different social functions (Szemerszki 2006: 56). The most notable dimension of the definition of operation is the articulation of the concrete and unique goals of the institution. By having surveyed the mission-declarations of higher educational institutions, we concluded that responsibility for mankind is generally among the distinctive goals of church related higher education institutions. Another differentiating character is the emphasis of freedom of research and thought contrary to the universities that are subordinate to state or market demands, therefore depend on politics and commerce. The third important element is the concept of personality development, which is broader than that of secular universities. This is done to prepare students not only for effective career but also for meaningful and rich personal lives.

We find the same thoughts and values among the goals of church related higher educations in the post-socialist countries but their identity is specially complemented with the emphasis of intelligentsia-training for the target community. A special role-expectation is associated with the term of intelligentsia due to the cultural traditions of the region, which has been fighting against underdevelopment for centuries, namely, highly qualified people not only outstand by consuming high culture but take the responsibility and fulfil the special mission for their communities as well. The national, ethnic or religious minorities of the region aim to establish educational institutions to be able to struggle against discrimination and underdevelopment and to preserve their identities (Kozma 2003: 39).

It is important which extra elements are included in the curricula compared to non-church related higher education institutions, which prepare students for this special role. The mission-declarations of the post-socialist region emphasize the religious interpretation of training material more than in those of Western-Europe. This is important because most lecturers at state universities train according to a partly eroded, intermingled but fundamentally Marxist or post-Marxist principle due to the socialist education-policy.

To be able to formulate the proper definition of church related higher education, we take into account training supply as well. It has been observed that the older denominational universities offer broader training supply whereas the newer ones operate with narrow training supplies – apparently owing to their younger age. Newly established church related higher education institutions do not offer economic and business trainings but pedagogical and social preparation is operated everywhere.

Actors in church related higher education

Having clarified the definition of church related higher education, we must introduce their education-political field of force. To be able to do that, we improved the Clark's triangle-model (1983: 145). To compare national education-policies, Clark formed this model which supposes three centres that convey pressure and expectations and influence higher education policies. The three centres include academic oligarchy, state bureaucracy and market, all of which have their own value-duals and expect higher educational institutions to fulfil their own values and requirements, respectively. During the 1990s, the critics of the model stated that the value-system of the state had shifted towards market logic, a state that requires accountability and assess achievement and that academic value-system was retiring whereas governmental/managerial logic began to dominate (Neave 1998: 264). After the millenary, the expansion of the nationally thematic mode of action was suggested because of expectations that were realized both internationally and locally more and more definitely and which were sometimes rather different. Besides, the Clark-model had to be supplemented because centres, which denoted different value-systems, were represented by authorities and organizations earlier but it is evident that we have to take into account collective interest groups or individual actors (lecturers, students) as well (Chen-Barnett 2000: 286, Marginson- Rhoades 2002: 291). Furthermore, higher education researchers noted that it is worth to analyze policies at local or institutional levels, too. We believe that a special model is necessary for drawing the field of force of church related higher education, which contains a fourth element besides the academic oligarchy, state bureaucracy and market centres. This fourth centre, which represents strong value-system, expectations and weight, is formed by churches. The power relation originating from denominations towards higher educational institutions is double-sided, which is derived from the organizational characteristics of denominations and the network characteristics of individuals who are joined on their own free-will. Besides, our model may be interpreted in three-dimensions, that is, the above mentioned relations are articulated differently at local, national or global levels. While the influence of local and national actors have always been easy to identify, global effects that shape higher education are becoming increasingly influential. This is exemplified by attempt to satisfy the apostolic regulations of Ex corde, which summarizes the operating principles of catholic universities. In some cases, concordant and contradictory interest may be articulated by actors of the same type.

Higher education is generally characterized by a relatively open goal-system, loose control-mechanisms and high fragmentation. The multiple connections of church related higher education may cause internal and external conflicts as well (Dee et al. 2004: 177). The relatively young church related higher education institutions of the region do not have rigid structures. Obviously, they could not return to the higher educational concept before socialism, so they had to synchronize several – so far unidentified - expectations in the new field of force.

On the one hand, expectations originating from the denominational characteristic of institutional mission may conflict with expectations aiming to achieve academic accuracy. According to the mission of church related higher education institutions, the majority of lecturers and executives must agree with the religious practices of the given denomination while high-quality academic performance is also expected from them. Prioritizing the two types of expectations is a difficult question everywhere but it is especially problematic in our region, where confessed piety was disadvantageous with respect to research supports, publicizing possibilities and acquiring academic degrees until the years of transition. If academic aspects are taken to the fore, the development of a more secular institutional intellectuality is unavoidable. In the post-socialist countries, the expansion of higher education passed late and extremely fast, hence lecturers with academic degrees are deeply lacked. Academic oligarchy controls the approval of the highest scholarly degrees here as well, thus several new institutions cannot command a sufficient number of qualified lecturers, rather, they pursue prominent professors who work at multiple institutions simultaneously. The image of this lecturer who travels and provides services temporarily cannot be compliant with church related higher education.

On the other hand, the second group of conflicts originates from the disagreement of denominational mission and state expectations. Institutional and departmental autonomy had been a fundamental characteristic of universities for centuries. The higher education of the regions had just disengaged from the strict constraints of socialist education-policy, it found itself in a worldwide changing system of higher education in which earlier academic autonomy and freedom was limited by states and international organizations (Altbach 2003). The space of higher educational institutions was restricted by extended governmental control. Secular obligations are the most aching for denominations while maintainers usually expect them to enhance their denominational-religious identities.

It also causes significant problems that denominations with diverse educational traditions were taken under state control due to the several political reorganizations of state-borders in the region. Subsequently, laws were modified according the educational roles of majority churches after the transition, which may hinder the educational attempts of minority denominations. This situation characterizes the non-orthodox minorities in Romania and the Ukraine whose church related higher education institutions do not receive state support, thus those are considered private in terms of funding as well. These groups are often ethnic minorities, which means that their church related higher education institutions constitute the only way to study in their mother tongues.

The third type of conflicts originates from the disagreement of denominational identities of institutions and market values. The region's market economy emerged as the result of a non-organic development through a redistributive economic system, for which the majority of population was unprepared in terms of business competencies and financial resources. As the standard of living of most families undersized those of the West, they could not invest significant money in their children's education. Institutions strive to sell their trainings as products and, therefore the ratio of places where students pay tuition fees has been increased. This endangers the principle of social justice, which is judged as fundamental by the social message of denominations. It would be necessary to support the underprivileged youths of social levels with scholarships, institutional places sponsored by denominations, student hostel or travel allowances. However, these societies lack the religious social groups and schools are not supported by sponsors and alumni.

As the different intuitions compete for students, universities and colleges attempt to prove their best. In their advertisements, they promise enjoyable campus-life, modern, consumer lifestyle and infrastructural improvements also aim this (net café, fitness centres, and student hotels). The concept of church related higher education institutions focuses on less commercial but rather pastoral and community-building values.

Institutions at short range

Church related higher educational institutions consider their duties to preserve ethnic and religious identities. This is exercised in a tolerant and constructive way through the membership of a universal religious community. Based on institutional histories, we concluded that local and regional churches are featured in the establishment of institutions. The most diverse role is played by the governmental actor. Because of the deficient structure of regional higher educational institutional network church related higher education institutions were established (and still operate) in denominational. Their operation is almost entirely supported by the state except for Romania.

Although clerics are appointed to heads of institutions at almost all denominational establishments, hierarchy of churches does not intervene into internal institutional affairs at the same rate. Every institution aims to focus on religious-denominational criteria. Institutions emphasize personal care towards students more than non-denominational establishments and the non-official tutor-student communication structures exemplify unique patterns.

The social contexts of the new church related higher education students are characterized by lower social-economic status, generally active religious practice, relatively high student ratio from denominational secondary schools. Students belonging to the respective denomination or exercising religious practice are heavily overrepresented among the students of each institution. However, students from the catchment area who belong to other denominations, students without affiliation and non-religious students also favour these establishments. The tutors of denominational institutions seem to be more overloaded than the average, which is the result of high class-load, conscientious educator-consultant duties, and correspondence to simultaneous academic, state and denominational expectations. However, institutions are very diverse in terms of the intensity to motivate their tutors for higher academic achievement.

Conclusion

The current situation of the Central-Eastern European church related higher education institutions of the region can only be understood through the Central-European and socialist historical models of higher education, then their current re-structuring, the social and cultural processes of the transition and the denominational and religious dynamics of the region. To model the current conditions, we added to Clark's triangle-model the fourth pole (church) that commands special expectation and values besides the state, academic and labour centres. This is to emphasize our research result that church related higher educational institutions do not belong to those private establishments that follow market logic. The most important result our empirical study is that church related higher educational institutions show strong individual images in addition to several common features.[1]

References and Bibliography

Altbach P. G. ed. 1999: *Private Prometheus. Private Higher Education and Development in the 21st Century*. Westport, Connecticut, London: Greenwood Press.

Altbach P. G. ed. 2003: *The Decline of the Guru: The Academic Profession in Developing and Middle-Income Countries*. New York: Palgrave Macmillan

Chen, T.M. - Barnett, G.A. 2000: Research on international student flows from a macro perspective: A network analysis of 1985, 1989, and 1995', *Higher Education* 39. 4. 435– 453.

Clark, B. R. 1983: *The Higher Education System: Academic Organization in Cross-National Perspective*. Berkley and Los Angeles: University of California Press.

Dee, J. R., Henkin, A. B., Holman, F. B. 2004: Reconciling differences: Conflict management strategies of catholic college and university presidents. *Higher Education* 47. 2. 177-196.

Hrubos I. 2002: *A „bolognai folyamat", Európai trendek*. Budapest: Oktatáskutató Intézet.

Kozma T. 2003: Minority education in Central Europe. *European Education* 35. 1. 35-53.

Kozma T. 2008: Political Transformations and Higher Education Reforms. *European Education* 40. 2. 29-46.

Levy, D. 1992: Private Institutions of Higher Education. In: Clark, B. R. & Neave, G. (eds.), *The Encyclopedia of Higher Education*. Oxford: Pergamon Press, 1183-1194.

Marginson S. – Rhoades, G. 2002: Beyond national states, markets, and systems of higher education: A glonacal agency heuristic. *Higher Education* 43. 3. 281–309.

1 This article was written with support from a Janos Bolyai Research Scholarship granted by Hungarian Academy of Sciences and a REVACERN FP6 Project.

Molnár, E 2008: The Conditions of Functioning of Denominational Educational Institutions in Ukraine. In: Pusztai, G. (ed.), *Education and Church in Central and Eastern-Europe at First Glance*. Debrecen: CHERD. 84-99.

Murvai, L. 2008: The Place of Denominational School in the Hungarian Education of Romania. In: Pusztai, G. (ed.), *Education and Church in Central-and Eastern-Europe at First Glance*. Debrecen: CHERD 100-109.

Neave, G. 1998: The Evaluative State Reconsidered. *European Journal of Education* 33. 3. 265-284.

Pusztai G. (ed.) 2008: *Education and Church in Central and Eastern Europe at First Glance*. Debrecen: CHERD.

Slantcheva, S. & Levy D. 2007: *Private Higher Education in Post-Communist Europe*. London: Palgrave-McMillen

Szemerszki M. 2006: *A nem állami felsőoktatási intézmények hallgatói*. Budapest Felsőoktatási Kutatóintézet.

Szolar, E. 2008: *Church Owned Higher Education and the Democratization of Romania*. Online Article: http://www.eric.ed.gov/ERICWebPortal/Home.portal?_nfpb=true&ERICExtSearch_SearchValue_0=szolar&searchtype=basic&ERICExtSearch_SearchType_0=kw&_pageLabel=RecordDetails&objectId=0900019b8038f257&accno=ED503866&_nfls=false

THE ROLE OF THE AUTHORITY IN THE RELIGION EDUCATION IN THE CONTEXT OF SURVIVAL

Andrej Šegula, Ljubljana

1. Introduction

Human beings are defined by relationships. In the period prior to birth, a person is in close relationship with his mother and with himself. After birth he enters the world of relationships, which grows every second. The close connection with his mother remains besides himself with him and his primary environment, meaning himself and those people and things first surrounding him (people and things). This circle widens with years and the relationships become richer: some deepen, some hurt, others free us and open us. Religious education also enters this net of relationships and opens a new world of relationships for a person. These are relationships which 'can' colour anew all the previously mentioned relationships and life itself. We start from the fact that in his essence, every human being is religious regardless of whether he admits it or not, lives by it or not. From here on we will substantiate the various forms of upbringing and the place of religious education in this process.

Authority (Mackey, 1994:35) and the relationship towards the Transcendent often go hand in hand. The relationship a person has toward the authority is often reflected in that person's relationship toward God. Thus we wish to build this article on the relationship toward authorities.

2. The place of authority in the process of upbringing

Authority is a vast concept. It can be found that young people in different circumstances (family, school, friends, parish, youth group, sports societies, various organizations, informal gatherings) form various models. The basic image of relationships (including also with the authority) is acquired by the youth within his family. According to the form of the family in which the child or youth was brought up, M. Gomboc (Gomboc, 2002) distinguishes between the following upbringing types: authoritarian (the complete power belongs to the parents, teachers), democratic (this type is a reaction to the change leading to democratic society), indulgent (permissive model, where parents and teachers give up their power completely), and the upbringing, which permits confusion and anarchy in the family (this model is also called the chaotic model since parents and teachers are not capable of clear attitude, their actions vary, and it swings between strictness and indulgence) (Gomboc a1, a2, a3, 2003). This experience serves as a base for the formation of all other relationships and the acceptance of authority in other circumstances of life.

When analysing the life context of present-day youth we, on one hand, deal with youth's perception of family relations, while on the other hand we also find images of his life in connection to God. A survey, conducted in the Maribor diocese[1], mostly portrays the exterior phenomena of religiousness (going to Sunday Mass, participation in youth meetings, reading of the Bible, exterior Christian symbols etc.), which to some extent also reflect the young person's inner relationship with God and his trust in Him. According to surveys among all the young, a certain degree of religiousness is shown which is not reflected in any particular religion.

3. Relevance of authority today

The foundation for perception of authority is given to the young within their domestic, family environment (Kroflič, 1997: 13-14). This is also the place, where (in the past more than today) the process of religious education begins. This is a formation which marks and accompanies a person throughout life. The outer forms of one's relationship toward authority and toward religion can change while the foundation remains. It can happen that a person brought up in a certain authoritarian and religious environment encounters a different environment. In this case, the confrontation of two forms ensues and the decision for one or the other has to be made. There is another way possible, namely the search for a compromise between the situation which marked a person and the one he encounters

1 V. Potočnik and B. Cestnik, Anketa, 2000. This survey was carried out among the young in the diocese of Maribor in the years prior to the plenary assembly of the Church in Slovenia. 3,200 survey sheets were sent out and 1,761 were returned. Included in the survey were only those young people who are actively involved in the life of youth groups (multiple answers were possible). The picture of the young and religiousness is also expressed by the survey among the young in the diocese of Murska Sobota (J. Bajzek, 2008: 179-245).

anew. Hereon we do not return to the basic environment of a youth as an environment in which he lives but rather to the environment in which he experiences authority and submission for the first time. Thus we speak about a parallel process with religious education. We have the place and the role of authority in the domestic environment and all other environments in life on the one hand and the relationship towards God, which is often the reflection of the relationship lived by a person in the given context on the other (for example someone who has a loving, patient, charitable father is likely to reflect this image onto God).

3.1 Authority in families with authoritarian upbringing

During the presentation of the various educational forms, we will firstly discuss authoritarian upbringing, which represents authority, assertion of power, status, respect, and influence (Kroflič, 1997: 13-14). The complete submission of a child or youth is characteristic of this type of upbringing. The parent is above the child and enforces his right through various forms of coercion. Parents or teachers (in various educational institutions) have all the power while the child, at least seemingly, has no say about his life whatsoever. M. Gomboc speaks about "the predomination of the teacher's irrational authority" (Gomboc a2, 2003: 37). This type of upbringing is founded on the willpower of the strongest, who demands submission. Thus the parent founds his authority on the statements like: "I know what is good for you and you know nothing" or "I know what is right and you do not". The analysis reveals the inequality of such a relationship (the authority of the strongest prevails, which uses physical as well as psychological coercion to achieve his goals). Parents and teachers who act according to this pattern are convinced that they are right and that only in this way they can do good for their children; they even perceive their coercion as their right and moral obligation. All these are typical features of authoritarian upbringing.

The other form of authoritarian upbringing is where parents and teachers assert their prestige and influence through knowledge, experience, and maturity. They take into consideration the child's ability. Their demands are explained and clearly defined. Their attitude reveals concern, warmth, and love, which significantly distinguishes them from authoritarian parents. Parents employing this form of upbringing are consistent, respectful, strict; they stick to the set rules and to their word. They depart from the above model in that they believe in their children and cooperate with them. Their children, later teenagers find it easier to integrate into a wider environment. They have a shaped attitude towards authority that serves as their advantage.

It is said for authoritarian parents that they have an authoritarian character. They can only function in a relationship of superior – inferior ("I know everything, you know nothing"; "I am stronger, you are weaker"). This is the need for the polarisation of relations: "I who know everything" on one side, and the one who is inferior, who needs learning, on the other. Educational procedures in this approach include criticising, reproaching, intimidating, shaming etc. This model often includes coercion of various kinds. M. Gomboc believes that "the authoritarian upbringing was more frequent in the past because it was only an expression or a reflection of the set, self-evident social relations" (Gomboc a2, 2003: 38). This type of upbringing was the consequence of the social order. Authoritarian relations in society formed the authoritarian upbringing in the family and other educational institutions (father – children, ruler – subjects, God – human). With socio-political change this model of upbringing changed. The consumer society no longer needs a 'slave' but a consumer, which also requires a different type of education. The mentioned upbringing retains the relationship of superior and inferior. The child can only escape this through resistance and not by simple protest. It can quickly happen that he develops from inferior to superior and thus continues the process of the authoritarian upbringing. The downside of this type is also the fact that the child acquires a negative self-image: feelings of inferiority.

While discussing education we are aware that there is no perfect example of a certain type of upbringing. Namely, almost all types display some elements of the authoritarian upbringing. The main question is which type of the upbringing is prevalent.

All these findings can be reflected into life in all other social environments, where a child or a youth continues his life, education, and later work. In cases where the young originate from the authoritarian families and environments, the question arises of how to approach such a person and how to include him into the new environment. Where and how to help a youth exit this basic relationship superior – inferior? How to help him avoid the desire to transfer in this educational process from the inferior to the superior?

The basic problem is the fact that many families have outgrown this model of upbringing (authoritarian or authoritative) and already live its democratic or even chaotic form. The question remains how to explain to the youth, who come from such backgrounds, about the 'healthy' authority (which is required in certain social and working circumstances), how to make it appealing without the authoritarian or authoritative connotation.

3.2 Authority and obedience in families with democratic upbringing

When discussing models of upbringing, we cannot disregard the fact that the form of upbringing in a family is in some aspect a reflection of the social order form (totalitarianism, democracy). "In the 20th century, the social development influenced the decrease of the meaning of authority in upbringing. The failure of permissive educational practices led to re-evaluation about authority in upbringing, which aims to be contemporary, thus democratic." (Gomboc al, 2003:34).

We are faced with many forms of upbringing. We have already discovered that with the authoritarian model, the power is completely with the parents. Democratic parents are aware of the problems and responsibilities regarding the division on power within a family. Everything is not always agreed upon in democratic upbringing. The essential component of the search for right balance within a family is the appropriate division of power (members can be equal, while their roles, statuses, responsibilities differ). "Authority without love, which includes independence, is dependence and violence. Solid boundaries are not unchangeable. In democratic family, rules and boundaries change, their creation includes all family members appropriately according to their age and maturity. Only thus can we speak about democratic upbringing and not authoritarian. In democratic upbringing authority of parents is necessary but subdued to a different, higher goal – the development and ever increasing independence of children." (Gomboc al, 2003: 35). This involves the appropriate division of power and clearly defined boundaries, within which a child can be shaped. The child needs these boundaries since only thus he can feel safe; this shapes his self-confidence, independence, responsibility, and also freedom. In the process of upbringing, parents and teachers gradually decrease their power and allow for the children to broaden their living and creative space.

Environments (family, community) which educate according to the principles of democracy offer more openness, understanding, acceptance of diversity and attendance to the needs of our fellow men. Democratic upbringing encourages individuality, autonomy, privacy, and initiative. Family or society, where principles of democratic upbringing are alive, is ruled by open, clear, and honest communication. Members of such family or community are interconnected, attentive to each other, and their relationships are relaxed; happiness and humour abide there (Gomboc al, 2003: 35).

Each of the models has positive and negative sides. While revising the democratic model we find that it comes very close to that ideal, which is supposed to fill families and environments, where people live and work. A youth who comes from a family with democratic model of upbringing carries solid foundations for his future life and work. It would be ideal if other educational institutions worked according to the principles of democracy: the candidate would be educated in the manner which enables him to grow, mature, and become increasingly independent. Namely, the democratic model of upbringing and the society we live in have a lot in common. This is also why the democratic model is becoming the ideal of monastic education. Nevertheless, there is still a great gap between the present and the ideal state of things.

3.3 Authority and obedience in families with permissive upbringing

From a historic point of view, education has mainly been marked by authority. The authority of a country was represented by a ruler, in the church the bishop (clerical dignitary), in the family a father, and in school a teacher. In the last century, great changes occurred: in the first half, authority still had an important place; we cannot state the same for the second half, during which authority lost its presence. When authority loses its role, we can speak about permissive education.

M. Gomboc describes five types of permissive upbringing.

The first one is indulgence, which lacks demands and boundaries. The child is indulged at any cost. This type often displays indulgence, convincing, pleading, explaining, negotiating, praising, reminding, the offering of help and protection also when not needed.

The second type of permissive education is the education subdued to the child's development. Parents and teachers stand by the idea that children know best what is good for themselves. They are afraid that they might hurt the child and not benefit him with their approach. Such teachers do not express demands. They observe and arrange the environment to enable the appropriate stimulation[s]. This upbringing requires a lot of time, energy, and attention.

The third type is the s.c. "what do I care" type, where teachers and parents display indifference; they have no personal relationship with the child. Here children are left to themselves. Teachers (parents) believe that freedom leads to independence but in reality they are just uninterested and preoccupied with other things. Children in this case feel the emotional distance, emptiness, often also guilt.

The fourth form of permissive upbringing is the seemingly democratic upbringing. Here children function at the level of a partnership; they are assigned burdens too great for them, which they cannot handle. They lack guidance, clear rules and boundaries, many things are unclear.

The fifth type is the Rousseau upbringing, which believes that a child should learn solely on the basis of his experience, on the natural or arranged consequences of his own actions. This upbringing prohibits punishing, criticising, disciplining or limiting the child in any way. Rousseau recommends that parents and teachers [to] study carefully all the factors in the environment of the child. This is a concealed enforcement of power, which is for children more difficult to resist than if it was overt (Gomboc a3, 2003: 36).

The permissive upbringing is mostly [the] reaction to the contemporary consumer oriented society. Namely, there are very few limitations in this type of upbringing. The child brought up permissively is much more easily convinced about this and that, which greatly promotes the consumer society.

But there is a question of the approach to a young person originating from such family. How does the educator speak to him about responsibilities, about boundaries?

4. Perception of authority and direct or indirect religious education

We can speak about direct education when a family lives the religious dimension. Within this dimension we can appoint certain subdivision. One of these subgroups could be those who live their religiousness as practical Christians (attending ceremonies, religious education of children within Church as educational institution, prayer, pilgrimages etc.), or those who declare themselves Christians but do not practice it (or practice it occasionally: bigger holidays, sacraments etc.). These two forms of religious education can be connected to the above presentation since the relationships that we live are of key importance to the formation of our relationship to God.

On the other hand, we can speak about indirect education when a person is touched, when something happens to make him think that there is something more in life than that which we can feel through our senses. This is one of the circumstances when a person looks at life from a different angle. Speaking about this type of education we primarily refer to extraordinary events.

We can also speak about indirect education with the usual upbringing, when a child or youth is raised in one of the educational forms (authoritarian, democratic etc.) and when he is raised for general human values (Gerjolj, 2006: 255-260). Thus two aspirations meet; on one side there is a person who wishes only the best for his child and wants to raise him 'properly', and on the other side a purely natural (God's) law, which is written into the human heart.

Thus we can find that both forms of education are close together. In this closeness we can also search for the answer why some people (raised 'past' the religious education) quickly find the way to believing in God. Even if this 'leap' does not occur we can define these two paths as similar and close.

5. Religiousness as "help" in life

Focusing on those who believe, who live their faith within their family, who are raised in the 'conscious' relationship to God, we see that they have certain advantage over others who do not believe and who live and build their lives without God. These two groups before us may not be regarded in terms of black and white. This distinction does not imply that those raised in faith have no problems while others who do not acknowledge God live in some disadvantage. We are dealing with one basic perception. A person close to God approaches life more easily. People who have been in distress testify to that (illness, death of a beloved person etc.) and have overcome these troubles more easily knowing that they are not alone, believing that God is with them and that he allows for this trial. Those who do not believe find this step, this realization, more difficult.

Religious education presents a big challenge for a believer. Where and how to deepen his personal faith? Where and how to learn? Then, how to transfer this experience onto your children? How to help them find anchor in God? How to transcend the rational dimension of religious education and move to experiential? What and how to live this "practical" dimension in an environment that does not acknowledge these values or is afraid to live by them? How to change from theory to practice? How to exceed that "fossil" feeling of subordination? How to live fully and breathe freely your relationship to the Transcendent? These are the questions encountered by everyone who take their religious education seriously.

If we aspire to answer these questions, we need to take a systematic look at the families (the forms of authority), in which we strive for religious education. Another very important area is the question, in what kind of schools are our youth being raised? What is the place and mission of Catholic schools and high-schools?

What do they bring to our environment? First and foremost, what do they bring to our children and youth?

The question of what and how much the "official" Church does also remains open. We have the acknowledged catechesis, preparation for sacraments, various groups, media, internet etc., on one side, but there is a question of whether this is really all we can do. How many people are included in our religious education and what is there to do to speak also to those who only occasionally come to us (on occasions of sacraments, bigger holidays)? Another question should also be posed: Do we bring a person in our religious education to such a level that this will help him with his "survival"? In other words, do we bring a person to a point where he "dares" to live his faith in his every-day life?

6. Conclusion

We have introduced the forms of upbringing in our families (from the strictest to the most permissive). We have found that the form of education received influences the subsequent relationships that a person enters into (Gerjolj, 2006: 270). But they also influence the relationship of a person (first a child then youth and adult) to God. The population could be divided into two groups; one group consisting of the believers, those who receive religious education; and the other group, those who do not "practice" their belief but in their efforts come close to the ideals of religious education (honesty, goodness, upbringing for beautiful etc.). The remaining question is to what extent the religious education actually contributes to the "spiritual survival" in our lives. To what extend does the Church, this official institution, provides or enable a person to reach the point, when this education is not only theory but above all practice?

References and Bibliography

Bajzek, J. (et al.). 2008: *Odiseja mladih*, Radovljica, Didakta.

Gerjolj, S. 2006: 'The relevance of moral intelligence in educational processes', in: J. Juhant & B. Žalec (eds.), *Person and Good: Man and His Ethics in the Postmodern World*, Münster, Lit, 255-274.

Gomboc (et al), M. 2003: 'Demokratične družine', *Vzgoja* 17, 34-35.

Gomboc (et a2), M. 2003: 'Avtoritarna vzgoja', *Vzgoja* 19, 37-38.

Gomboc (et a3), M. 2003: 'Obrazi popustljive vzgoje', *Vzgoja* 20, 36-37.

Gomboc, M. 2002: *Družbena pogojenost vzgoje v slovenskih družinah*. Maribor.

Kroflič, R. 1997: *Avtoriteta v vzgoji*, Ljubljana, Znanstveno središče.

Mackey, J.P. 1994: *Power and Christian Ethic*, Cambridge: University Press.

THE ART OF LIFE AND LEARNING IN THE PERIOD OF ADULTHOOD

Erika Prijatelj, Ljubljana

Introduction

The age of a person, whatever it is, is just right. Every year is unique and invaluable as it is lived only once. This is a sufficient reason to live with aging, the time being used as an opportunity to keep learning.

Rather than biological age, entering the period of adulthood presupposes the capacity for autonomous thinking, i.e. the ability of self-reference when it comes to reflecting one's own thoughts and actions. Such a person can control themselves and be responsible for their actions. Confronted with a choice or decision, they are able to consult their own selves. The experience of self-control and responsibility is the foundation of acceptance and life in accordance with the code of ethics that guides their thinking, emotions and behaviour, and form their conscience and desire (Guindon 2001, 110).

A person is never able to reach their full potential. Therefore, they never cease to be on their way to this goal. In their personal development through different life periods of adulthood, a person continues to transform and consequently change the way of adaptation to new external conditions. Their flexibility will vary according to the way they face events and changes.

The way of change prediction during adulthood, focused on the actualization of human mental power[1], takes into consideration both biological and psychological changes which result from human physical environment. The changes become

1 The expression of human life strengths is synonymous with human psychological power or a psychological virtue. They have been taken from E. Erikson, who first discovered them. He named them: hope, will, goal fulfilment, competence, originating in one‘s childhood, fidelity, characterised as the virtue of the youthful age, and love, care and wisdom, the three virtues of the period of adulthood (Erikson 1964d, 124–130). Forty years later, Jeannine Guindon, a Canadian psycho-education pioneer, supplemented Erikson's discoveries with the finding of essentially six human life powers with the last three Erikson's strengths expressed with differ-

an opportunity for growth. They are based on an individual's "self presence" and the environment, so that a person uses a central concept, the concept of self-representation in relation to the representation of the environment and other people. The change is a developmental one. Certain efforts prove transformative if their objective is growth based not on content or form but on clear personal conscience. A person engages in and manages the situation according to the meaning they give to the transformation depending on their current life period. The individual's way of becoming aware of the changes enables them not only to become responsible for them but the awareness of the new configuration of transition makes them initiators of changes (Alain 1988, 37).

For a person it is impossible to become a facilitator of their own development and growth if they are clearly unaware of the factors affecting their own personal development. These elements are: bodily and physical changes, search for meaning in one's life and in the outside world, knowledge, physical changes in the environment and different circles they are part of such as one's post, society in its broad sense, cultural centres etc. as well as various dimensions of interpersonal relationships, which help a person walk their unique and creative path. "Compatibility between their choices and refusals is deeply rooted in a person's values and priorities which have directed their choices in life" (Durkin 1995, 651). One's self-image helps the person to deal with changes, to choose what is possible, to refuse what is impossible and accept the inevitable. Thus, transformations arise from the very person and their work on themselves and enrich personal identity with a new quality. This means that a person is able not only to direct but also to cause changes. The ability to adapt enables a person to reach the integration of changes. The result is the modification of each expression of personal identity – that is, physical, executive, individual, psycho-sexual, psycho-social and spiritual – and a renewed inner structure of self in which a person matures in inner harmony and integrity (Atchley 1989, 184–185).

Every decade of a life cycle has its own specific dynamics, specific peaks and crisis together with the opportunity for freedom, growth and maturing in wisdom. The article will present fundamental challenges of individual life periods in the

ent expressions of the same power of love: mutual, caring or parental and wisdom or universal one (Guindon 2001, 29–37).

period of adulthood divided into early, middle and late life and draw attention to their interconnectedness as well as their impact on the development of the structure of personality.

1 The early years of adulthood: the twenties and thirties

The beginning of the period of adulthood is set between the end of adolescence, which is between the ages of eighteen and nineteen, and the beginning of the following decade, that is towards the age of twenty-eight. A person in these ages feels responsible to take life in their own hands. "A young person should enter the period of adulthood with an established code of ethics enabling them to direct their own choices and behaviour and start taking responsibility for their own life" (Alain 2001, 8).

It is good for one's own development to gradually start declining the financial and moral support of their own family in order to achieve their own physical independence and make a new step in the inner process of psychic and spiritual uniqueness (Schuster and Ashburn 1992, 169).

The first period of adulthood is thus marked by a double challenge. A person in their own twenties thus has to deal with the vital question of personal vocation and the choice of a particular occupation. In the first part of the twenties a person "becomes aware of the new configuration of their own self-image" (Berk 2004, 84), which is in interaction with the image of their own environment and other people. The period of asking questions accomplished by a quest for answers enables a person to specify the challenge which they will try to answer and to predict the path leading to it.

Work enables a person to consciously become part of a wider society. This requires a decision for a concrete occupation in accordance with one's interest, skills and values. "Study or work, which a person starts, opens them for their own environment and relationships with other people and help them discover their own identity and place in the world" (Gollnick 2005, 120). When a person accepts the decision about what they want to do in their own life, the process of clarification begins. A person needs to answer the question of what they want from life, which leads them to the search for harmony between their wishes on the vocational level (priest, religious, married, single) and their ambitions at the level of professional work. During these years, a person feels a strong need to perceive themselves competent for concrete choices and concrete realizations, which helps one to become self-critical and consciously enter into dialogue with the challenges of life (Parks 2000, 6).

Together with the criticism in the early period of adulthood a person becomes also "more analytical, experienced, diligent in achieving the set objectives and persistent" (Gollnick 2005, 121).

For the vast majority of young people a life decision gets its expression in relation to the person who they want to share life with. Some give priority to a specific mission which they completely dedicate themselves to; while others decide for a consecrated life, which is a decision for God and a person at the same time. Be it a decision for a specific person or a particular work, it is important that at the end of the adolescence a person is in accordance with their own personal values and tries to make sense of their own decisions. This helps a person "progressively develop the ability of openness to others and the availability regarding time" (Kelcourse 2004, 238) which they themselves decide who to devote to and to what extent.

When a twenty-year-old person carries out the changes in accordance with their own priorities, which they discovered to be important for them and is at the same time ready to acquire new knowledge, they mature internally in the process of differentiation of their own image in interaction with the image which they have about their own environment and other people. In fact, that signifies a "true transition from the youthful age/teenage life to adulthood, which may take about half of a decade" (Guindon and Alain 1992, 31).

In this life period a person feels "a strong need for approval from the people who are perceived as witnesses of interesting realizations from one's own perspective. A person takes such people as inspiring role models who help them get to know more precisely their own life goal and the way of giving their own share to the community" (Lerner 2002, 247). Such a person is kind of a mentor, an important personality, a companion who has a strong influence on the self-reflection of a young person besides their own family members. Their job is to help a young person deepen their own personal reflection and discernment about the choices so that they would lead them to greater inner freedom. It is important that such a person is not only an advisor but also an assistant to a young person in the process of self-discovery, self-revelation and self-appreciation (Monbourquette 1999, 105–111).

"Towards the late twenties a person sees that their own success is appreciated in their own environment. In that period, a young person feels that success is not as important as it used to be and that success alone brings no deep satisfaction. That is the source of personal questions which trigger a decisive turning point, namely the process of interiorization" (Guindon 1996, 3). That process is based on the reflection of one's personal values on the basis of which a person re-considers their own inner attitudes and choices. That enables them to see more clearly their own priorities and also refusals followed by the concrete choices. While a twenty-year-old is focused on action very much, a thirty-year-old person is more concerned about the discovery of meaning of their own work and life and consequently prefers quality to quantity. The fruit of this process is inner harmony expressed in the way of living one's motherhood for women and fatherhood for men at the psychical, spiritual, and physical levels and learning flexibility in relationship with persons of the same and different sex.

According to Fowler, a person aged 18 and over is in transition between the synthetic-conventional and the individually-reflective belief a religious level. That transition proceeds from a religious idealism to realism, where the rational side of religion is given more expression. Although a young person still values other people, their views, expectations and advices, they simultaneously undergo a process of inner reference points. Their faith becomes personal. At this level they take a critical attitude towards the previous system of values and gradually establish a new identity expressed and actualized by the choice of personal membership in a certain (religious) group and by the formation of one's own life style (Fowler 1981, 179).

Some contemporary writers, among them P. Feldmeier (Feldmeier 2007, 137), are convinced that many people of that age are involved in spirituality even more than they are encouraged by their own church community. It is important for them to be given room for creativeness and making suggestions. It is very valuable if they are accompanied by a person who accepts them, encourages them and helps them check their own religious vision. This also applies to young adult Christians who are "asleep and take no interest in anything. Spiritual leaders and communities should help them even more to face the questions such as 'What do you want in your life? What are your goals? What is worth living for? What is worth dying for? What do you carry in your heart?'" (Warren 1982, 122).

The early age of adulthood is a crucial stage for setting the foundations of genuine spiritual life of an adult. Whitehead refers to this time cairos, the time of grace, because that period is vital for the personal identity formation, releasing of imagination and the uncovering of personal dreams (Whitehead and Whitehead 1979, 67).

The twenties and thirties are transitional years from a great idealism to the realism of a complex reality. It is the time when an individual develops one's own "self" and discovers the potentials and borders of one's own power. A young adult often feels insecure. Therefore, they feel a need to uncover and see themselves in their own realizations. At the stage of "the recognition of the meaning of one's own realizations for them, a person is able to gradually make sense of their own being as well" (Bee 1997, 142).

The greater the wish to make progress in inner growth, the more internalized one's own share and closer to the discovery of the inner source. When a person decides to give meaning to what they do, they feel that they are completely themselves. A person discovers that it is up to them to define their own goals more precisely depending on one's own values, which lead one's own efforts. This may mark the beginning of the internalization process of who they are. It is only from the inside that a person is competent to give meaning to one's own realizations and row out into the deep water which has effects on every expression of one's own personal identity (Tostain 1999, 37).

2 Middle period of adulthood: the forties and fifties

The transition to the middle period is often taken as one of "the most important events in the life cycle" (Gollnick 2005, 159), which is quite reasonable in relation to the dynamics of the previous two decades. A person in their twenties is a researcher of oneself and the environment in which they live; thus, the emphasis is on action. However, if a person in their thirties does not enter the process of interiorization, they may experience the so-called "middle-age crisis" and desperately tries to find the solution outside themselves instead of inside, such as in the change of their partner in case of marriage, forgetting about the old friends and searching for new ones, holding on to reputation, giving to much importance to one's position etc. This confusion created by sudden changes in body and personal disintegration finds its expression in self-affirmation. Sheehy compares the need for self-affirmation with the adolescent behaviour which searches for balance and tries to find the right direction. The changes of profession, a divorce, a nervous breakdown and psychosomatic disorders are all indicators of the middle-age crisis.

"On the threshold of mid-life, a person consciously, although veiled in secrecy, stares into the time still remaining in life" (Bornstein and Lamb 1999, 46). One's look is directed towards the whole life cycle becoming increasingly aware that one half of life is already behind them and starting to question oneself how to lead the rest of it: Is that all what there is to life? What do I really want or need in life?

Why do I work that much? Why do I strive so much and can find no more time for myself? Why, what for, whom for? In the middle ages, these questions undermine one's life concept they have lived by then and relate with the question of meaning, which is a fundamental religious question.

From the religious point of view, the middle-age crisis brings a chance for spiritual growth and openness to God. While in crisis, one's suppressed bits and self-deceit come to surface as well as the wish for the source of life, healing and depth. Thus, the crisis is a critical turning point at which a person decides to remain close or to open oneself to God and his grace. A person is afraid to have a look at what is going on in themselves, to face the unrest in their own hearts. Instead, they project what is unsolved in them to the world outside, for example by trying to change first other people, surroundings and structures. Another less pleasant path is the path of self-revelation which makes a person free of masks, idols and self-complacency and leads them to the discovery of one's own truth. Especially in the moments of peace and silence, a forty-year old person may discover that they have only one life and that they are responsible for it. A person gradually gives up the expectations they have about other people such as parents, children, fellow workers, etc. and opens themselves unselfishly to the environment. The moments of solitude help a person start not only theoretically but also existentially "to accept the beginning of their own life, its passing, and its ending" (Guindon 1996b, 5).

At work, they become less dependent on the affirmations from other people or expressions of gratitude. For such a person, life becomes a newly found gift, which they are personally grateful for and in which they learn to find meaning and inner joy.

In one's fifties, in the years of renewed vigour, the acquired ability of taking *now* relatively and the reflection of who they become in the years passed by help a person more consciously discover the fruits of their life experience, achievements and knowledge and is ready to share them with others. Other people are no longer perceived as competitors. "The process of interiorization of one's own identity brings a person to the point at which they want to make another turning point in their life when they enter the following decade. They want to act in favour of other people and their personal" (Guindon 1996b, 13) growth both in the relationship with the family members and fellow-workers and the broader cultural, ecological, political and religious environment. Regardless of the kind of responsibility they hold, for a fifty-year-old person who has answered the challenges of their own life period a fellow person and their good become their own main priority.

However, if a fifty-year-old has not re-entered the process of interorization, that makes impossible for them to truly rediscover oneself as a person. Consequently, the perception of another person is distorted, as they are seen through the prism of events and roles which they have held and fails to see them first as a person.

On the religious level, Fowler notes that the unifying belief (Conjunctive Faith) usually does not occur before the middle period of adulthood. A person has already experienced disappointment and failure as well as the reality of their own efforts and irrevocable decisions" (Guindon 1996b, 13). God is no longer an external authority who controls people if and how they act according to the commandments; the ideal, people strive to, is gone, God has become internalized, experienced and a person may live from the experience of God's presence. If the previous level of faith was a more rational one, a person at this stage rediscovers the message and meaning of symbols, pictures, images and rituals and perceives them anew in interconnectedness and thus becomes part of them. Instead of arguing with other people in terms of view of the world, a person expresses openness to them, which surpasses strongly marked categories as formed at the previous level (Osmer 1990, 252). That stage may be described as balanced or inclusive belief and also as the stage of interdependence at which a person is able to be independent from others without losing their own autonomy. Individualisation, a life-long process, reflected in relation to the self as well as to others, exceeds the tension between autonomy and belonging and matures in the realization that a person is most autonomous when they belong most or when they devote themselves to God and people.

Middle period ages require a person to pay attention to contradictory poles which they carry in themselves, to accept the shadow not lived out and face their own inner self. Confrontation with one's opposites and shadows bring some people to the fear of opposites and consequently to the stagnation. Another possible reaction to the confrontation is the rejection of all values held dear by then in hope that everything suppressed would be able to live from then on. What happens may only be an exchange of the object of suppression, whereas one's inner balance remains disturbed. The inclination to deny all former standpoints in favour of their opposites is as exaggerated as the previous practice, where a person due to the set ideals ignores subconscious longings and fantasies which would question these ideals. The second half of life is not about the change of the life direction but about the maintenance of the previous decisions together with the recognition of their opposites.

A mature middle-age person takes the challenge of confronting the real self and nurturing a desire for the "inner journey" (Feldmeier 2007, 191) more seriously than a wish for self-promotion and productivity. The person is called not to put oneself into the centre any more as a psychological change occurs in this period by rule in comparison to the early periods of adulthood, characterized by great efforts to develop one's own identity, create one's own place, prove oneself and thus somehow turned inward. The middle-aged person starts preparing for the existence of the second half, in which they would finally leave one's youth and illusions behind.

3 Late period of adulthood: the sixties, seventies, eighties and over [2]

Is a sixty-year-old person an old one? Does it mean that a seventy-old one becomes an old person or even an elder one? The issue is a complex one. Therefore, the transition into the late period of adulthood will be taken the moment of retirement which for the majority of people means the beginning of the reorganization of work and life and thereby setting a new life structure. "A specific contribution of a sixty-year-old person is their focus on the essential and discovery of real needs of their human surroundings" (Sheehy 1982, 236). That is the way to become a person who is able to help without being burdened with the demand of immediateness and directness. A sixty-year-old places both their own life events and those common to the human kind in general in a new, more holistic context and has a more precise perception of their own surrounding and everything what may contribute to their own physical, psychical, moral and spiritual improvement (Schieman 2001, 154). The ability to "discover the inner meaning of events enables a person to recognize the factors which pave the way for the development

2 One way to acknowledge the variability in individuals who are aged 65 and over is to segment older adulthood into categories based on chronological age: young-old (ages 65-74), old-old (ages 75-84), and oldest-old (ages 85 +). Compared with individuals in the old-old and oldest-old categories, those in the young-old category have greater physical vigour and are less likely to suffer from significant sensory or cognitive decline. In fact, many young-old adults experience more of what are considered to be age-related changes in sensory, perceptual, and cognitive functioning.

of socially-culturally-religious environment and is at the same time aware of their borders" (Guindon 1993b, 3-16).

They are able to detect long-term consequences of the choices made by an individual or society and actively engage in the areas concerned with the quality of life and a better future for the next generations. It is interesting to observe that a sixty-year-old person usually finds it quite easy to express what they feel. However, if they do not develop an interest in innovations, they take a risk of boredom and difficult acceptance of their own borders when they reach retirement, which brings the cessation of a function.

"A seventy-year-old person sees all their life coming to the new perception of relations which make sense and encourage continuation" (Guindon 1989b, 15). Their discoveries contain a historical segment reflecting personal history. This differentiation brings them a better understanding of the ways trodden by other people as well. With the inner eye, that is with the contemplative gaze they read "the universal meaning of their own personal history" (Leduc 1999, 151) and uncover the meaning of live memory for future generations. "The time stops in contemplation. A person concentrates in the privileged silence and gives oneself completely into the hands of God. With this acceptance, the process of internalization starts almost passively and very peacefully. It affects the roots of one's being and all has been expressed." The way in which a seventy-year-old person who has retained psychological autonomy predicts problems shows that it covers the view of the whole person and includes sober assessment as well as the ability to generalize. It is important that they do not search for others to do the same as they or imitate them but want to discover their own path.

Erik Erikson aged 86 and Joan his wife aged 85 define this life period as "the final maturity which protects a person from despair which can be triggered by the constant physical disintegration" (Coleman 1988, 14). The Eriksons confirm that the latest period of their lives means "the culmination of wisdom to the extent in which every previous period finds its evaluation". A wise person has "admirable and moral behaviour, exceptional insight into life's problems, and the ability to consider multiple aspects of complex situations while maintaining some level of objectivity" (Erber 2010, 402). Wisdom sees both the good and bad sides with the intelligence of reason and the intelligence of heart. Humankind needs it every time they look for an answer to any question or problem which is only possible if relying on the heritage of those who have lived a long life (Koerbel 2000, 101-102).

For an eighty-year-old person memories are quite important but not as much as in the previous decade; yet their role is different. A seventy-year-old person who is rereading their own life makes connections and sees their own life story in the inner unity. An eighty-year-old one keeps only the essential parts of the memories, which help him make sense of the late period of life cycle. "Towards the end of life a person can find no other delight such as the taste of the truth" (Guitton 1988, 11). For an eighty-year-old one the essence extracted on the basis of their own history is more important than the history itself. Their own memories serve them only as an illustration of the essence reflected upon. Their message to the world can be seen in "making sense of their whole life" (Guindon and Alain 1990b, 21) – including the late period and time left and in the integrity of life experience. "An elderly person happy to have lived and without a wish to start living once again is a blessing for the family and all around them, for everyone in relationship with" (Feillet and Légaut 1976, 152).

"A person has pleasure to stay with oneself if they are aware of their own dignity" (Guitton 1988, 50). "Their mission is to become what they are in love. Only those, who have seen their own life and accepted it as a gift, are not tired out at the end of their own cycle from all the attempts and efforts. On the contrary, they feel gifted and happy to be God's dear sons or daughters and are invited to move to eternity" (Leduc 1999, 160). Légaut aged eighty talks about the experience of "taming" of death which only those who are spiritually and psychologically mature are able to do: "When the time comes a person does not see only their own destiny but also the necessity of death to give fertility to life by dying" (Légaut 1980, 91). Only the person who takes death as a law of life and approaches it as their own goal is able to live, remain alive and mature. A person who is unable to take that step and behaves like an adolescent looks like a thirty-year-old man according to Jung. They turn back to their own childhood remaining infantile which Jung describes as psychologically sick, unnatural. The problem of our society lies in the fact that the young man described in the example is pitied, whereas the old man who tries to look like an adolescent is admired.

We all wonder what will happen to us after we die. When a beloved one dies, we long to see them again after our turn comes. Will we have a glorious reunion with those we love or is death the end of all consciousness? St. Paul expressed the characteristics of the three major stages of life psychologically and spiritually briefly and clearly in his letters: childhood, adulthood and afterlife: "When we were children, we thought and reasoned as children do. But when we grew up, we quit our childish ways. Now all we can see of God is like a cloudy picture in a mirror. Later we will see him face to face. We don't know everything, but then we will, just as God completely understands us" (1Cor 13, 11-12).

The last period in the Fowler scale of religious development which fundamentally requires to be united with God and live in God features an exceptionally rare form of religion into which one matures only in the late period of adulthood. It is described as the unselfish religion. "The sixth level opens itself to the way of being in religion which is primarily giving completely in and surpassing oneself" (Astley 1992, 22). Fowler argues that such a person already reveals the fruits of "a strong kenosis or emptying of self" (Fowler 1986, 31). People at the level of the so-called universal religion live in the world in the way of transformed presence and are like bowls which contain universality in them. Due to this quality they have value in themselves beyond what the society says about them or how it judges their usefulness. People at this stage love life – without being attached to it too much (Fowler 1986, 76). "Despite numerous virtues, people of the sixth stage are imperfect – in the moral sense as well as in others. They have a typical new form of religion including the quality of freedom both in relationship to oneself and to other people" (Fowler 1980, 149).

Conclusion

Some writers (Andrilović, Zvonarević, Allport, Lowental) have been making efforts to relate the term adulthood with maturity. There are many who argue that the terms adulthood and maturity should be understood as synonyms; others (Havighurst, Guindon, Alain, Boutinet) again claim that the definition of adulthood cannot stand because maturity is a process not a state achieved once and for all. In addition, there is not only one kind of maturity, but at least five, namely: biological maturity which means the physical one; psychological maturity which means the optimal performance of motor skills and psychomotorics, the judging ability, control over emotions, abstract thinking ability; social maturity which involves the responsibility for one's starting and maintenance of interpersonal relationships, the balance between acceptance and giving, one's own system of values, flexibility and adaptability; professional maturity which is defined as the ability to choose the appropriate occupation for oneself and achieve success in it; spiritual maturity which is displayed in the decentralization of self and in the human ability to find meaning of one's life, in other words to discover the transcendental meaning.

Some people are able to achieve only the level of biological maturity, others the psychological but not the spiritual one as well. Every maturity contains also other elements of personality development. The age limit of achieving maturity is indefinable; some reach maturity in early years others not even in late years. That is why the theories which connect the concept of adulthood and maturity are less appropriate for the interpretation of personality development of adults in this age. The personality development and maturing is a process and not a state. Besides, they are less suitable also due to the inconclusiveness of chronological age.

Therefore, the concept of adulthood may be associated with social status, primarily with the psychological and spiritual maturity rather than by chronological age, especially considering the fact that in some countries the period of adulthood officially starts at the lower chronological age than in others. This fact is clearly demonstrated by an important recognition that the concept of adulthood and its related personality development are largely the products of social and cultural pressures and results of biological maturing. Also, the schooling ends by the age of 14 in some countries, in others at the age of 19 or even many years later. An individual crosses the threshold of adulthood when they assume new social roles related with different responsibilities and expectations as to the role of a learner. It is the elements of taking other social roles, assuming responsibility and expectations of the social environment that separate adults from children. The adoption of these new roles causes personality changes, changes in one's value system, inner attitudes, behaviour and beliefs.

In the process of personality development, a person unceasingly, their entire life seeks the formation and transformation of one's own identity, in other words, wants to find oneself. Permanent education and learning add new dimensions to their personality and therefore the concept of lifelong education is so much related with the personality development of adults.

The establishment of one's identity takes all life namely by managing some basic life skills such as receiving, giving, keeping, holding and liberating, working, cooperating, accepting oneself (Erikson, 1966) and opening to the o(O)ther. Learning the skill of receiving and giving in interpersonal interaction changes the original mistrust of others into trust. Mastering the skill of keeping, changes the original insecurity and dependence into autonomy and independence. We are no longer passive at work but take the initiative and thus action on one side alone turns into interactive cooperation. The most important element in the development of one's identity without which one's identity cannot be referred to as developed is the acceptance of oneself with all the gifts, advantages, limitations and insufficiency. "The condition for a person to take place in society is the knowledge of oneself; only then their own abilities allow them to open to the environment and people" (Desmarais 1994, 14).

Consolidation of the identity of self shows in three ways in the life of an adult: congruity between knowledge and decisions they take; temporary stability and positive emotional colour when they transform one's life in order to enable the growth of personal identity in all its dimensions; harmony with the meaning discovered in one's own life. The identity of self does not express a static concept which would be realized in a certain moment of one's life once and for all. On the contrary, every expression of identity keeps changing, developing and enriching according to the current life period which brings certain fruits and knowledge acquired in the previous periods. The greater the ability to differentiate, integrate and consolidate one's life powers the clearer one's own identity. It is defined by the personal awareness and opens up to the new horizons when a person is qualitatively present to oneself and to others. In adulthood, which is based on the integrated experiences from one's childhood and adolescence, a person has in every decade new chances to adapt and deepen the meaning of life which is the source of one's own personal priorities by taking responsible, free and appropriate decisions. Thus, a person identifies oneself with one's own life powers; whereas the internalization process leads them to a greater wisdom and inner freedom.

References and Bibliography

Alain, Julien. 1988. Les phases de vie adulte et la représentation de soi. *Sans frontières* 3:24-47.

Alain, Julien. 1991. Un processus de formation humaine. *Sans frontières* 6: 3-27.

Alain, Julien. 2001. En manque de défis. *Le magazine de la personne* 2: 15-24.

Astley, Jeff. 1992. *Faith Development – An Overview. Christian Perspectives on Faith Development.* Grand Rapids: William Eerdmans Publishing Co.

Atchley, Robert C. 1989. A Continuity Theory of Normal Aging. *The Gerontologist* 29: 182-196.

Bee, Helen. 1997. *Les âges de la vie – Psychologie du développement humain.* Saint-Laurent: Édition du Renouveau pédagogique.

Berk, Laura. 2004. *Development through the Life-Span.* Boston: Allyn and Bacon.

Bianchi, Eugene. 1992. *Aging as a Spiritual Journey*. New York: Crossroad.

Bornstein, Marc and Lamb, Michael. 1999. *Developmental Psychology*. Hillsdale: Erlbaum Associates.

Coleman, David. 1988. Growing into Wisdom. *The Gazette Living* 6: 12.

Desmarais, Marie-Marcelle. 1994. Un engagement social dans un projet. *La vie sans frontières, concertation stratégique* 2: 31-38.

Durkin, Kevin. 1995. *Developmental Social Psychology from Infancy to Old Age.* Cambridge: Blackwell.

Erber, Joan T. 2010. *Aging and Older Adulthood*, Malden: Wiley-Blackwell - Florida International University.

Erikson, Erik. 1964. *Human Strength and the Cycle of Generations.* New York: Norton.

Erikson, Erik. 1986. *Vital Involvement in Old Age.* New York: Norton.

Feillet, Bernard and Légaut, Marcel. 1976. *Patience et passion d'un croyant – Les interviews.* Paris: Le Centurion.

Feldmeier, Peter. 2007. *The Developing Christian.* New Jersey: Paulist Press.

Fowler, James W. 1980. *Moral Stages and the Development of Faith – Moral Development, Moral Education and Kohlberg.* Birmingham: Religious Education Press.

Fowler, James W. 1986. *Faith and Structuring of Meaning.* Birmingham: Religious Education Press.

Fowler, James W. 1986. *Faith Development and Pastoral Care.* Philadelphia: Fortress Press.

Fowler, James W. 1981. *Stages of Faith – The Psychology of Human Development and the Quest of Meaning.* New York: Harper and Row.

Gollnick, James. 2005. *Religion and Spirituality in the Life Cycle.* New York: Peter Lang.

Gouzes, André. 2003. *Le chant du cœur.* Paris: Cerf.

Guindon, Jeannine and Alain, Julien. 1990. L'octogénaire et l'essentiel. *Sans frontières* 5: 25-35.

Guindon, Jeannine and Alain, Julien. 1992. *Prendre sa vie en main – L'enjeu de la vingtaine.* Montréal: Éditions Paulines.

Guindon, Jeannine. 1988. Les étapes d'une phase de vie adulte. *Sans frontières* 3: 3-23

Guindon, Jeannine. 1989. Phase de vie du septuagénaire et contemplation. *Sans frontières*. 4b: 15-32.

Guindon, Jeannine. 1993. Phase de la soixantaine et réponse aux besoins de l'entourage. *Sans frontières* 8 b: 17-27.

Guindon, Jeannine. 1996. Donner un sens à son cycle de vie – L'enjeu de la quarantaine. *Sans frontières* 11b: 3-10.

Guindon, Jeannine. 1996. Favoriser la croissance des personnes – L'enjeu de la cinquantaine. *Sans frontières* 11b: 11-20.

Guindon, Jeannine. 2001. *Vers l'autonomie psychique.* Montréal: Médiaspaul.

Guitton, Jean. 1988. *Un siècle, une vie*. Paris: Laffont.

Holt, Bradley. 2005. *Thirsty for God (A Brief History of Christian Spirituality).* Minneapolis: Fortress Press.

Jones, Alan. 1999. *Exploring Spiritual Direction.* Boston: Cowley Publications.

Kelcourse, Felicity. 2004. *Human Development and Faith – Life-Cycle Stages of Body, Mind and Soul*. Missouri: Chalice Press.

Koerbel, Kurt. 2000. *Notre responsabilité les uns envers les autres – Pour un code universel des devoirs humains*. Québec: Fides.

Kübler-Ross, Elizabeth. 1981. *Living with Death and Dying*. New York: Macmillan.

Leduc, Louis. 1999. *Personnalité et relations humaines internationales – La personne et sa croissance – Fondements anthropologiques et psychologiques de la formation PRH*. Montréal: Médiaspaul.

Légaut, Marcel. 1980. *Devenir soi et rechercher le sens de sa propre vie*. Paris: Aubier.

Lerner, Richard. 2002. *Concepts and Theories of Human Development.* Mahwah: Erlbaum Associates.

Levinson, Daniel. 1978. *The Seasons of a Man's Life.* New York: Ballantine Books.

Levinson, Daniel. 1997. *The Seasons of a Woman's Life.* New York: Ballantine Books.

Liebert, Elizabeth. 2000. *Changing Life Patterns – Adult Development in Spiritual Direction.* St. Louis, Missouri: Chalice Press.

Monbourquette, Jean. 1999. *À chacun sa mission – Découvrir son projet de vie.* Ottawa: Novalis.

Osmer, Richard. 1990. Faith Development. *Encyclopedia of Religious Education. New York: Harper*: 248-256.

Parks, Sharon D. 2000. *Big Questions, Worthy Dreams,* San Francisco: Jossey-Bass.

Rainville, Pierre. 2004. Neurophénoménologie des états et des contenus de conscience. *Théologiques* 12: 15-38.

Rulla, Luigi. 2002. *Anthropologie de la vocation chrétienne.* Québec: Carte Blanche.

Schieman, Scott. 2001. Age, Education, and the Sense of Control – A Test of the Cumulative Advantage Hypothesis. *Research on Aging* 22: 153-178.

Schuster, Clara and Ashburn, Shirley. 1992. *The Process of Human Development – A Holistic Life-Span Approach.* Philadelphia: Lippincott.

Sheehy, Gail. 1982. *Franchir les obstacles de la vie*. Paris: Belfond.

Sheehy, Gail. 1996. *New Passages: Mapping your Life across Time*. New York: Ballantine Books.

Tostain, Manuel. 1999. *Psychologie, morale et culture.* Grenoble: Presses universitaires de Grenoble.

Warren, Michael. 1982. *Youth and the Future of the Church.* New York: The Seabury Press.

Whitehead, Evelyn and Whitehead, James. 1979. *Christians Life Patterns: The Psychological Challenges and Religious Invitations of Adult Life*. New York: Crossroad.

THE RELIGIOUS LIFE IN ROMANIA. LIVING TOGETHER AND PAINTING OF ICONS IN TRANSYLVANIA

Alina Pătru, Sibiu

Life has its marvelous happenings and a huge capacity to surprise. No day is like the other and settled plans are often exceeded by the occurrences. Christians say that life is a gift of God. That's why it is always new and goes beyond our expectations. Besides that, every historical and cultural context particularizes life. Life shapes its forms in relation with God and with the surrounding world. Life is communion, with both vertical and horizontal orientation. Christians know best that communion is the very ground of every life.

In my paper I am going to present a particular context in which life could develop. I shall refer to Transylvania, a landscape where several ethnical and religious groups have lived together over the centuries. This meant mutually enrichment, but also the need to overcome real and potential conflict situations. After that, I am going to focus on one specific phenomenon: the icon painting on glass, which the Orthodox Romanians of Transylvania have practiced on a large scale in the 18th and 19th centuries. This will be also illustrated as a reality of its context, which is multicultural.

I. The Context

Romania is, according to its Constitution, a national state, due to the fact that more than 89% of its inhabitants are of Romanian nationality. The same document records the fact that together with the former mentioned there are the recognised national minorities who live in the country and who have the specific minority rights, such as the right to preserve and develop their own culture and civilisation.

The part of the country where the most minorities live is Transylvania[1], the region in the North-Western of Romania, making up more than one third of the Romanian territory. There are here about 6.5 million Romanians, 2 million Hun-

1 When I am speaking about Transylvania, I mean the historical Principality of Transylvania, including regions as Banat, Crisana or Maramures.

garians, 90000 Germans (they used to be much more, but at the end of the 20th century the majority of them left for Germany) and some Gypsies, Serbs, Croats and Jews.

The confessional configuration of whole Romania is the following: 86% of the population is Romanian-Orthodox, 5% Catholic (either Roman-Catholic or Greek-Catholic) and 4% Protestant (the main directions are Lutheran, Reformed and Unitarian).[2] Traditionally speaking and having a significance primarily for Transylvania, we can say that the Orthodox and the Greek-Catholic Church are the Churches of the Romanians, the Lutheran Church is the Church of the Germans, while the Reformed (Calvinistic) and Unitarian Churches are Hungarian. Only the Roman-Catholic Church has a composite character. All these belongings are the result of historical developments.

II. Facts from the History of Cohabitation

Transylvanian Saxons (which are Lutherans) can often be heard describing the situation in Transylvania in terms like this: "It is a very particular context, where the Orthodox are in majority and the Lutherans in minority. You can hardly find this anywhere else in the world. And the most important thing about it is that they are getting along well with each other."

The fact is not only that they get along well, but they have also influenced each other considerably in the history. And they have done this only by living next to each other, even before deliberate measures were taken in order to intensify ecumenical contacts. How was this possible? The explanation is very simple: none of the two religious groups has led campaigns to convert the other to its own belief and, basically, there was no use of violence in the relations between the Lutherans and the Orthodox in Transylvania.

The Saxon population had been settled by the ruling Hungarian kings during the 13th century in the southern part of Transylvania, where they have built their own villages and towns among the villages of the Romanians. They had the mission to protect the border of the Hungarian kingdom and as a reward they were granted the rights of self-organisation and self-determination. Under these

2 See http://www.insse.ro/rpl2002rezgen/rg2002.htm, 26.05.2009, 13.45.

circumstances they have developed a strong awareness of their own communitarian identity. Already during Luther's lifetime they have imported the Lutheran ideas and embraced Lutheranism as a whole community. The way they have tried to spread their new religious convictions was by publishing Lutheran books in other languages than German. As they saw that the others were not interested in Lutheranism, they did not go farther than this.[3]

The result was that they have raised the appetite of others, e.g. the Orthodox Romanians, to have also published religious and liturgical books of their own. Soon after that, during the 1st half of the 16th century, the Romanians were publishing their first Orthodox books, in commercial collaboration with the Saxon printing-houses. Even nowadays the fact that liturgical and biblical texts were translated into Romanian and published so early is regarded as a consequence of the cohabitation with the Lutherans.

On the other hand, Lutheranism developed in Romania different as in other parts of Europe. I know pretty well Lutheranism as it is in Germany and as it is in Romania, and I have even had the meaningful experience to assist when German Lutherans from Romania and German Lutherans from Germany were talking about the similarities and the differences between them. One thing was generally accepted: the Lutherans in Transylvania have a deeper spirituality and a liturgy richer in symbols, thanks to the natural influences of the Orthodox neighbours.

Excepting a period in the 17th century when political leaders of Transylvania tried to impose Calvinism by force, the relations between the Calvinists and the Orthodox in the principality were peaceful. Almost the same can be said about the relations between the Catholics and the Orthodox. It is to mention here that the Habsburg royals, who where ruling Transylvania starting with the late 17th century, made even bigger efforts to impose Catholicism, with the result that one comparatively small part could be split from the Orthodox Church, and so the Greek-Catholic Church in Transylvania came into existence. The composite ethnical and cultural character of Roman-Catholic Church in Transylvania can also be regarded as a consequence of that.

3 For the historical information see Mircea Păcurariu, *Istoria Bisericii Ortodoxe Române (History of the Romanian Orthodox Chrruch)*, 3 vol., 2nd edition, 1992-1994 Bucharest: Editura Institutului Biblic şi de Misiune al Bisericii Ortodoxe Române.

Time passed, the Habsburg monarchs embraced the Enlightenment, and things settled. The period between the two world wars has best shown that people were able to forgive and forget what had happened to them, and to concentrate upon establishing normality in the social life. If the Communists hadn't interdicted the existence of the Greek-Catholic Church, the peaceful relations would have been continued. So we have after 1989 a re-born Greek-Catholic Church who has not yet overcome its traumas and has not healed its wounds, but who bears an aura of martyrdom, and an Orthodox Church who is frustrated in front of this, because it has also been suffering and it has also given its martyrs in the communist prisons. We cannot generalise, but there is a certain tension between the two Churches nowadays, amplified by the fact that they are both Churches of the Romanians in Transylvania.

III. Reflections

As we could see in the example about the Lutherans, violence and resentments as a consequence of it do not appear when a community (or even a person, it is the same psychological process) has a stable identity. Of course, this identity is not supposed to be a static one, but one which develops in a natural way, like every living organism which is changing itself in the interaction with the surrounding world. If the identity is so strong that the person or the community can say: this is me, this is my level now, my history consists of this and that, I feel comfortable with my past, my position among the others is acceptable, then the person or the community will be able to accept and to allow others to exist. Living together will then lead to mutual enrichments, in which everyone can develop, preserving the good feeling that he is in continuity with his past and in synchronisation with the actuality. Identities and mutual influences are not opposites under normal conditions, but aspects that belong together. Simply said, they are just the two sides of the coin.

The other examples show also several interesting things. The first I would like to mention is the fact that interreligious violence is often, very often a result of the intervention "in force" of factors who go away from pure religiousness. I consider that in absence of any intrusion from outside, religion[4] would not lead to violence, because religiousness presupposes the very basic acceptance of the others as they are. At all preoccupation for the others' spiritual wellness or for their salvation, a religious being does not go so far to force them to come to salvation, as God does not force anyone to come to Him.

The problem is that our religious existence, even if it is a good and a sincere one, often has also its limits. As religious beings, we all know that we are still on the way, and that we can grow in our relation with God, with all its implications for our relations with others, at least till the end of this life. But very often we also forget that, and act out of the conviction that what we do now is absolutely the best. So we can make mistakes out of religious enthusiasm. Such situations are already found in the Bible. Meaningful is the reflection of St. Paul the Apostle on this: "For I can testify about them that they are zealous for God, but their zeal is not based on knowledge. Since they did not know the righteousness that comes from God and sought to establish their own, they did not submit to God's righteousness." (Rom. 10, 2-3) The awareness of (political) power can become an even stronger temptation to made use of force in order to impose religious convictions. Preaching, praying, celebrating liturgy, living a proper religious life are modalities to help the others to find their way to religiousness which is proper for them.

The second conclusion I want to draw is that I have reasons to be proud of my Transylvanian ancestors! When I am talking about my Transylvanian ancestors, I do not mean only the Orthodox ones, but also the others. They were able to forget negative situations from the history. They did not need to find imaginary scapegoats in order to free themselves psychologically from feelings of guilt or from the feeling of being a victim. In Christ, the believers receive and develop their ability to forgive, which means to be relieved from the destructive power of the past, not to have the consciousness of a slave any more, but that of a beloved son who knows that he can be generous with the gifts of his father.

4 I follow that direction in the religious studies which understands the religious fact as being in connexion, in communion with the Sacred, be it personal or non-personal. This vertical connexion automatically involves a horizontal one, a connexion between the religious being and all the other facts and realities of the world, which he perceives as being themselves in relation to the Sacred, and whose liberty and dignity he learns to respect.

Third, we notice that this does not happen without concerted efforts. Thinking about the present situation of the Greek-Catholic and the Orthodox Church, we notice that, even for Christians, wounds are real and can be deep. The process of healing often needs time. Here we see how important it is to sustain it, be it on local or on general level. And to have patience until the good seed can grow.

Ecumenical efforts are welcomed to join the other modalities, which I have mentioned two paragraphs before. As long as there are believers who go one Sunday in the Orthodox church and every second Sunday in the Greek-Catholic one, as long as so many people on the street would tell you that all the Christian Churches must be good, because they all have the same God, and as long as they wonder every year why Orthodox and Greek-Catholic on the one side have one Easter date, all the other churches have another one and why it is not possible to put them together, I think we have reasons to hope that things will go on well. We can also hope that the ones from the church leaders or the theologians who know much more Church history than others, because they are much more involved in these things, will also be able to develop much better the Christian virtues in their lives, and that in Christian humility they will learn something from ordinary believers, which are together with them members of the body of Christ.

Transylvania is regarded to be a model of peaceful cohabitation between different ethnical and religious groups during the centuries. I think this perspective is realistic, because exemplary relationships are not where there is no conflict (it would be an illusion to expect that), but where people are able to overcome conflicts, working on establishing normality in their lives.

IV. Religious Life and Images of the Orthodox Romanians in Transylvania

The next part of my paper will be concerned with religious images, with the way of producing them and with their particularities which can only develop in such an ecumenical context. I shall focus again on the situation in Transylvania, describing a reality which is specific to that part of the world. It has to do primarily with Orthodox iconography, which is central for the life of the Orthodox Church. Let it be said first that a way of living and relating to the surrounding world necessarily produces a universe of representations. Our human existence tends to express itself, and therefore uses several artistic means. Images are known from the oldest times as being closely related to religious life, as the caves in Lascaux and Altamira prove.[5] „The experience does not shape any form for the human besides the symbolical mediation of the sensitive, or in absence of the capacity to read the story narrated by the image."[6]

Leonid Ouspensky believes that for Christianity image and theology are so closely related to each other, that the expression "theology of the image" represents almost a tautology.[7] For sure, this can be affirmed regarding Orthodox Christianity. "Very early on, iconography became an organic part of Holy Tradition and came to be nothing less than 'visual theology'."[8] Until today, the icons are central in the teachings and the worship of the Orthodoxy. For Orthodox people, the use of icons in their everyday religious life is so natural that it doesn't even need arguments. The Romanian-Orthodox theologian Dumitru Stăniloae affirms that "the depths of our soul manifest themselves through images. The total absence of them is equivalent with the absence of sense, of meaning, of consciousness. Intelligible is the same as imaginable. Spiritual life is not possible without images."[9]

When speaking about Orthodox icons, most Western Christians would immediately think about Byzantine art with its strict rules to be followed by any painter. They would probably say that the paintings do not change their shape in time, but they remain the same over the centuries. They would make a distinction between Western Christian art which adapted to the different cultural periods and Orthodox iconography which is not a subject of time.

All this is only partially true. The icons do show some particularities in space and time, so that an original art can rise and has often risen. Wilhelm Nyssen writes in his book about the Moldavian monasteries as follows:

"Since the earliest times there was a unquestionable possibility for everything that was fixed to become again an artistic event, so that one could have the im-

5 See art. *Lascaux Grotto* and art. *Altamira*, both in Encyclopaedia Britannica 2005 Ultimate Reference Suite DVD.

6 Tomaš Špidlík, Marko Ivan Rupnik, *Credință și icoană (Faith and Icon),* 2002 Cluj-Napoca: Dacia, 8.

7 Leonid Uspensky, *Teologia icoanei în Biserica Ortodoxă (The Theology of the Icon in the Orthodox Church),* 1994 Bucharest: Anastasia, 197.

8 Paul Evdokimov, *The Art of the Icon: a Theology of Beauty*, 1990 Redondo Beach: Oakwood Publications, 165.

9 Dumitru Stăniloae, *Ortodoxie și românism (Orthodoxy and Romanian Ethos),* 1992 M-rea Putna, 138-139.

pression that there has never been anything fixed before. The whole development of the Byzantine painting, starting with its early period and continuing with Ravenna and Parenzo, and later with the Serbian, Bulgarian and Macedonian monasteries, with the Moldavian frescoes and the Russian icon schools witness about that.

In Moldavia of Romania an unmistakable particularity of the painting appears, so that the dispute regarding the independence of that landscape was long ago decided in favor of Moldavia. ‚Byzantium after Byzantium'; everything is strictly byzantine but still very new. In the same time the obligatory canon which used to bound the artist was penetrated by the Latin spirit, so that one can only astonishly detect that here in the 16th century became clear again that there were two columns who sustain the dome of the Christian history. These two columns bear the names of the both 'ancient' cities Rome and Byzantium and indicate the quintessence of the whole Christian oikumene."[10]

I am not going to speak further about the well-known Moldavian monasteries, but refer, as announced, to a phenomenon from Transylvania: the glass-painted icons, produced by the hands of simple peasants. During the 18th and the 19th century a very rich art developed here, which is best testified in the Zosim Oancea Museum in Sibiel. "The Fr. Zosim Oancea Museum at Sibiel holds the largest existing exposition of icons on glass in Transylvania, a miracle of artistic creativity and religious inspiration born of the riches of the Orthodox Christian tradition and the imagination of Romanian peasant painters." [11]

Giovanni Ruggeri has recently dedicated a book to the above mentioned phenomenon.[12] He considers that "the emergence of the marvel of religious fervor and popular art represented by the icons on glass of Transylvania can be explained only against the background of the richness of the Orthodox Christian tradition and the imaginative gifts of Romanian peasant artists."[13] Most of the painters did not attend a school and were only hobby painters, learning

10 Wilhelm Nyssen, *Bildgesang der Erde. Aussenfresken der Moldauklöster in Rumänien*, 1994 Köln: Luthe, 18.

11 http://www.sibiel.net/Home_EN.html, 28.05.2009, 15.30.

12 Giovanni Ruggeri, *The Icons on Glass at Sibiel. The Zosim Oancea Museum*, 2008 Rome: CAEfor.

13 Ibid., 5.

from each other the way of writing with colors.[14] Even so, there are no less than six Transylvanian schools of painting[15] presented in the museum.[16]

More important is the fact that the icons represent a synthesis between Eastern and Western: "A unique fusion of Eastern tradition and Western technique, icons on glass emerged and spread throughout this extensive region of Romania in the first decades of the eighteenth century, reaching their apogee between 1750 and the end of the nineteenth century and almost vanishing in the period between the two world wars."[17]

Not only the technique was imported from the Western, but also contents, motifs, ways of representation. The *Coronation of the Virgin* is such a typical Western theme, as well as some representations of the *Holy Trinity*, which correspond to the Post-Tridentinian type. There are painters who are influenced by the Western art even in their style. Ruggeri writes about the *Last Supper* painted by Ion Morar (1815-1890) that it "displays a marked baroque influence, exuberant both in its colour and design... with a mixture of elements of high art (the composition being reminiscent of Leonardo's masterpiece) and of popular tradition (as in the radishes on the table)."[18]

Popular elements are very present in the icons which belong to several painters. "One definite element in the mergence of icons on glass in Transylvania is the fusion they represent between the inspiration of Byzantine iconography and a creative popular re-interpretation of this tradition, a reinterpretation which is also very significant on the socio-cultural level."[19] So, "in the case of Popa's *Madonna with Child* we can see, however, that the Virgin is wearing a folk-costume (şorţ) typical of the women of the Mureş Valley. This is an effective way of presenting the Mother of God as close to the people while at the same time raising the humble reality of the Transylvanian peasants' daily lives to a heavenly dignity."[20]

14 Ibid., 19.

15 The six schools are of geographical and historical expanse. They are the followings: Nicula and the northern Transylvania, The Mureş Valley, Făgăraş District, Braşov District, The Sebeş Valley – Alba Iulia, The localities around Sibiu.

16 See ibid., 23-47.

17 http://www.sibiel.net/Home_EN.html, 28.05.2009, 15.30.

18 Ruggeri, 45.

19 Ibid., 27.

20 Ibid., 30.

The art has also served as a way of releasing aggressiveness, so that conflicts did not rise. I would say that they have contributed in a certain way to the maintenance of the good relations between the different ethnical groups. Irony is a soft way of getting rid of inner tensions, and when it finds its place in art it helps the whole community. "Ţâmforea's icons in the museum at Sibiel… are evidence of the painter's mastery of illustration, his strong sense of justice animating many of his compositions. Thus, for example in the icon of *Dives and Lazarus*, Ţâmforea shows Dives and his companions in Hungarian dress, a clear condemnation of the contemporary Hungarian repression of the Romanians of Transylvania."[21] I want to underline that we have to do with interethnical, political problems, and not with interconfessional ones.

A fact that must be mentioned is that the museum is not a simple art collection, but it documents about a way of practicing Christian faith. All the icons exposed here are not just paintings, but places and means of worship. People were praying in front of these icons and they were experiencing communion with Christ, with the Mother of God and with the saints. The persons represented there have a spiritualized beauty, because "in iconography the face of each holy person replicates the face of Christ. Saints are images of Christ at different ages – old and young – different social categories, different colors, from every race and every age. Each human face, when it is full of the presence of the Holy Spirit, becomes the mysterious face of Christ."[22] So what we have in front of our eyes is "transfigured art, that is the spiritual beauty from beyond the material"[23].

The museum in Sibiel owes to its founder, Zosim Oancea, very much.

"The witness of Fr. Zosim Oancea (1911-2005) presents us with a man and Orthodox priest of extraordinary human and religious stature. It would be impossible to over-estimate his work: not only the importance of the project which is the icon-museum but also the spiritual qualities which inspired the life of this man."[24]

In order to understand the greatness of his life we shall not forget that the most decades of his active life were marked by communism, which represented a real

21 Ibid., 36.

22 Daniel Ciobotea, *Confessing the Truth in Love. Orthodox Perceptions of Life, Mission and Unity*, 2001 Iaşi: Trinitas, 55.

23 Ibid., 57.

24 http://www.sibiel.net/PadreZosim_EN.html, 28.05.2009, 15.45.

challenge for the churches. A world of terror was installed starting with the 50's. People were afraid to talk with each other on a sincere basis[25] and to witness their faith. Zosim Oancea had to endure 15 years of prison and forced labour because of his courage to name things as they were.[26] Those years he recalls as "the first miracle of my life"[27]. In prison he felt God as a neighbour and experienced true ecumenism, together with the priests and believers of the other churches, also imprisoned for their faith. After being freed, "the second miracle" came into existence: it has been not easy at all to build and to open an icon museum in the period of communism, being a former political prisoner and therefore being more haunted by the *Securitate* every moment.[28]

Zosim Oancea, which I learned to know personally short before his passing away, lived the last part of his life in the effort to retrieve the 15 years in which he could not be active in the Church.[29] The work for the museum was for him a way to serve the church. Sibiel was intended to become "a Transylvanian Voroneț"[30].

It seems that he has succeeded. Already in 1976, Horia Bădescu wrote:

"If you were in Mărginimea Sibiului and did not visit the museum of glass painted icons from Sibiel, whose power resides in the icon collection, it is as if you were in Paris and didn't visit the Louvre.

What you can find there is amazing. Perhaps only Voroneț can shock you like that, because only there you can see such a dissipation of pictorial genius, such a colour explosion which the peasant masters have put on the pieces of glass. I have written in the impression book: Sistine Chapel of Romania. Go and visit the Sistine Chapel from Sibiel!"[31]

25 For the situation in Romania during communism see e.g. the memories of Jessica Douglas-Home, *Once Upon Another Time. Ventures behind the Iron Curtain*, 2000 Norwich: Michael Russel, 130-224.

26 See Zosim Oancea, *Închisorile unui preot orthodox (The Prisons of an Orthodox Priest)*, 2004 Bucharest: Christiana.

27 Ruggeri, 52.

28 See for the description of this aspect of Oanceas life Zosim Oancea, *Muzeul de icoane pe sticlă ‚Zosim Oancea din Sibiel (The Museum of Glass-Painted Icons 'Zosim Oancea' of Sibiel)*, 2 vol., 2001-2002 Sibiu: Casa de Presă şi Editură Tribuna.

29 Ibid., 10.

30 Ibid., 37.

31 Horia Bădescu, in ibid., 76.

In front of the icons at Sibiel the different Christian denominations come together again in a new manner. As shown before, the painters of the icons drew from the tradition of different churches. Now, the members of the various churches, from Romania or from abroad, are inspired in the museum to see the Christian unity in a new light.

"By the middle of the 1970s Sibiel had become a kind of mini ecumenical centre. This was a source of great joy to Father Oancea who had published an original study on the important subject of unity between the Christian Churches. Groups of foreigners – not only Orthodox, but also Catholic and Protestant – prayed in the church with the local Orthodox community and important world dignitaries of the various Christian Churches visited the museum at Sibiel."[32]

In this way, elements that are specific to one culture or to one form of Christianity prove to be more than results of the one single culture in which they have developed. In turn, they have the ability to nourish all those who come in contact with them, independent of their religious or cultural belonging. Religious life is so rich in Transylvania because of the interaction of so many groups and cultures. Life is always based on communion, and only through lived communion it comes to fulfilment.

References and Bibliography

Ciobotea, Daniel (2001) *Confessing the Truth in Love. Orthodox Perceptions of Life, Mission and Unity*, Iaşi: Trinitas.

Douglas-Home, Jessica (2000) *Once Upon Another Time. Ventures Behind the Iron Curtain*, Norwich: Michael Russel.

Evdokimov, Paul (1990) *The Art of the Icon: a Theology of Beauty*, Redondo Beach: Oakwood Publications

Nyssen, Wilhelm (1994) *Bildgesang der Erde. Aussenfresken der Moldauklöster in Rumänien*, Köln: Luthe.

Oancea, Zosim (2004) *Închisorile unui preot orthodox (The Prisons of an Orthodox Priest)*, Bucharest: Christiana.

32 Ruggeri, 62.

Oancea, Zosim (2001-2002) *Muzeul de icoane pe sticlă ,Zosim Oancea' din Sibiel (The Museum of Glass-Painted Icons 'Zosim Oancea' of Sibiel)*, 2 vol., Sibiu: Casa de Presă şi Editură Tribuna.

Mircea Păcurariu, *Istoria Bisericii Ortodoxe Române (History of the Romanian Orthodox Chruch)*, 3 vol., 2nd edition, 1992-1994 Bucharest: Editura Institutului Biblic şi de Misiune al Bisericii Ortodoxe Române.

Ruggeri, Giovanni (2008) *The Icons on Glass at Sibiel. The Zosim Oancea Museum*, Rome: CAEfor.

Špidlík, Tomaš/ Rupnik, Marko Ivan (2002) *Credinţă şi icoană (Faith and Icon),* Cluj-Napoca: Dacia.

Stăniloae, Dumitru (1992) *Ortodoxie şi românism (Orthodoxy and Romanian Ethos),* M-rea Putna.

Leonid Uspensky, *Teologia icoanei în Biserica Ortodoxă (The Theology of the Icon in the Orthodox Church),* 1994 Bucharest: Anastasia.

*** *Encyclopaedia Britannica* 2005 Ultimate Reference Suite DVD.

http://www.insse.ro/rpl2002rezgen/rg2002.htm

http://www.sibiel.net/Home_EN.html

http://www.sibiel.net/PadreZosim_EN.html .

ABSTRACTS

Ulrich Beck
The Two Faces of Religion

In the introduction the author outlines his view that there are two faces of religion: 1. the human one; 2. the totalitarian temptation in religion which is inherent to it. There are two sides of the universalism as well: 1. A cosmopolitan fraternity which transcendens classes and nations and 2. A demonization of a religiously other which was happening throughout the history. Therefore the author claims that God can civilize but also barbarize people as well. Then he sets the question: If religion is the one that often divides us, why religion can't also be what enables us to bridge the divisions and separations among us? In the remaining part of the article he considers seven thesis of relevance for the question set above.

Key words: *two faces of religion, individualization, universality, cosmopolitanism, truth, peace.*

Wilhelm Schmid
Some Fundamental Questions of the Art of Living

Is the life we live our »own«? There are a lot of factors influencing our life, over which we have hardly any control. An art of living is far from being »easy«. It is confronted with some fundamental questions: In what contexts do I live? What choice do I have? Who am I? What understanding of live do I have? How can I conduct my life? What, specifically, can I do? Why form one's life at all? And what can »living well« mean in this context?

Key words: *art of living, guestions of life, context of life, choice.*

Karl Mathäus Woschitz,
The Life in the World of Dionysus and Apollo: The Greek Understanding of the Tragic and the Delphic Theology of the Humanity

The article deals with the dualism constituted by the reason (the Apollonian moment) and the will (the Dionysian moment). The two moments were understood by the ancient Greeks as the two sides of the man's striving for the life. However, they represent the main anthropologic problem of man as such.

Key words: *Greek conception of striving for the life; dualism constituted by the Apollonian and the Dyonisian moment; the main anthropologic problem as such; the tragic; Delphic theology of humanity.*

Janez Juhant
On Living with: Dialogue as the Way to the Art of Personal and Common Life

The article deals with the critical condition of humanity in present times: how can we find the balance between the greed for the goods at one hand and their scantiness on the earth at the other? Are we able to secure the foundations of living humanly or even of the survival at all? The author searches for the solution in the direction of the Christian way of life: 'Being with' means to share the goods, to cultivate the reciprocal empathy and to be ready to give our own life at disposal, to lose it in order to really gain it.

Key words: *life, man, foundations of life, Christian way of life, 'living with'.*

Bojan Žalec
Media, Reality Shows, Virtues, and the Pitfalls of the Internet

The paper deals with the importance of the media and of the internet. The author's reflection takes into account the huge importance of backgrounds, imitation and examples for the formation of personalities, for their (sub)consciousness and acting. The author considers foremost the dangers of media regarding the psychical mood of people, retrieving of information, education, creating of democracy, and cultivation of virtues (needed for these) as for instance courage or fortitude and tolerance. He stresses the importance of human body and physical contact, of empathy and genuine dialogue, of non-anonymity and exposure. Such relationships can't be realized by the means of the media or they are - because of their mediation through the media - importantly mutilated. The author uses in his consideration of the topics findings of Kierkegaard and phenomenology (Merlau-Ponty, Dreyfus),

Girard's mimetic anthropology, modern cognitive science and also findings of sociologists (Beck).

Key words: *media, internet, physical mood, retrieving of information, education, democracy, Kierkegaard, phenomenology, backgrounds, anthropology, Girard, imitation, examples.*

Zvezdan Pirtošek
Happiness and the Brain

Happiness is seen by many as a basic human emotion – innate, pan-cultural, evolutionary old, shared with other species, with a distinct feeling, physiology and behaviour. However, emotions are not experienced passively in response to elicitors but instead are active processes that modulate cognition and are themselves influenced by cognition. Basic aspects of happiness are functionally linked to deep ventral brain structures (mesocorticolimbic pathway, accumbens, amygdala) with dopamine as a central player in the evaluation of reward, sometimes causing addiction. Interaction with superficial dorsal brain areas (prefrontal cortex) and other neurotransmitters (e.g. serotonine) give happiness a distinctly 'humane' dimension when happiness can be felt in social interaction, arts, religion, science. Asymmetry of the hemispheres may also play a role: right posterior sensory areas probably in evaluating and frontal areas in experiencing and expressing either positive (left side) or negative (right hemisphere) emotions.

Key words: *happiness, emotion, cognition, brain, hemispheres.*

Santiago & Miriam S. Sia
Punctuating Life's Message: A Grammatical-Philosophical Exercise on the Quest for Meaning

The meaning of life has preoccupied the minds of many throughout the ages. In this article, the authors turn to their respective disciplines (literature and philosophy) and provide an interdisciplinary reflection on this fundamental concern. The claim that is made is that life presents us with a challenge: it can become a 'sentence' on us or it can be regarded as 'a series of sentences' which contain a message. However, just as in grammar, it is necessary to insert the proper punctuation marks to be able to make sense of the grouping of words in a sentence, so in life it is important to create 'punctuating moments' to facilitate the reading of life's message. The paper makes use of lessons that can be drawn from the study of literature and philosophy in understanding and interpreting the human quest for meaning in life.

Key words: *meaning of life, sentence(s), life's message, literary-philosophical approach.*

Vojko Strahovnik
The Art of Life: Kekes and Bauman on Attaining the Good Life

The paper deals with the more and more prominent topics of the art of life, the ataining of good life and pursuit of happiness. It presents the core thoughts of two authors that have recently dealt with these topics, namely John Kekes (2002) and Zygmunt Bauman (2008). Kekes uses a bottom-up approach and examines several examples of good lives in order to determine what constitutes the art of life and which conditions must be meet in order for us to attain a good life through it. Bauman on the other hand starts with a lucid examination of the modern society and then tries to give us answers on how to practice the art of life in it. At the end the paper points to some similarities and dissimilarities in both accounts of the art of life and tries to combine them.

Key words: *art of life, good life, personal excellences, values, happiness, liquid modernity***.**

Branko Klun
Life and the Question of Meaning. Some Phenomenological Considerations

Factical life prior to any theoretical objectification represents the point of departure for phenomenological analysis as developed by Heidegger in his early lectures. This life always includes an understanding of itself and of the world and is therefore intrinsically tied to significance and meaning. The constitution of meaning occurs as a modality of life and it has the character of possibility. However, if there is no "objective" meaning, the problem becomes especially urgent when dealing with the question of the meaning of life on the whole. How can we discern an authentic mode of life from an inauthentic one, along with their respective meanings? From the phenomenological point of view the criterion for this differentiation cannot be imposed from outside, but should be sought from within life itself.

Key words: *life, meaning, significance, facticity, phenomenological method.*

Tomas Kačerauskas
Art of Life from Phenomenological Point of View

The article deals with connection between philosophy and existence using phenomenological-existential concepts including M. Heidegger's „existential project", E. Husserl's „spiritual background (*Hintergrund*)", M. Bakhtin's „heroics of a story", as well H. Arendt's „*vita activa*". The author interprets the antique concept of philosophy as love of wisdom from phenomenological point of view. In addition to that, existence is treated as a unit story to be inscribed in the spiritual background (*Hintergrund*) of coexistence, while philosophy as a school of existence (*ex-sistus*) is a *technē* of this existential inscribing. This interpretation presupposes the life as a stream that we order when inscribing its events into a mobile existential story that emerges in the spiritual background. The author of an existential story is creating its hero, which inspires a rebirth of the author.

Keywords: *art of life, coexistence, existential story, spiritual background, birth and death.*

Gábor Kovács
Search for Identity as Art of Life in the Political Philosophy of Hannah Arendt

Hannah Arendt, the disciple of Martin Heidegger and Karl Jaspers, in her political philosophy as a starting point chose the notion of existence inherited from her masters. The point of gravitation of her doctoral dissertation entitled *Liebesbegriff bei Augustine* is the Augustinian question: 'Questio mihi factus sum', I became a question to myself. Is human existence capable to come out of his/her isolation and to find the way to the community of his/her fellow-men? This problem accompanied Arendt during her whole intellectual carrier. One of the central problems in her political philosophy is this searching for identity which in her theory is public or political identity. Private identity without political identity is a truncated mode of existence for human beings. Action which is one of the basic ontological characteristics for human beings is possible if only they enter the space of appearance. Arendt uses a metaphor: public realm or politics is a stage of theatre on which the actors must wear mask to hide their naked private existence.

Key words: *love, world, private identity, public identity, stage of theatre.*

Robert Petkovšek

Truths of Being, Truths of Life

In his phenomenological analysis of the phenomenon of life, Michel Henry refers to the present situation of the Western culture. Like Nietzsche and Heidegger, he considers that life in its authentic form is excluded from the modern culture where the concept of the world is considered as the horizon of visibility through which everything becomes visible and phenomenon for us. Truth, such as grasped in the Western tradition, is understood as the "world's truth". But, Henry points out that nature of the truth cannot be reduced to the natural horizon of visibility. Such an exclusively worldly understanding of man disregards man's inner experience as well as his experience of transcendence. The very essence of the life doesn't consist in its outward appearance and objectivity, but in its possibility of inner self-experience and self-revelation by which life experiences itself immediately and in a pre-worldly way. There is no revelation (world's truth) without auto-revelation (life's truth). Therefore, world's truths cannot express the truths of the life. Life is nothing other than that which reveals itself, the very fact of self-revelation as such that owes nothing to the truth of the world. Truth is to be defined as Life: life is self-revelation. Radical phenomenology is radical because it doesn't have for its object phenomena but phenomenological substance, i.e. phenomenalization of phenomenality, life. To the question: What is the truth? Henry answers in the sense of the St John's Gospel: "Life." Life experiences itself. It's the primordial capacity of self-experience, of self-revelation because there is no austereness, no distances in it. Life doesn't need the world to appear like things need to appear. According to Henry, "life that speaks not a word knows everything."

Key words: *Western philosophy, phenomenology of life, Michel Henry, world, truth, interiority, phenomenality, radical phenomenology.*

Zdenka Zalokar Divjak

Life as a Task in the Light of Frankl's Logo-therapy

Today's lifestyle requires that you become aware of it in all its complexity, coherence and integrity. Logo-therapy sees the essence of human conduct in his ability to rise himself above instinct reduction and lust for victory and tends to the meaning. His tendency for meaning signifies performing tasks that can be identified in every situation and are always focused on some work or interpersonal relationship. Man's spiritual dimension is the scope of its specific conscious and intuitive abilities. In practical life, this means that as individuals we are continually standing in front of different options which we can weigh up and of course choose the one we believe is the best in that situation. Likewise, our spiritual dimension also allows us to be able to overcome ourselves, to counter tragic nature and to correct wrong decisions. Man doesn't depend mainly on his genetic or behavioural patterns, although they may be of great importance for his development, but rather on how he is able to use his spiritual dimensions.

Key words: *task, logo-therapy, freedom, responsibility, meaning.*

Béla Mester

The Beatitude of Souls amongst the Things Indifferent. Adiaphora in the Stoic Ethics and in the Christian Thinking

In the history of the concept of adiaphora (indifferent things) in the European thought we can see the mirror of the changing ethical frames of the human life in our cultural heritage. My lecture offers an analysis of this term focussing on its three main aspects: (1) the use of this term in the Stoical ethics is purely individual, with some elements of an anti-political approach. (2) The Christianised use of the term adiaphora, especially in the religious debates of the 16-17th centuries, having a connection with the contemporary concepts of Christian liberty and iustitia civilis, is an ambiguous phenomenon. It concerns the individual consciousnesses of the believers, and refers almost directly to the public sphere. (3) Whether it is possible a relevant use of this term in the moral discourse nowadays, or it is a merely historical phenomenon.

Key words: *adiaphora, stoical ethics, Christian liberty, iustitia civilis, religious debates.*

Tadej Strehovec
The Meaning of Human Life

One of the most controversial spaces of modern society is the meaning of the human life. It is the space were different ideologies enter to the contest, confrontation among themselves and become the testing ground of different political opinions and convictions. Phenomena like euthanasia, abortion, in vitro fertilization, eugenics, embryo research etc. have a common point – that is to change previous view of human person and its nature and threw this new view to control (DNA) structure of the future human generations. Therefore scientific area like biotechnology, genetics and medicine become space where scientific expectations are mixed by philosophical and religious views and utopia. Many promises and messianic ideas which are created in such a space do not create only new hopes for patients and rich people. These promises and ideas are the source of many disappointments and new forms of despairs and fears as well. Demythologization of biotechnology in the so called bio-techno-theological process is one kind of the method which makes possible to see unseen world of social tensions, searching for innocent victims and sacrifices of innocent people in different periods of human life. The Rene Girard's approach is of the fundamental significance in such kind of the methodology and analysis. The main point in such kind of approach is to reveal the biotechnology and the modern society as part of the mimetic circle of violence and sacrifices; however on the other side the gospels become place where biotechnological cannibalism becomes visible and seen as a source of utopia and false messianism.

Key words: *biotechnology, demythologization, biotechnotheology, embryo research, bioethics, euthanasia.*

Tonči Matulić
Post-human Existence in the Atmosphere of the End of History

The author in this paper critically evaluates and makes enquiries about the ideas of the end of history, the last man and that what can be considered a system of post-historical thinking (post-histoire). The paper is divided in three sections. In the first section author questions the problem of the end of history in its intellectual-historical origins and in some philosophical and scientific-popular interpretations of it. In the second section are being analyzed closely some aspects of the ideas of the end of history and the last man in some works dealing with this topic of the American political economist Francis Fukuyama, one of the most notorious post-modern representatives of the ideology of post-historical thinking. In this context are being taken seriously the challenges and consequences of biotechnology revolution in relation to the idea of the end of history. The last part of the contribution, e.g. the third section, deals with a critical account of the traits of the so called post-human existence. The term post-human existence is being taken in the meaning of human existence reduced on mere conditio humana. This type or mode of human existence is being understood as culturally conditioned post-modern human existence historically deprived of any significant influence of the strong subjects of God, man, and the world on concrete human life. Post-human existence means simply human existence without sound and durable foundations. In other words there is no other meaning of humanity than that of free human projection. This approach is being criticized in this paper.

Key words: *the end of history, the last man, post-histoire, conditio humana, post-human existence, God, human person, disenchantment, exclusive humanism.*

Gunter Prüller-Jagenteufel

The Victims of Globalization and the Ethics of Life. Notes on Recent Latin American Ethics of Liberation

New developments in Latin American Theology are dealing with problems of Globalization from a new perspective. As Christian ethics needs to take up the preferential option for the poor, it has to start from the experience of the poor, the marginalized and the excluded. Therefore, the experience of exclusion becomes the starting point of a new ethics of liberation, which focuses on the "subject", the concrete living human being that can and should be the author of his/her own life's story. So the main task is to build up a society where all can participate as subjects.

Key words: *Christian Ethics, Latin American Theology, Theology of Liberation.*

Anton Jamnik
The Pilgramige as a Way of Life

Hope lies within the core itself of Christian faith. Our time with its growing feeling of futility of life and despair invites us to re-discover the broadness and the value of hope comprised in our faith and to base our life thereon. Hope as a Christian virtue essentially differs from a certain spontaneous and ill-considered optimism expressed by the words: it will go somehow, everything will turn out for the best. On the one hand, human hope is oriented towards the concrete reality, events and people, yet of fundamental importance is the hope as a state of mind, which is not bound to having or achieving anything, but means simply to be, to exist out of pure gratuity and generosity and to realize one's vocation. In the field of religious and ethical search one can see many signs of hope expressing man's longing for a fullness of existence.

Key words: *pilgramige, hope, faith, religious and ethical search, fullness of existence.*

Mateja Pevec Rozman
Postmodern Wo/Man in the Prime of Life; Living With or Without Virtues

In this postmodern moment of our civilisation, we all are artists of life. In individualized society we find out that different lifestyles are popular and acceptable. The following lecture consists of three parts: at first, I present a short outline of some characteristics of postmodern times, some of those outstanding characteristics, which denote us and our life. In the second part we are looking for what kind of lifestyle is more flourishing; I argue that virtues can give us a hand to make our life more fruitful and to make us the unique artists of life. Art of life is an art, because it requires individuals to make a creative effort that no one can make for other. Good life has to be constructed out of one's character, circumstances, experiences, and ideals which vary from individual to individual, tradition and society, times and places. For Art of life it is important to be personally engaged and devoted to our life task(s). The art of living is to live good and fruitful life; we must be active agents in this concrete moment. The art of life includes also others: the fullness of human existence is realised in a dialogic relationship. Life according to virtues for the wo/man in the prime of life of these postmodern times is still reasonable and leads us to good life.

Key words: *postmodernism, good life, virtues, active agents, community.*

Tomaž Erzar, Katarina K. Erzar
Whose Life is This? Art of Healing Trauma and Search for Disowned Self in Relationships

In this article, we discuss the antique idea of art of life in the context of attachment theory and intergenerational transmission of traumatic experiences. We argue that for children of traumatized parents living beyong trauma means to differentiate themselves from their parents and unburden themselves from the past they cannot repair. Since they tend to identify with their traumatized parents, children of these parents live out their lives trying to heal the wound their parents were unable to cope with. In order to reclaim their current life in the healing process, adult children of these parents have to reconstruct their reversed attachments to parental figures and see them as they are, i.e. insecurely attached children and dysfunctional adults.

Key words: *art of life, attachment theory, reversed attachment, trauma, intergenerational tramsmission, identity.*

Inna Naletova
Life as a Pilgrimage, Religious Messages of the Post-Soviet Russian Cinema

The paper approaches the topic 'Art of Life' from the perspectives of social anthropology, and it uses the materials of the post-Soviet Russian cinema to examine pilgrimage as an art of living (or rather an art to continue living) during problematic periods of human life. Specifically, it examines symbolic contents of 3 highly prised post-Soviet Russian films, *Nebesa Obetovannye* ("The Promised Heaven") by Eldar Riazanov, *Vosvraschenie* ("The Return") by Andrej Zvyagintzev, and *Ostrov* ("The Island") by Pavel Lungin, in which our contemporaries are shown as thinking and acting under the conditions of extreme personal or social uncertainty, in a kind of 'anti-structure,' bearing in itself a component of the sacred. By taking Viktor Turner's anthropological view on pilgrimage as an anti-structure – i.e. as a state of being in a reality beyond the established social norms – the paper applies the concept of pilgrimage to a broader spectrum of transitional life situations. It examines the concept of pilgrimage as a helpful cultural resource directly or indirectly guiding individuals during the period of transition, when other social resources are absent or inefficient. It proposes that an approach to human life as a pilgrimage is able to activate in individuals an intense spirit of community, a sense of moral responsibility and self-discipline, thus helping them to make a sense of life, to position themselves among others, and to create a new structure.

Key words: *pilgrimage, anti-structure, religion, post-Soviet culture, Russian cinema.*

Roman Globokar
Reverence for Life: The Currency of Schweitzer's Ethics

At the beginning of the twenty-first century, an increasing number of thinkers are referring to Schweitzer's ethics of reverence for life. This is particularly useful and applicable with regard to ethical attitudes towards the environment. Immediately after the First World War, Albert Schweitzer (1875–1965) diagnosed the decay of western civilization as a result of an excessive discrepancy between the material development of the world and man's moral responsibility. To reform western civilization, he proposed the ethics of reverence for life, which is based on the fundamental experience of man: "I am life that wills to live, and I exist in the midst of life that wills to live." Because man is indispensably connected to the surrounding living world, his moral responsibility extends to all living things. Schweitzer considered every being sacred, and therefore any destruction of life is an unethical act. The ethics of reverence for life, together with certain corrections and amendments, is also very relevant today in the search for answers to the challenges of the modern world.

Key words: *reverence for life, sanctity of life, will-to-live, responsibility, reform of western civilization, ecological ethics.*

Stanislav Slatinek
The Right to a Good Name

Our society is pervaded by information. We live in a media culture. The fundamental problem of the modern information society is communication. One can sense the penetrating influence of media on political and social order, on education, as well as religious and moral attitude of people. Printed matter or daily newspapers have an important role among media. Printed media today literally create and mediate culture. When reporting or informing public, it is of essence that ethical or legit means are used, otherwise public media (newspapers) fall prey to unbridled lust for profit. The first victims in this savage struggle are usually human rights, particularly the right to a good name. My paper wishes to draw your attention to the great peril posed by modern media (daily newspapers), which seek to serve the right to know, yet they neglect human rights, especially the right to a good name.

Key words: *medium, communication, daily newspapers, human rights, the right to a good name.*

Drago K. Ocvirk
The Art of Living as Proposed by Catholic Christianity and Sunni Islam

The majority of humanity understands and practises religions as propositions of the art of how to realize life individually and collectively. They do this through their doctrinal visions, ethical values and hopeful promises of life after death. This paper presents the art of living as proposed by Catholic Christianity and Sunni Islam. The former interprets Jesus' good news of God's love for human beings as a foundation of human dignity and of human person's central place in every thing. Sunni Islam as an art of living was elaborated and conserved - not without dissent - by ulama, Islamic scholars. Their doctrine affirms the reality of one God and his unique Messenger as massive evidence. For this reason a Muslim owes total submission to this evidence. S/he does it, on the one hand, by his/her unshakable allegiance to the Sunni community, and, on the other hand, by the public testimony of this evidence through the interpretation and action that are legitimated and approved by the Sunni community.

Key words: *religion as ars vivendi, Catholicism, Sunnism, centrality of human being, submission to Allah, ulama, relation collective – individual.*

Mari Jože Osredkar
To Be Saved in Relationship

The topic of my paper is the question: *How can my life be saved?* Religion speaks about life and death in writings on "salvation". Different doctrines of salvation are divided into two groups. In the first, an adept man can alone, without the help of others, discover the purpose and the goal of his life. The teaching of the second, where we find monotheistic religions, is based on the dependence on God's mercy. In reaching for salvation depending on God, conflict occurs between the "I" and the "other". To avoid tension, it must be recognized that persons are born into relationships that save them in three steps. In the first step, the relationship brings man from non-existence to existence. One cannot enter into relationship; he can just be aware that he is already in relation with another. The second step of salvation presents faith as the relationship between man and God. The believer is found in it while the "(O)other" is at the same time totally present and totally absent to the person. The third step of salvation happens when the believer recognizes the face of the Other in all others. Then he lives his relationship to God in relationships to others.

Key words: *religion, salvation, life, death, relationships, faith.*

Avguštin Lah
To Live with God in a World without God

By gaining control over nature, society and man's fate with the help of science and technology, an idea of a world where there is no place for God has gradually been growing since first establishing the subject centered paradigm and the subject's objectivistic rationality and autonomic freedom. The secularized world is an atheist world. To live with God in such a world and to understand His presence is possible only by evolving one's personal skills of dialogic rationality, by restoring the sense of superiority, by acknowledging the predominance of the concept of self in acts of giving and receiving, by respecting and appreciating others, by helping the poor, and in uncovering the secret of love in the communion of husband and wife.

Key words: *to live with God, faith, religiousness, atheism, subjectivity, personal relationship.*

Maja Milčinski
Asia and the Art of Living and Dying

The article deals with Asian notions of life, death, impermanence and universal love, and their difference to the European tradition. By analyzing the Mohist theories of Heaven, it evokes the notions of transcendence, which are described in the texts as the state of undifferentiated consciousness. Since the language is rooted in the differences, here the void space comes into play, as well as the mystical and meditative methods developed in Asian philosophical and religious traditions which might be necessary for a mature acceptance of impermanence and death, and for a full life based on it.

Key words: *impermanence, life, death, quality of life, universal love.*

Romualdas Dulskis
"Drifting as the Sea" – the Art of Life in the Daoist Tradition

The Daoist philosophy and religious tradition present exceptionally interesting and valuable insights into a person's vocation and life's purpose. From many perspectives, this is an entirely different world than the one we find in the Bible. Nonetheless certain aspects of the teachings in Daoism by the classics are very near to those in Evangelical texts. In Daoism the art of life relates closely with the idea of freedom. The Daoist purpose in life is to have no purpose, to be as free as the wind and sea and, along with that, to open completely to what inspires all life's processes—Dao. As per the stances of Catholic theology, discussions on divine inspiration regarding Daoist texts are out-of-the ordinary. Nonetheless, it would probably be difficult to deny the authenticity and subtlety of their wisdom.

Key words: *Daoism, the art of life, Christianity, inter-religious dialogue.*

Gabriella Pusztai
Church Contributions to the Transformation of Higher Education in Central and Eastern Europe

After the two decades of the transformation process in postcommunist countries the contributions of the churches to the new higher education systems and policies proved to be crucial. First of all they had new visions on higher education influenced earlier by party-ideology. Secondly they reached social-cultural groups that were dispreferred by former party-policy. On the third hand they put higher education closer to regions and territories considered not important by the former regimes (deprived territories with ethnic and national minorities, as well as religious minorities and minority denominations). With these inputs churches and denominations have become the important actors of the new higher education policies as well as the transformation processes in the countries of Central and Eastern Europe.

Key words: *church-related higher education, postcommunist transformation, actors in higher education, social function of higher education, ethnic and national minorities.*

Andrej Šegula
The Role of the Authority in the Religious Education in the Context of Survival

Educational approaches, within a family or in other circumstances of life, have a decisive influence on our perception of authority. The entire spectrum of upbringing is presented here: from the most authoritarian to the most permissive. Included in this context is also the perception of religious education, which is to a great extent dependant on the form of upbringing that a child or youth receives. We encounter two main groups of persons: (1) those trying to live according to the guidelines of religious education, and (2) those trying to educate in accordance with general human principles. In fact, these two essentially are identical, the only difference being their relationship toward the Transcendental. The Church strives to approach this issue in the manner that the education would be of help in a person's life, not only a theory. The question arises: did the religious education lose touch with life? This will demand a concrete answer in the times to come.

Key words: *authority, religious education, authoritarian upbringing, democratic upbringing, upbringing, survival.*

Erika Prijatelj
Art of Living and Learning in Adulthood

Rather than biological age, entering the period of adulthood presupposes the capacity for autonomous thinking, i.e. the ability of self-reference when it comes to reflecting one's own thoughts and actions. Such a person can control themselves and be responsible for their actions. Confronted with a choice or decision, they are able to consult their own selves. The experience of self-control and responsibility is the foundation of acceptance and life in accordance with the ethical code that guides their thinking, emotions and behavior, and form their conscience and desire. The focus of my presentation is adult maturing and how we imagine it. To change is to re-imagine, to realize that personal growth happens more deeply when we are able to foresee the next stage, as well as the challenges of a new period of life. A person never reaches the full potential of their abilities therefore they never cease to be on their way to this goal. By nature, a person is directed towards independence. However, personal autonomy in adulthood can only be achieved at the cost of life engagement in a particular profession and occupation, in relation to other people and in the case of a believer in a relationship with God. Each decade of adulthood has its specific dynamics, specific peaks and crises, but it is also an opportunity for freedom and maturation in wisdom. The presentation shall look at the fundamental challenges of individual life stages of adulthood divided into early, middle and late life. It will draw attention to their interconnectedness and impact on the development of the structure of personality.

Key words: *adulthood, personal development, crisis, process of interiorisation, maturity.*

Alina Pătru
The Religious Life in Romania. Living Together and Painting of Icons in Transylvania

The paper presents the situation of the coexistence of different ethnical and religious groups in Transylvania. The relations between them are exemplified, following a historical path. This is succeeded by a reflection upon identity and conflicts, religiousness and violence. After that, the paper focuses on a phenomenon specific for the Romanian Orthodox believers in Transylvania: the glass-painted icons of the 18th and 19th century. They represent a synthesis between Eastern and

Western and in the same time a form of inculturation of the Byzantine tradition into the Transylvanian context. Gathered in the Zosim Oancea Museum at Sibiel, they fulfil even in our days a bridge function in space and in time.

Key words: *Romanian history, Transylvania, cultural groups, identity, icons, peasant art, Zosim Oancea Museum at Sibiel.*

THE AUTHORS

Ulrich Beck
Prof., Ludwig Maximilian University of Munich/London School of Economics and Political Science
u.beck@lmu.de

Romualdas Dulskis
Prof. Dr., Catholic Theology Faculty, Vytautas Magnus University, A. Jaksto 1, LT-44279 Kaunas, Lithuania.
r.dulskis@ktf.vdu.lt

Katarina K. Erzar & Tomaž Erzar
Assis./Assoc. Prof., Faculty of Theology, University of Ljubljana, Slovenia; Franciscan Family Institute.
tomaz.erzar@guest.arnes.si;
lia-katarina.kompan@guest.arnes.si

Roman Globokar
ThD, Assis. Prof. for Moral Theology at the Theological Faculty of the University of Ljubljana; Štula 23, 1210 Ljubljana Šentvid, Slovenia.
roman.globokar@guest.arnes.si

Anton Jamnik
ThD, Bishop, Assis. Prof., Faculty of Theology, University of Ljubljana, Slovenia.
anton.jamnik@guest.arnes.si

Janez Juhant
PhD, Prof., Faculty of Theology, University of Ljubljana, Slovenia.
janez.juhant@guest.arnes.si

Tomas Kačerauskas
Prof. Dr., Head of the Department of Philosophy and Political Theory at Vilnius Gediminas Technical University, Saulėtekio al. 11, LT-10223 Vilnius-40, Lithuania.
tomas@hi.vgtu.lt

Branko Klun
Assoc. Prof., Faculty of Theology, University of Ljubljana, Slovenia.
branko.klun@teof.uni-lj.si

Gábor Kovács
Prof., The Institute for Philosophical Research of the Hungarian Academy of Sciences, Hungary.
kovker@t-online.hu

Avguštin Lah
Assis. Prof., Faculty of Theology, University of Ljubljana, Slovenia.
Avgustin.lah@guest.arnes.si

Tonči Matulić
Prof., Catholic Faculty of Theology, University of Zagreb, Croatia.
matulict@theo.kbf.hr.

Béla Mester
Prof., Institute for Philosophical Studies of the Hungarian Academy of Sciences, Hungary.
mester@webmail.phil-inst.hu

Maja Milčinski
Prof., Philosophy Department, Ljubljana University, Slovenia.
maja.milcinski@guest.arnes.si

Inna Naletova
Katholisch-Theologische Fakultät, Universität Wien, Austria, Inna Naletova received her MA and PhD in Religious Studies at Boston University. Currently she teaches sources in sociology of religion and coordinats a project at the Department of Practical Theology, University of Vienna.
inna.naletova@univie.ac.at

Drago Karl Ocvirk
Prof., Faculty of Theology, University of Ljubljana, Slovenia.
drago.ocvirk@gmail.com

Mari Jože Osredkar
PhD, Assis. Prof., Faculty of Theology; Poljanska 4, *SI-1000* Ljubljana.
Černetova 20, SI-1000 Ljubljana,
mari.osredkar.ofm@siol.net

Alina Pătru
"Andrei Saguna" Faculty of Theology, "Lucian Blaga" University of Sibiu, Romania.
alinapatru@gmx.at

Mateja Pevec Rozman
ThD, Assis., University of Ljubljana, Faculty of Theology, Slovenia.
mateja.pevec@guest.arnes.si

Robert Petkovšek
Assis. Prof., Faculty of Theology, University of Ljubljana, Slovenia.
robert.petkovsek@guest.arnes.si

Zvezdan Pirtošek
DSc. Prof., Medical Faculty, Department of Neurology & Faculty of Arts, University of Ljubljana, Slovenia, University Medical Centre, Zaloška 2, Ljubljana, Slovenia, Professor of Neurology at the Medical Faculty and Faculty of Arts (Department of Psychology) of Ljubljana and Head of Department of Neurology at the University Medical Centre in Ljubljana.
zvezdan.pirtosek@kclj.si

Erika Prijatelj
Asis. Prof., Faculty of Theology, University of Ljubljana, Slovenia.
Erika.Prijatelj@rkc.si

Günter Prüller-Jagenteufel
Assoc. Prof. of Moral Theology and Director of the Studies Programme of Catholic Theology, University of Vienna – Faculty of Catholic Theology – Department of Moral Theology, Schenkenstraße 8-10, A-1010 Vienna.
gunter.pruller-jagenteufel@univie.ac.at

Gabriella Pusztai
Ph.D. habil. (Sociology of Education) is a associate professor at the University of Debrecen and director of research of CHERD (Center for Higher Education research and Development). Address: H-4032 Debrecen Egyetem tér 1.
gabriella.pusztai@ella.hu.

Santiago Sia & Marian F. Sia
Professors, Milltown Institute, University of Ireland, Pontifical Athenaeum, Dublin, Ireland.
ssia@milltown-institute.ie

Wilhelm Schmid
Born 1953, lives in Berlin/Germany. He studied Philosophy and History in Berlin, Paris und Tübingen, and teaches Philosophy at the University of Erfurt / Germany, longtime also at the Universities of Riga/Latvija and Tbilisi/Georgia. Some years he worked as philosopher in a hospital near Zürich/Switzerland. Homepage: www.lebenskunstphilosophie.de.
mail@wilhelm-schmid.de

Stanislav Slatinek
Assis. Prof., Faculty of Theology, University of Ljubljana, Slovenia.
stanislav.slatinek@guest.arnes.si

Vojko Strahovnik
PhD, Assis. Prof. He is the head of research unit at IPAK institute and lectures at European Faculty of Law and Faculty for State and European Studies: Adress: IPAK Institute, Velenje, Slovenia.
vojko.strahovnik@gmail.com

Tadej Strehovec
PhD, Assis., Faculty of Theology, University of Ljubljana, Slovenia.
tadej.strehovec@gmail.com

Andrej Šegula
PhD, Assis., Faculty of Theology, University of Ljubljana, Slovenia.
Andrej.segula@teof.uni-lj.si

Karl Mathäus Woschitz Emer
University Graz, Faculty of Theology, Treeffelsdorf 28, 9064Pischeldorf.

Zdenka Zalokar Divjak
Assis. Prof., Faculty of Theology, University of Ljubljana, Slovenia.
zdenka zalokar@siol.net

Bojan Žalec
PhD, Senior Research Associate, the head of Institute of Philosophy and Social Ethics at Faculty of Theology, University of Ljubljana.
bojan.zalec@teof.uni-lj.si.